Tragicomic Redemptions

Tragicomic Redemptions

Global Economics and the Early
Modern English Stage

VALERIE FORMAN

PENN

University of Pennsylvania Press

Philadelphia

Published by
University of Pennsylvania Press
Philadelphia, Pennsylvania 19104-4112

Printed in the United States of America on acid-free paper
10 9 8 7 6 5 4 3 2 1

Excerpt from Patti Smith, "In Excelsis Deo." Written by Patti Smith © 1975 Linda Music. Used by Permission. All Rights Reserved.

Library of Congress Cataloging-in-Publication Data

Forman, Valerie.
   Tragicomic redemptions : global economics and the early modern English stage / Valerie Forman.
       p. cm.
   Includes bibliographical references and index.
   ISBN: 978-0-8122-4096-2 (acid-free paper)
   1. English drama—Early modern and Elizabethan, 1500–1600—History and criticism.
2. Economics in literature. 3. Literature and globalization. 4. Literature and society—England. 5. Drama—Economic aspects—England. 6. Theater—Economic aspects—England.
7. Theater—England—History—16th century. 8. Theater—England—History—17th century.
   PR658.E35 F67 2008
   822.3'093553 22   2008004163

In memory of Leonard Forman, who directed the first plays I ever saw

Contents

Introduction. The Economics of Redemption: Theories of "Investment" and Early Modern English Tragicomedy   1

Part I. Tragicomedy and Generic Expansion

1. Stasis and Insularity in *The Merchant of Venice* and *Twelfth Night*   27

2. The Voyage Out: *Pericles*   64

3. Poverty, Surplus Value, and Theatrical Investment in *The Winter's Tale*   85

Part II. Eastern Engagements

4. Captivity and "Free" Trade: Fletcher's *The Island Princess* and English Commerce in the East Indies in the Early 1600s   113

5. Balance, Circulation, and Equity in the "Prosperous Voyage" of *The Renegado*   146

Epilogue. Webster's *The Devil's Law-Case*, the Limits of Tragicomic Redemption, and Tragicomedy's Afterlife   186

Notes   205

Bibliography   251

Index   263

Acknowledgments   277

Introduction
The Economics of Redemption
Theories of "Investment" and Early Modern English Tragicomedy

This is a book about the productivity of loss in early modern economic theory and on the early modern English stage. In the closing decades of the sixteenth century and the opening decades of the early seventeenth, England was radically expanding its participation in an economy that was itself becoming increasingly global.[1] The highly profitable English East India Company, for example, made its first voyage in 1601. Fewer than twenty years later, just as that radical increase was really getting under way, England was suffering from an economic depression, blamed largely on the shortage of coin necessary to conduct those same very profitable trades. One of this book's objectives is to explore how early modern economic theory and drama negotiated the tension between these two phenomena. How could there be profit in the face of so much loss? Even more fundamentally, where does profit come from? This is not a book, however, about the attempts of English merchants to avoid loss or minimize costs or risks. Instead, this book argues that new economic practices required the English to reconceptualize loss itself as something productive. Early modern economic theories are thus somewhat Janus faced. They seriously engage with loss, but they also imagine those losses to be only temporary and ultimately transformable. Moreover, in these theories losses are reenvisioned as the source of something beneficial and positively valenced. The stories told and explicated in this study, then, pull in opposing directions, but also necessarily gravitate toward a particular end.

The other focus of the book is the early modern stage, especially the genre of tragicomedy, which has similar tensions at its core. At its most basic, tragicomedy, as the name suggests, is the product of a relationship between two potentially opposing genres—one that foregrounds loss, and the other resolution. Moreover and relatedly, because that relationship is narratively structured by the fortunate fall of Christian redemption, tragicomedy, as I argue throughout, is particularly well suited to reimagine losses as fortunate events. It is thus also an appropriate genre for mediating concerns about foreign trade in the early modern period. Indeed, one of the primary questions motivating this study is why so many plays interested in foreign trade and travel take the tragicomic form. In his prologue to the tragicomic *Midas*, John Lyly goes so far as to identify foreign trade as the reason for tragicomedy's existence: "Traffic and travel hath woven the nature of all nations into ours, and made this land like arras, full of device, which was broadcloth, full of workmanship . . . if we present a mingle-mangle our fault is to be excused, because the whole world is become a hodgepodge."[2] In part, Lyly defends the mixing of two genres in one play by blaming the very desire for multiple genres on foreign trade. While Lyly claims to view this contact as a form of contamination that leads to a fall from grace, he also scripts mixed genres, in general, and tragicomedy, in particular, as a form of art (an "arras") that develops through intercultural contact and commerce.[3]

This book takes Lyly's "analysis" one step further to argue for a strong relationship between new economic practices and new dramatic genres. My primary objectives in this project are to account for the frequency with which plays concerned with long-distance overseas trade take the tragicomic form and to explore the uses to which the tragicomic form is put in these contexts: that is, what work do tragicomedies do? The book's primary concern is thus the relationship between these economic theories and generic experimentation on the early modern stage. What I seek to demonstrate throughout the book are the ways not only that economic concerns and the attempts to theorize them led to experimentation with genre on the stage, but also the ways that the plays themselves participated in the shaping and development of economic theory and practices. Put most strongly, the book argues both that economic change could and did stimulate the production of new dramatic genres, and that the drama participated in developing new economic theories that *enabled* overseas trade and investment.

But the point of this study is not only to illuminate the mutual shaping of these otherwise seemingly disparate realms. What I hope also becomes clear is the way that reading these economic texts alongside tragicomic plays helps us to see more clearly what is at stake in the economic theories and in the plays, and why each developed along the lines that they did, that is, toward a narrative of productivity. Moreover, reading tragicomedy through the lens of economic theory and economic theory through the lens of tragicomedy helps to make visible the scaffolding upon which these texts were built. My approach is thus genealogical. Throughout, I examine the processes by which economic practices come into being and by which they develop interdependently with the discourses that explain them and the literary texts that mediate them. At its broadest, then, this project seeks to explain how ideas about productivity came to be significant in early modern England.

Overseas Trade and Discourses of "Investment"

The possibility of loss became an increasingly acute concern once England became actively engaged in long-distance overseas trade. But it was not only the risks of trade—piracy, shipwreck, and the like—that produced concerns about loss in the early seventeenth century. The very means for conducting long distance overseas trade—that is, the necessary expenditures—were themselves understood as losses. Such concerns might not have come to the foreground if not for the desperate economic situation of the early 1620s. Inflation, unemployment, and a huge drop in the sale of cloth (England's primary product) at home and abroad were some of the primary causes of an economic depression. The crisis was so severe that James I set up an advisory commission comprised of leading merchants to investigate the causes of the decay of trade and to make economic policy recommendations. Much of the resulting inquiry focused on the shortage of money in England, which was in turn understood to be the result of sending English coins and bullion out of the country to purchase goods abroad.[4] In short, long-distance overseas trade was considered primarily responsible for England's economic woes.

The relatively new East India trade was considered especially to blame. The English East India Company's trade, unlike that of companies that preceded it—for example, the Levant Company or Merchant Adventurers—was based not on the export of English goods, but on the import and re-export of foreign wares.[5] English goods themselves, especially wool cloth, were not particularly vendible in the East Indies; as a result, the trade could be conducted only by the export of coin or bullion. On the surface, such a trade could look doubly bad for England: first, initial expectations of a new market for English goods were quickly dispelled; second, to add insult to injury, coin or bullion had to be sent out of the country to purchase East Indian goods or to buy goods elsewhere that were more desirable in the East Indies and thus could be exchanged for spices and other goods from the region. As a result, a trade that would be considered extraordinarily profitable by modern methods of assessing benefit was instead accused of being a scourge that was draining the country of its resources.

Part of the conceptual problem was that what we would call expenditure was understood as an unredeemable loss. While "investment" seems an entirely natural concept today in our stock-owning culture, it was a concept that needed to be theorized and debated in the early modern period. Thus, Thomas Mun, the most influential participant in this debate, begins his chapter entitled, "The Exportation of our Moneys in Trade of Merchandize is a means to encrease our Treasure," by asserting that such a "position is so contrary to the common opinion that it will require many and strong arguments to prove it before it can be accepted of the Multitude, who bitterly exclaim when they see any monies carried out of the realm."[6] In fact, the analysis of James's committee on the decay of trade and the shortage of coin resulted in a war of economic tracts, the first public debate on economics that explicitly influenced government policy.[7] (We now call this pamphlet war the mercantilists' debate.)[8] What Thomas Mun and Edward Misselden, another leading merchant, introduced to address this misconception was the idea of a "balance of trade"; in short, according to both thinkers, as long as net exports exceed net imports, England would experience a "favorable balance of trade," more money would return to England, and the wealth of the country would be enhanced.[9]

This theory, which now seems like common sense, contained two major and related shifts in thinking that functioned to reenvision the economy as dynamic rather than as static.[10] Prior to this debate, the sending out of bullion was understood as an isolated action without a view toward its longer-term results. Thus, every time money was sent out of the country to purchase goods abroad, it was recorded as a loss that depleted the current quantity of treasure. As economic historians have pointed out, one of the radical results of the mercantilist debates was to reconfigure the economy as a system in which what mattered was not the *store* of treasure, but the *flow* of money and goods.[11] In the specific case of the East India Company, the export of bullion to pay for imports, according to this reconfiguration, would not produce a shortage of money as long as it was outbalanced by the receipts accrued from the re-export of those same wares, even if the money came back to England at a later time.[12]

But the shift in attention from the store of treasure to the flow of money and goods only shifts the way in which one accounts for these flows. It does not explain how profit itself is made. Thomas Mun, who seeks to demonstrate that exporting bullion to purchase foreign goods does not inevitably represent, or produce, a loss of English treasure, does more than shift our focus from store to flow. Mun, I want to argue, demonstrates that profits are possible, because what is sent out undergoes productive transformations: "For it is in the stock of the Kingdom as in the estates of private men, who having store of wares, doe not therefore say that they will not venture out or trade with their mony (for this were ridiculous) but do also turn that into wares, whereby they multiply their Mony, and so by a continual and orderly change of one into the other grow rich, and when they please turn all their estates into Treasure; for they that have wares cannot want mony."[13] That quality of transformability is the second major important shift in thinking about components of the economy. In this account, profits are the product of the "continual and orderly" transformation of those things sent out—be they wares or bullion—"one into the other."[14] The accumulation of wealth depends on not simply an exchange of wares for money, but the repeated transformation of one into the other. It is in these transformations that productivity lies. It is not only that wares have the power to "procure" money, as Mun argues in this same tract, but also that the transformation of money into wares back into money actually results in the production of more money.[15] The power of wares and money is thus that they can be transformed into each other, and the ultimate result of such a transformation is not only the procuring of money, but actually the production of more of it. Mun thus offers the transformative power of wares and money as the explanation of how expenditures are not losses, but are instead a source of accumulation—especially important given a depression blamed on the chronic shortage of coin and bullion.

The transformative powers of wares and money make loss the source of future accumulation.[16] Losses are thus reconceived as outlays or expenditures, and profits are not only justified, but also and even more significantly the *expected* result, merely what "naturally" accrues in the transformation of money into wares "back" into more money—a process that comes to be known as "investment." Significantly, the commercial usage of "investment" (the outlay of money in the *expectation* of a profit), previously a term for regal or religious endowment, was coined in 1613 in the correspondence of the English East India Company.[17]

Such transformations are at the root of the correspondence from the East India Company's factors (its agents) in the East in which the first commercial usages of "invest" appear. In almost all of the early examples of this usage, forms of "invest" appear not just to describe a simple purchase or exchange, but within the context of a complex, multipart transaction that emphasizes transformation. For example, in a letter of 28 February 1615 some of the company's factors say they will "invest *produce* of aforesaid goods and money in best sorts of Indicoes." In a letter of the twenty-fifth of the same month, Thomas Elkington, one of the company's factors, informs the company that "there is left with Mr. Thomas Aldworth and the rest in money, lead, quicksilver, vermilion, tin, etc. by computation a matter of 10,000l. sterling as it is there worth, which hath been thought fitting presently to *bring into money* as the time wil afford, and with the *proceed* thereof to go for Amadavar and there to invest itt in Indico to bee in Surrat before the raynes." On 7 March of that same year, after a detailed discussion of what will sell and what will be bought in various of India's ports, the factor concludes with, "for further advyse in particularising of the *sayles* of the Companies goods and *Investment*, of that and of their monies, I know your Worship shall have from the principal factors, to which refer me." In all of these examples, the idea of investing emerges primarily as part of a multi-stage process when goods or money are converted into a form that can be used to purchase different goods. Money and wares are re-employed, and money is transformed into goods that will be vendible, or convertible into spices that can be sent back to Europe and sold there. Not merely an outlay of money (for the purchase of Indian goods), an "investment" is a transformation of one form of ware or money into another that can then be used to produce a profit.[18]

The theoretical solution offered in this concept of "investment" is the reconceptualization of present loss as expenditure, that is, as a transformable source of legitimate, future profit. Mun's argument thus highlights that critics of the East Indian trade are mistaken because they look only to the beginning of the trade, the initial act of sending money out of the country, and not to the relationship between that beginning and its end.[19] What is significant here is the way that one's assessment of the results of the trade depends on not merely the difference between beginning and end, but on the transformation of that beginning into a different, more prosperous ending.

Tragicomedy and Tragicomic Redemptions

The story told, then, is not just "all's well that ends well," but all becomes better than it was before. Such a narrative of transformative prosperity is precisely what I argue is so crucial about stage tragicomedy, a genre that is sometimes misunderstood as a hybrid or mixed form. The critical history of tragicomedy is an interesting one: on the one hand, tragicomedy was much maligned, precisely for its mixing of disparate elements and thus its lack of propriety. Objecting to the genre in *The Defence of Poesy*, Philip Sidney referred to it as a "mongrel" that matches "hornpipes and funerals" without discretion.[20] On the other hand, it was arguably the most popular genre in seventeenth-century England, as McMullan and Hope point out in their collection of essays on the genre. Tragicomedy, however, has been given short shrift in current critical discussions of the early modern theater. With the exception of Shakespeare's late plays, which are studied under the redesignation of "romance," these plays are little discussed as a separate genre. When they are, they are often criticized, even dismissed, for their politics. This critical rejection is, in part, the result of a tendency to consider the genre either too conservative or even depoliticizing, given what is perceived as its inherent movement toward reconciliation and thus away from conflict, as if the plays give up on the tragic tensions and provide a comic resolution in their place.[21]

Tragicomedy, however, was not without its defenders. In "The Compendium of Tragicomic Poetry" (1599), the primary theorization of tragicomedy in the Renaissance, Giambattista Guarini defends tragicomedy against accusations of impropriety by arguing that it is not merely the addition of comedy to tragedy or vice versa, but a separate third kind: "for he who makes a tragicomedy does not intend to compose separately either a tragedy or a comedy, but from the two a third thing that will be perfect of its kind."[22] What is crucial in Guarini's defense and explication of the genre is that the play is not merely part tragedy and part comedy, or even a tragedy that becomes a comedy, but something categorically different. As Mimi Dixon argues in her insightful article on the roots of tragicomedy in medieval drama, to refer to the genre as a hybrid or mix is to "mistake its origins; or, alternatively, it is to grant tragedy and comedy logical priority."[23] Expanding both Guarini's and Dixon's arguments, what I want to highlight about the genre is that mistaking tragicomedy for merely a hybrid genre, rather than seeing it as a genre about the transformation of genre, will necessarily limit the ability to see how its productive potential derives from an engagement, rather than a disengagement, with the problems and conflicts it imagines.

Recent critical collections of essays have attempted a rescue of tragicomedy as well, largely by exploring the way individual tragicomedies and the genre as a whole can be understood to be politically engaged. My own purpose is less to redeem the genre in the moral sense than it is to explore the historical and cultural significance of a genre that depends on profitable transformations.[24]

Tragicomedy's productive potential has its roots in other genres, both theatrical and nontheatrical. While tragicomedy appears to be a new dramatic genre in the early modern period, it is actually both a theatrical development of the narrative romance, popular both during Elizabeth's reign and in medieval literature, and also a resurrected, though much revised, form of the forbidden medieval religious drama. Narrative romances tend to be filled with highs and lows, risks and rewards, or even tragic and comedic moments. In early seventeenth-century tragicomedy, however, these comedic and tragic moments are not just juxtaposed to one another. Instead, these plays depend on a more specific relationship between the tragic and the comedic aspects of the texts out of which, to quote Guarini, this "third kind" is produced.[25] This relationship derives from tragicomedy's source in medieval drama. Tragicomedy finds its narrative and structural basis in Christian redemption (the *felix culpa*), in which the temptation and fall of Adam and Eve produces the coming and sacrifice of Christ. This narrative arc was, of course, that of the cycle plays, whose providential plots traced man's fall and redemption in Christ. The productive potential of tragicomedy develops from its dependence on the narrative of the *felix culpa*, which is doubly "fortunate." Formally speaking, the coming of Christ is dependent on man's fall. Without Adam and Eve's transgression in the garden, mankind would never have benefited from Christ's sacrifice—the satisfaction. And the satisfaction is itself fortunate: what man loses in the fall is more than regained in God's act of becoming man. In other words, man does benefit from the transaction. The fall is thus fortunate in two interdependent senses—both formally and economically. The fall produces the redemption, and the state of redemption is prosperous. Similarly, in tragicomedy, especially the kind Guarini was defending, the tragedy (sometimes only partially) averted, becomes the means for its own tragicomic, even prosperous, conclusion.[26] In tragicomedy, the potential tragedy is thus reconceived as productive. Thus, rather than a hybrid of two genres, tragicomedy embodies a more dialectical relationship between the genres it employs, such that the presence of comic and tragic elements is not an impropriety, but a productive contradiction.

While I stated above that redeeming the genre of tragicomedy is not my primary concern, this project is nonetheless focused on the significance of redemption to the genre itself, both thematically and formally. To clarify the significance of the link between redemption and tragicomedy it will also be useful to articulate a primary difference between tragicomedy and romantic comedy, both of which, to put things simply, end happily. In romantic comedy, the plot is often initiated and structured by an obstacle that must be overcome (e.g., a father or daughter resistant to a marriage proposal, an inappropriately attired woman); in contrast, tragicomedy is structured by a loss (or potential loss) that needs to be redeemed. For example, in Shakespeare's comedy, *A Midsummer Night's Dream*, the marriage of the young lovers depends, in part, on overcoming the objections of Hermia's father, Egeus, and the authority of Athens, embodied in Theseus. In contrast, in the tragicomic *The Winter's Tale*, Leontes must redeem the loss of his wife and son, and the possibility for his (and the play's) redemption is embodied in the aptly named Perdita; according to the play's oracle, that which is lost must be found. In the redemptive formula of tragicomedies, lost or kidnapped wives, daughters, husbands, sisters, brothers, and the like, are found again, and resolution and conclusion are dependent not only on reunions but also on transformations that are significantly also understood to be prosperous, often in the most material, even commercial, sense of the term. Loss, unlike obstacle, I argue throughout the book, provides the possibility, as it does in the period's economic discourse, for a productive conclusion.[27]

I thus argue for an important further distinction between romance and tragicomedy. As I suggested above, romance itself has highs and lows, and even falls and rises. Thus, as Jonathan Gil Harris and others have suggested, romance is about avoiding hazards. Tragicomedy is less about dealing with or avoiding risk—adventuring—and more about the *transformation* of losses into profits, that is, "investment." In addition, in traditional forms of romance, redemption often might be thematically important, but the genre itself is not structurally dependent on redemption. In the romance, losses do not necessarily produce profits; they are temporally but not causally related. Moreover, redemption in the romance is a necessary response not so much to loss per se, but to a fall. Tragicomedy, even if it combines loss and fall, emphasizes the former. Tragicomedy, I would argue, is thus a reconfiguration of the romance form that registers and addresses specific historical, and especially economic, concerns. Indeed many plays about overseas trade represent an ambivalence with the romance genre. Massinger's *The Renegado*, for example, even stages a representation of its inadequacy and its consequent dismissal and replacement with tragicomedy. I am, in part, then suggesting a modification to Ania Loomba's identification of certain plays as "mercantile romances" and to Jonathan Gil Harris's discussion of the romance as providing the generic framework for representing a transnational economy. Instead, I argue throughout the book that tragicomedy (more than romance) becomes a genre that is particularly "appropriate" for negotiating concerns with the specifically economic aspects of overseas trade.[28]

In order to illuminate tragicomedy's productive potential it might also be useful to look at a play that is almost, but not quite, tragicomic. *Twelfth Night*, perhaps more than any other Shakespearean comedy, could be read as an intermediate step toward this genre, given that it is something of a hybrid between tragicomedy and romantic comedy. While the plot is structured more by the obstacle of Viola's disguise as Cesario than by the loss of her brother, the loss and the obstacle are intertwined in Cesario, who Viola admits is an imitation of her lost brother, Sebastian. Yet, the climactic reunion of Sebastian and Viola at the play's end is not redemptive. Though part of what is lost is found again, what is found does not exceed what is lost, as it does in the tragicomedy; in other words, the loss is not itself fortunate. *Twelfth Night*'s reunion of the siblings, to be sure, has affective power; but these reunions come at the expense of, or at least in contradistinction to, the possible profits the play imagines: Antonio's purse is never returned; the Captain who saves Viola and from whom she purchases her disguise is imprisoned; Malvolio's fantasy of social mobility is refused, perhaps even repudiated; and Viola's wedding to Orsino is deferred. Put succinctly, *Twelfth*

Night disavows the possibility for profits, that is, for both material and social gain. That *Twelfth Night* tries to imagine these profits might make it a precursor to tragicomedy, but not a tragicomedy. Indeed, the play emphasizes its own generic limitations as the inability to produce the profits it imagines. In contrast, tragicomedy, I will argue, has the production of profits, and more specifically the transformation of losses into profits as one of its main objectives. In tragicomedy, what is (potentially) lost is not only found again, but rematerializes as a gain.[29]

Twelfth Night is a useful example of a stepping-stone from comedy to tragicomedy also because it raises issues and problems that it then shows as irresolvable within the formal constraints of the comedic genre. Significantly, *Twelfth Night* represents its disavowals of profits as structurally necessary to the closure of romantic comedy. The result is an economy that is safely insular, but also static. Tragicomedy, by employing the dynamics of redemption—in which the tragedy averted is the means for its own resolution—can provide the possibility for an economy that is itself more dynamic and even open-ended. Rather than disavow its constitutive material forces, tragicomedy, for better or worse, imagines the possibility of transforming those limitations into productive ends. The dialectical aspects of tragicomedy are perhaps themselves redemptive; they allow for the possibility for a different, non-static future. Tragicomedy, then, works to break through the impasse of romantic comedy, by providing a more dialectical model that imagines extension rather than contraction.

One primary way to imagine such an extension is to engage with possibilities for travel and even foreign exchange, that is, to imagine extension beyond the local economy. (Significantly, the disavowal of economic historical forces that produces the static economy in *Twelfth Night* is represented in the bodies of foreign sea venturers who threaten the otherwise insular Illyria.) As I suggested above, tragicomedies, in fact, are very often engaged with such possibilities. Tragicomedy is thus doubly useful: it looks to foreign exchange as a way out of the cultural and generic impasse I describe above, and it provides the formal means for defusing threats represented in foreign exchange by providing the means to imagine losses as potential profits.

That tragicomedy took on these concerns and also provided a means to negotiate them is evidenced, for example, quite explicitly in the opening scene of Webster's tragicomedy, *The Devil's Law-Case* (c. 1617–19). The proof of the excessive wealth of the primary merchant in the play is ironically how much money he sends to the Indies: "for Silver, / Should I not send it packing to th'East Indies / We should have a glut on't."[30] The recurrent economic concern (too much money flowing out of the country) is thus presented as a cure for an imagined flood of it at home.[31] Rather than view trade with the East Indies as a potential source of harm or loss, for Webster it is a necessary outlet. Webster's irony makes clear that the connection between the shortage of coin in England and the East Indies trade must have been pervasive enough for its inversion to be a theatrically effective joke and for it thus to serve ironically as a sign of the merchant's excesses and the threats he poses. Moreover, Webster invokes tragicomic inversion, in which the potential tragedy transforms into the solution. He does so not by having the loss transform into a solution within the context of the play's unfolding, but by having his character insist that the sending of money out—the loss— is actually the solution. In doing so, Webster's parody of the form highlights, even thematizes, the imagined potential of the tragicomic form simultaneously to imagine expansion and profit as interdependent concepts, a revision necessary if losses are to rematerialize as gains.

The Economics of Redemption

It is in this productive relationship between loss and gain that I locate important historical connections between the genre of tragicomedy and new economic practices. As I explain in the book's chapters, the relationships among new economic discourses, economic practices, and tragicomedy have much to do with the religious discourse of redemption. In the above section, I highlighted the "fortunate" aspects of the Christian narrative in the formal sense, but the Christian narrative has a much stronger connection to the economic that would make the staging of redemption an even more powerful means for engaging with economic concerns.

Christian redemption, at least since St. Anselm's eleventh-century *Why God Became Man*, has been understood in explicitly economic terms. In these terms, not only still current in the Renaissance but perhaps even strengthened by Reformation debate, man owes an infinite and ultimately unpayable debt to God for an original sin understood as the result of defrauding God, of robbing him of what rightfully belongs to him.[32] Man is unable to pay, but cannot be saved without paying. Christ's sacrifice—the "satisfaction"—is explicitly understood as the price of mankind's sins and, importantly, more. The debt to God is repaid, even overpaid, by Christ, who is both man and God and whose life has infinite value.[33] Thus the idea that what man loses in the fortunate fall is more than regained in the coming of Christ the redeemer is not just formally economic, but is instead an idea that is steeped in economics.[34]

This connection is evidenced throughout early modern religious texts. That Christ "purchases" mankind is an idea repeated with regularity in early modern sermons and other religious texts. The King James

Bible, for example, enlists Christ as "the ransom for many" (Mark 10:45), an idea central to early modern notions of the satisfaction and to the idea of "redemption" itself. Etymologically, "to redeem," from *re-dimere*, is "to buy back," and its meanings all derive from this base. According to the OED, to redeem means "to make payment for (a thing held or claimed by another)"; "to regain"; "to free (mortgaged property), to recover (a person or thing put in pledge), by payment of the amount due, or by fulfilling some obligation"; "to buy off"; "to ransom, liberate, free (a person) from bondage, captivity, or punishment"; "to save (one's life) by paying a ransom"; "to rescue, save, deliver"; "to make amends or atonement for, to compensate"; and "to deliver from sin and its consequences." Building on these connotations in his 1609 sermon, Lancelot Andrewes (Bishop of Winchester and one of the leading authorized translators to work on the King James Bible) frames mankind as a kind of expensive property:

> *Redeeming* (as the word giveth it) is a second buying, or buying backe of a thing, before *aliened* or *sold*. Ever, a former *sale* is presupposed before it. . . . Our *Nature aliened* in ADAM, for the *forbidden fruit*; a matter of no moment . . . the first *end* is, *To get us rid*, from under this estate. He did it: Not by way of *entreaty*, step in and beg our pardon: That would not serve. *Sold* we were, and *bought* we must be: A *price* must be layd downe for us. To get us from *under the Law*, it was not a matter of *Intercession*, to sue for it, and have it. No, He must *Purchase* it, and *pay* for it. It was a matter of *Redemption*. And, in *Redemption* or a *Purchase*, we looke to the *Price*. For if it be at any easie rate, it is so much the better. But with a high *price*, He *Purchased* us; it cost Him *deare* to bring it about. At a higher rate it was, even *Pretioso sanguine*. His precious blood, was the *price*, we stood Him in. Which He payed, when *He gave His life a ransome for* man.[35]

Emphasizing the price paid to redeem mankind, this sermon highlights the excessive cost. Mankind, as other texts attest, may be expected to similarly expend all for this benefit: to "receive Christ as our onely *Redeemer* . . . we are ready to forsake all things to gain him."[36]

But the logic here, of course, is that the gain will exceed what is forsaken; gaining Christ is of infinite value. The cost to Christ is infinite; Christ, imagined to act as both surety and repayment, overpays, but the return to mankind is prosperous. Such stakes are made clear in doctrine explaining how Christ's sacrifice is actually an act of mercy bestowed on a mankind that can only ever be unworthy. For example, Richard Greenham, a preacher and minister, explains how God's mercy in Christ exceeds all expectations:

> *There is with the Lorde plentifull redemption:* and therefore *Israell* need not to feare to finde mercie; if our sinnes be great, our redemption is greater; though our merits be beggarly, Gods mercie is a rich mercie. If our peril be not come even to a desperate case, and that wee be as it were utterly lost, and past hope of

recouerie, there is no praise of redemption. Heere then is the power and profit of our redemption, that when all sinnes goe over our heads, and heaven and earth, the Sunne and Moone, and the Starres come as it were in iudgement against us, yet a cleare and full raunsome shall be given into our hands, where-with to purchase our redemption, and so to procure our perfect deliverance be-yond all expectation: and so as it were to fetch something out of nothing.[37]

Greenham's conclusion returns us to the logic of investment, if in a slightly different form. Though nothing and loss are not quite identical in his formulation, what we can see is the idea of a prosperous return; it is not only that loss does not remain loss, but that redemption by defini-tion contains within it a transformative power, one that makes some-thing out of nothing or, as in the realm of overseas trade, profit out of expenditure. While we often associate Protestantism with a work ethic based on sowing in order to reap, the logic of redemption, a logic I argue is at the heart of mercantilist texts, inverts the conceptual frame-work that underlies a logic of deserving. On the one hand, it is possible to equate loss/expenditure with sowing. But on the other, the logic of infinite return in exchange for nothing emphasizes not a restricted economy, in which there is a need for return because of scarcity, but instead the potential for profit, growth, and expansion that is not de-pendent on man's own deserving or labor, but on the grace of God.[38]

That potential contradiction is perhaps at the heart of attempts to un-derstand and to justify profits in the early modern period. In the open-ing section of this introduction, I focused on the primary concern raised by new economic practices—that of coin and bullion leaving the realm. But there was an additional older concern that tragicomedy's basis in re-demption also helps to mediate. While losses of bullion were a newer worry, the idea of profit, especially profit made from money alone, had long been considered troublesome. In our current moment losses need to be explained, but profits and returns are as familiar to us as the air we breathe: the very definition of "investment," as I mentioned above, is the outlay of money in the *expectation* of a profit.[39] But this comfort with prof-its made from money was not the norm in the early seventeenth century, as the proliferation of discourse against usury demonstrates.[40] Thus mer-chants, especially those engaged in foreign trade, were in the position of performing an unusual balancing act. On the one hand, they were ac-cused of causing, or at least exacerbating, economic crises in England be-cause of their export of bullion; thus they needed to demonstrate that their activities ultimately increased the wealth of the commonwealth, rather than depleted it. Yet, given that there was also great suspicion of profit in the period, they also had to demonstrate that profits were justi-fied and thus not excessive or fraudulent. The developing genre of tragi-comedy is useful for balancing these concerns precisely because its reliance on redemption provides a model to explain not only how loss (reconfigured as expenditure) can rematerialize as gains, but also how those gains are legitimate.[41] While Christian doctrine traditionally opposed the production of usurious profits, it might be the case that "investment" appears justified, in part, because it follows Christian example.[42]

This book demonstrates how merchants, economic theorists, and tragicomic playwrights all resolve the problem of present loss by reconceptualizing it as a transformable source of legitimate, future profit. The book's focus thus is not primarily the religious dimensions of these plays, but instead the ways that redemption is partially secularized then redeployed both in the economic realm and in dramatic form.[43] Of course, as I suggest above and as John Parker and Peter Stallybrass have demonstrated, Christianity was long steeped in economic thought.[44] But what I want to demonstrate are the ways that economic discourse borrows back some of its own terms and processes from the religious, with modifications. The point of this study is not to argue for a one-to-one mapping of religious discourses onto economic discourses or dramatic form. In fact, what interests me throughout is the way that the various deployments of religious doctrine make apparent the way that these discourses are recoded in order to mediate, or even accommodate, new economic practices. While I address these points in detail as needed throughout the book, I want to highlight some of the salient differences and speculate on their relevance here.

There are three main, interrelated differences between the economics of religious redemption and that of theories of investment that I want to introduce here. As in the doctrine of Christian redemption, what is crucial to theories of a favorable balance of trade and ultimately to the concept of "investment" is that the beginning (loss/expenditure) transforms into a different ending (profit/capital accumulation). But unlike the doctrine of Christian redemption, that of "investment" imagines that difference from the very beginning. Losses—that is, expenditure—are profits in potentia. Indeed, this proleptic (even slightly oracular) vision is what separates the concept of "investing" from that of "venturing," the prior term used to refer to the activities of long-distance overseas traders. A "venture" is "an enterprise of a business nature in which there is considerable risk of loss as well as chance of gain."[45] The difference between the two terms is, in fact, in the expectations. When one ventures, there is "considerable risk of loss *as well as* chance of gain." When one invests, there is only "expectation of a profit." Of course, the story of the fortunate fall does and does not share this logic. It is providential; it was always going to happen, but it is not repeatable, that is, intended for repetition.[46] In the Christian narrative the fall is fortunate retroactively, that is, when viewed from an end point, and it is not to be repeated. Investment takes that retroactivity and also makes it proleptic: when you invest you imagine what you send out now not as a loss but as an expenditure expectant of a future profit. I refer to this theory of investment as proleptic prosperity. It is as if you fall with redemption, and maybe even resurrection, already in hindsight. In the strictly economic version, the whole point is that one invests only because one anticipates a profit (in part because such an event has been repeated before).

Embedded in this difference between economic and religious redemption is yet another divergence. Though Christ purchases mankind's sin with his blood, this expenditure, like God's mercy, is a gift freely given. Discourses against usury repeatedly cited Jesus's injunction to his disciples to loan expecting nothing in return. As Scott Shershow notes, the Geneva Bible's marginal annotation to this passage makes even more explicit that loss ought to be an end in itself: lend "not onely not hoping for profite, but to lose the stocke and principall, for as much as Christ bindeth himselfe to repay the whole with a most liberall interest."[47] It is not only that one ought not to anticipate or expect a profit, but also that the very intention of profit making is contraindicated. Loss thus is valued not because of its transformative properties, but as a means either to accrue (for Catholics) or represent (for Protestants) moral/spiritual worth. The Biblical version encourages its readers to imagine themselves in Christ's position of always losing more. But the economic theory allows for a more literally profitable conclusion—one that more closely resembles the outcome for mankind as a whole.[48]

The third difference between economic and religious redemption might help to explain why the other discrepancies both matter and also cease to matter. While Anselm's discourse provides the economic language of debt and repayment, the model his text represents is largely static. Anselm's focus, as his title suggests, is on explaining why God had to become man in order for man to provide satisfaction to God. The emphasis thus is not on what the Fall produces, but how, in layman's terms, it could be rectified. Anselm begins with the Fall as a *fait accompli*; his interest is not in why man had to fall, or even exactly the benefits of that fall, but on how God can redeem man and thus on how man can repay God. In contrast, religious discourse that describes the Fall as the *felix culpa* formulates the fall as productive, but it does not necessarily contain an explicitly economic component. Early seventeenth-century economic theory combines the idea of the productivity of loss that grounds the very paradox of the *felix culpa* with the economic language inherited from Anselm, then takes the resulting potential even further. Applying the logic of cyclical productivity to the idea of excessive return, Mun produces a model with a dynamic understanding of the relationship between loss and profit in which the continual transformation of money and wares into more money leads not only to investment, but also to the self-generating potential of capital.[49] As I argued above, it is in the circulation, that is, in the very repetition, that value is produced. As a result, the injunction to lend hoping for nothing in return might become meaningless since the concern for one's brethren, which was at the heart of much discourse against usury, is no longer relevant. If value appears to come not from the labor of others, but from the money and its circulation, then the expropriation of value is no longer an issue.[50] "Investment" is thus perhaps itself redeemed in very the moment of its conception.

Reading economic practices both genealogically and through the insights gleaned by thinking about the relationship between tragicomedy and redemption has significant implications for the way we understand the relationship between religious doctrine and economic practices. This book revises two conventional lines of wisdom about that relationship. Because Christian doctrine traditionally opposed usury, most critics argue that merchants tried to justify overseas trade and early capitalist practices by insisting on the differences between those practices and usury. But my analysis demonstrates that the mercantilists and the theater (at times also organized as joint-stocks like the newer trading companies) take a very different tack. The theorization of new economic practices, which is only partially motivated by moral concerns, instead of directly addressing Christian doctrine, borrows from Christian models of redemption. The result is a new way to conceive of loss and expenditure, as well as a legitimation of these practices and the profits they produce. I want, then, to offer a potential alternative to the influential narrative derived from Max Weber—in which the Reformation is responsible for producing potentially capitalist subjects—by suggesting that the new economic model recodes a narrative foundational to Christianity's earlier forms.[51]

Redemption, Investment, and Tragicomedy

I suggest that tragicomedy and economic theories of investment address concerns about loss and legitimate profit by putting the two problems in productive relation to each other. My point, then, is not just that tragicomedy's transformation of limitations into productive ends—its generic structure—formally resembles that of redemption, but that many of these plays take a tragicomic (that is, redemptive) form precisely because they are concerned at various levels and to various degrees with economic practices and problems. Indeed, the primary questions motivating this study are why plays concerned with overseas trade so frequently take the tragicomic form, and why tragicomedies insistently return to the theme of redemption in the midst of economic crises. The simultaneity of experiments with this genre and the radical increase in long-distance overseas trade, I believe, is not co-incidental. Instead, tragicomedy, criticized in the early modern period for being a mongrel, is for that very reason a particularly appropriate historical "response" to problems with overseas trade and to new theories of value. What is crucial about the genre and its basis in redemption is that the two genres are not merely mixed or attached, but are placed into a dynamic, even dialectical, relationship in which potential losses rematerialize as (legitimate) gains and otherwise static economies can be imagined, as they also come to be in Mun's account, as more dynamic and thus open-ended. I thus want to add to my earlier argument about theories of investment and their engagement with the transformability and productivity of loss in order to put them in dialogue with the above insights about tragicomedy: what matters in these discourses is not only that the assessment of trade's profitability depends on the difference between the beginning (the potentially tragic loss) and the end (the comedic profit), but also that this assessment depends on the *transformation* of the beginning into a different, but legitimated, tragicomic ending.

Though many of the book's insights develop from the ways that tragicomedy and discourses of overseas trade share common ground, methodologically, I do not read the two as mere analogues of one another. Moreover, though I read the plays as taking up economic concerns in their form and sometimes in both form and content, I am not arguing that the plays are in the service of economic concerns. Though the plays take up economic issues, they have their own purposes—to entertain and to make a profit—and they are often also exploring their own interests and problems, for example, the limitations of comedic resolutions. This book's interest is in precisely what happens when these kinds of theatrical problems intersect with the economic ones. This book is also interested in the dialogue between the epistemological effects of tragicomedy on the one hand, and those of economic discourses on the other—for example, the dialogue between tragicomedy's spectacular transformations and the analytical explanations that differentiate the mercantilist texts from earlier economic thought.

This book thus brings economic theory, the works of early mercantilists, narrative accounts of merchants in the "Indies," and documents of the English East India Company and the Levant Company into dialogue with early modern drama in order to explore rigorously how the redemptive form of tragicomic theater provides a model and even a means for managing as well as mediating material challenges presented by shifting economic and social forces. This book seeks to demonstrate how a genre based in redemption and thus on the power of losses engages with debates about economic practices. The kinds of questions I ask in the book's chapters are: how is the idea of redemption, precisely because it understands the religious as economic, employed in these plays? How do the processes of redemption make it available to negotiate concerns about shifting economic forces and conflicting modes of production? What does analyzing these economic discourses through the lens of tragicomedy, that is, as fundamentally dependent on transforming "nothing into something," reveal about the way economic discourses are produced? To what extent and with what effects do early modern economic discourses alter the more magical transformative processes of tragicomedy into a different kind of discourse?

Clearly, my intention is not to provide a taxonomic study of the genre of tragicomedy. Unlike most other full-length studies of the genre, I am not providing a survey that attempts to account for all of the genre's permutations or to provide a definitive description of the genre's features. One might object that not all tragicomedies take precisely the form I outline here (some do rely more on mixing aspects of the genres than on a dynamic relationship between them) or foreground loss in the same way. I am not arguing that all tragicomedies take precisely this same form and that tragicomedy is a genre whose only thematic concern or formal influence is overseas trade.[52] Instead, my interest is in what work tragicomedy can do and how it becomes a genre that productively engages with economic concerns. I have thus selected plays whose form and content highlight different ways that tragicomedy and economic concerns were in dialogue with each other. I have also specifically selected the plays in this study in order to explore how tragicomedy engages with different economic problems and in different geographical regions.

Moreover, I am interested in exploring both tragicomedy's potential and its limitations as a model and means to manage material challenges. Given that tragicomedy as a genre foregrounds generic flexibility (it is, after all, a genre about the ability of genres to transform), it might provide a test case for understanding the relationship between generic development and material practices, that is, for the historicity of form in both senses: that form develops within specific historical contexts and that form makes historical interventions. By placing the genre of tragicomedy in relation to contemporary economic texts, my intention is to develop a reading practice that both contexualizes the genre and argues for its role in the newly developing public discourse of economic theory. This project thus is interested in redeeming genre itself—which of late has been relegated to the poor cousin of historical context—as important to the study of literary and cultural history.[53]

The book is divided into two parts. The first part (Chapters 1–3) explores how the formal qualities of tragicomedy provide a model for managing the material challenges presented by shifting economic and social forces—it does so by exploring the movement from Shakespearean comedy to tragicomedy and transformations within Shakespearean tragicomedy itself.[54] In Chapter 1, I set up tragicomedy's potential by arguing that comedy fails to accommodate new economic pressures. The chapter focuses on two plays—*Twelfth Night* (1600) and *The Merchant of Venice* (ca. 1596)—that struggle to imagine possibilities for profit, but fail to do so. These comedies, which I read as intermediate steps on the way to tragicomedy, produce safely insular, but also static, economies. Concerns about the economics of redemption permeate *Merchant*; the infamous pound of flesh as forfeiture grotesquely literalizes Anselm's explanation of why God became man, transforming the ideal of Christian redemption into a narrative of revenge. Productivity is thus prevented in the play as the comedic resolution (oddly steeped in revenge) depends on a folding-inward, a logic of return that refuses, rather than enables, expansion. *The Merchant of Venice's* imposition of comedy on a revenge tragedy leads to a kind of insularity that would ultimately prevent not only profitability, but also the very trade that the world of the play initially seeks to accommodate and make safe. The play is thus more of a revenge comedy than a tragicomedy. *Twelfth Night*, I argue, stages the limits of comedy by representing its disavowal of both losses and profits as a refusal necessitated by the logic of the comedic form itself. This chapter's purpose is, in part, to show how comedy—given its structural need to eliminate sources of tension and conflict—necessarily refuses expansion. These comedies, then, cannot formally solve the problems that motivate them.

The second and third chapters demonstrate the capacity of the tragicomic form to break through this impasse. Chapter 2 examines a play explicitly dedicated to overcoming the related problems of insularity and the absence of proper forms of exchange: Shakespeare and Wilkins's *Pericles* (ca. 1607). *Pericles* explores the possibilities of expanding economically by expanding geographically. The chapter first shows how the relationship between inward collapse and outward movement that drives the play forward is necessary to tragicomedy's expansive potential. I begin the book's discussion of tragicomedy with *Pericles* because, perhaps more than any other play, it represents and then resolves the problems of a closed economy. It does so by placing incest (reconfigured as too much commerce with the self) in dialectical relation with the "properly productive" travels of Pericles that this sin sets in motion. I argue that this expansion is particularly important because it enables the play to reimagine isolated economies structured by the static relationships among scarcity, wealth, and charity as a productive economy redeemed by more dynamic relationships among loss, profit, exchange, and credit. This imagined economy rewrites the defensive categorizations in which poverty is foreign and wealth is native, thus defusing the kinds of threats posed by foreigners in the comedies discussed in the preceding chapter by imagining contact with other countries as a source of productivity rather than as a form of violation. Finally, *Pericles* is an important play for this study because it, unlike *Merchant*, recodes the Anselmian model in order to rethink problems previously deemed moral as primarily economic problems.

The purpose of Chapter 3 is to explore how the tragicomic form and its theatrical manifestations can address a question only begged by *Pericles*: if loss is to be transformed into profit in this newly imagined dynamic economy, where does the added value come from? The chapter focuses on a reading of Shakespeare's *The Winter's Tale* (ca. 1609–11), a play that juxtaposes competing models for value production and that repeatedly asks how value itself and especially surplus value can be recreated out of nothing, absence, loss, and even material poverty. I argue that the play imagines a model of "investment" that derives from and then supercedes that of religious redemption in order to locate value in the very transformation of those things that are lost or discounted. Speaking formally, *The Winter's Tale* provides a quintessential example of how the dynamic relationship between loss and profit can be materialized in the crossbreeding of genres, then absorbed into theatrical practices. The play imagines theatrical re-creation as "investment," that is, as producing surplus value out of the poverty of the very mediums from which it borrows. Thus, at the play's end, the vivification of Hermione's statue can be represented as "surplus" grace that not only redeems the play's losses, but also overcompensates for the deficiencies the play attributes to seemingly less profitable and less significant methods of value production. This chapter shows how Shakespeare illuminated the process by which a play's diverse sources—in this case, repentance, narrative romance, and even labor—could be transformed into something more valuable: the theater itself.

Building on the more general questions about value and the economics of foreign trade raised in the first three chapters (i.e., how can one profit from interactions with foreign economies; how can loss be made productive; how can we envision an economy more dynamic than static; where does value come from), the second part of the book explores how tragicomedy's redemptive processes manage concrete problems that arise out of trade within specific geopolitical formations. The second section of the book thus focuses on two plays, Fletcher's *The Island Princess* (the first English play to be set in the East Indian Spice Islands,

1623–24) and Massinger's *The Renegado* (set in the Ottoman pirate and market community of Tunis, 1624), which represent the complexities of England's engagement with cultures that are sources for coveted goods and thus also sites of fierce competition.

Chapter 4 reads English East India Company documents regarding trade relations with the rulers of the Spice Islands and the company's Dutch competitors in the region alongside both historical narratives of captivity written by English merchants and the narratives of redeemed prisoners central to Fletcher's play. Analyzing these texts' dual foci on profit and imprisonment, I argue that England develops a discourse of "free" trade that allows it to imagine the islands and their goods as valuable without possessing them outright, that is, without colonial possession. The chapter explains how narratives of redemption are employed to convert a colonial model into a strictly economic one that imagines value as transferable and envisions trade not only as compatible with liberation, but also as its very source. This chapter has two primary and related objectives: the first is to explore how and why the two states of "freedom" and "prosperity" develop interdependently from the complex situation of England's trade in the early 1600s; the second is to explain the role that tragicomic narratives play in their development.

Chapter 5 turns to Massinger's *The Renegado* (1624), a play set in Tunis—a market community and home to the Barbary pirates, who threatened to make England's trade in the Levant and Ottoman Empire nearly impossible. While many critics of the play have focused on either the potential threat or the alluring temptations of the Ottoman Empire, my reading demonstrates that the play showcases the inventiveness of the newly developing balance of trade theory by rethinking the unacceptability of both loss and profit simultaneously. Tragicomically rewriting the threats of trade with Tunis—impotence and obstruction—as restraint and protected circulation, the play reimagines not only loss as legitimate profit, but also profit as itself a form of equity. I conclude my analysis of effective tragicomedy with this play in part because this rewriting serves to redeem the economic realm itself. Reversing Catholic doctrine, in which renouncing worldly goods could lead to redemption, this tragicomedy employs religious redemption as a more profitable alternative to revenge and the virtuous guarantor of economic prosperity. Through an inversion in which the economic register borrows back its discourses of redemption from Christianity in order to accredit itself, this play most explicitly demonstrates how discourses of redemption can be productively recoded. It thus serves as fitting subject matter for the concluding chapter to a book that explores how tragicomedies develop in relation to other genres and how tragicomedies variously redeploy discourses of "redemption" in order to engage a series of related economic problems.

The book's epilogue explores the limits of tragicomedy through a reading of Webster's *The Devil's Law-Case* (1617)—a play that stages the failures of tragicomedy's transformative possibilities. While all of the other plays discussed in the book appear to be heading toward resolution, this play seems hell-bent on exposing tragicomedy's scaffolding and its accommodation of new economic practices. Attempts within the plot to reincorporate the foreign and its profits within a domestic setting lead to contraction rather than expansion, to revenge and not redemption, and ultimately to a vision of economic forces as perverse rather than natural. Even the family is a dead end. These attempts fail not because of limited resources but because productivity is taken too far. I argue that *The Devil's Law-Case* raises the questions of tragicomedy's limits by exploring productivity's excesses. It thus interrogates the positive valence seemingly assigned to productivity by the other plays. Writing against the tragicomic genre in which the play participates, Webster's play demystifies the intrinsic productive power accorded both to capital and theater. The book concludes by turning away from the early modern theater and toward twenty-first-century geopolitics in order to explore how the logic of redemption continues to rein in or make use of capitalism's excesses in our current time.

Before proceeding, I want to make some observations about this book's own doubleness. On the one hand, this study explores the productive potential of tragicomedy as containing within itself a kind of optimism, a potential for resolution, for averting tragedy, and for making its characters, to quote Paulina in *The Winter's Tale*, "winners all." Yet, the notion of productivity is something of a double-edged sword in these narratives: while the transformation of loss into something "better" could include things like the amelioration of poverty, the insistence on productivity suggests a potentially unrelenting progress narrative, one that could eliminate other sources of pleasure as a possible end in themselves, while productivity and profit take their place as the only natural conclusions. To put my point simply: productivity is not always a good thing. It has its own costs, and the insistence on it, even the desire for it, is historically produced. Moreover, the emphasis on productivity and profits obscures the very processes by which value is produced. Since the very circulation of money appears to produce more money, the value of labor necessary to transform loss into profit and create the surplus value that enables capital investment disappears from view. I take up this problem in depth in the penultimate section of Chapter 3, but it might be the case that all of the tragicomedies discussed in this book reproduce (sometimes critically) the magic by which gains that result from extracting value from an exterior source appear as inherent to the transformed outcome.[55]

Though "investment" (one of capitalism's most significant and visible practices) and tragicomedy might be in dialogue with each other throughout the book, I am not therefore arguing that capitalism represents utopia or the end of history. On the contrary, throughout the book I engage both with the plays' hopeful potential and their implicit or explicit critiques of the economic practices they also seem to be accommodating. At times, the tension between the two is itself irresolvable; sometimes the discrepancies are, well, productive.

Second, the first half of the book focuses primarily on plays by Shakespeare, while the second half focuses on plays by three different playwrights. Tracing a single playwright's struggle with the limitations of a particular genre (in this case, comedy), then his progressive development of another genre (which we can see in the movement from *Pericles* to *The Winter's Tale*), allows us to see more clearly how the form develops as a result of both the internal pressures of the stage and in relationship to a particular set of historical issues relating to the development of economic thought in the early seventeenth century. The benefit of focusing on Shakespeare in particular in the book's section on the historicity of the transformation of theatrical genre has to do with his tendency to represent things of his own time and place only implicitly if at all. For example, in *The Winter's Tale*, the clown's contemplation of the purchase of currants (the primary import from the Levant) with the proceeds of the sheep-shearing (wool was England's primary export) potentially raises a variety of historical questions, but it does so only implicitly. It might seem that focusing on plays that do not explicitly call attention to themselves as historically engaged would be a detriment to, rather than a benefit for, such a study. But focusing in this book on a playwright with a tendency toward abstraction, who reduces thematic content to forms, is particularly useful for demonstrating how debates about economic practices and particularly the development of the idea of investment could be rendered as tragicomedy. We could then invert the claim that Shakespeare's limited use of explicitly historical referents makes his plays timeless, to say instead that the very limited use of those referents points to the historicity in the form. Indeed, one of the main points of this study is that these texts do not need to display their historicity on the surface in order to be so. My argument about form throughout claims just the opposite: what I hope the readings throughout demonstrate is that literature in general, and the theater in particular, register and address historical concerns, not only with mimetic and thematic representations (in this case of economic practices) but also in the forms themselves. The plays in the first half of the study provide the foundation for reading the relationship between form and economic practices in the later tragicomedies—tragicomedies that address specific economic problems deriving from their geographical locations—in precisely this way. The Shakespeare plays and the others in this study as well demonstrate the ways that economic practices become embedded in, and are even managed by, generic forms and theatrical practices. The history is in the form—in the very shape of the plays themselves—and the plays are of their time.[56]

Part I
Tragicomedy and Generic Expansion

Stasis and Insularity in *The Merchant of Venice* and *Twelfth Night*

The Merchant of Venice and *Twelfth Night* might at first appear an unusual pairing. *The Merchant of Venice* is deeply steeped in economic questions and concerns, and it could be said that the plight of its main lovers, which is resolved early, is in many ways in service to the economic concerns that dominate the play.[1] Given the role of a pound of flesh as collateral for a loan at the center of a conflict between Jews and Christians, it, unlike *Twelfth Night*, seems a play one could not possibly leave out of a study on the economics of redemption. *Twelfth Night*, though it has its dark moments, could easily be described as a comedy whose focus is on pairing off its lovers into acceptable couples. Given this focus and its seeming lack of interest in foreign trade in particular, and economic concerns in general, *Twelfth Night* might even seem an odd play to include in a study about the relationship between genre and economic practices.[2] Yet what unites these otherwise divergent plays and what makes them important to begin this study is their relationship to the tragicomic. I begin with these plays because both gesture toward a tragicomic pattern in which losses can be redeemed, but then do not stay on that course. I read both plays as partial generic hybrids that ultimately foreclose their tragicomic potential, not by being too tragic but by conforming too closely to the conventions of comedy. Both plays seem to imagine possibilities for profit, but fail to do so because comedic closure requires the elimination of sources of tensions and conflict. These comedies, then, produce safely insular, but also static, economies. As a result, neither play fully recognizes the redemptive, that is, fortunate, potential of loss to lead to productive transformations.

This chapter's purpose is thus, in part, to show how the limitations that develop from comedy's insistence on closure as a form of resolution prevent the plays from formally solving the problems that motivate them. And yet in pointing to what the genre lacks, these plays—as I will argue throughout this chapter—nonetheless serve as stepping stones to the genre of tragicomedy, which tries to imagine expansion as a safe source of profitability, precisely by transforming potential loss into profit. In my reading of *The Merchant of Venice*, I explore how the play's implementation of the economic logic of Christian redemption in the infamous pound of flesh reinvisions the play's economic problems and helps to illuminate the formal limitations that keep the play from resolving those problems. I then turn to *Twelfth Night*, a play that abstracts similar economic problems into the form as a means of more explicitly representing the problems as the limitations of comedy itself.

Loss and Redemption in *The Merchant of Venice*; Or, Who Needs Shylock

Of all the plays in this study, *The Merchant of Venice* is the one in which trade most explicitly threatens to have tragic consequences, that is, in which trade itself is explicitly foregrounded as a potential cause of great loss and suffering. Indeed, the play opens with Salerio and Solanio speculating that the cause of Antonio's sadness is the potential danger that his ships and all of the goods within them face on the seas. Putting himself in Antonio's place, Solanio insists,

. . . had I such venture forth
The better part of my affections would
Be with my hopes abroad.
. . . And every object that might make me fear
Misfortune to my ventures out of doubt
Would make me sad.[3]

Salerio reinforces and intensifies this connection by going on to note that, were he Antonio, anything that might remind him of his ships and the dangers on the seas would make him sad—for example, his own breath cooling broth would remind him of the wind, or the "holy edifice" of stone he entered when he went to church would remind him of dangerous rocks. Harmless, even beneficial or sacred, things become reminders of things potentially tragic. Thus, he imagines that the rocks / holy edifice would "scatter all her [the ship's] spices . . . / Enrobe the roaring waters with [his] silks, / And, in a word, but even now worth this, / And now worth nothing?" (1.1.33–36). In his account, overseas trade provides a potentially tragic perspective; in a world that trade dominates, all things can be signs of loss. In such a world, a rich cargo—so rich as to be indexed sufficiently by the all encompassing "this"—can, in a moment, be transformed into nothing.

The opening scene does not, however, imagine loss to be a permanent condition. The scene's focus shifts from Antonio's ships to Bassanio's plan to "get clear of all the debts [he] owe[s]" (1.1.134).

Bassanio's plan is to borrow money from Antonio in order to woo Portia, a "lady richly left" (161). But before he gets to the literal details, Bassanio explains his plan through an analogy to boyhood games of shooting arrows. In those days, if he "lost one shaft," he would shoot another the same way, watch it more carefully, and thus by "adventuring both," find both (140, 143). Connecting the analogy to Antonio, he explains, "That which I owe is lost; but if you please / To shoot another arrow that self way / Which you did shoot the first, I do not doubt, / As I will watch the aim, or to find both / Or bring your latter hazard back again, / And thankfully rest debtor for the first" (147–52). After finally revealing the content of his plan (i.e., Portia) he concludes: "I have a mind presages me such thrift / That I should questionless be fortunate" (175–76). Bassanio's plan, then, is primarily one to redeem losses. Portia is rich. Bassanio, however, emphasizes not only his future wealth if he wins her, but especially the possibility of redeeming himself from his debts. Indeed, he emphasizes his future wealth as the outcome of such a redemption. What is most significant in this moment is the potential to redeem loss and to transform potential loss (the second arrow) into a source, even a means, of redemption.[4]

Bassanio's arrows thus might be, in part, a response to Antonio's potential losses discussed in the play's opening exchange: the arrows signify an alternative to the permanence of loss (even if it is not exactly the same loss). More explicitly, the need for another arrow, that is, to borrow money from Antonio, returns the scene to its opening discussion in a more practical sense. All of Antonio's money is already at sea invested in ships conducting foreign trade, most likely bringing foreign goods to Venice. Thus, while it might seem that the loss foregrounded in the scene's opening is not directly connected to Bassanio's plan to redeem himself, I want to suggest that it is intimately so. My aim here is in part to call our attention to two interrelated functions of the first scene. First, from its opening moments the play is already ruminating on the relationship between loss and the possibilities for redemption. Second, what the two parts of the first scene suggest is that the play might resolve its primarily economic problems (here introduced as the tragic potential of trade, but complicated throughout the play) through the logic of redemption in which a further loss or expenditure can "pay back" what is owed, or ideally even lead to a greater profit.[5] Thus, even before the play's conflict is introduced through Shylock and the infamous pound of flesh, we can see how the play sets up both the need and the possibilities for redemption, even if precisely who needs to be redeemed and why alters throughout the play.

As the play continues, the tragic potential of trade seems to recede from the foreground and is displaced, in part, by the pound of flesh, which is at the center of the agreement Antonio makes with Shylock. In place of interest on the loan, Antonio agrees to give up a pound of flesh if he cannot repay the principal on time. Of course, Antonio is at risk of having to give up his flesh only if his ships do not return. But when he defaults, the pound of flesh occupies the center of the play's conflicts as if the trade itself has ceased to be significant. In what follows, I argue that the pound of flesh both takes the place of the tragic potential of the ships and is the vehicle through which that loss remains and, even becomes, meaningful. If symbolically the pound of flesh registers the deeper fears that the loss of the ships would invoke, it contains within it the cultural contradictions surrounding the early modern understanding of overseas trade. How then does thinking about the pound of flesh within this context add to our understanding of the play's interest in the problems, especially the economic problems, it raises? If Shylock's bargain with Antonio becomes the lens through which foreign trade is viewed, a new potentially comic perspective as opposed to the purely tragic one of Salerio and Solanio, how does this substitution of a pound of flesh for ships allow the play to resolve its concerns about foreign trade—about the ubiquity of loss and illegitimate profits—differently?

Collateralizing Christian Flesh

The Merchant of Venice seems to have three major interrelated problems: first, the religious conflict between Christians and Jews; second, the tragic potential of trade; and third, the related concern about the ethical basis of commercial profit, especially, but not only, profit made through usury. Though the pound of flesh partially signifies the tragic potential of trade, it is introduced into the play oddly not as a problem, but as a solution to the conflict between two different ways of doing business that the play essentially divides along religious lines. To oversimplify, the Christian way is to lend money as to friends without charging interest; the Jewish way is to charge interest, that is, to profit financially from the transaction. In order to reconcile the conflict between the two ways of doing business, the pound of flesh needs to serve as the means by which Jews give up interest or needs to make profit compatible with Christianity, or both. On the surface, the pound of flesh provides an easy solution to the conflict between these two ways of doing business by allowing Shylock a means of forgoing interest. Antonio insists that he only lends money gratis. According to their arrangement, Shylock will imitate Christian behavior and principles and he, too, will forgo interest on the loan. In exchange, Antonio agrees to give up a pound of flesh only if he cannot repay the loan on time. In effect, Antonio's flesh would serve as repayment of the debt—not as interest, but as a substitute form of redemption: Antonio substitutes for Bassanio, and the pound of flesh substitutes both for interest (in the very idea behind the arrangement) and, if Antonio defaults, for the money that cannot be repaid. Antonio accepts the arrangement against Bassanio's better judgment, because he is certain that he will be able to repay the loan; enough of his ships should come in by that time. Moreover, he remarks that the Hebrew grows "kind"—that is, more like Christians—because in this instance he lends money freely, the practice that according to the play's Christian characters differentiates Jews from Christians. While it has become commonplace to say that Antonio acts as a sort of Christ figure by offering his flesh as the means for redeeming another, what is more important here is the way that Christ's self-sacrifice serves as a model for resolving economic conflicts. Antonio's insistence that he lends money gratis (and thus Shylock's offer to do so in kind) is very likely modeled on Christ's blood freely given. Indeed, the early modern injunction to lend expecting nothing in return was explicitly modeled on Christ's own charitable behavior.

In effect, the model of Christ's redemption is already on the table before the pound of flesh, which, in turn, I want to argue, even more explicitly instantiates the logic of Christian redemption. The Christian model of redemption is deeply embedded in the pound of flesh in particular, and the play's economics in general. The pound of flesh as collateral seems shocking; as many critics have suggested, it is evidence of Shylock's inability to distinguish properly between categorically different domains—the personal and the economic.[6] As evidence, critics often point to the conflation in his simultaneous lament over his two seemingly incommensurable losses when his daughter Jessica runs off to marry the Christian Lorenzo: "my daughter! O, my ducats!" (2.8.15). While the pound of flesh most certainly seems intended to highlight Shylock's inability to distinguish between the spiritual and affective on the one hand, and the economic on the other, it would also have signified differently given that the religious and the economic were not so explicitly separate in the early modern period. For a modern audience perhaps nothing seems more remote, that is, categorically separate, from Christian redemption than an economic transaction. "Redemption" ("the act of buying back"), though, as the word itself suggests, had long been an economic concept, that is, understood in economic terms. As I discussed at some length in the introductory chapter, the redemption of mankind by Christ was at least since Anselm understood explicitly as the repayment of a debt to God for the price of mankind's sins, for mankind's defrauding or robbing God of what was owed him. Christ's flesh and blood were (and still are) the "satisfaction."[7] While the situation among mankind, God, and Christ is obviously not identical to that among Bassanio, Antonio, and Shylock, one could understand Antonio's paying freely with his flesh to cover the debts that Bassanio owes to Shylock as analogous to Christian redemption. Clearly the play does not intend to make Shylock God, but the value of the comparison is in understanding the pound of flesh not as a villainous outrage with no analogue, but as a way of bringing the Christian model of redemption to bear on the economic problems and conflicts the play has already raised with its discussion of perilous trade.[8] The pound of flesh refocuses trade through the lens of the economics of redemption.

While there is a long critical tradition of reading the play's economic conflicts in dialogue with its religious conflicts, there is almost complete critical silence on the stronger connection between the economics of the play and Christianity itself, that is, that Christ purchases mankind's sins. This omission is striking given the frequency with which a connection has been made between Antonio's flesh and Christ's flesh. Critics have focused on the categorical differences the play ascribes to the economic practices of Jews and Christians, differences the play then undermines. However, it is not just the case that the religious conflict plays out through the economic one or vice versa, but that the narrative of Christian redemption becomes a means to think through economic problems. One exception to my representation of the critical history is Peter Stallybrass, who has insightfully noted the relationship between the pound of flesh and the economics of redemption.[9] To my knowledge, however, no critic has linked the connection between Christian redemption and Antonio's offer back to the play's concerns with perilous trade, nor has the connection been linked to the play's genre and formal properties. In what follows I seek to demonstrate how an analysis of Christian redemption reworks our understanding both of the play's economics and of the play's formal limitations to resolve those economic problems.[10] My intent is not merely to illuminate an economic theme (e.g., whether the play promotes or is resistant to certain kinds of economic practices). Nor am I attempting only to provide a context (e.g., the emergence of capitalism or reformation doctrine) to illuminate the play's thematics. Instead I am interested in exploring both the way that the thematics of trade and redemption are impacted (and even limited) by formal questions and how the play works through formal problems by thinking through religious and economic questions. I am thus reading the play's thematics in the context of formal negotiations. In particular, I read the play as a comedy whose formal problems relate to, and even anticipate, problems faced by early modern economic theorists in their attempts to understand and explain why financial losses can be impermanent rather than unredeemable.

Revenge and Fortune

As I discussed in the Introduction, the story of Christian redemption has a particular narrative arc. The fall of mankind (a tragic loss) and the resulting debt to God are not only paid but also overpaid by Christ, who is both man and God. Anselm's rebuttal of the argument in which the devil has the right to man not only reassigns man to God but also emphasizes the plenitude of God's grace and mercy and the profit that man accrues through Christ. What man loses in the fortunate fall is more than regained in the coming of Christ the redeemer. The narrative arc is thus doubly fortunate: man accrues a profit, and that profit is the very result of the transformation of loss itself. In other words, the coming of Christ is not an arbitrary windfall but is dependent on man's fall itself, which then retroactively appears to be fortunate, a fortunate fall.

In this context, the implementation of the pound of flesh in *The Merchant of Venice*'s narrative could produce a happy ending, one that might imagine trade as fortunate rather than tragic (thus addressing the play's first and framing concern) while at the same time making commercial profit compatible with the Christianity whose narrative serves as the very model for the trajectory from tragedy to (divine) comedy. Christ's model for charitable behavior—lending without interest—thus serves as a potential springboard for the use of the narrative of Christian redemption within the play as a whole. In this case, it is not just that Christians are defined by their adherence to a model deemed "kind," eventually a synonym for "Christian" itself, but also that the model of "kindness" itself is fundamentally Christian. In this case, a fortunate, profitable ending *is* a Christian ending.

The narrative of redemption explains how loss can rematerialize as gain, but in *The Merchant of Venice* loss leads first to an attempt at revenge that not only prevents profits, but also brings trade to a halt. Though the play begins by highlighting its tragicomic potential and suggesting that generically speaking its narrative arc is based on the story of Christian redemption, it then foregrounds a perverse version of the story of redemption such that the site or sign of redemption itself comes close to making the play tragic, or even a revenge tragedy—specifically, a revenge tragedy that also threatens to undermine the possibility of a return on investment on which capitalism depends.[11]

Though the play always hints at the pound of flesh as potentially a means of revenge, the flesh transforms into a tragic vehicle at the play's center—that is, at the beginning of the third act. Act Three begins with a reprise of the play's opening, as Solanio and Salerio reflect once again on the dangers Antonio's ships suffer. This time, however, the dangers are not just potential, but actual. Antonio has lost a ship, a loss Salerio hopes "might prove the end of his losses" (3.1.15). As the scene progresses, losses of a variety of kinds compound. When Shylock enters the conversation he first speaks of a different loss, that of his daughter, who has recently taken flight with the Christian Lorenzo and who has taken with her a casket of jewels and money. It is "flesh" that the play uses, perhaps metonymically, to link the two sets of losses and their consequences. Reflecting on the state of her soul for her flight, Shylock exclaims, "My own flesh and blood to rebel," and then repeats again, "I say my daughter *is* my flesh and my blood" (30, 32, emphasis added). Seemingly changing the topic of conversation, Salerio asks Shylock, if he has heard "whether Antonio have had any loss at sea or no" (36). Connecting this loss to that of his daughter, Shylock responds, "There I have *another* bad match! . . . Let him look to his bond" (37, 39–40, emphasis added). Making the connection even tighter Salerio says, "if he forfeit thou wilt not take his flesh. What's that good for?" Shylock's answer is "revenge" (43–44, 46). The pound of flesh thus explicitly transforms from a potentially Christian form of resolution to the sign of the difference between Christians and Jews, ironically by transforming what was the solution into an overly literal version of Christian redemption itself in which Antonio's flesh is now "good for" redeeming Bassanio—but as a commensurate exchange, rather than a gift of plenitude.

The next section of the scene makes the connection between the two losses and the play's shift to revenge even tighter. Tubal, a fellow moneylender, brings Shylock two sets of news—one about the money Jessica has spent while escaping and the other about Antonio's losses. Shylock responds with glee to the good news about Antonio's losses and impending bankruptcy, and with despair to the bad news of the prodigal actions of his daughter. But Shylock's responses to these pieces of news are not separate. That the news of Antonio's failure is not bad luck but good for Shylock is dependent on Shylock's loss of Jessica. Certainly critics have noticed previously that Shylock insists upon revenge because Jessica is lost to him, and lost to him in favor of Christians who are also closely allied to Antonio. More important here is the way that Antonio's losses signify for Shylock not negatively as losses, but also positively, even fortunately, as compensation for the loss of Jessica. Antonio's losses provide a means for Shylock to redeem what is otherwise unredeemable. When Tubal says that he could not find Jessica, Shylock concludes the rehearsal of the losses associated with her by lamenting, "Why thou, loss upon loss: the thief gone with so much, and so much to find the thief, and no satisfaction, no revenge" (3.1.78–79). In this way, the pound of flesh is no longer only a symbol of redemption. Instead it becomes a means of revenge, or more precisely it is simultaneously a way to redeem losses and to take revenge, which means that revenge and redemption, the "satisfaction," have collapsed into each other. The pound of flesh thus becomes a means of perverse redemption. It serves as a grotesque literalization of the Christian narrative of redemption, a perversion of the ideal of Christian redemption into a narrative of revenge.

This collapse is central to the irony of Shylock's oft-quoted "hath not a Jew eyes" speech. Often misconstruing Shylock's speech as an argument for shared humanity, critics ignore the turn in the speech's conclusion. "If you tickle us do we not laugh? If you poison us do we not die?" turns into: "And if you wrong us, shall we not revenge? If we are like you in the rest, we will resemble you in that. If a Jew wrong a Christian, what is his humility? Revenge. If a Christian wrong a Jew, what should his sufferance be by Christian example? Why, revenge. The villainy you teach me I will execute, and it shall go hard but I will better the instruction" (3.1.54–61). Shared humanity thus becomes the ability to inflict commensurate harm. Revenge is the mirror image of Christ's satisfaction, the supreme exemplum, the model that all Christians are expected to follow. By mirror image I mean both the reflection and the inversion. When the pound of flesh becomes real, that is, materializes as an actual plot device, it does so both as a repayment that redeems Bassanio and as a source of revenge. The pound of flesh thus begins its dramatic life as tragicomic potential and as the inverse of tragicomic potential. As it takes the place of and intensifies the tragic potential located in Antonio's ships (that is, the tragic potential in foreign trade) it suggests not a fortunate ending but increasing loss. I said above that shared humanity is really commensurate attack. But in fact, the best revenge is not commensurate, an eye for an eye, but rather one that "betters the instruction." Instead of imagining the profits that might come from foreign trade (something never explicitly mentioned in the play), the play imagines a vortex of loss ("loss upon loss")—not an abundant repayment, but an excessive taking back.

Trade thus does not lead to mutual exchange and advantage.[12] On the contrary, it is replaced by revenge that actually disrupts the economic activities the play otherwise imagines. Thus, in the courtroom scene, instead of accepting Bassanio's offer of two times the principal Antonio owes, Shylock insists on the pound of flesh. Antonio still must redeem Bassanio, but only flesh and not money will do. The economic solution is refused for the personal, spiritual one. Whereas earlier Shylock confuses categories, here he refuses to allow the model of spiritual redemption to become a model of explicitly economic redemption. In this case it is the insistence on categorical separateness, or the refusal to allow for a crossing of categories, that blocks the play's resolution.[13]

Moreover, as a result of Shylock's insistence on revenge and on categorical separateness, the relationship between credit and trade is stymied and the circulation of money and goods must come to a halt. The play's plots—Bassanio's fortunes, Antonio's fortunes and bond, and Jessica's elopement—crash into one another, but instead of dialectically producing a fortunate "third kind" out of their confluence, they produce a potential revenge tragedy that rather than transforming loss, clings to it. Revenge leads not to profitable potential, but to a nonexpansive folding inward, a logic of return that refuses, rather than enables, expansion.[14] In revenge's partial replacement of repayment, excessive taking back is highlighted over the repayment that Antonio's flesh represents. The possibilities for economic redemption and profit thus transform into their opposite all within the context of religious difference and religious doctrine.

Nothing and Something

Though I have argued that the pound of flesh is a grotesque literalization and perversion of the Christian narrative of redemption, the strong irony might be that the play's turn to revenge depends also on following the deeper potential of this narrative. In order to think through the ways the play does and does not get out of the impasses I have described above, it will be useful to explore how the play inherits some of these contradictions or opposing potentials of the pound of flesh (i.e., revenge or redemption) from Christian discourse itself. The collapse of redemption into revenge is not just the result of Shylock's villainous thinking, but is already a problem of early modern Christian thought, one that arises out of the complexity of Christian discourse regarding the satisfaction obtained via Christ's sacrifice. According to this doctrine, Christ's blood is a blessing and gift freely given to man by Christ, who is both God and man. Looking at this narrative from just a slightly different angle, we can see that while Christ's blood is a gift from God, it is also repayment to God from man. If God requires Christ's blood, then God exacts a price from man as repayment for the violated justice of God.

Writing in the late sixteenth century, Faustus Socinus challenged this doctrine of the satisfaction precisely on the basis that it was vulgar to suggest that God required repayment and thus would not or could not forgive sins by sheer mercy.[15] It is perhaps easy to see how repayment, in the form of a sacrifice, is not a far cry from a form of revenge. So what looks from one perspective like a kind of redemption, because Christ provides the repayment as a hybrid third party, is also a form of taking back. To redeem is to pay back in order to get back into God's good graces, but the one who insists on repayment can be perceived as vengeful. The New Testament God is thus dangerously close to the Old Testament God. To paraphrase Othello: a sacrifice may be made into a murder. Even if we grant that repayment to God is not exactly revenge, Socinus's objections still remain. How can God be merciful if he exacts flesh? To answer these questions, I return to two figures I cited in the Introduction regarding the economics of redemption that might be particularly relevant for understanding the play's movement back and forth between redemption and revenge.

According to early modern interpretations of the economics of the doctrine of redemption, man must be willing to lose everything; as theologian George Lawson put it in the middle of the seventeenth century: in order to "receive Christ as our onely *Redeemer* . . . we are ready to forsake all things to gain him."[16] It is not only that Christ is the model for man's willingness, even obligation, to lend with the expectation of nothing in return, but also that one is willing to give up everything in order to receive Christ in the first place. As I suggested above, it is unclear precisely how God is merciful within this context of, if not infinite, then at least complete loss.

The theological response is, in part, to invert this formulation and to configure God's mercy as precisely the opposite of man forsaking all. Thus, the preacher Richard Greenham argues:

> *There is with the Lorde plentifull redemption:* and therefore *Israell* need not to feare to finde mercie; if our sinnes be great, our redemption is greater; though our merits be beggarly, Gods mercie is a rich mercie. . . . . . Heere then is the power and profit of our redemption, that when all sinnes goe over our heads, and heaven and earth, the Sunne and Moone, and the Starres come as it were in iudgement against us, yet a cleare and full raunsome shall be given into our hands, wherewith to purchase our redemption, and so to procure our perfect deliverance beyond all expectation: and so as it were to fetch something out of nothing.[17]

But how do these two disparate yet paradoxically related understandings of the economics of redemption help to explain how *The Merchant of Venice* makes use of the economics of redemption to work through its economic conflicts? Lawson's injunction to "forsake all" is strikingly similar to the much-discussed inscription on the winning, lead casket: "who chooseth me must give and hazard all he hath" (2.7.9). Of course, the casket's inscription says nothing of the benefits of such an act. In fact, as many critics have pointed out, the point of the inscription seems to suggest that one is worthy of Portia only if one is willing to take a risk. One cannot *expect* to profit, although one may hope for it. Similarly, according to Protestant doctrine one cannot earn or deserve God's mercy, though one's acts or profits can express that one has God's favor. Paradoxically, then, God's mercy can only ever be understood as a free gift, regardless of how much one has paid for it. One then only has to be willing to lose all; one does not actually have to lose all. Greenham, however, goes further than gift giving; he is interested in how the gift becomes possible, that is, in transforming what little man is worth into the exorbitant profit he reaps from his relationship to God and God's presence in Christ. Greenham's formulation of God's mercy thus provides another alternative for creating a fortunate end both to the losses that man must be willing to undertake and to his theft from God. Man gets out of God's debt through Christ's repayment of mankind's debt to God—a repayment figured as "to fetch something out of nothing." To "fetch," here, most likely means to "draw forth," "to borrow from a source," or "derive from an origin." In reference to a commodity it could also mean "to 'bring in,' realize, sell for (a certain price)"; or of money: "to purchase, procure (commodities)."[18] According to this logic in which something is derived from nothing and thus that nothing is transformed into something, mercy itself is imagined as a form of prosperity, that is, as a way of not only redeeming loss, but also of transforming that loss itself into a form of prosperity. Greenham's conception of mercy still rehearses the logic of the redemption as understood at least since Anselm, but it puts in starker terms the way that mercy pulls gain out of loss. Even more to the point, it shows how mercy could be understood precisely as the transformation of what was lost into a gain. The transformed loss, then, no longer signifies as loss; and Christ's sacrifice is man's fortune. Inverting Salerio's fear that the churchlike holy edifice of the rocks will transform riches into nothing, God's mercy, by fetching "something out of nothing," depends on and offers an economic model that could both reverse the tragic trajectory and rewrite revenge as mercy that offers mankind fortunate prosperity.

(Un)Fortunate Mercy

Soon after Bassanio chooses the right casket, he is finally forced to admit to Portia that in fact his state is not "nothing," as he had previously stated, but "worse than nothing" (3.2.258, 259). He has engaged his friend "to his mere enemy / To feed [his] means" (261–62). The motivation for his confession is a letter from Antonio explaining that all his ventures have failed, a letter whose every word is as "a gaping wound / Issuing life-blood" (264–65). Only about one hundred lines earlier, however, Portia gave all to Bassanio ("what is mine to you and yours / Is now converted") on the condition that he never give away her ring (166–67). The romantic plot, though temporarily comic in itself, fails to fulfill its initial purpose and resolve the economic problems. Bassanio is no longer worth nothing, but his new worth proves inadequate to redeem the losses that both Antonio and Shylock have suffered.

On a literal level, Shylock refuses Portia's generosity. The play thus separates to some extent the two plots (the romantic and the economic) and insists that the economic plot requires a form of resolution other than the resolution conventionally and traditionally provided by comic marriage. The conventional marriage plot usually works by taking existing, isolated or separate characters and creating pairs out of them. There are often economic reasons to do so, as there are in this play. Comic marriages, however, merely move money and property around. This redistribution might be particularly useful for getting one out of debt, but it is not transformative; it does not make nothing into something, even if it replaces nothing with something. Similarly, in terms of the genre itself, the romantic comedy provides us with an enclosed world with a set number of characters to be paired off and moved around, but this redistribution is about making things even, not necessarily profitable. While feminist critics insightfully have pointed to the unease with which romantic comedy resolves itself and the resulting discomfort, especially with the fate of its often silent female characters, my concern here is not so much to object to the genre's means of resolution, but instead to demonstrate the way that comedy is inadequate to the very problems it poses. As a hybrid of comedy and revenge tragedy, the play moves back and forth between revenge and redemption, but the comedic form cannot imagine the expansive world in which payback is ultimately productive of the prosperity necessary to negotiate between revenge and redemption. In other words, the comedic form keeps the play from taking advantage of the profits of mercy that would resolve both its religious and economic conflicts.

If the Christian injunction to forsake all reminds us of the inscription on the lead casket that seemingly entitles Bassanio to Portia in the first place, then we might expect that the resolution and response to the play's impasse in revenge, as well as to its concerns about tragic losses and ethical profits, could be found in what is according to Christian doctrine the opposite of revenge—fortunate mercy, for which forsaking all, or at least the willingness to forsake all, is not just a loss, but a constitutive loss. As every reader or audience member of the play knows, mercy is precisely what is pitted against revenge in the play's courtroom scene in which Shylock insists on taking the pound of flesh rather than repayment or multiple repayments of the bond. Immediately after Shylock's entrance the Duke, who presides over the trial, begins by stating that mercy is what he and all of the world expect of Shylock:

Shylock, the world thinks—and I think so too—
That thou but lead'st this fashion of thy malice
To the last hour of act, and then 'tis thought
Thou'lt show thy mercy and remorse more strange
Than is thy strange apparent cruelty,
And where thou now exacts the penalty—
Which is a pound of this poor merchant's flesh—
Thou wilt not only loose the forfeiture,
But, touched with human gentleness and love,
Forgive a moiety of the principal,
Glancing an eye of pity on his losses,
That have of late so huddled on his back . . .
We all expect a gentle answer, Jew. (4.1.16–27, 33)

In its very first invocation, mercy is positioned explicitly as a willingness to forgive debt. The Duke expects that Shylock will not only "loose the forfeiture," that is, waive the pound of flesh, but also "forgive" some of the principal. He wants Shylock to reverse his course, to take in effect what might be, if not the beginnings of a tragicomic turn in which losses could be transformed into profit, then at least a turn that puts an end to losses. Shylock, as audience members might expect, refuses to "loose" anything and instead insists on his "losing," unprofitable suit. The insistence on revenge is thus explicitly the unprofitable alternative to mercy's profit, one that clings to loss as loss—just as Shylock hopes to compensate for, or redeem, his loss of Jessica through revenge, that is, by producing more loss or investing in loss, both Antonio's and (by his admission here) his own. Shylock refuses the tragicomic turn only to insist on unprofitable revenge.

It is not only Shylock, however, who refuses the tragicomic potential for prosperity, but also the play as a whole. Critics often point to the way that Portia (disguised as Bellario) relies on the letter, rather than the spirit, of the law to turn the direction of the trial, a framework aligned more with Old Testament thinking than with New. But the way that she begins to turn both the scene and the play's direction also recalls the economic model associated with Shylock's revenge plot. She insists that Shylock shed no blood, nor cut less or more than the pound of flesh. Portia stops Shylock's revenge, but she does so by reminding those present in the courtroom (as well as the audience members) of the restricted economy in which they participate. Shylock is to receive only what is explicitly nominated in the bond—no more, no less—no loss, no profit. If he takes more or less even by a hair, then, he dies and all his goods are subject to confiscation.

Shylock is at the mercy of the court, since he, an alien, has at least indirectly attempted to seek the life of a Venetian citizen. The punishment for this intended act is the seizure of his goods and his life, unless the

Duke is merciful. At the scene's end, mercy takes the form of sparing Shylock's life and reducing the economic punishment: half of his goods will go to Antonio in use to be given upon Shylock's death to Lorenzo, Jessica's Christian husband, and the seizure of the other half is to be reduced to a fine. But this mercy is not a gift freely given. Antonio finishes explaining his conditions:

Two things provided more: that for this favour
He presently become a Christian;
The other, that he do record a gift
Here in the court of all he dies possessed
Unto his son, Lorenzo, and his daughter. (4.1.381–85)

How do we read these terms for mercy rendered onto, or executed upon, Shylock? Is mercy a gift? Does Shylock pay for his own redemption? Moreover, does he purchase his Christianity? Are the latter two questions essentially the same in this context? One could argue from a Christian perspective that his conversion is what redeems him; in this case, it is not a price he pays. But that reading is undermined by the fact that the benefit emphasized by the Christians in the play is not the gain of Shylock's soul, but the seizure of his wealth. Moreover, Antonio makes clear that the conversion is the price Shylock pays to keep some of his goods. If the objective is the conversion of Shylock, then Shylock purchases Christianity and redemption in a way that vulgarizes Anselm. Inversely, if the objective is to let Shylock keep some of the means by which he makes a living, then Christianity is the price paid for that possibility. In either case, mercy is configured as exactly what mercy is not: part of a commensurate exchange, and one that makes literal money, not figurative debt, the equivalent of Christian redemption.

Rather than read the execution of mercy upon Shylock as just mercy or revenge, to borrow a phrase from Harry Berger, Jr., I read it as "mercifixion."[19] Berger uses the term to refer to the excessive passive-aggressive way in which mercy and giving in the play work to rack up more emotional debt from their recipients than the so-called gift might really be worth. I want to extend the meaning of "mercifixion" here to think about it also in relation to the mercy extended to Shylock, which renders mercy as the equivalent of forcing the forgiven to repay the debt. Mercifixion makes the recipient of mercy also the one who performs the actual satisfaction; Shylock is thus simultaneously the recipient of mercy and he who receives the punishment—both combined in the same act. Unlike the Christian narrative in which mercy is rendered unto man through the crucifixion of Christ (a third party, who repays the debt for man), in this version he who repays the debt and is the recipient of mercy are one and the same. It thus becomes harder to see mercy as fortunate or prosperous, as something that transforms something into nothing. While this resolution eliminates Antonio's financial problems, it leaves the play ever more enmeshed within the potential contradictions of Christian discourse on redemption, precisely because revenge is not distilled from mercy and the comic resolution imagined does not go beyond that of the romantic comedy in which property is redistributed from one family to the other. If anything, the conversion of Shylock—the making of the Jew into a Christian at precisely the moment of the repayment (perhaps recalling Jesus's own fate)—makes this figurative marriage resolution more endogamous than exogamous and makes Venice not just xenophobic, but also claustrophobic, an enclosed world without a model for dynamic economic process.

Gentle, Generic Mercy

In order to see the implications of this mercifixion for both the play's generic development and its limitations, I want to return to an earlier character on which Shakespeare's play piggybacks: Marlowe's similarly implemented Barabas, the title character of *The Jew of Malta*. Doing so will help us to see how *The Merchant of Venice's* imposition of comedy on a revenge tragedy leads to a kind of insularity that would ultimately prevent not only profitability, but also the very trade that the world of the play initially seeks to accommodate and make safe. Marlowe's revenge tragedy, first performed in 1592 and revived in 1594 (perhaps because of the trial and execution of Elizabeth's Jewish physician, Dr. Lopez) begins with the Knights of Malta issuing a decree that the Jews of Malta will be responsible for paying back-tribute owed to the Turks. According to the decree, all Jews must pay half of their estates. Anyone who refuses to pay shall straight become a Christian, and finally anyone who denies the decree shall lose all. This decree revises a historical one: in 1492, the Jews of Malta could avoid expulsion only by purchasing Christian baptism at the price of 45 percent of their wealth.[20] In Marlowe's play, the merchant/usurer Barabas refuses and thus loses all of his wealth (at least all of which the Knights are aware). Here begins the cycle of revenge and repayment. The conditions of mercy rendered unto Shylock by Antonio (that he give up half his goods and convert) are thus strikingly similar to those that initiate Barabas's revenge rampage. Explicitly invoking the logic of Christ's sacrifice and the role of the Jews in the choice of Barabas over Jesus, Marlowe's Barabas responds with horror at the threat that he will have all of his wealth taken away if he does not acquiesce to the giving up of half of it: "*Corpo di Dio!*" he ironically exclaims.[21] To drive the connections home between Christ's sacrifice and that of the Jews in the play, Marlowe has the governor of Malta rebut

Barabas's resistance by paraphrasing the High Priest whose words were responsible for the plotting of Jesus's death: "we take particularly thine / To save the ruin of a multitude; And better one want for a common good / Than many perish for a private man."[22] Marlowe makes clear the scapegoat logic by which Malta operates; indeed, Barabas calls specific attention to it, asking if he should be "tried by their [the members' of his tribe] transgression?"[23] Conflating Jesus's role (dying for mankind's sins) with the punishment of Jews for their role in Jesus's death, this scene, like that of the trial in *The Merchant of Venice*, highlights the difficulty of distilling revenge from mercy and satisfaction.

But whereas these events in *The Jew of Malta* initiate Barabas's revenge rampage, in *The Merchant of Venice* they are offered as a resolution. *The Merchant of Venice* thus rewrites *The Jew of Malta* as a comedy; more precisely, it revises what is a tragic initiator of Barabas's revenge plot into a comic ending or resolution, one that makes the fall of Shylock fortunate for others. The fall of Shylock (the loss of half of his estate and his forced conversion) works in contrast to the beginning of Barabas's plotting by both marking the end of Shylock's revenge and leading to a transfer of wealth to the Christian characters in the play, even equating the end of his revenge and that transfer. His fall is thus formally fortunate for the play and economically fortunate for its Christian characters.

Reading *The Merchant of Venice* as a rewriting of a revenge tragedy into a comedy that does not really change the logic of the primary tragic component reveals the ways in which the play's use of the economics of redemption superimposes a comedy onto a revenge tragedy. In Marlowe's play, unlike in Shakespeare's, Barabas remains the focus (as Shylock does not) immediately after his wealth is taken away and thus continues the play on its unprofitable course. The governor of Malta invites Barabas to "Live still; and if thou canst, get more."[24] Barabas responds to such a plan with disbelief: "Christians, what or how can I multiply? / Of naught is nothing made."[25] In Barabas's pessimistic response we can hear the inverse of Richard Greenham's formulation of mercy. In Christ's redemption of mankind, nothing is made into something, but Barabas's skepticism points to the difficulty of transforming loss into something of value, of making loss pay. Shakespeare's play foregrounds this very issue, as I have been suggesting. Departing from Marlowe's play, Shakespeare's makes use of Barabas's question and the discourses of the economics of redemption it invokes in order to rethink the tragic perspective associated with foreign trade, and tries to resolve the dilemma of ethical profits by imagining a comic ending to the tragedy that has preceded it. *The Merchant of Venice* does so, however, only through coercion—of both Shylock and perhaps the genre of the play itself. It passes off revenge tragedy as comedy. Immediately after

Barabas asks his question, Marlowe's play returns to the idea of Barabas's (and his people's) sins as if to remind the audience of the costs of re-demption. Shakespeare's play instead turns away from Shylock toward the ideas of miraculous productivity and immaculate re-production in which lost things can miraculously reappear.[26]

Most of the final act of *The Merchant of Venice* is taken up with the ring plot through which Portia manages to transfer Bassanio's indebtedness from Antonio to herself, but the play ends with a quick yet definitive end to the financial problems (if not the conflicts and contradictions) plaguing the play. It does so by returning to conventions of romance with which the play's marriage plot begins. In the play's final moments, Portia hands Antonio a letter informing him that three of his ships have "richly come to harbor suddenly" (5.1.276). Nerissa, Portia's maid, then gives Jessica and Lorenzo the "deed of gift" in which Shylock bequeaths to them upon his death all of his possessions. Both Antonio and Lorenzo make remarks that provide a perspective for how these events are to be understood, even if how the events came about is inexplicable (the return of the ships) or left unexplained (the deed of gift). Anto-nio, with lines that echo and revise both Barabas's and Shylock's con-cerns about the theft of their wealth, says, "sweet lady, you have given me life and living" (5.1.285).[27] Lorenzo remarks, "Fair ladies, you drop manna in the way / Of starved people" (293–94). Much removed from the play's opening speeches, in which the mere invocation of foreign trade led to a tragic perspective, what we have here is a vision of plenty and largesse.

It would be possible to read this ending, as Scott Shershow interest-ingly does, as speciously representing loss with return, thus as contribut-ing to the "ruse with which capitalism, both then and now, grounds itself in economic restriction (investment with 'return') and at the same time cloaks itself with an ethic of generosity."[28] We can certainly read the play's concluding gifts that way, especially given the way this resolution ultimately envisions these returns as Portia's gifts that are understood in turn through the metaphor of an Old Testament form of abundance, manna. The quality of gift giving and largesse is absorbed into the fortu-nate, magical ending. The play seems to get to have it both ways. In this model one does not have to give up on accumulation of wealth as an objective, because the system through which it is acquired is ultimately ethically generous. While we do not usually think of capitalism as a gift-giving economy or particularly based in the magical, what the two might share, at least in terms of the play, is the fantasy of magical production. Fundamental to capitalism and the concept of investment in particular is that the expenditure itself—what you invest—is what is productive of future profits. The expenditure magically increases without effort or labor. But as that expectation becomes the norm—the definition of "investment," after all, is the "outlay of money in the *expectation* of a profit"—one appears to earn or even deserve more money simply because one has expended some amount.

This reading certainly has some explanatory power, and though the play interestingly glimpses these possibilities, I will argue that it falls short of fully imagining them for three related reasons. First, though the ending is certainly fortunate (for the Christian characters), profit itself is still largely disavowed. The ships "richly come to harbor." But the adverb "richly" disavows the profits that might be contained in the hull as much as it suggests them, for it invokes a quality of the ships themselves—a way they move or are—just as Antonio's wealth is embodied in him (he is a "good man," a man of credit) and as Portia is a "lady richly left" (1.1.161). What we get in the final act is a return of his ships, but not necessarily a profitable one. Indeed, profits are not mentioned anywhere in the play except negatively in relation to usury and the breeding of coins. Profits and the circulation that might produce them are still nowhere to be seen. Instead what we have is a quality that seems to be inherent to the ships themselves rather than the result of effort and movement.

Second, even the transfer of money from Shylock to Lorenzo is not profit; it is merely a transfer. The real mystification, or ruse of capitalism, is that it is productive, that value is created, and thus that one can gain without anyone else's losing, because value is created through the mere circulation of money and goods. Thus while Portia's magical largesse might seem to hide the loss from view, the reminder of Shylock's deed of gift in this last scene (as does the invocation of Old Testament abundance—manna—divorced from works, merit, or productivity, one that enables Jews to escape from persecution) recalls that on the whole nothing has been gained. It is still a zero sum game.

The play then is ultimately a revenge tragedy-romance comedy or, for short, a revenge comedy. But to see this genre and the contradictions it highlights as merely interested in representations of hypocrisy is to miss the point. Instead, I want to argue that the play keeps bumping up against the limitations of its generic form, and thus is unable to get out of its impasses, or can get out of them only by fudging, creating mirror images of its initial problems.[29] The attempt to make a comedy out of what would otherwise be a revenge tragedy can lead only to irony or the hypocrisy that underlies the play's representation particularly of its Christian characters.

Moreover, forcing comedy onto tragedy requires a scapegoat, and the logic of the scapegoat is by definition not productive, it is insulating. As a comedy that requires closure, the play can conclude happily only by eliminating Shylock and his insistence on the pound of flesh.[30] In return it gets manna, the return of Antonio's ships (the pound of flesh was always the image of their loss), and magically produced benefits. For all its rhetoric of fairness to aliens, the play ultimately shuts its doors and insists on insularity. The play thus ends with an impasse not unlike the one with which it began. There is no way to account for or even imagine productivity within a genre that insists on closure—which here includes forced conversion, transfer of funds, and a scapegoat/sacrifice—the costs of which, generically speaking, are very high. Because the play requires closure in the form of a resolution that is protective, it has no way to imagine gain except as the result of revenge or its mirror image—free gift.[31] Formally speaking, the play never severs redemption from revenge and, practically speaking, the resulting scapegoat logic on which the play depends forecloses on the credit economy, eliminating the source by which money could be found and circulated. Thus there is no way to imagine productivity—only transfer/repayment/retribution/satisfaction or a free gift that is ultimately unrepayable. In other words, the play leaves itself with no way to imagine gain that is not at the expense of another or the result of divine generosity.[32]

While the play ends happily, a future for trade is hard to imagine. While recent critics have usefully demonstrated the ways that it is actually Antonio, rather than Shylock, who might be the figure for capitalist energies and processes in the play (Michael Ferber, for example, argues that in this play Shakespeare "tied capitalism to a sort of anti-Calvinist Christianity that encouraged uncalculating acts of sacrifice and risk"), the play's turn to generosity actually prevents the imagination of profits just as the play bumps up against formal limits.[33] Even the return of the ships is subsumed under Portia's generosity, thus is actually a return to the original marriage plot, which points not toward expansion but toward redistribution. Figured as largesse, the return of the ships, like manna, might be a free gift, but it also functions as a way to disengage with economic processes and with the future. What is done is done; an end has been achieved. The play's events are a one-time occurrence. The comic form thus does not allow for the kind of transformation that Greenham imagines when he defines mercy as the transformation of nothing into something.

It will take the genre of tragicomedy along with the mercantilists and their more secular thinking about the logic of redemption to imagine a model of productivity that does not depend on the gift or revenge alternative. *The Merchant of Venice* is certainly a generic hybrid in that it incorporates romantic comedy and revenge tragedy. But by merely superimposing one over the other or embedding one inside the other, it does not imagine a dialogue among them. In addition to the disavowal of profits and the use of a scapegoat, the lack of dialogue between the two genres is the third reason that the play does not fully imagine the profitability of loss. The play uses the Christian narrative of redemption to explore economic questions, but does not go as far as tragicomedy does to make that narrative the generic foundation; instead the play keeps the genres from dialectically engaging with each other. By insisting on the priority of comedy/romance over tragedy, it does not make use of the tension between the two primary genres; instead it disavows profit and it does not make use of tragedy's loss. As a result, the unwanted element (Shylock) is merely excluded even as the value he embodies is transferred to the remaining characters. Thus no tension has been resolved; it has only been eliminated. The play ends strangely; after so closely intertwining the strands of its plots (making Bassanio's romance dependent on the borrowing of money in the Venetian credit market, for example) the play merely re-separates them at the end, leaving Shylock behind.

My project here has not been to figure out whether the play is pro- or anti-capitalist, or who is the figure for capitalism, or even whether the play is anti-Semitic. Instead, the significance of reading this play through the lens of the economics of redemption, in part, is to explore the limitations of the structure of comedy for thinking through and resolving contemporary economic problems. The remainder of this chapter focuses on the slightly later and less explicitly historical *Twelfth Night* to demonstrate how similar problems are abstracted into the comic form itself as a means of exploring—even dramatically representing—the limitations of comedy's mechanisms for resolution, as if the comic genre itself has used up its own stock and resources such that it can no longer account for or resolve the economic conflicts with which it particularly engages.

Potentially Tragicomic Investments

With the exception of discussions of social mobility, *Twelfth Night* is not usually read as a play with significant economic concerns.[34] Yet it is a play very much concerned with the relationships between loss and profit, especially forms of loss that cannot quite be made into profit. In what follows, I argue that the absence of critical reflection on the play's economics and the play's own inability to imagine profits stem from the same cause, the play's suppression of its material contexts and those of its literary sources. In the consequent derealized noneconomic world it imagines, the play disavows the very conflicts that are at its center and thus loses the opportunity to imagine that profits can be made out of the losses the play earlier sustains.

Like *The Merchant of Venice*, *Twelfth Night*, as I suggested in the Introduction, is a play that intertwines comedic obstacles (especially, in this case unrequited love) and more profound losses. The play opens with Orsino contemplating his own unrequited desires for Olivia, but loss and the attempts to redeem loss set the play's tone and drive the plot forward. Moreover, though the play does continue to try to overcome the comedic obstacles it presents, it in part does so by first foregrounding the potential for loss. In fact, the play is both haunted and framed by losses—threatened, imagined, and actual. Going a step further than *The Merchant of Venice*, *Twelfth Night* begins not only with imagined and suspected losses, but actual ones. *Twelfth Night* foregrounds both Viola and Olivia's loss of a sibling (a beloved brother) and in Viola's case, an "identical" twin, her double—a version of herself—lost in a storm at sea. While *The Merchant of Venice* begins with a discussion of the nautical dangers of foreign trade, *Twelfth Night*'s plot is initiated by an actual shipwreck. The main plot develops from these losses: Viola, who finds herself alone and unprotected on a foreign shore, decides to cross-dress in order to serve Count Orsino, because she cannot serve Olivia; she cannot serve Olivia because Olivia is in mourning and will thus admit no suitors.

In her first scene, Viola emerges on Illyria's shore as a survivor of a shipwreck. Her conversation with that ship's captain sets up the possibility for the redemptive pattern in which these losses and maybe loss itself can be imagined to be redeemed. By the end of this scene, she has discovered a plan to find a place for herself within Illyria: she will pretend to be a eunuch, serve Orsino, and perhaps even woo him for herself. Furthermore, by cross-dressing, she will take the place of that very lost brother in a substitution/resurrection. In other words, she will take on a disguise that will lead to potentially more loss and difficulty but with the possibility of reward at the end—the recovery of her brother (who might perchance be saved as well) and a marriage to the Count of Illyria. This plot's larger design seems to provide a microcosm of the tragicomic: first shipwreck, continued wandering/suffering, and then the reward produced out of that loss. The play thus holds out tragicomic potential.[35]

Viola's plan itself (which then drives/structures the rest of the play) embodies the tragicomic design. It leads to further tribulations and also contains within it the hope for profit or reward. But tragicomic potential is even further embedded in the specificity of this plan. Though critics usually refer to Viola's disguise merely as cross-dressing, when she presents her plan to the Captain she says not that she will play the part of a man or page, but that she will play a eunuch. Most critics and editors have ignored this comment or written it off as the result of revision or error, since s/he does not explicitly present him/herself to Orsino as a eunuch, and s/he does not literally sing.[36] More recently, however, both Keir Elam and Stephen Orgel have provided important readings of the implications of the eunuch for *Twelfth Night*.[37] Both have begun by questioning the peculiarity of her choice given her desires. As Orgel points out, the eunuch is an apposite figure for Viola/Cesario whose desires, especially regarding Orsino, are frustrated throughout the play.[38] As a result, Viola's decision to impersonate a eunuch is paradoxical, because she chooses this disguise precisely to overcome her frustrated desires—in order to gain opportunity, not to deprive herself of it. It is this aspect of the eunuch figure that Elam seeks to illuminate when he asks, "why should she posit disfigurement and loss, in the form of castration, as a mode of gain, something to her advantage?"[39] Elam answers the question in part by tracing *Twelfth Night*'s debt to the stage history of the eunuch from Terence's *Eunuchus* to Italian Renaissance *commedia*. In *Eunuchus*, the lover, Charea, poses as a castrated servant in order to get access to his beloved, an inversion "whereby what looks like the neutralizing of male sexuality turns out instead to be a triumphant assertion of virility."[40] The theatrical figure of the eunuch is interesting, then, because it paradoxically empowers the character that takes up the position of impotence. The (impersonated) eunuch, then, is a figure that inverts its own constitutive limitations and transforms those limitations into possibility. The significance of the trajectory of the plan itself, which Elam insightfully notes, is that loss is imagined to be not only the source of advantage, but also *transformable* into profit or gain.

In Viola's plan, we might see a link to the tragicomic design as well as to the economic models developing in this period in which loss was reconfigured as expenditure, thus as a source of future profit.[41] Moreover, we might see her plan as evidence of a developing, though ambivalent, link between loss and profit. These connections are present not only in the general outline of her plan, however, but are also embodied in the very materiality of Viola's exchange with the Captain. Paying considerable attention to Viola's cross-dressing, critics have glossed over both her initial notion to pretend to be a eunuch and the very transaction that leads to it. In the lines that precede Viola's decision to impersonate a eunuch, she makes a request for the captain's assistance and a generous financial offer:

There is a fair behaviour in thee, Captain;
And though that nature with a beauteous wall
Doth oft close in pollution, yet of thee
I will believe thou hast a mind that suits
With this thy fair and outward character.
I prithee (and I'll pay thee bounteously)

Conceal me what I am, and be my aid
For such disguise as haply shall become
The form of my intent. I'll serve this duke;
Thou shalt present me as an eunuch to him.[42]

Though Viola's solicitation of the Captain is steeped in the language of courtesy, what seems to be at the heart of her request is an offer to pay him a good deal of money for his assistance and participation in her disguise as well as the clothing itself, which will be necessary for her to enter the Duke's service as something she is not (that is, a eunuch).

Curiously, the information regarding that she will pay the Captain and pay him bounteously is subordinated in this dialogue (literally placed in parentheses in the First Folio). Grammatically, the financial offer is suppressed; from within the parentheses, however, the offer still puts pressure on courtesy's "beauteous wall." The parentheses mark the way that Viola's attempts to redeem her situation embroil her within the play's financial economies and highlight the play's interest in marking the economic as only parenthetical.

It might first appear that the play's interest in redemption, unlike that of *The Merchant of Venice*, has little to do with the economics embedded in the concept. On the contrary, the connection here is also significant, if not quite explicit. Viola's purchase of clothing, in particular, could be read as a literal (in)vestment that functions as a rematerialization of the partially disavowed expenditure. Prior to the early seventeenth century, "to invest" did not yet have the now dominant economic meaning it now has in English, nor did it have economic connotations. The *OED* offers the following definitions, all tied more closely to clothing (i.e., to vestments) than to money: "to clothe, robe, or envelop (a person) in or with a garment or article of clothing"; "to clothe or endue with attributes, qualities or a character"; "to establish in the possession of any office, position, property"; "to endow or furnish with power, authority, or privilege"; "to clothe with or in the insignia of an office, hence, with the dignity itself"; and "to install in an office or rank with the customary rites or ceremonies." All of these meanings are in some way relevant here.

Viola's disguise, however, also gestures toward the soon-to-be minted economic meaning of "investment": "the outlay of money in the expectation of a profit."[43] For an early modern audience, perhaps no object would appear as steeped in the economy as did clothing. As Ann Rosalind Jones and Peter Stallybrass have convincingly argued, clothes were themselves a significant form of currency (i.e., an accepted medium of exchange) in the early modern period; they were circulated, detached, reassembled, and pawned in a society without a functioning modern banking system or much liquidity. The circulation of clothing for economic purposes, they argue, was not an exception but the norm.[44] Clothing was also at the center of debates about England's economic stability in the period. Wool cloth was England's primary export, but it was becoming increasingly unpopular both abroad and at home and was often blamed for England's negative trade imbalance, thus for the emptying of its coffers.[45] This unpopularity stimulated the search for new markets for wool and in some instances led to the development of new trade routes.[46] The increasing importance of fashion, the subject of much anxiety in the period, was also stimulated by and was a catalyst for these expanding markets.[47] Furthermore, as the available style of clothes and the fabrics out of which they were made proliferated, domestic production itself was stimulated and transformed.[48] Clothing also became an important part of England's multilateral trade for East Indian spices. Because England's wool cloth was not particularly vendible in the warm climate of the East Indies, the English traded for calico and indigo at East Indian ports in order to exchange these goods for the spices that were in great demand at home.[49] As a result of these changes, there was an increased speed in the circulation of clothes—both new and second hand—and of other goods from newly tapped foreign markets. It is not just that clothing was a sign of wealth or status (as sumptuary laws suggest), but that clothing was enmeshed in the economy.

This link is evident in the very extension of the range of meanings of the term "investment" from something one does with clothing to something one does with money, an extension that takes place in the early part of the seventeenth century. To invest begins to mean not only to clothe or bestow in an office, but also "to employ money in the purchase of anything from which profit [or interest] is expected." Perhaps the term picked up economic resonances in part from clothing's centrality to the economy and especially its relationship to foreign trade. Significantly, the *OED*'s first two examples of the commercial usage of "to invest" and the first three of "investment" are from the East India Company's correspondence; most of the examples through the eighteenth century are explicitly about overseas trade. Furthermore, the *OED* speculates that the economic meaning emerges in English through the Levant or Turkey Company prior to the East India Company. So the new financial meaning of "invest" is a result of developing markets in foreign trade in which clothing was central.

The explicit etymological connection between clothing and the outlay of money in the expectation of a profit lies in their shared transformative possibilities: to "invest" is to give "the capital another 'form.'"[50] In fact, all of the early examples of the new economic meaning emphasize the *transformation* of money into goods into more money, or money into goods, into different goods, back into more money.[51] As Viola's plan suggests, clothing has transformative powers; in Elam's terms it can turn dispossession into advantage, loss into gain. The possibility for that gain to be explicitly material and economic is alluded to in the substance of the exchange: both the clothing purchased and the money used to make that purchase. In other words, Viola's plan boils down to the transformation of money into a form of wares, which would then produce an even greater gain. While I do not want to elide the symbolic value of her purchase, what I want to illuminate is what is less often discussed: how the material aspects of her plan follow along the lines of tragicomic investments.[52] Her plan is to transform her initial unanticipated loss into a gain and a further planned loss or expenditure (her outlay of money and the taking up of the position of the eunuch) into gain as well. This is precisely what was new about the very use of the idea of investment in the early seventeenth century. Investment was a concept developed to explain that losses (bullion sent out of the country) were not really losses, but instead should be understood as expenditure that would lead to a greater inflow of bullion (i.e., profit) at a later time.

"What You Will"; Or, What We Don't Want to Know About Viola's Clothes

Given the material considerations of Viola's plan as well as the fact that a focus of recent criticism has been *Twelfth Night*'s interest in social mobility and the relationship between subjects and objects in early modern culture, why do critics seem to slip past Viola's purchase of clothing from the Captain?[53] As I mentioned earlier, the parentheses mark the information as subordinate. They also, at least for a reader if not an audience member, set off the transaction, thereby making it more visible and thus harder to miss. Why, then, do the gendered and sexual readings of Viola's cross-dressing predominate? A partial explanation could be made by referring to current critical concerns (e.g., cross-dressing and what it tells us about the connections between gender and sexuality). An even more persuasive explanation is that the play invites us to slip past the transaction, and that this invitation has much to do with the relationship the play sets up between its formal and thematic concerns.

First, the point of Viola's disguise within the plot of the play is to allow *her* to get past the play's material contexts and the limitations they would otherwise impose. It is not only that she takes on a disguise that conceals her position, but also that she does so in order to avoid all of the constraints posed by the circumstances of Illyria itself: Orsino already has an object of desire, Olivia will accept no suitors, Illyria is not an altogether safe place. On the one hand, the point of Viola's plan is to transform loss into gain; the vehicle of her plan registers the material world in which doing so would be possible. On the other hand, the plan's purpose is not to make use of her material contexts and constraints, but to avoid them. Illyria becomes increasingly anti-topic, rather than utopic (that is, the play rejects the constraints of place) and Viola/Cesario operates throughout the play according to an autonomy effect in which s/he seems unimpeded by material reality, even if her desires are temporarily frustrated. Though we might argue that she is making use of the loss of her brother (through a partial imitation of him), most of the play's characters proceed as if unrestricted and unaffected by losses: for example, Olivia stops mourning to pursue Cesario; Sir Andrew keeps pouring money into his pursuit of Olivia long after it becomes evident that he has no chance to win her; and Antonio stays in Illyria to be with and protect Sebastian, even though it is Antonio himself who can not walk the streets there safely.[54]

These tensions help to explain what a number of critics have noticed about the play and put it in a different light. Eric Mallin, for example, argues that the play keeps the real at bay.[55] Similarly, Keir Elam notes that the play is full of enigmas and that it does little to resolve the questions it poses about meaning and reference.[56] Stephen Booth has demonstrated with great insight how the difficulty of the play's language requires that the audience become like Malvolio, who is shamed for interpreting signs so that they are in his favor; they foretell the fantasy he is already having.[57]

If we put these critics' insights together we can see how the play's refusal to fully acknowledge the historical constraints within which it works leads to its inability to resolve the very questions it poses. In other words, the inconclusivity and illegibility of the text are linked to the disavowal of the play's material contexts. Looking at the play's sources and not its future potential, Cristina Malcomson notes that the play suppresses its merchant roots in order to focus on the master-servant relation.[58] Comparing the play to the early modern mercantile Italian contexts of its sources, Keir Elam argues that the play "reflects the more static world of landowners."[59] While I agree that England's economy might not have matched that of some of the Italian city-states at the time, nonetheless I think Elam understates the concerns about movement of people, objects, and money in early modern England. I would thus also want to revise Malcomson to suggest that the play stages this shift in focus not just as a form of nostalgia for master-servant relations, but as a way to imagine a happy ending, a reality in which losses are less visible and can be deemed derivative of the bad behavior of characters like Feste, Sir Toby, and Malvolio, dependent members of Olivia's manor household, rather than from the socioeconomic material conditions that are kept just underneath the play's surface. The play can thus disavow the kinds of conflicts and losses that the play's organizing action—the shipwreck—might entail and proceed to its comic resolution.

The disavowal that I am analyzing here is actually what makes the play a comedy rather than tragicomedy, that is, the disavowal marks the play's inability to move toward, or fulfill the promise of its tragicomic potential. In his discussion of the limits of comedy, David Kastan explains that "according to the generic definitions derived from the late classical commentaries on Terence, comic action—unlike tragic—is to be feigned rather than drawn from history, testifying to comedy's freedom to shape its fiction into comforting patterns of wish fulfillment."[60] This distinction provides useful insight into the workings of *Twelfth Night*, a play that stages the disavowal of its material concerns, especially the losses that it transforms into more comedic obstacles. The play thus stages tension between its more tragicomic potential, in which losses could transform into gains, and its more comedic structure, in which loss and material constraints are disavowed rather than being a source of productive contradiction.[61]

I want to argue that Shakespearean comedy, and *Twelfth Night* in particular, is especially interested in demonstrating these costs, of showing us the tension between the reality principle and that of the pleasure principle, to use the psychoanalytic terminology Kastan borrows for his analysis. The cost of comedy, to paraphrase Kastan, is that it denies reality. Critical conversations on *Twelfth Night*, as I suggested above, repeatedly point to the way that the play stages a gap between its referents and the contexts to which they ought to be pointing. I want to suggest that the play is primarily interested in this gap, in what comedy does and fails to do by not fully engaging with its context—that is, by almost engaging but then swerving away in order to follow a comedic pattern.

Though the focus of this reading is not on the play's concern with the relationship between ontology and representation as it is worked out in the play's thematic concerns—for example, with identity (a concern of much recent criticism on the play)—I am particularly interested in exploring the formal implications of the gap between the play's referents and what is represented.[62] One of the further benefits of this reading is that it brings into focus that the play has other pressing thematic concerns (that is, economic ones) but that it represses them, because it cannot fully engage them within the form of comedy. In illuminating the play's formal concerns in relation to its repressed economic concerns, part of my project here is to provide a material context for Kastan's insight about the subordination of the reality principle to that of the pleasure principle, one that demonstrates the costs of denying reality within an increasing mercantile economy. *Twelfth Night* might be a particularly good example of such costs since it suppresses the play's merchant roots through Viola's and Sebastian's parentage (noble in this play, but mercantile in its most immediate dramatic source, *Gl'Ingannati*), through the play's highly conventionalized romantic and courtly pursuits, and through the highly affective qualities of Viola's disguise. Thus to say that the disguise allows Viola to circumvent material restrictions is to acknowledge its relationship not only to the plot, but also to the contexts from which the plot develops. Yet, as I suggested above, the disguise also embodies the historical, especially economic, concerns within which it also embroils her. This tension, the simultaneous registering and denying of material concerns, organizes the play and is what makes it comic rather than tragicomic. Or more precisely, the denial of material concerns is what makes *Twelfth Night* comic, and the simultaneous registering and denying (that is, disavowal) of both loss and material, economic concerns (especially material forms of loss) is what makes it a stepping-stone to the tragicomic. It is a play that highlights even as it undermines its own comic wish-fulfillment and thus makes the comic limitation more visible. Eric Mallin observes that the play's "general shape, in which shipwreck leads to further tribulation and finally to reward, parodies the Christian redemption story."[63] But the play does not parody redemption so much as swerve away from redemption precisely because as a comedy, it cannot engage fully with the problems it raises. Viola's disguise makes use of the play's losses and avoids them simultaneously. It embodies both possibilities, but stops short of making use of the contradiction, and the play, as I will argue below, chooses instead to follow the path of its subtitle: "what you will."

Failed Redemptions

The costs of the path of wish-fulfillment—that is, stopping short of fully engaging with the material contexts—are registered in a parallel plot about the other twin's interactions with a sea venturer and in the fate of that venturer.[64] In order better to understand the significance of *Twelfth Night*'s disengagements from its material contexts, we need to turn our attention to this character, especially to his relationship to the possibilities for redemption.

The only place in the play in which redemption appears explicitly is in Sebastian's relationship with Antonio. In their first scene, Sebastian twice mentions that Antonio has "recovered" him from the sea, that is, Antonio has saved Sebastian's life by taking him from the sea's "breach" (2.1.37, 22). Antonio thus enters the play explicitly as a redeemer. Though Antonio seems to be all about generosity and sacrifice (like that other Antonio in *The Merchant of Venice*), when he finds himself in trouble he is quick to remind others of his prior redemptive actions and insist upon their significance. Toward the end of the third act, Antonio mistakes Viola/Cesario for Sebastian and comes to his/her defense in the duel s/he is trying not to fight with Sir Andrew. In this moment, Antonio is recognized and apprehended by Orsino's men for previously attacking Orsino's ships. Upon his arrest, Antonio turns to Viola/Cesario and after informing her/him that "This comes with seeking you," he asks, "What will you do, now my necessity / Makes me to ask you for my purse?" (3.4.340, 342–43). Of course, Viola/Cesario does not know to what purse he is referring, since he gave the purse to Sebastian and s/he thus only offers him some money, exactly half her/his "coffer" (355). Incensed by the ingratitude, Antonio refuses this offer and asks again for his purse, worrying that if his request is not granted he will upbraid his friend for "those kindnesses/That [he has] done" (360–61). Unable to redeem himself, that is, unable to purchase his freedom from his captors (conceivably why he needs his purse), he asks his captors permission to speak in order to tell his story:

This youth that you see here
I snatch'd one half out of the jaws of death,
Reliev'd him with such sanctity of love;
And to his image, which methought did promise
Most venerable worth, did I devotion. (368–72)[65]

In the play's final scene, he again points to Viola/Cesario as the ungrateful boy whom he did "redeem" from the "rude sea's enrag'd and foamy mouth," but who now will do nothing for him in return (5.1.77, 76). This tale ends with the accusation that the boy even denies him his own purse. Thus, in the places that redemption is explicitly invoked, it is represented as failed or disrupted; in particular, its future profits (or returns) are denied.

I want to backtrack a bit to think about why Antonio's purse, which is also invoked in each of these encounters, becomes the vehicle or sign for the impossibility of recompensatory redemption.[66] In the Introduction and throughout this book I ask why tragicomedies return to the theme of redemption in the midst of economic crises. Antonio's frustrating encounters provoke a related but slightly different set of questions: why do these turns to redemption fail? Specifically, what might the failure of redemption represented in the purse tell us about both the economic crises with which the play seems to want to engage and the play's inability to address these crises?

Though Antonio gives his purse to Sebastian as a gesture of affection, even of love, the purse is not only an expression of Antonio's personal feelings. While the circulation of any purse would seem to be at least in part about the circulation of money, the very source of this purse's con-

tents is particularly telling here. Antonio makes his offer of the purse immediately after his partial admission that he is in danger in Illyria for an
act of piracy. He also acknowledges that the real source of his danger in
Illyria is that he alone has stood out and did not repay what was stolen,
which he explains, "for traffic's sake / Most of our city did. Only myself
stood out, / For which, if I be lapsed in this place, / I shall pay dear"
(3.3.34–37).[67] I suggest that this purse has a history, one that makes its
contents particularly significant. The purse represents what was stolen
from Orsino—stolen, the play repeatedly suggests, in an act of piracy. In
fact, each of the three times the purse is invoked (in 3.3, 3.4, and 5.1) it
follows upon the suggestion, or even direct accusation, of Antonio's
piracy. In 3.3, as I discussed above, Antonio gives his purse to Sebastian;
in the following scene he asks for it back from Viola/Cesario, who does
not have it. In this scene there is logic to the simultaneous mention of
purse and piracy: Antonio is being arrested, thus needs his purse. In the
final scene, however, there is no such causal connection. The officers
who hold Antonio remind Orsino that their prisoner stole their ship and
its freight from Candy (i.e., Crete). Orsino then recognizes Antonio as a
man who posed a serious threat to even their best ships. He then accuses
Antonio, calling him a "notable pirate" and "salt-water thief" (5.1.67). In
his defense, Antonio denies being a pirate, then adds that the boy by the
Duke's side he did "redeem. A wrack past hope he was. / His life I gave
him" (5.1.77–78). He concludes his defense by paradoxically accusing
Viola/Cesario, who he thinks is Sebastian, of denying him his purse,
which presumably contained what was stolen from Orsino.

My point is not that the play is primarily concerned with piracy per
se.[68] The repeated invocations of piracy (along with the shipwreck that
begins the play) in conjunction with a purse filled with money taken outside of Illyria's boundaries and then brought back within them, however,
do materialize the concerns surrounding England's economy of foreign
trade. Indeed, referring to traffic in 3.4, Antonio explicitly calls attention to piracy's potential to inhibit trade.[69] But the purse also invokes
other less visible, or less easily traceable, costs of foreign trade. One of
the primary accusations against foreign trade in the early seventeenth
century was that it would deplete national resources by emptying England's coffers, as Antonio depleted Orsino's coffers. The exact reasons
for this loss of currency, however, were hotly contested. Many blamed excessive imports. If more coin and bullion than domestically produced
goods were sent abroad in exchange for imports, many argued, there
would be a net loss of money from England.[70] Relatedly, this loss was also
blamed on the disparity of the value of silver and gold at home and
abroad, as well as on the inconsistency of the weight of coins that were
often debased and clipped.[71] If silver and gold were valued more highly

abroad, they would more likely be sent out of the country. Though piracy was a very serious threat and, as I suggested above, one that was partially blamed for the loss of wealth from England, it could also be invoked as a way to locate a threat that was otherwise hard to define. Antonio and his purse could serve that function here by standing in for the potential losses associated with foreign trade, of which piracy is one. The purse, which is itself both unredeemable and incapable of providing redemption, is a sign of how trade could be disrupted (Antonio alone did not return what he stole) and how trade itself provides the occasion for loss. The missing purse doubly signifies the possibility for loss from which the world of the play needs to protect itself, especially the loss of money from the country's coffers.

The purse thus represents not simply the threat that foreigners pose when they enter the country, but the concern that the country itself is permeable—that unwanted elements could come in and currency could leak or be taken out. Though a full-blown debate about currency leaving the country would not occur for almost two decades, these concerns were discussed in some of the earliest mercantilist documents. In his 1601 tract, for example, Malynes rails against the "bringing in of superfluous commodities at a deare rate" as a result of which the "kings treasure is like water powred into a sive or basket, which presently runneth out, and is never filled" and against the false weight and measure of coins as a cause that "carieth out our treasure in bullion and money, empoverishing our commonweale."[72] Antonio's purse, then, represents the shadow side of Viola's purchase of clothing (both an export and an import item in England at the time); her purchase/investment seems potentially profitable, but it also contains within it the specter of loss.

Though the purse is an object of exchange, its primary role in the play is as something that cannot be returned. While the truth of the matter is that Viola/Cesario cannot return the purse because it was actually given to her twin brother Sebastian, what appears to happen from Antonio's perspective is a refusal on the part of the ungrateful Sebastian not just to return the purse, but also to acknowledge its very existence. The play thus stages a disruption to the purse's circulation or re-circulation that parallels and furthers Viola's previous refusal to acknowledge material constraints and the losses they might produce. In her purchase of the clothing she tries to circumvent the material restrictions of Illyria, to get past the play's material world; here, though s/he does not know it, what s/he is doing (or, what the world of the play is doing) is refusing to acknowledge the significance of Antonio except as a threat to be contained. When Viola/Cesario denies the existence of the purse, the loss that is contained in it and the potential resources it contains to produce future gains are denied participation in the world of Illyria. Refusing to acknowledge one act of redemption prevents another more literally profitable one.

The significance of disavowing these losses emerges in the play's unusual bipolar ending. On the one hand, the play unties the knots of its romantic plots and more. Rather than a recognition scene, this is an authentication scene: Malvolio tries to authenticate the letter he believes was sent to him by Olivia professing her love for him; Olivia tries to prove that she is legitimately married to Cesario; Sebastian tries to determine whether Cesario/Viola is truly his sister Viola, and Viola/Cesario tries to determine whether the copy of herself is really the original—him whom she imitates. In the final scene, all of these confusions are cleared up. Moreover, Orsino offers to marry Viola/Cesario, and we find out that Maria is married to Sir Toby. All of the potential couples are confirmed and deemed appropriate.

Yet, the play's closure is not without its costs. The final act of the play could be characterized as a series of interruptions followed by a series of deferrals. Orsino is distracted from Antonio when Olivia enters, and "heaven walks on earth." Orsino's attention never returns to Antonio, who is left imprisoned and immobilized, like the Captain, the other seafaring foreigner, and perhaps merchant, who is held in prison at Malvolio's suit, the substance of which is never explained. In the play's final moments, then, the two plots are for the first time brought into contact with each other, since we find out that the Captain still has Viola's "maiden weeds," and Orsino will continue to call his page "Cesario" until he sees him/her in her original clothes. The confirmation Viola/Cesario promises Sebastian rests on a return of the clothes that never takes place. The Captain is prevented from returning to Cesario the "woman's weeds" that would allow her to become Viola again, Sebastian to claim his sister, and Orsino to claim his wife to be. At the last moment, Malvolio's indirect possession of Viola's clothes produces a chain reaction that works its way backward through the events of the play.[73] Not surprisingly, the ending is deferred to a fantasized, nostalgic future— when, as Orsino puts it, "golden time convents" (5.1.381). If Viola is the means by which the play swerves to avoid the historical and material concerns, she gets tied back into its knot in the play's ending. While the deferral of profit is inherent in investment, the deferral of this profit to a nostalgic future suggests that Viola will not be able to get the hoped-for return on her investment.

I would thus want to modify Ann Rosalind Jones's and Peter Stallybrass's observation that the play ends by introducing a whole new narrative about Viola's maiden weeds.[74] Their formulation suggests that the play gestures toward further productivity, at least narrative productivity. But what seems most striking about this ending is that everything stalls just before the ending. If the original two plots are first brought together here at the play's end, they are also brought to a halt, as this conjunction makes Viola's identity dependent on Malvolio, who holds the Captain, who holds Viola's "maiden weeds."[75] Circulation is prevented, and the ending that ought to occur is prevented along with it; what remains is stasis. While there is potential for a whole new narrative, the play blocks off that future and simply comes to a halt. So rather than having a dynamic relationship between plots, as occurs in the slightly later, tragicomic *The Winter's Tale*, when these plots are brought together they stop dead in their tracks. What seems most important is not just that the play's resolution depends on leaving some things unresolved, but that the closure produces and depends on stasis. The play thus emphasizes its own generic limitations as the inability to produce the profits it imagines. In fact, the reunions and marriages come at the expense of, or at least in contradistinction to, the possible profits the play imagines. While the Viola/Sebastian pair seems to make use of an early loss to provide the excess necessary to enlarge the imagined world and thus to imagine a more profitable resolution than the standard conventional romantic comedy, the failure of Viola's transformation back into a woman keeps the play limited. The play gestures toward the tragicomic potential, but does not fully materialize it.

Instead, this play stages the costs of closure, showing the limitations of comedy especially for engaging with economic forces and foreign trade. The play's economy is static, however, not because all of the contradictions have been resolved (and thus there is no "work" left for the comedy to do) but because the forces of change and history are literally immobilized, and the contradictions have been swept under the rug. It thus seems particularly significant that Viola's clothing is not returned to her and that the obstruction to circulation results from the imprisonment of a sea captain, one whose occupation is about mobility and who would very likely also be involved in the movement of goods and money. It would be possible to take the Captain's imprisonment as pure coincidence and not relevant to the argument I made earlier about the connection between her clothing and foreign trade if it were not for two other salient details about the play's ending. The first is that the only other character imprisoned at the end of the play is also a sea venturer/pirate, that is, Antonio. His fate is left undetermined at the play's end. Second, like Viola's clothing, Antonio's purse is not returned.

Why is it that the two seafaring foreigners are imprisoned at play's end—one on stage for the entire final scene and one off stage—and that the two crucial objects previously under their control remain out of circulation? Imprisoning the two sea captains at the end keeps Illyria insulated, figuratively preventing traffic to and from areas outside of Illyria's boundaries, thus also preventing the losses associated with that trade. The lack of resolution around the purse has a similar function. Just as no one actually asks Malvolio about the Captain, even though Malvolio is remembered precisely for this purpose, Antonio does not ask Sebastian for the purse that was so crucial to him and which he demanded of Viola/Cesario only earlier in the same scene. It is still missing. The reason the play cannot accommodate its return might lie in one final set of contradictions the purse embodies. When Antonio gives the purse to Sebastian he suggests that he might need it to purchase a "toy," something unnecessary, a luxury. But when he asks for it back, he needs it to pay for his ransom, that is, to redeem himself, or perhaps to pay back what was stolen from Orsino. The reality of needing ransom is actually an outgrowth of the world of trade and piracy on which the import of those luxury items depend. Two seemingly different worlds—one of commerce and one of friendship—collide here, and Antonio's generosity is doubly indebted to the world of global commerce in which he participates. Moreover, though Antonio insists that Sebastian make use of the purse, when Antonio asks for it back he imagines that there will still be sufficient funds to pay for his ransom. The play's mix-ups depend in part on the fact that Viola does not have the purse to give back. But what makes Antonio think that there will be sufficient funds left in it to ransom himself even if he did get it back? If Sebastian has done what Antonio suggested, might not the purse be empty? Antonio's logic is that he can give, and money can be spent on luxury items, yet there will still be money left for ransom and payback. To stretch the reading just a bit, the purse might embody the very tensions in the logic of Christian redemption I discussed earlier in this chapter; the purse contains within it the matter for a gift (like that of God's mercy in Christ) and funds for payback. The situations do not map onto each other perfectly, but the connections are suggestive, especially since Antonio's logic (spending and still having) is similar to that of capital investment in which expenditures are productive of future profits.

From a narrative perspective, Antonio's reunion with Sebastian should include the return of the purse; its return is necessary to the resolution of their conflict and the mistaken identities. However, it is not so much that the narrative of the purse is left unresolved as it is left unacknowledged, as if nothing in the plot actually depends on it. Actually, nothing in the play does depend on it. Unlike the handkerchief in *Othello* or the chain in *Comedy of Errors*, whose circulations are crucial to the plot, the purse in *Twelfth Night* has no causal relation to the events of the play. The purse occupies an unusual position in that it is simultaneously central to the plot complications—a sign of mistaken identities and of Antonio's identity or history—and irrelevant to the plot itself. Perhaps its very irrelevancy is what makes it paradoxically relevant, a sign of the disavowal through which the play's "festive" quality is constituted.[76] While earlier in the play the redemptive potential of the purse is cut off by Viola/Cesario's inability to produce or return it, in the final scene it is as if the play itself has forgotten all about the purse. This very lack of recognition of the purse and all it represents is staged by the play as necessary to its own form, as a sign of the way that the play's insistence on closure depends on disavowing the very contradictions that are at its center and would otherwise drive the play toward more productive conclusions.

The play thus turns away from its earlier tragicomic gestures, refusing possibilities for redemption and offering a more static if somewhat happy conclusion in its place. Formally speaking, it is the play's refusal to engage with its own productive contradictions that lands it in stasis. Thematically speaking, it is the denial of loss that leads the play to be unable to recoup its profits. One might say that endings necessarily produce stasis because all is supposedly finished at play's end. But this play is conspicuously and uncomfortably both unfinished and stalled.[77] *Twelfth Night* thus explicitly stages the way that movement toward closure and the disavowal of losses that such closure requires prevent imagined profits from ensuing. Given the play's already partially submerged problems regarding foreign trade, this staging demonstrates how such closure and disavowal lead toward stasis—to an economy in which circulation is prevented rather than enhanced—and produces a world safe, because of insularity, rather than safely expansive and potentially profit-producing.[78] Generalizing from these observations, we might conclude that the genre of comedy itself, given its emphasis on closure rather than expansion, is formally inadequate to engage with new concerns and theories about foreign trade as they were being formulated in the early seventeenth century.

While in *The Merchant of Venice* the scapegoating of Shylock functions thematically to protect Venice from aliens at the cost of foreclosing on the credit economy, in *Twelfth Night* the scapegoating of Malvolio functions (through the imprisonment of the Captain who has Viola's maiden weeds) more formally to prevent the dialectical engagement of two genres necessary to a tragicomic, expansive profit. What is a more thematic problem in *The Merchant of Venice* is thus represented more explicitly as a problem of the form itself in *Twelfth Night*. In other words, Malvolio's "revenge" points to the very limitations of the scapegoat function in the genre of comedy.

As I suggested earlier, my analysis of these two "comedies" is not intended to point to the way that the ending is unsatisfying (e.g. that we know nothing of Olivia's thoughts about being married to the brother of her object of desire, or that Malvolio gets no satisfaction) or even to the fact that some pieces or issues of the play are left unresolved (e.g., that the play does not want to deal with problems of sexual identity or social mobility). Instead I am interested in the way that the play represents closure itself as something that works against sufficient resolution, in part by protecting the world of the play from historical forces.

While *Twelfth Night* stages its disengagement with historical and, in particular, economic concerns, it nonetheless engages with the potential for thematic content and generic forms to converge. The play thus provides the groundwork for thinking about how plays can register and address socio-historical concerns not only mimetically and thematically, but also in dramatic forms themselves. *Twelfth Night* in particular provides adumbrations of the genre of tragicomedy itself—a genre that develops in part by engaging with losses more seriously, thus requiring the development of a more dynamic—even dialectical—model.

Chapter Two

The Voyage Out: *Pericles*

Unlike *Twelfth Night,* which ends with insulation from foreigners and obstruction of profits, *Pericles* explores the possibilities of expanding economically by expanding geographically. So, while the ending of Shakespeare's late plays might seem conservative in the strictest political sense (of reunion and restoration) as critics have long suggested, the play's focus is on expansion, both geographic and economic. These are not opposites, but different models. This play (and other of Shakespeare's "romances" as well, I will argue) are not only interested in restoration or conservation, but also in exploring the relationships among production, profit, and the accumulation of value that expansion enables.

Pericles, in particular, is a significant play for this study because it actually demonstrates how the Christian model of redemption (which since Anselm has been understood in economic terms) is transformed back into an economic model in which losses can be understood to be productive of profits.[1] As I argued in the Introduction, Christian discourse of redemption, that of the fortunate fall, had long been steeped in economics. Christ purchases mankind and serves as a repayment to God for mankind's act of defrauding God. Prior to the Reformation the relationship between the economic and redemption at the individual level could be strikingly straightforward. For example, one could remit sins through the purchase of indulgences and acts of charity as well. This play takes a traditional formula—charity as a means to redeem the self through an act that aids others—and rewrites it so that newly imagined dynamic economic processes become their own form of a partially secular redemption.[2] This chapter thus has a threefold purpose: to demonstrate how the genre prefers expansion over insularity; to show how *Pericles* imagines a shift from a static model of scarcity and charity to a dynamic model of loss and profit, which has the added and necessary benefit of making expansion not only safe, but also a source of material accumulation; and third, to show how the play makes use of the economic valences in the theological concept of redemption in order to make the economic practices seem ethical as well as to rewrite the ethi-

cal questions so that they are imagined from the perspective of the economics themselves, that is, in order to think of them as economic rather
than as primarily moral problems.

Economic concerns are at the play's center. Critics have long devalued
the play for its episodic structure and lack of thematic coherence. Yet,
what the play lacks in dramatic buildup for being so episodic it gains in
thematic and structural momentum. All of Pericles' destinations and all
of the play's episodes have economic undercurrents if not explicitly economic foci—a point that seems to have been strangely lost on critics of
the play. Almost none of the criticism seems to notice the centrality of
the play's economic concerns.[3] If any thematic strain unites what some
critics complain is an incoherent and episodic plot, it is concerns about
charity and scarcity and the imagination of loss transformed into gain.

This transformation of loss into gain is also absorbed into the play's
formal structure to some extent, even staged in it. While the play's
episodic structure might seem to disrupt a narrative arc in which loss is
redeemed, I provide a different reading that perceives the episodic as
necessary to the play's concerns rather than as a drawback. In *Pericles*,
loss and gain continually follow on the heels of each other as if the les-
son needs to be relearned over and over. While critics have maligned the
play for this atheatrical, episodic quality, it might be the case that the
play also stages in this episodic quality a stepping-stone toward a model
in which profit can actually be the anticipated outcome of loss, anticipated because it has occurred repeatedly in the past. The episodic structure, I will argue, is thus not an impediment to the play's coherence. On
the contrary, it is the very means by which its thematic content is explored. In order to demonstrate this connection, this chapter follows the
course of the play's geography through three of its primary locales—
Antioch, Pentapolis, and Myteline—in order to show how the play's
episodic structure enables it to return to particular economic problems
and rework them.

Beyond Incest and Charity

Pericles has as its central underlying concern the possibility for extending outside the self that *Twelfth Night* disavows. The play begins with Pericles' arrival at the court of Antioch, where he hopes to win the king's
daughter by correctly solving a riddle presented by Antiochus, the king
and father of the desired bride. A wrong answer would cost Pericles his
head, as it has many prior suitors, but a correct response requires the
dangerous recognition of the incestuous relationship between Antiochus and his daughter. The play thus begins with its hero's engagement with an explicit sin that stems from the failure to properly extend

beyond the familial economy; as a result, it thematizes and literalizes the importance of intercourse beyond such a localized and insular economy.

The play here is reworking a problematic in the relationship between incest and economic gain. The unnatural breeding to which incest leads has a long association with illegitimate economic activity. Beginning with Aristotle, unnatural breeding has been a figure for usury (in ancient Greek, *tokos* is the word for both interest and offspring), and any kind of commerce whose end is profit rather than the satisfaction of need.[4] Aristotle begins his discussion of "unnatural acquisition" by comparing these unnatural methods to what he considers the most "natural" means of fulfilling need—maternal nourishment. Here is a late sixteenth century English translation of Aristotle: "it is most necessarie to have goods prepared by Nature, whose dutie it is to provide foode for all thinges that are engendred: For that which resteth and remaineth of that whereof every thing is engendred, is the foode unto it."[5] The same passage in a modern translation reads, "the offspring of animals always gets nourishment from the residuum of the matter that give it its birth."[6] For Aristotle, then, it is natural for the offspring to get its nourishment from the parent. He explains that the antithesis of this form of "naturally made" is making a profit at the expense of other men. As Eric Spencer insightfully argues in an essay on *The Merchant of Venice*, usury results in "stagnant *repetition* or *duplication*, rather than teleologically meaningful *fertility*, which implies change, development, and qualitative growth."[7] For Aristotle, commerce for profit is a perversion of means and ends, because money is supposed to be only a medium of exchange to obtain those things that are necessary for good living; money is thus not intended to be an end in itself. Usury, the most egregious form of profit making, thus results in the perverse and unproductive formula of "currency, son of currency."[8] Both usury and trade for profit (rather than need), because they have the accumulation of monetary wealth as their goals, could result in a form of social stagnation given the identity of means and ends. This stagnation is evident in Aristotle's formula, in which the parent and the son are one and the same.[9] Though Aristotle's objection to monetary gain for its own sake has been understood to be primarily ethical, the terms of that objection suggest that monetary gain also expresses another economic problem—that of stagnation.

In *Pericles*, unnatural breeding is also configured as incest, which is rendered in turn as an economic problem. Incest is represented as too much commerce with the self and the self's offspring. The sin of incest that begins the play significantly appears in the riddle as a form of improper consumption—feeding on the flesh of one's own family:

I am no viper, yet I feed
On mother's flesh which did me breed.
I sought a husband, in which labour[10]
I found that kindness in a father.[11]

To counter this sin of self-consumption, the play offers Pericles' next significant action. After he escapes the murderous attempts of the incestuous Antiochus (who realizes that Pericles has solved the riddle), Pericles brings a ship full of corn to the starving people of Tharsus. Their hunger is so extreme that mothers "are ready now / To eat those little darlings whom they loved" (1.4.43–44). His escape releases him from the dangers of one insular regime and saves another realm from the same cannibalistic fate. In contrast with the flesh-devouring act of incest, Pericles' ships—"stored with corn to make your needy bread, / And give them life whom hunger starved half dead"—are life producing (1.4.93–94). This fantasy of the regenerative profits that result from economic contact with others in a world whose economy is based on charitable expenditures intensifies the riddle's sense that incest is the sin of too much commerce with the self.[12]

The problem with incest in the play is not so much that it is an unnatural form of reproduction (Aristotle's formulation), but that it results in a form of self-consumption: "Feed[ing] on mother's flesh which did me breed."[13] Aristotle's formulation of the natural phenomenon (getting nourishment from the residuum of the matter that gives the offspring its birth—e.g., the placenta, or perhaps breast milk in mammals) is startlingly similar to precisely what is so unnatural in the incestuous relationship of Antioch. The play, then, revises Aristotle, for whom unnatural forms of acquisition (retail trade for profit rather than need and use) result in stagnation and redundancy, suggesting instead that too much commerce with the self is what is unnatural and stagnating.[14] The upshot of this alteration is that stagnant, self-devouring incest sets up extensions beyond the "immediate" economy as a solution to the problem, that is, as a way to avoid the stagnation threatened by the formula, "currency son of currency." The play turns Aristotle upside down so that what Aristotle defined as the problem (profiting from trade) becomes the solution.[15] This perversion of the already perverse usury (the play's perversion is that it turns Aristotle's criticism of self-reproduction into a criticism of self-consumption) serves as a means to accentuate incest's insularity and to introduce its potential opposite—an idealized fantasy of the abundance that comes with incorporating others into a world of economic exchange—precisely what Aristotle defined as unnatural.

Pericles inverts the problem of romantic comedy, and sometimes tragedy, by making the play's first problem not enough difference rather than too much difference—of race, or economic status, for example. The play repeatedly transforms this internal focus in its episodic travels and encounters.[16] Given the play's initiation with a scene of incest, it is not surprising that the play distinguishes between forms of endogamy and forms of exogamy. But the play uses incest as a means to figuratively represent the need to expand out. Exogamy, in general, can provide access to a larger economic world. Of particular interest here is the way that the play employs this insight in order to engage with questions about the importance of foreign trade.[17]

The closed economy of incest is contrasted throughout the play to Pericles' wandering and "commerce" with others. If tragicomedy, as I argue in the Introduction, works to break through the impasse of romantic comedy by providing a more dialectical model that can at least imagine an extension outside of a localized economy, then *Pericles* might be the play that explores such possibilities most explicitly. I therefore begin my discussion of tragicomedy with *Pericles* because more than any other play it represents and then resolves the problems of a closed economy by placing in dialectical relation incest—that is, too much commerce with the self—and the "properly productive" travels of Pericles that the sin of incest sets in motion.

As a brief plot summary will indicate, the initial sin of incest sets in motion a series of literal long-distance sea journeys to other "worlds" in order to provide the opportunities through which the play's initial transgression can be redeemed and this fundamental economic problem can be recast and resolved. After leaving Tharsus, the charitable Pericles is shipwrecked in Pentapolis where his own impoverishment is the focus until he wins over the King and the King's daughter, Thaisa. On his way back home to Tyre, Thaisa dies in childbirth due to a terrible storm and by necessity is thrown overboard in a coffin laden with coins and spices. It turns out that she is not dead, and is revived by Cerimon on the shores of Ephesus, unbeknown to Pericles. The despairing Pericles returns to Tharsus where he eventually leaves his daughter, Marina, in the hands of those whom he relieved from starvation. Envy results in a plot to kill Marina, but she is "rescued" by pirates who take her to Mytilene and sell her into a brothel that is represented as both the site of redeemed profits and moral conversion. All of these events are in some sense the outcome or product of the original sin of incest and are also thematically placed in dialogue with the issues of insularity and expansion that incest raises.

Incest, especially a riddle about incest, provides an extraordinary instance of the dialectic between insularity and expansion—opposing terms in the debate about the commercial contact with distant countries and cultures. The riddle about incest, while it is devised in order for Antiochus to keep his daughter to himself, is also devised for the purpose of marriage. Moreover, while incest seems closed off and insular, the riddle, by inviting suitors from the outside, also contains the seeds for a model of extension. While its content is about closure, the form is about exposure—that is, a riddle in general presents something to be revealed or unmasked. Pericles, however, cannot expose Antiochus publicly for fear of losing his life. But it is precisely this threat, a result of Pericles' unpacking of the riddle, that initiates his travels and thus his economic contact with several different cities, almost all of which suffer from a form of scarcity. So, like the tragicomic form, in which the averted tragedy becomes the means of its own resolution, here the insularity of incest is precisely what motivates Pericles' redemptive journey.[18]

To underscore the relationship between these economic relations and incest, the play refers back to Pericles' charity when he needs Cleon, the governor of Tharsus, to take care of his own daughter, Marina. But in doing so he also raises questions about charity's efficacy as a long-term economic solution. Cleon reassures him that his charity will not be forgotten:

Your grace that fed my country with your corn—
For which the people's prayers still fall upon you—
Must in your child be thought on. If neglection
Should therein make me vile, the common body,
By you relieved, would force me to my duty.
But if to that my nature need a spur
The gods revenge it upon me and mine
To the end of generation. (3.3.19–26)

"Your grace, must in your child be thought on" revises the notion of the father-daughter relation such that rather than the father's stagnating in the daughter, or the daughter's consuming the flesh that bred her, the father's good deeds are now embodied in the daughter. Moreover, according to Tharsian morality, if the recipient of charity is unnaturally ungrateful (in this case, not himself charitable in return), the gods will take revenge on him and his future generations as well. Charity thus begets charity: it entitles one's future generations to charity and obligates the recipient to be charitable in return. Consequently, he who does not act charitably after receiving charity dooms his offspring until the "end of generation"— forever to the end of his posterity or, as might be thematically most appropriate here, with the effect of putting an end to his generative capacities.

Charity, first presented as a solution, contains within itself the seed of another problem. If charity begets charity (as currency is the son of currency), it also threatens annihilation—the end of generation. The forcing of Cleon to perform his duty by the "common body" "relieved" by Pericles sounds as much like a form of domination as it does a form of justice. Though on the surface the lines represent Pericles as nurturing parent of the people who, if need be, will force Cleon to repay Pericles' charity, the sexual innuendo also casts him as their sexual partner. Thus, when all is said and done, Pericles' charity might mirror the incest it initially counters and not provide the relief it originally seemed to offer. Indeed, the play's economy of charity is so entangled within itself that it starts to seem incestuous and to produce the same problem (self-consumption) it was intended to solve.

My point, of course, is not to suggest that Pericles is as guilty as Antiochus, or that he has committed a form of incest. The contradictory representation of Pericles' charity is significant because it reveals how charity (even if it seems temporarily beneficial) and the economic system that underlies it might lead to stagnation. It thus forces the imagination of a different economic system. I want to return, then, to the play's initial representation of Tharsus to explore how the play substitutes loss for scarcity in order to counter this threat of economic stagnation, which seems to be at the foundation even of the model for a seemingly exogamous charity.

Just prior to Pericles' arrival in Tharsus, Cleon discusses with his wife Dionysa the good old days in terms that are highly suspect, especially in their representation of the relationship to foreigners:

This Tharsus, o'er which I have the government,
A city o'er whom plenty held full hand,
For riches strewed herself even in her streets;
Whose towers bore heads so high they kissed the clouds,
And strangers ne'er beheld but wondered at;
Whose men and dames so jetted and adorned,
Like one another's glass to trim them by—
Their tables were stored full to glad the sight,
And not so much to feed on as delight.
All poverty was scorned, and pride so great
The name of help grew odious to repeat. (1.4.21–31)

While Cleon tries to represent the difference between a past and present Tharsus as that between plenty and scarcity, these lines suggest that the issue is not, and never has been, scarcity *tout court*. If plenty reigned, why was poverty scorned, and why would the "name of help" be odious (and not obsolete) to repeat? Why would there be poverty or a need for help at all? What these contradictions suggest is that this image of pre-crisis Tharsus is based on a nostalgic fantasy of plenitude, haunted by the fear (and reality) of scarcity. Accordingly, poverty in the old Tharsus is not absent but "scorned," that is, repudiated. The fantasy of plenty seems to be based on the exclusion of the very possibility of poverty, that is, of a form of economic (or class) difference mapped onto a difference between native plenitude and foreign lack.

The vehemence of this exclusion of poverty suggests the very fragility of the image of plenitude conjured up by the nostalgic reflection. In the present Tharsus, the fear of poverty rematerializes as the possibility of loss due to a prevailing economic weakness that makes Tharsus vulnerable to attack from the outside. The repudiated economic difference within Tharsus reappears as the threat of economic difference between Tharsus and its "neighboring nation" (64). When Cleon first sees Pericles' ships coming from Tyre, he assumes that they have come to take advantage of his relatively weak position. Intuitively perceiving this concern, Pericles assuages it by saying that his fleet is no Trojan horse—the quintessential symbol of perverse invasion, that is, infiltration and violent takeover through a pretense of generosity. Instead of posing a threat of devastating incorporation, however, his ship is stuffed with corn. Though Pericles insists that this transaction will not result in a violently produced loss, the concern that a relationship with strangers is potentially productive of a loss is lurking barely beneath the surface of this scarcity-weakened Tharsus that finds "help" odious.

In Cleon's speech cited above, the exclusion of those who might be poor and in need of help is mirrored in the wonder of strangers who "ne'er beheld, but wondered at" the majesty and plenty of Tharsus; both are necessary components of the fantasy of Tharsus's past plenty as well as its relative wealth and greatness. According to this fantasy, Tharsus would have no need of foreign charity or commerce. In this economy, strangers are necessary only to reassure the people of Tharsus, that is, to shore them up by esteeming them, by reflecting them back to themselves—a fantasy further reflected in the circularity of the passage's literal reference to mirroring in which the adorned saw themselves in each other's images. Like the incestuous Antioch of the opening scene, Tharsus is self-enclosed and insular, perhaps made even more so by the strangers necessary to reinforce their narcissistic insularity. If they were not feeding on each other's flesh before the famine, they were feeding off of foreigners in a more figurative sense. While Tharsians might engage with strangers, they do so only to reinforce their insularity.

Yet this insularity depends on the poor they exclude and the foreigners who shore them up and thus is vulnerable to those who exist outside them, precisely those who also come to help them. Like the incest of the riddle, their closed economy is subject to disturbances from without. But the resemblance between the two "economies" (of incest and of Tharsus) is not merely formal. The content, too, is paralleled. The result of Tharsian insularity is starvation, scarcity, and the threat of self-consumption that, in turn, threatens to end generation, thus requiring the (odious) help of Pericles to open it up and relieve it.

It therefore is not surprising that their insistence on hyper-insularity would lead to ingratitude for the help to which they become subjected. Regardless of how much Cleon insists that Marina will be well treated by them (that Pericles' grace and generosity will in his "daughter, be thought on"), she becomes the locus of Dionysa's evil actions and ingratitude. What Pericles introduces into Tharsus is help, and Marina becomes a constant reminder—"always thought on"—of the need for that help. She is a stranger perceived as a constant threat to the city's well-being. Instead of a reflection of Tharsus's own greatness, for Dionysa, Marina is the image against which her own daughter pales by comparison. Like the poverty of pre-crisis Tharsus, Marina embodies the possibility of (hierarchical) difference and, by extension, the possibility of economic difference and loss that must be expelled. The relief Pericles provides to Tharsus, now embodied in his next generation, thus rematerializes a previous, if disavowed, loss.

I want to highlight two particularly salient points from this analysis of Tharsus's fears. The first is that Tharsus's understanding of its economy as a static state—even if there are two options, scarcity and plenty—is specious and misguided. Instead, what the rematerializations of the repudiated poverty as threat from the outside reveals is that the economy is not defined solely by scarcity, but also by losses that are themselves the result of more dynamic, even diachronic, forces. Moreover, it is the relationship with the non-local economy that exposes the possibility for loss. Pericles' travels thus reveal the truth of a nonstatic economy. This shift is represented formally in the play's episodic structure in which loss and profit repeatedly follow on each other's heels. It is also represented thematically through the play's wanderings and the potentially threatening exchanges with foreigners. While an economic system structured by scarcity and plenty is endogamous, that of loss is exogamous. Loss is the unspoken fear of economic contact with foreign lands.

This fear of loss through contact with foreign economies is not a concern the play primarily inherits from Aristotle, ancient Greece, or even its sources. The play addresses a contemporary concern of England's—that over-consumption of foreign goods would reduce the demand for domestic production and result in a drain of money from England to pay for imports.[19] While much of the discourse in the period expressed concern about wasteful expenditure on luxury imports, loss of coin was associated with imports of necessities as well.[20] A shortage of grain in England in 1608, the year *Pericles* was entered in the Stationers Register, for example, resulted in a fear of just such a loss: "the dearth of corn in England of late hath been a great cause of trans-portation of our coin beyond the seas."[21] The result was a decrease in the money supply and an experience of even greater poverty. As B. E. Supple argues, because a supply of ready money was so important to an economy without advanced forms of credit, overseas commerce could be a real source of instability.[22] Thus, in the early part of the seventeenth century, there was a resurgent interest in methods for keeping money within the country. For example, both the privy council in 1616 and members of James's commission on trade proposed resurrecting the statutes of employment, which required that money made by foreign merchants from the sale of their goods in England be used to buy English goods for resale abroad.[23] These methods to counteract loss suggest that foreign trade, even if necessary, could be understood as ultimately loss producing.

In its attempts to imagine geographic and economic expansion, *Pericles* also works to figure out a way that the resulting exchanges need not be tragic. The reconfiguration of the static economy of scarcity and plenty into a dynamic economy of loss and, as we shall see, also profit is not necessarily as tragic as Tharsus's (or England's) fears suggest; it is also potentially tragicomic. This is so because the transformation of scarcity into loss is necessary—from both a tragicomic and capitalist perspective—to the imagining of profit. Through "foreign exchange," the schematic and stagnant relationship between scarcity and plenitude is transformed into a more dialectical and diachronic relationship between loss and profit. A diachronic notion of loss (as expenditure) is necessary to get to a notion of profit. In order simultaneously to counter fears about loss and rewrite the Aristotelian problematic in which economic gain is stagnating, the play needs to recast foreign exchange and loss into redeemable, productive potential. To do so, the play will also need to rewrite Tharsus's schematic categorizations in which poverty is foreign and wealth is native, even autochthonous. Such assignations must be inverted for overseas trade to be redeemed as profitable.[24] A profitable economy is thus one that benefits from trade with others, that is, it imports wealth. In order to do so, money must leave the country, but that "loss" is newly understood as part of a dynamic process that is importantly productive.

If the play has Pericles' charitable act mirror Antiochus's incest, as I suggested earlier, it in part does so in order to imagine Pericles truly as mirror, that is, as inverted image of the sin, loss, and self-consumption that defines Antiochus and perhaps even Tharsus as well. Gower's monologue following the first scene at Tharsus represents Pericles as antithesis to Antiochus precisely because Pericles' travels, unlike Antiochus's actions, are a dynamic and productive (that is, redemptive) process:

Here have you seen a mighty king
His child, iwis, to incest bring;
A better prince and benign lord
That will prove awful both in deed and word.
Be quiet then, as men should be,
Till he hath passs'd necessity.
I'll show you those in troubles reign,
Losing a mite, a mountain gain. (2 Chorus, 1–8)

Pericles, as this prologue foretells, will repeatedly sustain significant losses—of his kingdom, his wife, and then his daughter. Pericles thus will be the character that embodies possibilities for redemption not because he himself has sinned, but because he will suffer losses that will also be more than regained ("losing a mite, a mountain gain").

The play simultaneously transfers the need for redemption onto Pericles and suggests that redemption will take place in economic terms that match the social concerns the play has been representing. The play—and the genre as a whole, I will argue—thus alters its focus from the need to redeem a sin to the need to redeem a loss. Like the riddle's content—incest as self-consumption—this prologue foregrounds replacement of sin with economic crisis as a function of the genre.

Pericles, in its shift from Antiochus to Pericles and from incest to economic deprivation, calls attention to—even stages—this revised focus. What seems crucial about the play's first act is the way that the play converts a moral and religious problem—the sin of incest—into an economic one (though one that still retains a moral component). As I argue in the Introduction, the substitution of loss for sin makes use of Anselm's understanding of Christian redemption (in which Christ's sacrifice is understood as a repayment to God through which mankind prospers) as an economic process. It also lays the groundwork for the play's scenes of redemption to take the form of Pericles' prosperous voyages in which what is lost is more than regained in explicitly economic terms. To sum up the effects of these early scenes: the play simultaneously shifts its focus from sin to economic loss, identifying the losses it substitutes in sin's place as transformable sources of productivity that come from foreign contact understood as explicitly not charity.

Recasting Poverty: From Begging to Borrowing

In the next locale that Pericles visits, he rewrites this understanding of loss by taking advantage of it and transforming it into a form of profit, making his averted tragedy a source of prosperity. Immediately after leaving Tharsus, Pericles suffers shipwreck and lands as the sole survivor, with only the clothes on his back, in the kingdom of Pentapolis. As Antiochus's sin was figuratively displaced unto Pericles, Tharsus's need for help and the possibility of loss and poverty are now transferred onto Pericles, who, I will argue, similarly rewrites its potential so that he is not devoured like Tharsian children.[25] Upon landing, Pericles overhears a conversation among fishermen that emerges out of the Master of the fishermen's regret that they could not help those they saw drowning, as they "could scarce help [them]selves":

THIRD FISHERMAN. Master, I marvel how the fishes live in the sea.
MASTER. Why, as men do a-land: the great ones eat up the little ones. I can compare our rich misers to nothing so fitly as to a whale: a plays and tumbles, driving the poor fry before him, and at last devours them all at a mouthful. Such whales have I heard on o'th' land, who never leave gaping till they swallowed the whole parish, church, steeple, bells and all . . .
THIRD FISHERMAN. But if the good king Simonides were of my mind—
PERICLES. [aside] Simonides?
THIRD FISHERMAN. We would purge the land of these drones that rob the bee of her honey. (2.1.26–34, 42–46)

Class difference—only adumbrated as a possibility in Tharsus—enters this scene along with a revised understanding of scarcity: scarcity produced by unequal distribution. But "unequal distribution" is perhaps too neutral a phrase for the class conflict represented in both analogies of the rich to whales that devour the poor fry and to drones that rob the bee of her honey.[26] Together they produce a fantasy of retaliatory justice in which the king (no small fry) shares the philosophy of the fisherman and thus purges, not the poor, but the rich from the land.[27]

Economic difference (the poverty), repudiated in Tharsus, rematerializes here as a form of antagonistic class conflict in which the odiousness of needing help can be further explored and even eliminated. When Pericles first participates in the fishermen's conversation, he makes a request for pity that does and does not situate himself within this hierarchy of impoverishment. Speaking of himself in the third person, Pericles says, "He asks of you that never used to beg" (61). His entreaty, which also seems to be an act of disavowal of the position he must occupy, nonetheless produces a conversation about begging:

MASTER. No, friend, cannot you beg? Here's them in our country of Greece gets more with begging than we can do with working.
SECOND FISHERMAN. Can'st thou catch any fishes then?
PERICLES. I never practiced it.
SECOND FISHERMAN. Nay, then thou wilt starve, sure; for here's nothing to be got nowadays unless thou canst fish for't. (2.1.62–68)

In response, Pericles reflects on his want, saying he has only enough life in him "to crave [their] help," which produces further reflections on begging:

SECOND FISHERMAN. Hark you, my friend. You said you could not beg?
PERICLES. I did but crave.
SECOND FISHERMAN. But crave? Then I'll turn craver too, an so I shall scape whipping.
PERICLES. Why, are all your beggars whipped then?
SECOND FISHERMAN. O, not all, my friend, not all; for if all your beggars were whipped I would wish no better office than to be beadle. I'll go draw up the net. (2.1.83–91)

Given their critique of the treatment of the poor by the rich, the harsh treatment of beggars in their mouths might appear a bit surprising. What the fishermen's dialogue with Pericles lacks, however, is the logical link between the exploitation (cum consumption) of the poor by the rich and the production of those who then beg out of necessity. Instead, the fishermen see the beggars and the rich as committing the similar transgression—that is, the sin of idleness; the rich are drones that rob honey from the worker bee, and "begging" is directly opposed to "working." But it might not be so much that the rich and the beggars (those on opposite ends of a hierarchy of wealth and needs) are merely linked; instead, it seems that the status of not working is displaced in the course of their conversation from the rich onto the poor.

In his analysis of work and the gift in the early modern period, Scott Shershow demonstrates how this displacement is particularly central to forms of capitalist practice and ideology developing in the period.[28] Such a displacement, I will argue, depends on the reconfiguration of notions of poverty themselves. Pericles' acceptance of his newly impoverished state and with it the actions available to those without resources (i.e., begging) is at best ambivalent. But the play rescues him from such a fate when the fishermen pull up not the big fish they are expecting, from the difficulty they have getting it out of the net properly ("like a poor man's right in the law"), but the lost armor that Pericles inherited from his father (2.1.113). Initially Pericles' gratitude is directed toward Fortune, whom he thanks for giving him "somewhat to repair myself," though he is quick to add, "it was mine own, part of my heritage" (2.1.118, 119).[29] Pericles concludes the discourse of his father's legacy to him by summing up the situation: "my shipwreck's now no ill, / Since I have here my father gave in's will" (2.1.29–30). When asked what he means to do (perhaps because the fishermen do not easily see how the armor belongs to him) Pericles explains: "To beg of you, kind friends, this coat of worth, . . . / And if that ever my low fortune's better, / I'll pay your bounties, till then rest your debtor" (2.1.132, 138–39). The discovery of the armor seems to eliminate Pericles' previous discomfort with the position of beggar that he now happily occupies. Pericles' newfound comfort results from his new relation to property. The "coat" he now begs (in comparison to the one given to him freely by the fishermen's Master in response to his previous entreaty and shivering body) is already his own; it rightly belongs to him. Moreover, it is the sign that he is not impoverished, but a man of property and inheritance. This time, his beggarly action receives no comment from the fishermen; perhaps because it comes with a contractual promise to repay a debt. Over the space of three lines, begging thus becomes borrowing. As a result, he is not a dishonorable, literally worthless beggar, but a man of credit.

If the position of the beggar is kept alive in the latter part of this scene, it is only to be rewritten as that of the debtor, even more specifically as one who enters into debt not so much out of necessity but, as we will shortly see, in order to reap a profit. This distinction is crucial. No longer in a world of ambivalent charity in which the name of "help" is odious to repeat (prior to the appearance of Pericles' armor in this scene, repeated it was—five times), we have a world of loss and material profit, in which the former, in tragicomic fashion, can be transformed into the latter. To return to Shershow's insights regarding the anxiety about the idle rich (those who invest rather than labor) being displaced onto the poor, in this scene we have an implicit rewriting of the devouring whales into justified debtors and maybe even creditors.[30]

Pericles is not an unproductive beggar or even an unproductive borrower. He is first a borrower who shortly becomes an investor, who accumulates considerable wealth when he employs the armor to win King Simonides' benevolence (which partially takes the form of material gifts) and the love of his daughter, Thaisa. He "wins" them through the most conventional (in the literary sense) means possible—a chivalric knightly tournament. The harsh economic undercurrents of the scene with the fishermen are swallowed up, temporarily disappeared by the romance that enables the profits of Pericles' loss, now recast as debt or expenditure, to ensue.[31]

The remaining discomfort, however, is represented, if only as a pretense of an obstacle to Pericles' success. King Simonides pretends to be the typical objecting father of comedy even though he himself chooses Pericles for his daughter. His pretended objection, not surprisingly, is that Pericles is not her equal. (He has not revealed his true status, and he is dressed in his shipwreck attire.) But difference is dismissed in a parody of the comedic obstacle; Simonides ends his threat, "either frame your will to mine, either be ruled by me," with the punishment that will ensue if Pericles does not heed his admonishment, "or I shall make you man and wife"—literally, then, for worse or for better. In a revision of the relationship between Antiochus and his daughter, in which Antiochus prevents his daughter from being given away by keeping her for himself, Simonides keeping his daughter and giving her away is collapsed into a single gesture. In tragicomedy, the averted tragedy is transformed into the profitable resolution. Illuminating that process, Simonides' threat is literally also the solution—his promise—just as losses of a more economic kind are made into profits.[32]

In the play, sin is first recast as loss, then loss is recast as expenditure. Instead of suffering from the self-consumption that derives from incest and threatens Tharsian children and Pentapolian beggars, Pericles transforms what was his own (his armor) and the property of others (the wealth that comes with Thaisa) into his own accumulated possessions. It is not only the case that Pericles' "wreck is no ill," but also—to paraphrase the prologue to this act—losing a mite, he has a mountain gained. Pericles' loss is thus fortunate. It might be worth recalling at this point that the possibility of turning loss into profits appears for the first time in the same locale where the possibility of class conflict also first made itself explicit. Poverty, along with class difference, are repudiated again as they are in Tharsus, but this time by their rematerialization in profit rather than by their displacement onto foreigners.[33] As a result, Pericles can embrace his position as debtor, whereas Cleon of Tharsus's statements about repayment are repeatedly couched in the hypothetical negative of possible ingratitude.[34] To account for the difference, it is necessary to recognize that Pericles' fortunate fall produces him as a legitimized and profitable investor.

In its reworking of Christian discourse of redemption and attuning its logic to specifically economic uses, *Pericles* anticipates the arguments of mercantilists that I outlined in the Introduction. In that argument, money sent to the East Indies does not represent loss because it is productive of future profits made on the re-export of imported goods that it claims as its own, as if they were the inheritance of the company's initial expenditures. Of course, the play (and the genre of tragicomedy), unlike the mercantilists, do not have the justification of profits as an explicit goal. Instead, while trying to address the economic problems that are its thematic focus, the play is also trying to get beyond the limitations imposed by comedy's dependence on closure discussed in Chapter 1. Pericles' profits in Pentapolis depend on the combination of a tragicomic transformation and comedic marriage—a combination that could signal closure. But rather than end here, *Pericles* continues on, making use of its episodic structure to imagine further transformations of loss and a resolution that by opening outward supports, rather than eliminates, expansion.

Virtuous Redemption and Infinite Exchange in the Brothel of Mytilene

In the play's final significant locale, the brothel of Mytilene, the play intensifies its attention to explicitly economic problems. In this locale of prostitution, the play shifts its attention from the more abstract concept of expansion presented in the opening scenes to the more explicit economic ends of such a model—the possibility of infinite accumulation—which was precisely the economic goal to which Aristotle most vehemently posed ethical objections. While *Pericles* here might seem to be working to address the morality of such accumulation, it also works to illuminate the way ethical and religious questions transform to economic questions. I have been arguing that the play throughout transforms Anselm's religious model of redemption back into an economic one. The play's conclusion goes a step further to demonstrate how the ethical questions are reimagined from the perspective of the economics themselves and how the play itself requires a similar framework in order to continue to imagine and enable its own narrative expansions—not the closure of comedy, but the open-endedness and accumulations of tragicomedy.

These final scenes rework the moral/economic binary by bringing the terms into direct contact with each other. Whereas earlier in the play, in the representation of incest, for example, the economic and the moral are complexly entangled, in the brothel they are (at least initially) contrasted and juxtaposed.[35] The brothel is also the only site in the play that is represented as explicitly morally corrupt, perhaps even evil, precisely because of its economic content, for the explicitly vulgar form of its economic problems, of which it has many. In fact, it would not be a stretch to say that it explicitly offers variations on almost all of the economic problems running below and on the surface of the play. If incest is too much commerce with the self and an exchange that is none, the brothel recreates and inverts that problem in a slightly different form in which the exchange has no end point but can be repeated ad infinitum, at least theoretically. These perversions of proper exchange bookend the play. In addition, the brothel is a site of scarcity, perverse charity, and class conflict. All of these problems, however, are conflated and reduced to a hyper-vilified economy of questionable commercial profits based on deception, exploitation, and dehumanization. In other words, it is the making of actual commercial profits (through pandering) that takes the blame for all of these other economic ills and becomes the representative of what it means to engage in an economic endeavor. The displacement of ill will onto profit making, counterintuitively but not paradoxically, coincides with the privileging of profit making as the primary objective of economic activity. (This objective is precisely what was so upsetting about commercial activity to Aristotle—it confused means with ends—but is what is considered most natural in capitalist ideology.) The brothel is thus the dumping ground for the play's economic concerns and the site where displaced anxieties about profit and loss rematerialize.

The brothel provides the material resources for the play's resolution both by re-commercializing the relationship between loss and profit foregrounded in Pericles' interaction with the fishermen and by explicitly linking it to forms of moral redemption. While the economic problems of this scene and the play as a whole become crystallized and displaced onto the making of illegitimate profits, the scenes in the brothel become equally focused on possibilities of redemption. Because the brothel is the locale where profit is most vilified by its association with prostitution, it is also the location where profit is most available to the moral benefits of redemption.

The need for redemption in the brothel results primarily from the means by which financial profits are accumulated and the consequent incommensurability between the profits and those means. If we examine the complaints and strategy of Pander and his wife, Bawd, as they prepare for a stable and secure future, it becomes clear that economic accumulation is actually a threat to their salvation. Pander thus explains to his wife the advantages of retiring early:

Our credit comes not in like the commodity, nor the commodity wages not with the danger. Therefore if in our youths we could pick up some pretty estate, 'twere not amiss to keep our door hatched. Besides, the sore terms we stand upon with the gods will be strong with us for giving over. (4.2.27–32)

To paraphrase this difficult passage: "Our reputation (i.e., our credit) does not accumulate like our profit (i.e., our commodity) does, nor is the profit commensurate with the danger.[36] So, if we could acquire sufficient property, it would not be a bad idea to close up shop. By the way, we are on bad terms with the gods and so would benefit if we quit soon."[37] Pander seems to recognize the immorality of his position, but interestingly he cannot seem to get outside the commercial and contractual terms even in his discussion of altering the terms, especially those of his agreement with the gods. Pander has two different problems, but they are closely related. The first is that infinite profits can be accumulated (as prostitutes can be circulated), but the accumulation of reputation or credit is limited. The moral problem is that profit and credit are not equivalent. The problem, then, is not only the means by which he makes his profit, but also the resulting incommensurability of reputation and profit.[38]

Pander's reputation is not good precisely because profits (especially in a world with a expanding economy) can continue to grow, thus exceeding credit or reputation. This expanding economy, the opposite of the play's figurative "incest," raises a different problem—that of figurative "prostitution," which is, literally speaking, infinite circulation and accumulation. As a result, Pander and his wife, Bawd, are in debt to (i.e., "on sore terms with") the gods. While Pander invokes "gods" in the plural, his problem is a Christian one: mankind's account with God has been unsettled as a result of fallen status; thus mankind must return to God what the sinner has stolen from him.[39] Mankind, like the Pander family, must try to repay what he has stolen from God(s) in order to right the account and rebalance the equation. The anti-commercial aspects of the scene therefore are tied directly to an understanding of one's account(ing) with God. As one accumulates infinite profits beyond his or her credit, s/he becomes increasingly indebted to God. In a parodic inversion of the economics of Christian redemption, the more business Bawd and Pander do, the more indebted they become.

The scene addresses both Christian and Aristotelian concerns. Recall that for Aristotle it is infinite accumulation that is morally corrupt because it confuses means with ends, and the proper end is attaining the necessities for good living, which is by definition not infinite. Accumulation, as opposed to the fulfilling of needs, has no clear stopping point.[40] In Christian terms, however, the infinite exists in the grace of God, but it is out of man's reach, or at least out of man's agency. Only Christ (the God/man) can remit the debt incurred by man's sins and return to mankind that which his transgressions had forfeited. Prior to the Reformation one could right one's account with God through the giving of alms and the purchase of indulgences,[41] but the Reformation's separation of works and grace makes that impossible on an individual level.[42] In other words, the doctrine of works and indulgences provided a loophole of sorts in the doctrine of undeserving; one could acquire salvation, for example, by abandoning the economic (e.g., by the giving of alms/charity) in the earthly realm. But this loophole is closed by Reformation doctrine. Given these limitations, what the play needs to do in order to save the forms of profit making it represents earlier in the play is to imagine the possibility of accumulating credit equivalent to its profit (what Pander and Bawd admit they cannot do) so as to properly balance the moral and commercial accounts, thus addressing both the Christian and Aristotelian objections to profit in a Reformation world.

The play embodies these possibilities in Marina, who is not only Pericles' daughter, but is also, as her name indicates, a symbol of the sea—a source itself of loss and profit.[43] At this point, the play still seems to be concerned with addressing the morality of profit making, but as we shall shortly see, morality drops out of the equation. Marina's function in the brothel and the play as a whole is to reverse unfortunate processes by making virtuous redemption and expanding accumulation comparable practices.[44] While Bawd and Pander are right about the fact that Marina will bring them the profits they have been waiting for, they are not quite right about how her virtue will serve, or even save, them. In fact, Marina's virtue exceeds their attempts to turn her into a "creature for sale"; rather than be brought down (what happens to others at the brothel) she converts all of the men who come to corrupt her. Following in her father's footsteps, Marina might say of her capture by the pirates and consequent experience in the brothel, "this wreck's no ill." Marina not only escapes the fate of other "poor bastards—brought up only to be brought down"—she inverts it (4.2.12–13, 14). Marina's actions serve to highlight the redemptive qualities of the tragicomic formula; she brings up those who tried to bring her down.

Marina's tragicomic inversions rewrite the values of the brothel so that infinite returns, rather than serve as a counter to redemption, are more or less equated with it. Marina is told that the governor, Lysimachus, is prepared to line her apron with gold if she uses him "kindly," that is, if she sells herself to him (4.6.56–57). When she refuses to do so and instead converts him with her virtue, he nonetheless lines her apron with the same gold he would have given her if she had prostituted herself. Indeed, immediately after he professes that her speech has altered his corrupted mind, he gives her gold coins: "Hold, here's gold for thee. / Persever in that clear way thou goest / And the gods strengthen thee" (4.6.109–11). In effect, he pays her for her virginity (precisely what he would have done had she not been virtuous), that virginity that is so valuable to the brothel.[45] Only nine lines after Lysimachus pays her the first time, he does so again: "Thou art a piece of virtue, and I doubt not but thy training hath been noble. Hold, here's more gold for thee" (4.5.116–18). She converts Lysimachus, who then "rescues" or "redeems" her, literally buying her back (the meaning of "to redeem") by making two deposits in her earthly account and that with the gods as well. She responds to his injunction to "persever" and his wish that the gods strengthen her with an anagrammatic wish: "the good gods preserve you." In their "perverse"—the missing anagram—exchange, mutual redemption is underwritten by a transfer of coins in which credit and commodity flow equally. Marina accumulates virtue, converted men, and coins as more or less indistinguishable profits, even interrelated profit. Through this process, credit, like the kind Pericles acquires in Pentapolis, becomes as much an economic term as an ethical one.

Unlike the profits of Bawd and Pander, Marina's are not foul because they do not exceed her credit (i.e., her moral value and reputation).

Her reputation grows with the profits; so it is not the case that profit exceeds credit—a sin perhaps in which what one accumulates exceeds what one deserves. It is not just the case that Marina and the economic processes she practices are deemed moral and redeemed, but that accumulation itself acquires positive associations, just as the two meanings of credit (social reputation and belief in one's ability to repay a debt at a later time) become interdependent and interactive. If earlier the play demonstrated how the religious model of redemption can be transformed back into an economic model, enabling sin to be recast as loss that is productive of a future expenditure, through the extreme version of the tragicomic model that enables infinite accumulation, morality paradoxically drops out of the equation altogether. If any ethical question about economic profit remains, it is instead reimagined from the perspective of the economic practices themselves.

Unlike *The Merchant of Venice*, which ultimately cannot imagine a form of profit making (in which loss or nothing is transformed into something) that is compatible with Christian ideals of redemption, *Pericles* refunctions the Christian model of redemption not so much to justify economic practices, but to rethink economic problems as economic rather than moral problems. This retuning of the Anselmian model of religious redemption eliminates the explicit need to make the economic practices compatible with moral concerns (what *The Merchant of Venice* cannot do) because the transformation of loss into profit (here represented in Marina's acquisition of gold at the brothel to which she is sold against her will) is already modeled on notions of religious redemption, on the trajectory of fall to fortune.

Though some of Marina's profit making in the brothel scene might seem hyper-redemptive and thus potentially parodic, this potential does not hinder the coins' circulations or their importance to the play's profitable resolutions.[46] Nor does the play repeat *Twelfth Night*'s practice of sweeping the commercial concerns under the rug. Marina gets coins; she gives some to Bolt; and she must continue to give her earnings to the Bawd (cursed as she might be). Moreover, when Pericles arrives in Mytilene, the play makes a forced effort of having him continually insist on paying for the provisions that he is given; he does not become indebted to foreign largesse—quite the contrary. The affective reunions among father, daughter, and rediscovered mother are, if anything, accompanied by the accumulation, or the hint of accumulation, of the rule and property of several cities as well. Pericles and his family not only regain each other, but also Tyre (which Marina and Lysimachus will rule), Mytilene (through Marina's marriage), Pentapolis (through marriage and the death of Thaisa's father), and possibly Tharsus (to which Pericles was on his way in order to seek revenge when Diana spoke to him in a dream and sent him to recover Thaisa). In this tragicomedy, nothing has been forfeited; every loss has produced more than compensatory, or even, commensurate gain. Recuperation is, if anything, excessive.

The play, then, is interested in both the figurative economies that the need for redemption sets in motion and the literal economics. In some ways the play looks like a conventional romance; Pericles' journey produces a series of emotional losses that are individually (and then jointly at the play's end) recuperated. But the play is not only interested in the recuperation of affective losses. As I have argued throughout, what unites the play throughout is its repeated concern with the economic and its interest in exploring how losses can be transformed into gains.

I began the book's study of tragicomedy with Shakespeare's and Wilkins's *Pericles* because it engages with a variety of fundamental economic problems that will be at play in the book's remaining chapters: how to overcome economic stagnation; how to understand trade with foreigners as profitable rather than threatening; and how to understand the resulting profits. *Pericles* is also a useful starting point because it uses the model of the economics of redemption—in which losses are transformed into profits—to think through these economic problems, and even to think of them as economic problems at all, that is, not as primarily moral problems. This chapter thus lays the groundwork for understanding why the plays examined in later chapters repeatedly return to the theme of redemption just at the point when economic crises seem to be verging on the irresolvably tragic. In the next chapter, I continue to lay this groundwork by turning to a play, Shakespeare's *The Winter's Tale*, which explores questions that *Pericles* only begs: if loss is to lead to profit, from where does that added value come, and how do the redemptive processes of theatrical tragicomedy provide the means to manifest that value?

Chapter Three

Poverty, Surplus Value, and Theatrical Investment in *The Winter's Tale*

How is it that something can come from nothing or, even more perplexing, from loss itself? This chapter focuses on Shakespeare's *The Winter's Tale*, whose engagement with redemption addresses this very question. As I argued in the preceding chapter, *Pericles* is very much concerned with the relationship between loss and redemption. *The Winter's Tale* not only shares this concern, but also intensifies it. This intensification is in part a result of the way that *The Winter's Tale* forges a more specific relationship between its tragic and comedic components and thus between its losses and its gains. While both plays are now usually classified under the category of Shakespearean romances, they are actually quite different structurally. *Pericles* is largely episodic in its structure. As a result, the play represents a series of highs and lows, fortunate and unfortunate events, even if the play also has a final resolution that appears to redeem all that is lost. In contrast, *The Winter's Tale* does not present the "painful adventures" of Leontes, the primary father figure in the play. Instead, its opening acts present a more continuous narrative in which a series of losses in a downward spiral serve to intensify the power of the losses and the redemption they require, as a brief plot summary will indicate: Leontes, through his suspicion and jealousy of his visiting childhood friend, the king of Bohemia (Polixenes), with his wife, Hermione, loses his entire family and more. His son and heir, Mamillius, dies when separated from his accused mother; Hermione, who has just given birth to a daughter, appears to die after hearing of her son's death; Leontes sentences his newborn daughter, whom he believes to be the result of the adulterous liaison, to be abandoned in some strange land; Camillo, his trusted Lord, leaves him, fleeing to Bohemia with Polixenes after warning Polixenes of Leontes' plan to have him murdered; and his other Lord, Antigonus, is killed by a bear on the shores of Bohemia just after abandoning the babe in compliance with Leontes' demands. Even after the oracle acquits Hermione, Leontes nonetheless continues to insist upon Hermione's guilt until the news of his son's death arrives. Only after all of these early losses in Sicilia does Leontes make a vow of daily repentance.

The possibility for redemption, however, is dependent not on repentance, but on a model provided by the oracle, which not only acquits Hermione, but also reveals that the king will be without an heir unless that which is lost is found. Whereas in *Pericles* the means of redemption— extending beyond the local economy—seems at times to displace the need for redemption itself from center stage, in *The Winter's Tale* the thematic focus remains on the losses as the very means for redemption, even in its more comedic sections. Attention thus shifts to the lost daughter, who is found and raised by a shepherd. Polixenes' son, Florizel, falls in love with the daughter, but Polixenes vehemently objects to his son's marriage to a lowly shepherdess and threatens her father and brother with death. Camillo, who wants to return to Sicilia, helps them to escape. Once they are back in Sicilia, the daughter's true identity is revealed, and the play ends with the transformation of the father and brother into gentlemen and the seeming miraculous transformation of a statue of Hermione back into her living self. Antigonus and Mamillius, however, remain dead. As this selective plot description suggests, many of the early losses are employed to produce the play's more profitable resolution.

Throughout this chapter, I argue that the transformation of the play from tragedy to tragicomedy depends on a transformation of loss that is embedded in both the play's theatrical practice and generic structure and that it is through these transformations that value is produced. After Hermione collapses on stage, Paulina (Hermione's lady and Antigonus's wife) condemns Leontes to despair, retracts the condemnation, and then, in a quintessential example of *praeteritio*, lists all of the losses of which she swears she will speak no more. Leontes, however, attempts to respond to Paulina's condemnation (and the events it rehearses) with equal force: he will daily visit the graves of mother and son where the tears he sheds will be his "recreation"—that is, not just his daily activity but his re-creation, what reconstitutes him (3.2.238).[1] Even though repentance is ultimately not the only, or even the primary, means of addressing loss in the play, Leontes' formulation adumbrates the centrality of transforming losses and making them productive through "recreation."[2] The daily visit, of course, will not be at the play's center. Though repetition might make for an interesting sonnet sequence, as theater, a daily repetition might itself be deadly. Re-creation, on the other hand, has considerable theatrical and tragicomic possibilities. Re-creation characterizes both theatrical representation as medium (as in to re-create a scene or event on stage) and the formal qualities of tragicomedy as a genre, in which tragic or potentially tragic events must be "re-created" in other forms. These kinds of productive transformations are at the heart of the primary defense of tragicomedy in the early modern period. In this model, two genres—tragedy and comedy—are brought together to produce a third kind.[3] Moreover, for tragicomedy to "work," the genre itself must undergo a prosperous transformation as the play proceeds. Putting the theatrical and the generic together: in tragicomic theater, things/persons that "disappear" from the stage return in reconfigured forms (or even are reconfigured as returns) to produce new and desired effects. This connection is evidenced in the play's repeated use of the word "issue," which according to the *OED* means not only "prog-eny," and "that which proceeds from any source; the outcome or prod-uct of any practice or condition," but also "an action of going, or flowing out," including, but not limited to, an exit from the stage. The play makes use of theatrical performance and "re-creation"—its issues—as a means to think through the genre of tragicomedy and represent its po-tential. Linking redemption to re-creation in its attempts to understand how loss can be productive of value, the play stages, even theatricalizes, the formal potential of tragicomedy.

Even though *The Winter's Tale* is more dramatic than *Pericles* and less maligned by critics, it is generically speaking more disquieting. As my students repeatedly point out in dismay, the play seems to shift genres abruptly in the fourth act from tragedy to pastoral comedy. In what fol-lows, I explore the productive potential of this transformation and the productive power of redemption by placing the shift in genre in dialogue with the other shift that accompanies it: from an interest in affective losses to an interest in the exchange of commodities and the accumulation of material wealth. In *Pericles*, scarcity is reconfigured as loss that is produc-tive of future profits within specific episodes. *The Winter's Tale*, in contrast, transforms loss into profit through its generic structure, I argue, in order to account for the production of value, that is, the added material or mon-etary worth necessary to the making of profit. To return to my opening question, the play imagines the productivity of loss by tying redemption to the production of material value. While previous critics have read the ro-mances before as thematically focused on redemption, my concern is to show how that focus is material in both senses of the term: redemption is crucial both to the play's medium—its use of theatrical spectacle and the way it places tragicomedy and comedy into relationship with each other—and to the economic questions it registers and addresses, about how loss can transform into profit and beyond that how the value of things is itself created.

Recent critics have also explored the play's interest in economics—particularly the way its language is steeped in economics and its symbolic representations of capitalism's long-term investments.[4] To my knowledge, however, to date no critics have made a strong connection between the play's structural and thematic interest in redemption, on the one hand, and its interests in these economic concerns on the other. Exploring the strong connection between the two enables me to demonstrate how this play in particular and tragicomedy in general owe their structure to the economics of redemption and how tragicomedy through a partial secularization makes the Christian discourse of redemption available to think through a variety of explicitly economic issues related to loss, profit, and the production of value, all of which are crucial to the conceptualization of capitalist investment.

In order to work through the implications of tragicomedy's structural indebtedness to the economics of redemption and to explore the play's interest in economic concerns, I begin by juxtaposing the play's inadequate models for value creation to the more effective model offered by a combination of the play's oracle and the Christian model of redemption. I then turn to the way the play materializes these models, especially in the fourth act, transforming them into the more explicit economic model of investment. In the final sections of this chapter, I explore how the material or monetary worth necessary to the making of profit depends on the surplus value expropriated from the character of Autolycus (who does not exist in Shakespeare's sources) and then rematerialized in the theater's own spectacular effects.

Valuing Loss and Making Investments

Even before Leontes begins to suspect Polixenes and Hermione of adultery, the play's characters understand their world as structured by potential losses and the ways in which they might be rematerialized—a problem understood specifically as one of creating worth out of loss itself. The play begins with the Lord of Bohemia expressing the inability of Bohemia to pay Sicilia the debt it is owed for its hospitality because there is a "great difference" between the two kingdoms (1.1.3). Bohemia is marked by its "insufficience" in relation to Sicilia (1.2.69).[5] In their dialogue the economic disparity between the two kingdoms is represented as potentially unredeemable debt.

But the scene quickly modifies its terms so that difference and unredeemable debt are replaced by loss.[6] The Lords' conversation abruptly shifts from the debt owed by Bohemia to Sicilia to a mutual loss the two have shared as a result of their separation from each other: "they have seemed to be together, though absent; shook hands as over a vast; and embraced as it were from the ends of opposed winds" (1.1.25–27). These affective supplements that reproduce the lack they seem to fill are quickly replaced in the Lord's conversation by the king's son, who is mentioned immediately after as "an unspeakable comfort" (29). He thus functions as the necessary heir and the means to fill the gap—of both the distance and the economic difference—between the two kingdoms. As the rematerialization of the kings' losses, he compensates for the gap between the two kings, which though tied to their lost innocence, is reconfigured as temporal and geographical distance. Leontes' later concern with whether or not Mamillius is his "copy," then, is directly tied to the older men's nostalgia for themselves as "boy[s] eternal" (1.2.66). Leontes' concern with Mamillius's legitimacy is not simply a matter of having a proper heir, but of re-creating himself in his son who serves to counterbalance his own deficiencies. While this reading might seem to make a more psychoanalytic point about masculine interest in (self) reproduction, what is particularly significant is the way that Mamillius is the indirect answer in the scene to the problem of incommensurable exchange and debt.[7] To restate the shifts in this opening scene: incommensurability leads to debt, which is converted to loss, which is then redeemed by the son, whom the very thought of "makes old hearts fresh" (33–34). Indeed, to "restore or make fresh" is one of the primary definitions of "re-create" (what Leontes and the play will need to do after Leontes obliterates most of the world around him). It is not simply that power needs to be transferable to heirs (at this moment in the play, Mamillius), but that incommensurability is reconfigured as loss that is then (productively) rematerialized in heirs. This is so precisely because the play's primary concern, as it is in this scene, is not so much how to pass on power or to whom but, in tragicomic fashion, how to make up for what is lost and how to make that loss productive.[8] In its movement from incommensurability to debt to loss to re-creation, the first scene outlines the structural and thematic trajectory for the play as a whole. While in *Pericles* the emphasis is on exchange and the need for expansion in order to create dynamic (rather than static) relations through which losses might rematerialize as profits, *The Winter's Tale*, in part through its intensified focus on losses and the means to transform them, focuses instead on the very question of how loss can be made productive. In some sense, one could say that the play is trying to understand how tragicomedy as a genre of re-creation could be possible.[9]

The play begins to address this possibility by bringing different models of value depletion and production into dialogue with each other. In Leontes' model (which I will call the "value elimination" model) nothing produces only more nothing; in Polixenes' model (which I will call the "cipher" model) nothing multiplies unnaturally and uncontrollably; in the repentance model in which Leontes attempts to overcompensate for his sin, value is depleted. Finally, in the model offered by the oracle,

redemption is reconfigured as profitable and even certain to rematerialize out of the loss that has already ensued. It is the latter model that
helps to imagine the productivity of loss that is crucial to tragicomedy's
re-creations. In the remainder of this section, I detail the play's movement among these models and its turn to the latter in order to demonstrate how the process by which the productive power located in heirs is
reconfigured in explicitly material and economic terms.

While there is no explicit incest in this play, like *Pericles*, it begins with
future promise illegitimately perverted by the father figure. In this case,
Leontes' jealousy destroys the promise embodied in his son. When
Leontes falls into a jealous rage as a result of his suspicion and Camillo's
inability to confirm what he believes to be positive evidence, he argues:

> Is whispering nothing . . .
> . . . Wishing clocks more swift,
> Hours minutes, noon midnight . . .
> . . . Is this nothing?
> Why then the world and all that's in't is nothing,
> The covering sky is nothing, Bohemia nothing,
> My wife is nothing, nor nothing have these nothings
> If this be nothing. (1.2.286, 291–92, 294–98)

In this proof by contradiction, Leontes tries to show that his suspicions
are authentic, because based on evidence of material transgressions. If
these events are not significant (i.e., material), the ridiculous conclusion is that all is nothing; thus the logic of Leontes' speech is that these
nothings are actually something. While his speech insists that these
nothings actually do produce something, because these things (including Hermione) are not nothings, the emotional tenor of his speech suggests the opposite. If whispering is something, then Hermione actually
is nothing. What materializes out of his reiterations (really repeated accusations) of "nothing" is the devaluation of Hermione and of the world
in which Leontes exists, including Mamillius, on whom the future depends. The repetition of nothing therefore threatens to produce nothing by undermining the future potential embodied in both the son and
the as-yet unborn daughter. Like the "babe" he is soon to reject, the future is condemned because the accusation against Hermione is itself
configured as the impossibility of reproducing not only something of
value, but also value itself.

The language of his accusation against Hermione frames the transgression it misrecognizes as itself a problem of the absence of value. Redemption is necessary then not only because Hermione is believed to
have sinned (or because Leontes has), but also because all has been reduced to naught. Moreover, the play needs doubly to make up for the

loss of Mamillius, the future heir, who was already understood to be the replacement for prior losses and the compensation for insufficiencies. Perhaps Leontes' configuration is accurate: nothing does produce nothing, or even more nothing—if such a possibility exists. The state of nothing is thus contagious; it blocks out all else. The world of the play is deeply in debt, in need of a form of redemption that would re-create value.

An even earlier model the play offers for the production, rather than the elimination, of value will help to put Leontes' concern with the elimination of value into context. Just before Leontes' suspicion emerges, the soon-to-be-suspected adulterer Polixenes tries to get himself out of perpetual debt for Leontes' hospitality. Revising the conversation between the Lords in the first scene, he thinks of a way to express proper and sufficient thanks. He will multiply his thanks with ciphers (that is, zeros) which he imagines "standing in rich place" (1.2.7). By simply adding ciphers onto the end of his singular thank-you, he will create thousands of them. Quite literally, Polixenes presents a model for transforming nothing into something that relieves his situation of debt in "perpetuity." In the process, he converts his indebtedness, the result of a lack of value—what the ciphers themselves represent—into a means to produce value by putting those ciphers in rich place. While value here is produced out of nothing it depends on rich place, which Polixenes can and cannot lay claim to (as king, but of the less wealthy Bohemia). In that case, perhaps, his model of value creation raises mores questions than it answers.

What was initially presented as the proliferation of value in Polixenes' mind above turns into its opposite in Leontes' accusation of Hermione: all is transformed into nothing. As Stanley Cavell points out, Polixenes' model is a kind of breeding (unnatural breeding, I would add) that makes Leontes suspicious in the first place. If Leontes' indirect response to this model is to imagine its very opposite, the annihilation of value, then to counter Leontes' response the play's resolution would require a model that would legitimize the production of value. The play needs to create something, if not out of nothing, then out of what has been lost and returned to its proper place.

Polixenes' model also contrasts with that of Leontes' repentance. As I noted above, Leontes will daily visit the graves of his wife and son, inscribed with the causes of their death to his "shame perpetual" (3.2.236). Through his action he will re-create himself, if not his lost loved ones, not by adding ciphers, but through his repeated action. At the opening of the fifth act, we find out from one of Leontes' Lords that the King has been true to his word: "No fault could you make / Which you have not redeemed, indeed paid down / More penitence than done trespass" (5.1.2–4). Though Leontes says that he cannot forgive himself—as long as he remembers her virtue, he cannot "forget [his] blemishes in them"—the suggestion of his Lord is that he has more than paid back the debt of his sins through his penitence.[10] The Lord's figurative economics are intended to suggest that Leontes has redeemed himself by paying more than he had to; he thus has moral excess in his account.[11] But from a more literal economic perspective, Leontes has simply overpaid: the flow of value out is greater than the value coming in. In the language of credit and borrowing, the trespass (i.e., debt) is less than the sum or value he has paid back. While this model of individual redemption through repentance might give Leontes high moral standing, from an economic perspective it provides a model for value depletion rather than creation. Thus, it is more like than unlike the transgression (the accusation of Hermione that transforms all into nothing) for which it is intended to compensate. The play needs to put aspects of both Polixenes' unnatural value creation model and Leontes' value depletion model together so that the mode of redemption itself can be reconfigured as a means to produce legitimate value. The play would thus reimagine Guarini's aesthetic model for tragicomedy—in which the putting together of tragedy and comedy leaves behind the excesses of each in order to produce a third kind—in more explicitly mathematical, if not, economic terms.[12]

The Winter's Tale's third kind is structured by the play's oracle: there will only be an heir (what will restore and replenish the kingdom, make even old hearts fresh) if what is lost is found, that is, put *back* into rich place. The conversation between Leontes and his Lord shifts to the importance of Leontes remarrying so as to produce an heir, an argument successfully countered by Paulina's reminder of the oracle: the lost child must be found. As if to discount Leontes' model of repentance, Paulina (and the play as a whole) is insistent on the means of redemption: the answer is not repentance; nor is it the creation of something entirely new—a new wife (or heir) would not be sufficient; the (re)solution must rematerialize out of loss that has already ensued. While this discussion seems to shift the focus away from the value of repentance as a means of redemption, I will argue below that the substitute it provides is at its foundation based on the same economic formula, but only in inverted form, so that what is returned exceeds what was lost.[13]

As in *Pericles*, the possibility for redemption is embodied in the daughter, this time aptly named Perdita, after her position of loss, abandonment, and ruin. She is the lost thing that must be found according to the play's oracle and thus contains the power to invert the nothings of Leontes' suspicion and make them into something, that is, something legitimate and valuable. This possibility for value creation is evident from her beginning, even at the moment when she is made into the lost thing. When Leontes orders her abandonment, Antigonus hopes Leontes will "be prosperous / In more than this deed does require" (2.3.189–90).[14] Though Antigonus refers to her as the "poor thing, condemned to loss," he hopes for "blessing / against this cruelty to fight on her side" (191–92).

Antigonus's language gestures toward the shift that occurs almost immediately after he leaves Perdita on the shores of Bohemia—from the more personal and affective losses that occur in the first three acts to the more explicitly economic, even commercial, losses and gains of the fourth and fifth acts. If the economics of loss and redemption discussed so far seem to be in part only figurative, the literal economics come to the surface at the very end of the third act when the play begins to shift genres and changes location. Perdita's first recovery, that is, her recovery by her new father, depends on an explicitly literal version of the economic relationship between lost and found that Antigonus imagined: in search of his lost sheep, the shepherd finds the babe and the box of gold that is sent out with her. When the shepherd's son finds out about the gold he responds appropriately: "You're a made old man. If the sins of your youth are forgiven you, you're well to live. Gold, all gold!" (3.3.110–11). Perdita is not only the loss that is found, then, but also loss turned boon, a maker of an old man. She thus fills Mamillius's earlier role as geriatric supplement and re-creates, even revives, what is lost. In Perdita, the mathematical and spiritual models of the opening acts become decidedly economic, and the model of religious redemption—though partially rejected for its insufficiency, especially by Paulina—is nonetheless employed to provide the model by which value lost can be re-created. In other words, the religious model begins to be reconfigured as an economic one as the sins of youth are put in relation to the discovery of gold. I say that this process is only beginning at this point in the play because the shepherd's son does not actually say what we expect: that the gold will redeem the sins of his youth. He says that his father will "be well to live" *if* the sins of his youth are forgiven. The value of the gold is thus initially dependent on religious redemption. Only later in the play will the economic actually have absorbed the transformative power here ascribed only to the religious. (I will return to this point later.)

The material things that Antigonus leaves with Perdita are key to the process in which loss can be understood to transform into profits. When King Leontes condemns Perdita to loss, he insists that his servant "commend it [the babe] strangely to some place / Where chance may nurse or end it" (2.3.182–83). But Perdita's future is not left entirely to chance. Fortunately, Perdita is left with a bundle of things that will later authenticate her birth and serve as evidence that she, unlike her mother, is not naught. This bundle, not mentioned as such until late in the fourth act, is then repeatedly referred to as the key to the play's profitable resolution. This bundle, or "fardel," is referred to six times near the play's end: for example, "let us to the King. There is that in this fardel which will make him scratch his beard"; "what's in the fardel"; "there lies such secrets in this fardel"; and "I was by at the opening of the fardel" (4.4.687–88, 731, 733, 5.2.2). Significantly the word "fardel," meaning bundle, comes from an Arabic word for burden, which it could also mean, especially figuratively, as in a burden of sin or sorrow; that is what Leontes carries throughout the play after realizing both his errors and losses. Another word, "fardel," spelled and pronounced the same as the other "fardel" but which derives from the Dutch word for advantage ("*vordeel*") means profit. A "fardel" is a burden or a profit, or in this case, both. I argue that in this tragicomedy the fardel is the sign of averted tragedy as the means for its own resolution. As in the fortunate fall itself, in which the transgression of Adam and Eve in the garden produces the coming of Christ, the fardel represents the burden that leads to an even more fortunate future. In more economic terms, the fardel serves as the sign of the rematerialization of loss as a profit. Yet, in contrast to Leontes' individual repentance that (over)pays loss,[15] the fardel and the box of gold that come with it will transform the play's loss into profit.[16]

Not just a daughter or heir on whom the future of the kingdom rests, Perdita is thus the embodiment of expenditure sent out either to prosper or to become naught—"to nurse or end." Sent out across the sea along with the box of gold mentioned above, she is the source of a series of future profits, especially for the shepherd who finds her and grows to an "unspeakable estate"—the sins of his youth actually never to be mentioned again (4.2.35).[17] The box of gold and the fardel that accompany her are thus not simply a dowry necessary to make a good match. The significance of these objects shifts given their placement in the play's Bohemian world, one that is marked by the sale and purchase of foreign commodities and the production of domestic commodities necessary to create the wealth necessary for those purchases. Indeed, just before the play introduces the adult Perdita, her clownish adopted brother (i.e., the shepherd's son) is trying to figure out how much of his wool (England's primary domestic product) is necessary to purchase the imported spices desired for their sheep-shearing festival. I will thus argue that the objects left with Perdita represent not primarily her future inheritance, but the expenditures necessary to an economy of overseas trade and investment.

Michael Bristol draws a similar, though not identical, conclusion about the play's economics. He says, "Leontes' redemption is not brought about by grace and forgiveness but is rather the result of his own bold risk-taking decisions combined with his patience and enormous capacity for deferral."[18] In his reading, in which redemption is only incidental, "Time"—especially the play's sixteen-year interval—is crucial: "Leontes' initial sacrifice takes on the surprising character of a successful long-term investment."[19] My reading here shares much with Bristol's, especially in its analysis of Perdita and the box of gold with which she is left. But I think it might be worth reading Bristol literally (perhaps too literally) and thus to note that Leontes does not take a risk, that he has no strategy, and he is not particularly patient either (at least not initially).[20] Instead, Leontes carelessly tosses away his babe and sends her out of his country. His activities thus resemble not legitimate investors, but the negative characterization of long-distance overseas traders. It might be useful to remember that the accused merchants theorized investment as expenditure productive of future profits in order to defend themselves against claims that they were carelessly and wastefully sending English bullion abroad and thus producing losses.[21] Leontes' actions, like those of overseas merchants, are initially potentially loss-producing.

Though Bristol refers to Leontes' "investment," what he describes is something more like venturing. According to the *OED*, when one ventures, there is "considerable risk of loss *as well as* chance of gain" (emphasis added). When one invests, there is only "expectation of a profit." While the possibility of loss might still exist, the emphasis has shifted to profits and to expectations. Rather than serve as justification, risk is deemphasized so that the relationship is not that of a balance between two possibilities—loss and gain—but between outlay and profit, as we saw in Pericles' experiences in the previous chapter. An outlay, as Thomas Mun (one of the East India Company's directors) argued, is not a loss but an expenditure that is productive; this distinction is crucial.[22] The logic of investment depends on the *transformation* of losses and expenditures into expected profits, rather than on risk taking. Value accrues, then, as a result of what is expended (i.e., capital) rather than as a return for risk per se.[23] The distinction I am making between my own argument and Bristol's matters because I think it helps us to answer an additional fundamental question the play asks: how does loss lead to a profit? How is value created by the expenditure? According to Bristol, Leontes' redemption is not brought about by grace or forgiveness (or, I would add, repentance); with this statement I agree. I also agree that the play does represent the economy as one of investment, even if Leontes himself does not act like a careful investor. What I want to add, then, is that the play must work to transform the effects of his loss-producing actions into profits. Moreover, while I agree with Bristol that Leontes' (or the play's) redemption is not achieved by Christian means, the character of "investment" is itself modeled on the Christian notion of redemption—the fortunate fall—in which the loss is reconceived not simply as an alternative to gain, but as an expenditure whose function is to produce future profits. Redemption thus does not drop out of the play; instead it becomes a reconfigured vehicle for imagining the play's resolution, a resolution that depends not only on the rediscovery of Perdita and her return to her proper place, but also on imagining the production of value out of loss. The play, then, is neither dependent on the unnatural and insubstantial breeding that Polixenes' model imagines nor on the vagaries of fortune that venturing implies. Instead, what guides the resolution of the play is the expectation that the losses will transform into material profits.

The difference between the models of venturing and investment is also made clearer by looking at the difference between the treatment of loss and gain in the play and in its primary source, Robert Greene's narrative romance, *Pandosto: The Triumph of Time* (1588). The plot of *The Winter's Tale* follows that of *Pandosto* fairly closely. As in the play, the babe in *Pandosto* is committed to the "charge of fortune" ("to nurse or end" in the play), but then the narrative romance stays focused on the vagaries of fortune rather than on the transformation of loss into profit. What Greene represents are (possibilities for) reversals of fortune: the shepherd, for example, only keeps the child because he is poor and the gold found with her will "relieve his poverty." In the play, this relief is divided between the shepherd and the character, Autolycus, who does not exist in Greene's text. Furthermore, the prince and princess only end up back in the Sicilia equivalent by chance (a storm), not by design; the Perdita equivalent fears that by "climbing high she will fall too low." Even more striking, the Florizel equivalent, Dorastus, muses in depth on his willful occupation of a lowly position in order to woo Fawnia (the Perdita equivalent): "A strange change from a Prince to a pesant? What is it? thy wretched fortune or thy wilful folly? Is it they cursed destinies? Or thy crooked desires, that a pointeth thee this penance?"[24] Even though he uses the language of repentance, what the prince contemplates are reversals of fortunes. Change is the product of fortune and destiny. In this model the low does not produce the high; they are temporally, but not causally linked. In contrast, I will argue that the play employs the redemptive narrative to transform a narrative of high and low fortune into a theatrical representation of loss transformed into profit. While it is not the case that chance does not exist at all in the play, it is subordinated to—even displaced by—the economic model dependent instead on outlays. While it has become commonplace in current criticism to argue that mercantilist or capitalist profits were differentiated from usury by referring to risk, I am arguing here that the capitalist model tries to eliminate risk, in the practical sense and theoretically, even if merchants did sometimes argue that their profits were justified because their activities were risky. Similarly, though the babe is sent out to "nurse or end," the play's oracle, though conditional (the king will only have an heir *if* that which is lost is found) suggests that the babe will "nurse,"[25] given that the play's resolution depends on these recoveries. Put otherwise, the prophecies of oracles come true: they produce, like investment, expectations. Moreover, this specific oracle sets up a dependent relationship, like that between outlay and profit, not a set of options as in loss or gain. As a result of the oracle, the play's structuring perspective actively orders loss into return.

The actual model for "investment," unlike the model for venturing (which depends on chance), is the religious model. Central to the concept of investment is that value is actually created, though somewhat magically, through the return(s) of what has been lost.[26] Cavell reads Leontes' reiterative "nothings," through which he condemns Hermione, within the framework of skepticism and nihilism to claim that Leontes has a desire for plenitude in a world free of debt. Perhaps Leontes has an "unconscious" nostalgic wish for that kind of innocence, but the play, instead of continuing to "disown knowledge" as Cavell suggests, makes disavowal productive by employing a model of religious redemption in which nothing can be turned into something. In that model, one is not free of debt; instead one understands debt as something that can be made into a profit. As in *Pericles*, debt is not poverty but a means to future returns. Thus, though repentance is not the means to redemption in *The Winter's Tale*, the religious model does not completely disappear. Instead, as in *Pericles*, it yields to the economic model for which it also serves as a basis. Inverting the (cash) flows of repentance, in which Leontes ultimately "paid down more penitence than done trespass," less is expended than is returned, a point evidenced in Bohemia by the ability of the shepherd's son to purchase spices for the sheep-shearing festival. Whereas it is conventional to turn to a pastoral location (like the forest in *As You Like It* or *A Midsummer Night's Dream*) to provide an imaginative space to work through the play's problems, what is unusual here is that Bohemia is a space with a greater material, rather than ideal, focus. It is as if the gravitational pull of the Mediterranean economy is so strong that it pulls Bohemia, which is actually landlocked, into its commercial economy.[27] That economy pulls the play as a whole along with it, so that the play's originating concerns with loss and redemption are worked out in economic terms. The play thus shifts its focus from the concern with spiritual redemption to economic redemption within the context of foreign, if not global, trade. This shift has three primary results. First, for the play itself, the result is that it works through its problems of loss, debt, and incommensurability by thinking through the lens of foreign trade. Second, that working through has additional implications for the genre of tragicomedy and the future conceptualization of capitalist practices: by demonstrating how Christian discourses of redemption can be reconfigured to resolve economic problems, the play imagines the productivity of loss that is fundamental to both the genre of tragicomedy and capitalist investment. Furthermore, by imagining the importation and integration of foreign goods and wealth in dialogue with the domestic economy of production, the play demonstrates how the religious model yields to the economic one and begins to explore some of the tensions within the model, particularly the difficulty of accounting for value creation when losses are transformed into profits. It is to the latter problem that I turn now.

On the Uses and Disadvantages of Poverty

Though the play borrows from the model of religious redemption to explain how value is created, the answer—expenditure—seems to beg the question nonetheless. How does expenditure itself create value?[28] If we want to answer this question and explore the possible sources for additional value, we must turn to the character Autolycus, who makes his first appearance in the fourth act at the moment that Perdita's foolish brother is struggling with his calculations. Autolycus is a seeming itinerant peddler of sheets and ballads—a masterless person, whose occupation also provides cover for his thieving activity. While Perdita represents loss reconfigured as expenditure that is productive of future profit, the possibility for specifically economic loss as well as for the production of value, I will argue, is embodied in Autolycus. He is thus crucial to understanding how investment is profitable, that is, how expenditure produces a return by creating surplus value out of the poverty it employs.

Autolycus is a figure for economic loss in two senses. First, most simply he is a thief and thus responsible for losses of property. His first and primary target is the foolish brother who appears, as I discussed above, engaged in a mathematical quandary, trying to figure out how much of his wool will be necessary to buy the imported goods (currants, and the like) for the sheep-shearing festival.[29] Autolycus dupes the brother by pretending to have been his own victim—that is, Autolycus claims to have been robbed by Autolycus, who has supposedly forced him (self) into the rags of Autolycus. (I will return to this exchange later.) When the clown tries to help him, Autolycus takes advantage of this opportunity to pick the pocket of the clown, who then leaves "Autolycus" to go "buy spices for our sheep-shearing"—though how he will be successful with his empty pockets is unclear (4.3.106–7).

Second, if Autolycus is the agent for loss, he is also one who suffers from loss. We are told by Autolycus that he had once worn "three pile" (i.e., velvet) when he was in the service of Florizel, the king's son (4.3.13). He is now "out of service" (14). We are not told why, but the play implies that he has been cashiered. He is thus a masterless man, potentially a vagrant, beggar, or thief. Masterless men were feared to be some combination of the three.[30] It is in relation to Autolycus's masterlessness that the sheep-shearing and the sale of wool are particularly significant. One of the most visible causes of masterlessness in the period was the enclosure of land for the grazing of sheep, necessary to wool production—England's primary domestic product and export. Enclosures pushed poorer farmers off common land, leaving them to find other means of survival. It is to this problem that Thomas More refers in the *Utopia* when he says that men are being devoured by sheep.[31] And it is partially to this process of enclosure that Marx refers when he argues that primitive accumulation—the divorcing of the worker from the ownership of the conditions for the realization of their labor—is necessary for the creation of a wage labor force.[32] Autolycus's status is tricky. He is identified with the sheep-shearers, but was also once in the service of the prince. Being dismissed from service makes Autolycus of no value within the aristocratic system, but it makes him, like the victims of enclosure, available to be of value within a system dependent on wage labor and capital.[33]

As a masterless person, Autolycus is a specific sign or embodiment of loss, that is, of the casualties of capital, concealed in the production of wage laborers who seemingly benefit from their employers. While this does not fully justify Autolycus's claim to have been his own victim, the status of "robbed" does nonetheless seem to be his own, even as he steals both from the clown whose father owns the sheep and from the sheep-shearers themselves. As Bristol interestingly points out, sheep-shearing depended on a significant amount of temporary wage labor and, I would add, the very wage laborers that the enclosures enforced.[34] Such circularity is reproduced in the clown's purchase of imported foodstuffs as partial payment for the laborers who (according to More's *Utopia*) the sheep themselves devour.[35] Moreover, theoretically these spices would be paid for with the proceeds of the previous sale of wool and thus would be the fruits of prior labor—that is, surplus value (labor which remains un[der]paid)—re-employed as largesse to feed and thus reproduce more labor for future sheep-shearings in order to generate even more profits that would accumulate from them.[36] We might then rewrite the question the play asks—how is value created, that is, how is something made out of nothing or loss—to ask, in Marx's terms, how is surplus value created? In other words, what is the relationship between the value "created" and the value extracted from un(der)paid labor?[37]

The production of surplus value (at least symbolically, if not literally) in the play also depends on a reading of Autolycus, who is not only the sign of the play's losses but also the means by which its genre-based profits are accumulated. Just as Autolycus was both agent of loss and the sign of it, he is an agent of the play's profit and a sign of it as well. Autolycus is crucial to the play's profitable resolution in two ways—at least. First, when the play shifts to comedy in the fourth act, Autolycus, or at least Autolycus's clothes, become the means for its resolution. Polixenes has forbidden the marriage of his son, Florizel, to Perdita, who, unbeknown to everyone is actually the daughter of Leontes. Polixenes thinks her a lowly shepherd's daughter and thus unworthy of his son, the prince. Florizel stumbles upon Autolycus, who has just made considerable profits for himself by selling wares and picking pockets at the sheep-shearing. Upon seeing Autolycus, Camillo (Leontes' ex-Lord now seemingly trying to help Florizel escape from *his* father) strategizes: "Who have we here? / We'll make an instrument of this, omit / Nothing may give us aid." And to Autolycus he says, "for the outside of thy poverty we must make an exchange" (4.4.608–10, 617–18). In accordance with this plan, Florizel and Autolycus change clothes. Made into a tool of their profitable resolution, Autolycus is here instrumentalized, even commodified, like the wage laborer of the sheep-shearing from whom he was just stealing in the earlier part of the scene and with whom he is also identified as masterless person. Conflating the commodity—the thing exchanged—and the wage laborer, the play makes Autolycus doubly the source of its profit now reconceived as added value gifted to him: "what an exchange this had been without boot! What a boot is here with this exchange," Autolycus says, reflecting on his new finery and the additional money given to him for "discasing" and providing Florizel's disguise (657–58).[38] Through him and in him, the nothing (that may give "aid") is transformed into something. If Perdita is capital, Autolycus is the (re)embodiment of surplus value itself, simultaneously extracted from and then rematerialized in himself.

He is barely finished with the reflections on the change in his fortunes when the clown reenters, this time with his father, the shepherd, who is carrying the soon-to-be-infamous fardel—that is, the sign that losses can be transformed into profit. In Florizel's clothes and now as an agent of profit, rather than its tool, Autolycus has a second "job" to do to ensure the play's resolution. The shepherd and his foolish son have been threatened by the King for their relationship to Perdita and now fear for their lives. Preying on their gullibility, Autolycus says that they will be flayed out of their "cases" (i.e., skins). He thus tricks the shepherd into giving him more money and leaving his son as a pawn in order to plead their case to the court. It is not entirely a deception, however, for he does plead their case, in a sense. Autolycus brings the two "rustics" and the fardel aboard the ship sailing for Sicilia; he is thus responsible for the reconciliation and reunions of the two families. Without him, the lost heir would not have been found; she would have remained only Perdita. In addition, the shepherd and his son are not only forgiven their trespasses, but made gentlemen after Perdita's identity has been authenticated. To return to my original description of the relationship between the comedic and tragic components in the plot: the initial "losing" of Perdita produces the situation in which Polixenes is able to object to the marriage of his son to her, which provides the necessary conditions for the profits of the resolution to ensue. Autolycus is the means by which these profits are brought to fruition.[39]

Given the complexity of Autolycus's roles in the play, a summing up is in order. How do we account for Autolycus's double, doubled role: as thief and robbed, as embodiment of surplus value, and agent of profit? Revising Bristol, Barbara Correll calls attention to the permanent losses of Mamillius and Antigonus as well as to the lost time to argue that "Leontes' initial sacrifice amounts to robbery rather than investment."[40] But could we not put these two readings together to make even more explicit what is implicit in Correll's reading in order to argue that the play depends on robbery and investment—even investment as robbery? Borrowing from the clownish brother's assessment of his and his father's condition as "gentlemen newly born," which he describes with the malapropism "preposterous estate," I would like to call the play's resolution one of preposterous prosperity, not primarily to account for its temporal disorders, but for its transformations of losses into profits on the one hand, and for the relationships it establishes between theft and investment on the other (5.2.131–32). "Preposterous estate" refers primarily to their new status as gentlemen. They already had an "unspeakable estate" as a result of the way they employed the gold that they found with Perdita. But since they keep the profits they have already "earned," I would argue that the malapropism here reflects back on the way that the profits they have earned are the result of the transformation of previous losses. Reading the play's resolution as one of preposterous prosperity helps to explain further how Autolycus, in effect, could represent himself as robbing himself. Calling Autolycus a "scene stealer," Correll says that he competes with, rather than enables, the aristocratic family romance.[41] But again, I would like to suggest that he does both.[42] As a quintessential counterfeit (who copies himself), he rematerializes what is lost and serves as the (instrumentalized) agent of the transformation of those losses into legitimized profits. In other words, he is not only agent and instrument of capital; he is also its surplus. By "surplus" I mean to communicate both the added value and the extra, excluded population that society cannot prosperously absorb. "Preposterous prosperity" might also capture the redundancy of Autolycus's imitation of himself in order to rob himself—that is, he acts as usurper of his own surplus value. (After all, "Autolycus," from the Greek, means "self wolf.")

It will be useful to explore not only the terms of his relationship to the aristocratic family romance, but also the ways in which he is instrumental in the generic transformation from romance (with its primary focus on the aristocratic family) to tragicomedy (which focuses also on productivity). The questions therefore are how does he enable or compete with the family reunion and how does he mediate or disrupt the workings of capital? How does he participate in the production of surplus value? Finally, how is that production dependent on Autolycus's dismissal of his own value? Of importance here is that Autolycus is a sign or embodiment of surplus value, but never exactly the producer of it—not in the most literal sense. What is so peculiar and perhaps distinctive about Autolycus is that he is repeatedly represented as almost producing value, but in the end steals value from others and perhaps even extracts it from himself. He is an itinerant peddler of material wares and ballads. But the wares he sells are most likely stolen, and his singing of ballads is employed as a distraction of his audience's senses so that he can pick their pockets. Moreover, some of Autolycus's songs are not ballads per se; instead, as in the first song he sings at the sheep-shearing, the content of the songs is the wares he wants to sell: "gloves as sweet as damask roses, / Masks for faces, and for noses" (4.4.216–17). Thus, even further removed from anything like use-value, the wares become the contents of songs, which are themselves also for sale. The processes of exchange in this scene transform means into ends; the result is not only unnatural reproduction (as Aristotle argued) but, as Marx argued, commodities whose value appears to inhere in them. The latter is signaled by the way that wares are collapsed into the medium through which they are seemingly made valuable.[43] The point of Autolycus's thieving activity is not simply that one man's gains are another's losses, but that the gains are the result of extracting value from an exterior source—a process mystified by the logic of investment, in which the source of value appears to be the expenditure itself and thus in which the value seems to inhere in the object itself, rather than in the labor—of sheep-shearers or lacemakers, for example. We could say that Autolycus represents the disavowal of labor. His thieving activity is not a disruption of capital, but an often excluded sign of it.

The distinction between means and ends is further collapsed in the first ballad Autolycus offers for sale. Set to a "doleful tune," he tells his audience, is the story of a usurer's wife, "brought to bed of twenty money-bags at a burden"; she gives birth (her burden) to money-bags (4.4.253–54). Autolycus thus offers to sell a tale whose content itself (usury) was considered the worst form of confusing means and ends. The tale serves as an example of unnatural breeding for sure, but also of a prosperous "issue" (a word repeated throughout the play). The story of this ballad serves as mirror and contrast to the one told by the play as a whole; but the ballad, in general, as a commodified art form might serve as a stepping-stone to the model for the play's generic structure. Like the fardel—a burden that produces a profit—the ballad (whose refrain was called a "burden") has that transformation of loss (the doleful tune and the "burden") into profit (twenty money-bags) as its means (the content of the ballad of the usurer's wife) and ends, though perhaps not yet legitimate ends.[44]

The play's tragicomic resolution (enabled by Autolycus and the fardel) is engendered, however, by a form of better breeding; generic grafting, an issue raised at the sheep-shearing festival, produces a "third kind" that is both artfully and naturally prosperous. In his discussion of how one properly mixes tragedy and comedy to create the perfect kind that is tragicomedy, Guarini explains that art imitates nature: "while nature alters the parts after they are united, art alters them before they are joined in order that they may be able to exist together and, though mixed, produce a single form."[45] Might Shakespeare have had this explanation in mind when he wrote the debate on art, nature, and grafting between Perdita and Polixenes? Regardless, the debate comments on the generic structure of the play and the necessity of altering Perdita and Hermione (perhaps along with Autolycus, Florizel, and the shepherd) through art, in order to allow for proper and prosperous breeding. Tragicomedy in this model is thus explicitly a transformative genre.

It might be useful to remember that the model for such a transformation exists in not just Autolycus's acts in this play, but in his heritage as well. In his first appearance, Autolycus tells the play's audience that he is the issue of Mercury—the god of commerce and the market, a protector of traders, whose occupations are those of messenger and thief. Mercury's very first theft is of Apollo's herds—a theft perhaps mirrored in Autolycus's treatment of the clown and the sheepshearers. To make up for his theft, Mercury gives Apollo a lyre. According to this story, the compensatory issue of theft is thus poetry, the repayment, if you will, for Mercury's sins.[46] What will be the repayment for Autolycus's thefts and those of the play as a whole? To what extent will the compensation the play offers depend on the interdependence of the aesthetic and the commercial, and what will Autolycus's role be in that compensation?

Re-creating Theatricality

I conclude by looking at the relationships the play sets up among redemption and art, specifically the ways that redemptive processes are employed so that legitimate value-added (as opposed to that congealed in ballads or produced by the clown's gentlemanly swearing on Autolycus's account) is the product of tragicomic theater.[47] The play's final scene returns more explicitly (and somewhat more seriously) to the religious model of redemption. Paulina refers to Leontes' visit to her home to see the statue of Hermione as "a surplus of your grace which never / My life may last to answer" (5.3.7–8). According to Paulina (who conjures the statue—"Bequeath to death your numbness, for from him / Dear life redeems you") the return to life "require[s] you do awake your faith" (102–3, 95). While clearly incorporating allusions to the resurrection, the play is not presenting an allegory as such. Instead of a resurrection, I read Hermione's return to life, which requires not that one's "sins are forgiven," but that one has "faith," as the play trying to imagine a future that is not made static by the disavowal of its losses, and thus as a counterpart to the implementation of Autolycus. Borrowing from, but revising, the diction of the oracle so that it is both more Christian and more economic, the revival represents belief in future profits.

Unlike the ending of *Twelfth Night*, the play employs the economics of redemption to imagine a future that is anything but static. But how does it do so? In this concluding section I argue that the play itself must exchange the outside of *its* poverty for a form of theatrical credibility that would not only guarantee "surplus" value, but also be productive of it. Except for the staging of the statue come to life, almost all of the play's problems are resolved in its penultimate scene. In that scene, the characters learn that Perdita's true identity, as the daughter of Leontes and Hermione, has been revealed as a result of the opening of the fardel, which represents the fulfillment of the oracle. None of this discovery is staged; it is only recounted. In this recounting, poverty is reconfigured as theatrical absence—specifically the inability to see, represent, and interpret adequately. The scene alludes to these problems repeatedly: "Were you present at this relation"; "I make a broken delivery of the business, but the changes I perceived in the King and Camillo were very notes of admiration"; "there was speech in their dumbness, language in their very gesture. They looked as they had heard of a world ransomed or destroyed . . . but the wisest beholder that knew no more but seeing, could not say if th'importance were joy or sorrow. But in the extremity of the one, it must needs be";[48] "ballad makers cannot be able to express it"; "this news which is called true is so like an old tale that the verity of it is in strong suspicion"; "that which you hear you'll swear you see, there is such unity in the proofs"; "did you see the meeting of the two kings"; "you have lost a sight which was to be seen, cannot be spoken of"; "they were to be known by garment, not by favour"; and "I never heard of such another encounter which lames report to follow it and undoes description to do it." This section of the scene finally ends with the gentlemen's decision to go see for themselves, because, as they say, "absence makes us unthrifty to our knowledge" (5.2.1, 8–10,12–18, 22–23, 25–26, 29, 36, 38–39, 43–44, 50–52, 100).

For what then does the play exchange the outside of its poverty? Or how, or for what, is it redeemed? One answer is the theatricality of the scene that follows, in which Paulina brings the statue of Hermione to life, made all the more stunning by the absence of theatricality that precedes it. But given the previous scenes' repeatedly expressed concerns about the transparency and profits of representation, should we not be skeptical, if not of the scene's profits then at least of the claim that the experience of profit is shared by all onlookers? The "awakened" Hermione does ask for a recounting of events (the real audience would find this redundant since it is the material of the play they have just seen), but Paulina intervenes and says to her audience: "Lest they desire upon this push to trouble / Your joys with like relation. Go together, / You precious winners all" (5.3.130–32). Paulina wants to prevent any troubling narratives from detracting from joy. She thus pushes them aside in order to promote her profitable version of events.

One way this version is credited is by the removal of Autolycus (a ballad seller and process-server) from any kind of authorial role—not surprisingly, by Autolycus himself. Immediately after the gentlemen who recount the events in the penultimate scene leave to partake in the thrifty spectacle to come, Autolycus regrets (though not in a very serious tone) his past wrongdoings given that they now serve as an impediment for him to share in the profits: "Now had I not the dash of my former life in me, would preferment drop on my head. I brought the old man and his son aboard the Prince; told him I heard them talk of a fardel, and I know not what" (5.2.102–5). Conceiving himself as incapable of redemption—significantly defined here as the remission of sins *and* the partaking of profits[49]—Autolycus generously disowns his role in these discoveries: "But 'tis all one to me, for had I been the finder-out of this secret it would not have relished among my other discredits" (109–10). Autolycus preposterously immaculates—that is, redeems—the narrative in order to let its theatrical and aesthetic profits ensue. Otherwise, it might peter out into "I know not what." If Autolycus's earlier transformation into an "instrument" could be understood to register his commodification and echo (if only ironically) his potential as a vehicle for God's word (what "instrument" often signified), then Autolycus's self-representation reconfigures himself as a usurper of his own surplus value and a false prophet. But he enacts this latter transformation to lend the resolution credibility, guarantee the play's surplus value, and undo the stasis that the circularity of self-usurpation might produce. (While Perdita is restored to her proper place, it is not entirely clear whether Autolycus remains cashiered.)

As I argued in Chapter 1, disavowal leads to a static economy in *Twelfth Night*. But here "poverty" is put to use and disavowal (which by definition does not acknowledge loss) appears to be transformed into redemption (which makes use of loss) that is both credible and productive. Again, Autolycus robs himself, but this time of authority. As in the relationship of capital to surplus value, the play's prosperous ending depends on not a mere elision of the actual labor that is performed, but its transformation. The value of Autolycus's labor is discounted only to be re-counted for the sake of profitable accumulation, just as the low elements are made necessary to the resolution of the high: not "hornpipes *and* funerals," as Philip Sidney negatively declaimed of tragicomedy, but funerals *into* hornpipes, or births, as the case might be.[50] If the value of Autolycus's wares and the labor necessary to produce and sell them is congealed in the ballads that represent them, in the play's ending the discounting of Autolycus by Autolycus serves to enable that value to rematerialize elsewhere as surplus.

The actual profits that accrue to the play's main aristocratic characters reside primarily in the union of the two kingdoms. But this union is not merely a gain in territory; affectively it is the elimination of distance and separation. It eliminates the very need for the kinds of exchanges that open the play and thus rids the play of the fundamental problem of exchange—incommensurability[51]—as well as the possibility for "trespass."[52] Perhaps that is what it means to be "precious winners all." Not only do all gain, but they are also worthy. (The root of "precious" is price.) All are also worthy because they have seen the play—that is, the redemption of Hermione from death by life, and moreover, by faith and surplus grace.

The play provides a further aesthetic parallel to these unifications. Even though the penultimate scene repeatedly emphasizes the difficulty of proper expression and adequate interpretation, there is one event that is perfectly legible: the spectacle of Perdita's response to the recounting of the story of her mother's death. The theatrical audience is several layers removed from the immediacy of the events, but they are told that all members of the spectacle's audience have an identical response: "Whom was most marble there changed colour. Some swooned, all sorrowed. If all the world could have seen't, the woe had been universal" (5.2.80–84). Not only are the kingdoms unified, but also difference is eliminated by the recounting of stories (as long as Autolycus does not do the recounting). No longer does Bohemia suffer from insufficiency vis-à-vis Sicila. It does not seem, however, that the theatrical fully supplants the religious, *pace* Cavell, but that the theatrical makes use of its poverties, and thus rematerializes and will "relish," unlike Autolycus, the economic and religious models it employs—and to its credit.[53]

My aim is not to represent the theater as identical to the commercial, global economy. But the theater is represented here as trying to redeem the economic in general and lost value in particular, with its own supplements. It seeks to capitalize on its own spectacular effects. Of course, this reading is complicated by the fact that the spectacle that produces universal affect is only recounted and not staged; what the audience sees is a staged recounting of a theatrical event, upstaged by the revival of Hermione that follows it. Like Autolycus, the theater steals its own scenes. Profits and surplus value are thus rematerialized in the theater itself, which "borrows" from narrative romance only to reconfigure it into a more profitable medium: both tragicomedy (based on redemption) and theater (based on re-creation). Unlike its source, *Pandosto*, which ends tragically (with the death of the Leontes figure and without the revival of its Hermione), the theatrical form provides both re-creation and relish. Theater is what is represented as a profitable medium, more profitable than the semi-tragic romance of *Pandosto* or even the "painful adventures of Pericles." Comparing *Pericles* and *The Winter's Tale*, we can see that the relationship between profit and loss thematized in *Pericles* is absorbed into both the generic structure (no longer episodic highs and lows, but a continuous fall made fortunate) and theatricality of *The Winter's Tale*. We can thus see a progression from the comedic *Merchant of Venice* and *Twelfth Night* that have difficulty imagining expansion while achieving closure, to *Pericles* whose dialectical structure enables expansion, to *The Winter's Tale* whose dialectical relationship between its two locales and genres enables the thematics of transformation to be absorbed into a structure and theatrical practice deemed valuable.

That profitability in *The Winter's Tale* might be modeled on the earlier form of profitable art: the commodified ballads rematerialized in the spectacle of the theater from which they are and are not elided. Howard Felperin suggests that Autolycus's art is a low parody of the high art of the play itself, but I would like to suggest that it is also a model for the profitability of tragicomic theatricality, materialized in the spectacle of the statue come to life.[54] The statue is credited at first precisely because of the disavowal of its status as commodity: it is "a piece many years in doing and newly performed by that rare Italian master Giulio Romano" (5.2.86–88). Moreover, it is "masterly done," the product of the "carver's excellence" (5.3.65, 30). But the value of the statue as a statue (that is, as a pure work of art) gives way to the theatrics of its coming to life, which is the mixing of art and life—that is, theater, a medium that depends on the literal embodiment of artistic value. What is important is not the masterfully carved statue, which it is and is not, but the performance of the return to life; it is tragicomic theater itself. If the play distances itself from Guarini's recommendation for limiting tragicomedy to near deaths through the fates of Mamillius and Antigonus, in the statue it provides a meta-theatrical version of the limitation as potential surplus. The statue's movement as well as its wrinkles force the audience to "awaken" their belief, precisely in order to reconcile art as a historical event—not timeless, but participating in and making use of time.

Furthermore, rather than making its audience senseless, thus ripe for theft (what Autolycus's ballads do), the stone (because it is and is not real, is art and is not art, but a grafting of life onto art) "rebuke[s] Leontes, for "being more stone than it" (37–38). The effects of tragicomic theater are (disciplinarily) redemptive and, I would add, also profitable: Leontes follows this observation with the exclamation, "O royal piece." His performative speech (as in "it's a girl," or "I pronounce you man and wife," or "it's my wife") re-creates Hermione as Leontes' issue, that is, the issue of his mint.[55] (A royal piece could be a gold coin whose value would be guaranteed by the impression of the monarch's face stamped upon it.) The progeny is not "twenty money-bags at a burden," but a legitimate utterance. Leontes' next performative could be understood as an instantiation and simultaneous legitimization of the (prosperous) theater itself: "let it be an art lawful as eating" (110–11). Of course, what one eats (e.g., one's own progenitor, ballads, spices, currants, sheep, corn), as we learned from both this play and *Pericles*, is a remaining "issue," a pun used repeatedly throughout the play to refer simultaneously to offspring, profit, expenditure, and even an exit from the stage—a pun that returns us to the question of how value is produced, reproduced, and represented.[56]

If, as I have argued, the genre of tragicomedy anticipates the mercantilists' argument that money sent out of the country is only misrecognized as loss because it is actually transformable into profit, here what we might be witnessing is not only the play working through economic problems of its time (and even of its near future) but also the reimportation of the lessons learned by addressing these economic problems back into theatrical practice. The theater (or Shakespeare, at least), like Leontes, learns not just that money can be made through the "rational" process of investment, but also that there is profit to be made from spectacle-effects. These effects are the surplus value the theater can produce when it transforms art into life and life into death into life through its own mystifying labor. That labor has as its goal the production of profit and the very concealment of the labor necessary to produce the aesthetic pleasure on which the theater's own profits depend.

What I hope has become clear in this chapter and in the preceding one as well are some of the ways that these plays employ the dialectics of tragicomedy and the economic undercurrents of religious redemption to explore the perceived need for foreign exchanges and to rewrite the perils of such expansions as sources for profit and accumulation, which in turn are reabsorbed into the tragicomic theater. By explaining why the genre of tragicomedy is particularly well suited to engage with economic problems related to loss, profit, and the production of value, these chapters on earlier plays serve as a foundation for the later chapters that explore how tragicomedy's redemptive processes manage concrete problems that arise out of trade within specific geopolitical formations, such as those developing in the complex and competitive arenas of the East Indies and the Levant.

Part II
Eastern Engagements

Captivity and "Free" Trade
Fletcher's The Island Princess *and English Commerce in the*
East Indies in the Early 1600s

> *On the Last Day the Redeemer himself shall say, I was in prison and you*
> *redeemed me. What better work can man perform for Christ than that*
> *which was the best work which Christ performed for man? And what was*
> *that but Redemption. . . . What had all this profited us if he had not*
> *redeemed us? How can that work but be most acceptable unto him which is*
> *the best resemblance of the best worke he ever did for us? Redemption!*
> *Redemption! . . . So would they say to themselves of their wastfull and,*
> *commonly, sinfull expences, I might have chosen whether I would have lost*
> *this money: I might have saved it by bestowing it either towards the*
> *redemption of my enthralled brethren in Barbarie, or on the relief of their*
> *wretched wives and children at home; and so have made a more*
> *advantageous returne, then any of our Merchants do by their most thriving*
> *adventures into any parts of Barbarie.*

—Three Sermons: Compassion Towards Captives . . . in miserable
bondage in Barbary *(1636)*

> *There is no happiness on earth that can equal that of regaining one's lost*
> *liberty.*

—Cervantes, *"The Captive's Tale" in* Don Quixote *(1605)*

> *The English did endeavor to defend them with whom they had free trade*
> *and trafficke.*

—An Answer to the Hollanders Declaration, Concerning the
Occurrents of the East India *(1622)*

The previous chapters focused on Christian redemption as a model for
how tragicomedy might turn potentially unredeemable losses into
sources of anticipated future profits. This chapter turns to how tragicomic narratives of captivity might provide a means and a model for
reconfiguring trade itself as a source of redemption. In the previous
chapters, I argued that tragicomedy unblocked the impasses produced

by romantic comedy's insistence on closure. In this chapter, my argument is that tragicomic historical narratives and plays work not only to imagine a larger, noninsular and thus prosperous economy, but also an economy that imagines trade as having a purpose beyond that of prosperity. In these texts, trade is represented as a source of liberation.

In order to make this argument about the development of discourses of "free trade," this chapter reads economic and historical documents of the English trade with the East Indies in dialogue with stories of merchant captives and a play whose tragicomic trajectory depends on movement from imprisonment to liberation: John Fletcher's *The Island Princess*. These early seventeenth-century texts not only represent an increasing concern about captivity, but also make use of the potential of imprisonment in order to imagine a trade that is by contrast both free (even freeing) and prosperous. This chapter thus has two primary and related objectives: to explore how and why the understanding of these two states—freedom and prosperity—develop interdependently out of the complex situation of England's trade in the East Indies; and to explain the crucial role that tragicomic narratives play in their development.

Developing a Noncoercive and Valuable Trade in the East Indies

The conceptual links among a profitable trade, free trade, and freedom develop out of the unique political and economic situation of England's trade in the Indies. As Michael Neill has pointed out, English objectives in the East were explicitly more mercantile than colonial, that is, England did not plan to take over, or even inhabit, the lands with which it was trading.[1] Indeed, the English repeatedly contrasted themselves to their predecessors—the Portuguese, Spanish, and Dutch—whose trade practices (at least according to the English) were much more dependent on restrictions and physical coercion. Instead, the English represented the trade in which they participated as noncoercive in several respects. The English claimed to support a nonmonopolistic trade in the area, so that the Indies could enjoy multiple European trading partners (in contrast to the English end of things, where the East India Company merchants insisted on having a monopoly on East Indies trade). As well, the English promoted the notion that trade should neither produce nor depend on the subjection of those with whom they traded.

A powerful promoter of this logic was Samuel Purchas, who collected narratives for an ambitious five-part, multivolume work on England's trade. He introduces his history by offering the wisdom of Solomon's fair-trading policies as a model for England's practices, emphasizing that Solomon did not "make a monopoly of the ocean, as if the whole East had been created for Ezion-geber."[2] Most likely, Purchas is writing not about a future worry that the English will set up monopolistic practices abroad, but against the de facto monopolistic practices of those Europeans who had already been trading in the Indies—the Spanish, the Portuguese, and in the current moment, especially the Dutch. Purchas immediately connects this nonmonopolistic, generous approach to a policy of noncoercion: "And as he sought not to prejudice Egypt, or any of his neighbours, if out of their own ports they intended to seek the world abroad, no more did he prove injurious to the Ophirians, with whom he dealt either in their wealth, hindered, by prohibiting all others to trade with them; or . . . by erecting forts against their wils, as prisons of their libertie and fetters of their captivity."[3] Other historical documents similarly associate nonmonopolistic trade with freedom for both the English and their trading partners. For example, a pamphlet defending the English against Dutch accusations that they had helped the Bandanese break their treaty with the latter emphasizes the difference between English and Dutch trading practices: "the English did endeavor to defend them with whom they had free trade and trafficke; who lovingly and with free consent sold to the English their spices, &c, who put themselves under the protection of the English. . . . Thus hitherto it is plainly acknowledged, the Hollanders never had any lading, any castle or fort, any trading in the Ilands of Banda, but what was gotten by force and absolute constraint."[4]

Given recent scholarship on the Black Legend of a bloodthirsty and rapacious Spain, it would be easy to dismiss this contrast as England's attempt to extend their disparagement of Spanish trading practices to the Dutch and thereby represent their methods of conducting trade as more honorable.[5] But the English insistence on their trade as a purely mercantile, rather than a colonial endeavor, is not all ideology. Some of the distinction drawn between the English and the Dutch methods is a matter of practical economics. The text that I just cited is a pamphlet defending the English against Dutch accusations and thus takes a moral tone, highlighting the more ethical dimensions of English trade. Letters from the English East India Company's factors writing from the East back to the company insist on a similar distinction in their trading practices, but they do so to argue for a noncolonial form of trade for reasons of profitability, not honor, that is, for materialist, rather than idealist, reasons. For example, in 1615 George Cockayne wrote to the company that "the trade that comes by compulsion is not profitable . . . [the Dutch] have many castles with much trouble and little profit."[6] So, it is not only that the English traders distinguish themselves from the Dutch because the Dutch are in their way, but also because the Dutch model is less profitable than, say, Solomon's more honorable trade with the Ophirians.

Since the English had to negotiate with the Dutch to trade in many areas in the Indies and were forced ultimately to agree to support some of the costs of the Dutch colonial methods, the sting of Dutch colonial and monopolistic methods was doubly felt. Sir Thomas Roe, for example, wrote against signing an agreement with the Dutch for precisely these reasons: "their garrisons, charges, and losses by negligence will engage the company to bear part of their follies for no profit."[7]

The rejection of the colonial model for a strictly mercantile and thus more profitable trade, however, created a significant problem for merchants at home. Given that the objectives of the English East India Company did not include a takeover of the islands of the East Indies themselves in the strict sense, the islands were not incorporable into any notion of England or Britain. English merchants had to argue then that the products of a distant and unincorporable land could be of value to England and thus could justify the considerable outflow of bullion from England necessary to purchase them. From our postcolonial perspective—that is, with the history of western colonialism in hindsight and economic imperialism virtually synonymous with contemporary globalization—this problem might seem to be nonexistent. It is now not much more than "common sense" for Western nations to imagine a profit made by obtaining valuable goods from what is now the Third World at a low cost, then reselling them in other locations in the First World. But this viewpoint in early modern England had to be argued, in part, because it required a new understanding of economics (especially the flow of money) and the relationship between the commercial undertakings of individuals and the well being of the commonwealth as a whole.

These problems with representing long-distance overseas trade as beneficial for England became particularly acute and visible in the trade of the East India Company, because unlike many of the trading companies that preceded it, the English East India Company did not primarily expand markets for English goods. Instead, it developed a multilateral trade in order to make profits from its imports and re-exports, rather than from its own exports.[8] In order to acquire bullion for these imports and make a profit from them, the East India Company (chartered in 1600) engaged in an elaborate set of exchanges that would have little to do with goods produced in England or destined for consumption there: Spanish rials (made of New World silver) procured elsewhere in Europe were used in the Indies to purchase calicos that were exchanged for spices that were then re-exported to Europe, or even the Levant, in order to acquire more Spanish rials, with which the cycle would begin again. But if goods from the Indies are brought into England only to be re-exported, clearly they have no use-value as far as England is concerned. The trade is not supplying England's needs, at least not in any direct way. East India Company merchants had to demonstrate that there was value for England in these trades even if the trades had no direct effect on the sale of English products or availability of additional products for use in England. The whole project, then, raised questions regarding the benefit for the nation that simply selling English goods abroad did not.[9]

This complicated set of arrangements thus required justifying such trade as profitable in the strictest economic sense. In order to do so, merchants and economic theorists argued that the East Indies trade would lead to what was newly understood as a favorable "balance of trade" (in which net exports exceed net imports).[10] In fact, when Thomas Mun makes his argument for the idea of a favorable balance of trade, he does so by emphasizing that *Indian* wares, in particular, could be of value to England in this way: "There is the *same* power in these Indian wares, to procure other sommes of ready moneyes, to be brought into this kingdom."[11] The benefit for England thus does not depend on trade in wares that are the product of English industry, and it does not depend on their use in England. Mun's argument depends instead on value alone. Indeed, Mun is trying to reconfigure the value of these foreign goods as potentially England's own in order to be able to conceive of the expenditures on Indian wares as producing profits for England. This reconception is necessary, in turn, to reconfigure expenditures on Indian wares as investments in future profits rather than as simply a drain on the nation's bullion.[12]

The East India Company thus was faced with both a practical problem—the need to find ways to establish purchasing power and to make the trade profitable—and a conceptual one—the ability to represent Indian goods as valuable to the English. Given the rejection of the colonial model, the English had to reconceive of the products of the Indies as of value to their nation without imagining the lands themselves as potentially English possessions. Doing so requires imagining the value of the Indies as transferable and thus alienable from the Indies themselves. In the remainder of the chapter, I argue that theatrical tragicomedy and the tragicomic structure of many narratives of early modern trade address this multipronged problem through their reliance on discourses of redemption that serve to reconceive trade as a source of liberation, that is, as having the very opposite effects of colonial endeavors. In these narratives, it is the very liberating effects of trade that enable value to be transferred and profits to be made. Thus, while most of the current criticism that explores issues of "free trade" in the early seventeenth century focuses on the debates over the merchant companies' monopolies at home or on the question of government intervention, my focus here is on the way that ideas about a prosperous and free trade developed in relationship to policies of coercion and threats of captivity far from home, and in relation to ideas about what it meant for persons and things to be free.[13]

Trade: Redeemed and Free

Early in Purchas's introductory chapter, he argues that "God hath given to every man and to every Nation, a kind of proprietie in their peculiar possession." But there are and are not limited cases to this natural order. God has "determined the bounds of their [men's] habitation. But not so straitly of Negotation." Thus he understands trade as the result of "mutual necessitie, the mother of mutual commerce, that one should not be hungry, and another drunken, but the superfluitie of one country should supply the necessities of another, in exchange for such things, which are here also necessary, and there about; that thus the whole world might be as one body of mankind, the nations, as so many members, the superabundance in each, concocted, distributed, retained or expelled by merchandising whereby not without mutual gain one may relieve others wants."[14] In this reapplication of the body politic metaphor, the emphasis is on the supplying of wants. The several countries are like one body, made up of different members whose functions are now envisioned as the products they supply. By the end of the introduction, however, the emphasis has shifted considerably to a model of the unification of the world through trade. Concluding with a discussion of charity, Purchas claims that the

chiefest charity is that which is most common, nor is there any more common than this of navigation, where one man is not good to another man, but so many nations as so many persons hold commerce and intercourse of amitie withal; Salomon and Hiram together, and both with Ophir; the West with the East, and the remotest; parts of the world are joined in one band of humanitie; and why not also of Christianitie? . . . That as there is one lord, one Faith, one Baptisme, one Body, one Spirit, one Inheritance, One God and Father, so there may thus be one Church truly Catholicke, one Pastor and one Sheepfold? And this also wee hope shall one day be the true Ophiran Navigation, when Ophir shall come into Jerusalem, as Jerusalem then went unto Ophir. Meane while, we see a harmonie in this Sea trade, and as it were the consent of other Creatures to this consent of the reasonable, united by Navigation, howsoever by Rites, Languages, Customes and Countries separated.[15]

Disturbing, but not surprising, is the wish for the unity to be unity as Christians. Even more important for my analysis here is the understanding of the harmony of commerce and the consequent unification of the world—the much repeated "one"—as a New Jerusalem, when "Ophir shall come into Jerusalem." Reading together these two quotations that bookend the introduction to Purchas's multivolume history of trade and discovery, we can see how the going out and expanding of discovery and trade is imagined as a universal conversion that results in the redemption of mankind. The frontispiece of the text makes a similar argument. As Michael Neill has astutely demonstrated, Purchas's frontispiece represents the merchant (rather than the soldier or colonist) as the truest type of pilgrim and the English nation as the Chosen People whose voyages will unify all and accomplish the "millennial destiny of humankind."[16] But it is not only that all things become potentially English or Christian, but also that trade itself is represented as redemptive.

This argument is made even more explicitly in the documents that could be said to launch England's participation in the East Indies trade. When the first ships of the East India Company set sail in 1601, they had in hand a circular letter from Elizabeth I addressed to six kings of the Indies that emphasizes the redemptive value of trade:

Whereas almighty God in his infinite and unsearchable wisdom and gracious providence hath so disposed of his blessings and of the good things of this world created and ordained for the use of man, that the same, however they be brought forth, and do either originally grow and are gathered, or otherwise composed and made some in one country and some in another: yet are they by the Industrie of man directed by the hand of God dispersed and sent out into all the parts of the world, that his wonderful bounty in his creatures may appeare unto all nations, his Majesty having so ordained that no one place should enjoy (as the Native commodities thereof) all things appertaining to man's use, but that one Countrie should have need of another, and out of the abundance of the fruit which some region enjoyeth the necessities or wante of another should be supplied: By which means men of several and far remote countries have commerce and traffic one with another, and by their interchange of commodities are linked together in amitie and friendship.[17]

This argument shares a similar logic to Mun's understanding of the potential value of foreign wares to the English and Purchas's view of the unifying effect of trade. Elizabeth's biblical perspective on how losses produce potential profits, however, takes an even wider view on how goods from one place may be valuable to another. Going a step further than Purchas in her use of the model of redemption, the queen's letter argues for a proleptic relation between the original dispersal and the consequent unification. Her story is in effect tragicomic: the diaspora of goods is fortunate, because it produces (with the help of God) the "industry of man," which then redistributes these goods and unifies countries.

Moreover, while Purchas argues that the trade is redemptive because it is unifying, Elizabeth's letter again goes a step further by implicitly arguing that the trade's redemptive potential is precisely the result of her nation's refusal of imperial objectives. In order to establish the good intentions of the English traders, the letter juxtaposes them to their predecessors—the Portuguese—who pretend "them selves to be the sovereigne Lorde and Prince of all your Territories, & gave it out that they held your Nation and People as Subjecte to them: & in ther stiles and Titles doe write them selves kinge of the East Indies."[18] Instead of mastery and subjection, what Elizabeth's letter emphasizes is the possibility for more honorable and equitable friendship.

The prologue to Elizabeth's narrative of global trade as a form of redemption is thus the story of the Portuguese who hold the East Indian "nation and people as subjecte to them." Elizabeth's ideological vision of global trade as a form of redemption works on more than one level. First, it redeems Indian goods from the hold of the Portuguese and thus makes them available to the English.[19] Second, it imagines a repair of the fallen distribution that is simultaneous with (and even causally related to) the redemption of the Indies and its people from the hold of the Portuguese. The ideology of free trade is offered as countering, rather than causing, the subjection of one people to another. Moreover, *free* trade is not just an alternative to subjection; it is offered as the very means to freedom. We might say that the people and goods of the Indians are purchased back (the meaning of "redeem") by free trade itself, which benefits all. Elizabeth's letter, by opposing English practices to the coercive practices of her predecessors in the Indies, also argues for the liberating effects of trade. In her document, the condensation of free trade and liberation reconfigures trade (the original source of the subjection) in tragicomic fashion, as the saving grace.

If what we can see in Elizabeth's letter is an argument for the benefit of trade for the whole world as a result of man's redemptive industry, in Thomas Mun's defense of trade written for an English audience we can see its mercantilist counterpart being argued in order to justify investment on the part of the English. In Mun's text it is not so much that the countries are linked, but that the commodities themselves become valuable and profitable for the "industrious" English—a point only partially subordinated in Elizabeth's narrative written for a different audience.[20] Elizabeth's notion of benefit still depends on understanding the goods as necessary and useful to those nations that procure them from abroad. What becomes important in Mun's argument is that a "continual and orderly" change of money and wares "one into the other" leads to more money.[21] I would argue that Mun's argument for exchange-value and accumulation makes use of Elizabeth's argument for the productive effects of trade, but in doing so it ultimately eliminates the necessity of the goods' use-value for England on which her argument depends. The "power" of Indian wares to bring profits to the English is the result of a reconception of lack or want as productive (Elizabeth's version) and value as something transferable. Given the East India Company's more practically motivated rejection of coercive policies, we might read Mun's understanding of the transferability of value as dependent on the liberating effects Elizabeth's letter imagines. Value, like the goods themselves, can circulate freely and accrue as a result of the redemptive trajectory of trade. As a result, goods not of use nor produced by the English can be understood to be profitable not just for the company members, but also for the nation. By reading Elizabeth's letter and Mun's treatise in dialogue with each other we can see how the East India Company's arguments for the profitability of its trade produced the two ideas of trade as a liberating force and value as transferable as interdependent concepts. This combination is the manifestation of trade as free trade, that is, as redemption. The remainder of the chapter focuses on redemptive trade narratives and a theatrical tragicomedy, Fletcher's *The Island Princess* (1623/4), that address these concerns by employing narratives of captivity tragicomically in order to imagine, as Mun and Elizabeth do, both value and people as free to circulate and trade.

Productive Redemptions

Fletcher's *The Island Princess* is significantly the first English play to be set in the East Indies. Taking a familiar romance narrative in which the princess is the source of competition among a number of suitors, the play relocates the genre within the context of the Portuguese colonization of the Spice Islands and the continuing conflicts among the islands. All of the European characters are Portuguese (technically speaking); when the play opens the most explicit current conflict is actually between the two neighboring islands of Ternate and Tidore. Early in the play Quisara, the King's sister, offers herself as the prize for whoever can redeem her brother the King of Tidore, who has recently been imprisoned by the Governor of the neighboring island, Ternate. After Armusia (a newcomer to the Indies and a Portuguese man) redeems the King, Quisara's previous suitor plots against him as does the Governor, who disguises himself as a Moor-priest and warns the King of the dangers of marrying his sister to a Christian European whose intentions toward the island and its goods might not be honorable. The redeemer, Armusia, is thus imprisoned until the other Portuguese characters, including the first suitor, destroy the town and reveal the priest to be the Governor of the enemy island whose imprisonment of the King initiated all of the action described above.

As one might imagine from the above plot description, the play repeatedly calls attention to its characters' need for redemption. Compared to many other tragicomedies of the period, however, *The Island Princess* is less concerned (at least initially) with the avoidance of losses per se than with captivity and liberation and thus with reconceptualizations similar to those I outlined above in my discussion of the interdependence of discourses of freedom and trade. Accordingly, the need for redemption, repeated throughout the play, recalls not primarily the religious or moral necessity of compensatory (or overcompensatory) action. Instead, almost every time the word "redeem" is used it serves (as it often did in the period) as a synonym for the need to rescue a character from imprisonment—first the King of Tidore, who is imprisoned by the Governor of Ternata, then Armusia, who is later imprisoned by the very King he had previously redeemed from the Governor of Ternate's hold.

The use of "redeem," with its economic connotations, rather than the synonymous "rescue" is noteworthy. These connnotations resonate in the play's first usage of "redeem" when Quisara, the island princess, offers herself as a reward to whomever redeems her brother, the King:

> If I were covetous, and my heart set
> On riches, and those base effects that follow
> On pleasures uncontroul'd, or safe revenges,
> There he [the King] should dye; his death would give me all these . . .
> Yet . . . These golden dreames of greatnesse cannot force me
> To forget nature and my faire affection.
> Therefore that man that would be known my lover,
> Must be known his redeemer, and must bring him
> Either alive or dead, to my embraces.[22]

When Quisara offers herself to her brother's redeemer, she does so as part of a repudiation of the possessions and power that would be hers if he remained imprisoned. The parallel construction in which she offers herself, however, makes her not her brother's future subordinate, but an equivalent substitute: he who is "to be known my lover," she says, "must be known his redeemer." The line that follows does even more; it places him in her possession—either "alive or dead" in her "embraces." Significantly, the contract that motivates the entire plot associates redemption with a material and physical transfer. Redemption, the movement from imprisonment to liberation, depends on an exchange, in particular, an exchange in which the object of liberation (i.e., the King) is transferred from one person's hold to another—in this case from the Governor to the King's sister, whose promise of a self-initiated exchange (her marriage) provides the occasion for the initial exchange.[23]

The associations among redemption, liberation, and exchange continue in the consequences of her initial offer. The King's redemption, which would return him to Quisara's possession, occurs only through the offer in which she gives herself away. But it is the King himself, after he is redeemed and safely returned to Tidore, who takes on the responsibility of enforcing her promise. Referring to his debt to Armusia for redeeming him, but before he knows of his sister's promise, the King asks if "anything like recompense has been invented" (2.8.143). This "invention" is necessary for the exchange to serve to free the King from the status of possession that was, more or less, the original intention of Quisara's offer. Indeed, the King says that he will "feel no liberty" until he knows of a way to repay Armusia. The discussion of how to materialize the exchange of Quisara continues to focus on questions of liberty. When the King tries to enforce Quisara's promise, Armusia invokes the necessity of liberty *to* these exchanges, that is, not only as their result, but also as their source. He insists that Quisara not be forced into his embraces, echoing Quisara's initial insistence that she cannot be forced by "golden dreams of greatness" to wish that her brother remain imprisoned. In order for the King fully to experience himself as free, that is, redeemed (the point of Armusia's forceful liberation and Quisara's promise that motivated it), he must repay a debt. That repayment depends, according to Armusia, on the free consent of Quisara.[24]

Even prior to Quisara's offer, the play hints at these kinds of associations between liberation and exchange. Armusia's first extended speech, a description of the island's plenitude, is a striking example. This description depends on a fantasy in which the rivers "throw up their pearls, and curl their heads to court us" (1.3.28). Simultaneously auto-subjective and also "auto-jective," the rivers give up their goods of a free will further demonstrated, rather than contradicted, by their willing subjection. Such a possibility requires that they, like Quisara, not be coercively subjected. The transfer of the island's products to the Portuguese, like that of the King to Quisara and Quisara to Armusia, depends on the forms of liberty they also produce. My intention here is not merely to highlight the metaleptic quality of these exchanges—the inversion of cause and effect—but to call attention to the way the play imagines exchange and liberty as interdependent terms. The promise of the exchange of Quisara liberates the King, who insists that he will not really be free until Quisara repays his debt, which Armusia, the redeemer, insists must be the result of her free consent. I want to argue that it is the very association between redemption and exchange (in which exchange is a form of redemption and redemption is a form of exchange) that serves to reconceive exchange as not only dependent on liberation, but also as its source. Significantly, the contract between Quisara and her suitors, which motivates the rest of the plot, is at the center of an overdetermined relationship between liberty and ex-change, in which the exchange both depends on and produces libera-tion. Perhaps going even a step further than the historical documents I discussed above, the play represents exchange itself (rather than the satisfaction of needs outlined by Elizabeth) as the actual source of the liberation.

I am thus building on the insights of Mauss's theory of gift exchange in order to highlight the potentially liberating and prosperous effects of the King's position of imprisonment—even if the profits are initially imagined in romantic terms. To repay a debt in this play is not so much a point of honor or power (as in Mauss's theory), but a means to libera-tion.[25] As I hope to demonstrate, the connection between repayment and liberation prepares the way for the play's insistence that value is cre-ated out of imprisonment. Freedom then emerges as a prosperous state. In other words, the play can make explicit use of its narratives of cap-tivity by transforming them into fortunate narratives. In doing so it engages with developing theories of trade that grow out of the compli-cated tensions and conflicts among the European and East Indian coun-tries vying for economic power, especially those theories of trade that seek to explain how to make value transferable without engaging in strictly colonial endeavors.[26]

Before returning to the play's tragic problems and its tragicomic po-tential, I turn briefly to the kinds of available captivity narratives from which tragicomedy could borrow. Captivity narratives abound in the pe-riod in both the fictional and non-fictional literatures.[27] Already a poten-tial staple of romance, given that the lover is conventionally represented figuratively as an enchained prisoner, narratives of captivity no doubt underwent a resurgence in the period as a result of increased contact with religious and cultural enemies, which was a result of the increased contact and competition brought by commerce.[28] Indeed there is rarely a fictional or historical narrative of English trade in the period that does not involve an actual imprisonment, or at least the threat of it. Of course, captivity narratives were ripe for this association; even those cap-tives not taken as a result of trade were traditionally redeemed—that is, ransomed—in the most literal sense. In addition, prisoners were often taken for use as slave labor. Thus, it was rare to find a captivity narrative without an economic component.

But the connections between merchants and prisoners became stronger and more complicated as more merchants traveled farther abroad and across seas to compete with merchants of other nations for access to the goods of yet other nations. The English, whose trade is my focus, became subject to imprisonment not only from long-term rival Turks, Portuguese, and Spaniards, but also, in the Indies, from even the

Dutch, who were their friends at home. Merchants repeatedly wrote of the risk of enslavement or captivity that came from their enemies' attempts to eliminate them as competition. For example, Ralph Fitch, one of the first Englishmen in India in the late sixteenth century, was captured in Ormus and imprisoned in Goa after being accused by an Italian of spying on the Portuguese. Fitch claimed that the Portuguese were taking revenge because Francis Drake had shot at a Portuguese galleon in Maluco and because Fitch himself posed a commercial threat to the Italian trade. He claimed that if not for his imprisonment, it would have been possible to make as "good" (i.e., as profitable) "a voyage as ever any man made with so much money."[29] Writing of his attempt to escape with fellow detainees after the Portuguese said they had "more matter" against them, Fitch says, "we determined rather to seek our liberties than to be in danger for ever to be slaves in the country."[30] Hakluyt's *Voyages* includes the narrative of Jon Fox, who was captured by Turks on his way to traffic with Spain and brought to Alexandria with other Christian captives to serve as galley slaves in 1577. His escape along with "266 prisoners delivered out of captivity" is compared to the parting of the Red Sea, and even though he is captured on his way to traffic, his redemption is explicitly contrasted with commercial profit. In this narrative, those who steal treasure during their escape are weighed down and killed by the "wicked treasure of the infidels" with which they "stuffed themselves so full as they could between their shirts and skins."[31] In contrast, Fox seeks only liberty and the honor of God. He is nonetheless "liberally" rewarded by the Pope, the King of Spain, and the court of England, both for the loss of his youth and for serving as an example for all "true hearted Christians."[32]

Closer to the scene and the date of *The Island Princess*, the English were engaged in fierce competition for trade in the Indies with the Dutch. Many documents detailed feared and actual Dutch abuses that led to the imprisonment of English merchants. In 1622, the East India Company published a response to a document that the Dutch had published in English, accusing the English of helping the Bandanese break its treaty with the Dutch. This response includes the depositions of men who were captured by three ships from the Netherlands and imprisoned in 1619. According to one of them, Bartholomew Churchman, his captors "have many times termed us slaves to the King of Holland, and that we should all be sent to the Moluccas to rowe in their Gallies, and so be kept bond-slaves under them during our lives."[33] His deposition includes descriptions of deprivation and torture not entirely unlike the deprivations *The Island Princess*'s imprisoned King of Tidore suffers at the hands of the Governor of Ternate. The East India Company's text also contains descriptions of twenty-five Englishmen who were captured by the Dutch in Banda and brought to the Moluccas where "they were very hardly and inhumanely used, being fettered and shackelled in the day time, and close locked up at night. And from the moneth of May, until the end of September, they were compelled to carrie stone and lime for the building of forts there."[34] The Dutch General, they claimed, had grates and cages made in their ship and put the men in them and carried them "bound in irons from Port to Port amongst the Indians and thus in scornfull and deriding manner and sort spake unto the Indians, as followeth: 'Behold and see, here is the people of that Nation, whose King you care so much for. But now you may hereby plainly behold how kindly wee use his Subjects,' making them believe that Englishmen were their Vassals and Slaves."[35] In 1619, after burning down the town and English house in Japara, the Dutch forcibly took away the English flag and trailed it in the dirt through the town. What is crucial here are the tactics of humiliation and the attempts to lessen the English in the eyes of the islanders with whom the English (and the Dutch) wanted to trade. These tactics are significant because the islanders often made trade agreements with a European country in return for protection from other European powers that threatened their sovereignty and even in return for protection from other islands. This latter is also the case at the time for the historical Tidore and Ternate, who made alliances with European powers to protect them from other European powers and to protect them from each other. For example, a letter from the King of Ternate to James expresses his sadness that he cannot allow the English to set up a factory because of a prior treaty with the Dutch in which the Ternatans agreed to trade with the Dutch exclusively in return for help against the Portuguese. They say that they are thus "enforst against [our] liking" to say no. A letter from the island of Tidore, in contrast, asks for help from the English against the Dutch who have sided with Ternata against them, and who "jointly together have overrun and spoyled part of our country . . . and are determined to destroy both us and our subjects."[36]

After many years of hostile relations in a Dutch-dominated trade, the English and Dutch signed a treaty in 1619 with the hopes of putting an end to the strife and interference. In return for a promise by the Dutch not to prevent the English trade in the East Indies, the English agreed to share some of the Dutch expenses for maintaining their trade, especially the men and forts necessary to "protect" the islands. Though the English themselves did not want to participate in a coercive trade for economic reasons, as I discussed above, they were coerced into participating in—or at least contributing to—the coercive trade of the Dutch. Incensed by what they thought was an unjust requirement to share the costs of the Dutch trade, President Fursland and his Council writing to the East India Company from Batavia said they were "quite tired out living in this kind of slavery."[37] While I have chosen these examples because they highlight certain aspects of the threats of captivity, they are not exceptional in the literal sense; they are instead representative of common complaints, narrative structures, and discourses. They represent not only real and imagined threats and consequences of trade, but also the strong associations that existed among imprisonment, slavery, and mercantile activity.[38]

But the relationship among these terms is not identical in all of the narratives. In the captivity narratives of Jon Fox and Ralph Fitch, the connections between the economic activities and the states of captivity are more straightforward, even as the texts disavow these connections in order to provide moralistic readings. Both Fox and Fitch, like those abused by the Dutch, are captured because of the economic threats they pose. Yet, both authors disavow their economic intentions (especially Fox, who refuses to take infidel jewels), and claim that the primary rewards for their suffering (though partially financial) are honor itself and the liberty they achieve through their escape. In some sense, both forfeit opportunities to prosper in order to obtain liberty, or a more honorable form of liberty. In these earlier texts redemption seems to require the disavowal of prosperity. In contrast, in the years just preceding *The Island Princess*'s first performance, the coerced and unjust costs the English incur in order to trade in the Indies are themselves equated with slavery. When the company's President says that they are "quite tired out living in this kind of slavery," he refers not to actual imprisonment, but to the realities of competing with, and even sharing expenses with, the Dutch for their forts as detailed in their 1619 treaty. In this case it is not simply that captivity is a possible result of long-distance overseas trade, but that unfair trade practices (as we might call them) are themselves reconfigured as slavery. The straightforward relationship between exchange and captivity in the earlier texts (i.e., captivity is a possible outcome of trade) becomes mystified such that unfair trade and captivity are collapsed into one another. It is in these kinds of moments that I would locate the beginnings of the development of interdependent discourses of profitable trade, free trade, and freedom.

While I began this chapter by highlighting the English insistence on a trade that is non-coercive vis-à-vis the native inhabitants, what is clear is that the threat of coercion, captivity, and even slavery extended to the English within their relationships with other Europeans, especially the Dutch, and even with natives of the East Indies, as I will discuss below. The English concern with free trade is thus multidimensional. To say that England would trade with the Indies without compulsion meant that they would have greater profits because the people of the Indies "lovingly and with free consent sold to the English their spices," and that English merchants too would not suffer from compulsion. Complexly intertwined in the relation between the English and their trading partners, and by extension in the notion of "free trade," is the relationship between the English and the Dutch. Any argument for the freedom of England's trading partners (and thus for the prosperity of the trade) must be read in relation to these merchants' own sense of freedom or lack of it. It is within this context that a complex ideology of free trade develops especially in relation to the Indies, in order to address the problems raised by Mun, Elizabeth, and, as we shall see, *The Island Princess*'s "evil" Governor of Ternata.

Tragicomic Liberty

With their emphasis on captivity, the accounts of Fox and Fitch enable a tragicomic narrative in which an initial loss or sacrifice is ultimately rewarded by liberty. The East India Company texts that equate slavery with limitations on trade raise problems that could not be solved simply by providing rewards. Instead these problems and their conceptual associations require the development of the kind of tragicomedy, I will argue, that *The Island Princess* provides—one in which captivity is made useful, even productive, in order to make trade simultaneously liberating and prosperous. Given that the play begins with the imprisonment of the ruler of one island by the other and concludes with the liberation of the King's redeemer, a Portuguese, from a similar imprisonment and with the transfer of town of Ternata to the Portuguese, we could say that the play is engaged with the problems of captivity as well as the uses to which captivity can be put.

The examples of captivity I cited above could be useful in providing a historical context for the imprisonment of the King's redeemer, Armusia, and perhaps even for that of the King of Tidore by the Governor of Ternata. But I want to combine this analysis with that of other questions surrounding liberty in the period, such as those raised by Armusia's fantasy of objects that give themselves up freely and his related fantasy that Quisara give herself up willingly. These are fantasies of the freedom by which the inhabitants of the East Indies could trade with Europeans and the freedom or alienability of the objects themselves to be exchanged. In some cases, the subjection of the people of India by other Europeans produces a third relation of coercion/imprisonment: the native inhabitants imprison the English because they (wrongly, from the English perspective) assume that the English, like their precursors, the Dutch and the Portuguese, have come to do them harm. For example, in 1610 David Middleton feared that the people of Banda would be distrustful of him and his men and thus take their goods and imprison them because of the bad treatment they suffered at the hands of the "Portugals and Hollanders."[39] In *The Island Princess*, all of these possibilities are intertwined in Armusia, a newcomer who is seen as a threat to those Europeans already there, but who is imprisoned by the King of Tidore because of the actions of those who preceded him.[40] In this instance, it is the disguised enemy of the King, the Governor of Ternata, who instigates the imprisonment, making Armusia's captivity the result of a fourth complication: enmity between the islands, here played out, however, in relation to the potential enmity between one of the islands and the Europeans with whom it trades.[41] The imprisonment of Armusia is thus at the center of a number of actual and potential conflicts over the value of the island. As I will argue below, the focus on Armusia is not coincidental, given he is also the one who imagines the freedom of the inhabitants to participate in exchange and the freedom of the objects of exchange.

After Quisara agrees to uphold her offer to marry Armusia because he redeemed her brother, the play is rid of its comedic obstacles and the play's romantic plot is largely resolved.[42] But the play is still left with a conceptual problem that is not immediately apparent given the early associations between the exchange of the king and liberty. How can the *value* of the island's goods be transferred to the Europeans while maintaining the possibility that such a transfer would result in liberation and not subjection? This conceptual problem is raised by the Governor of Ternata, whose rage at Armusia for liberating the King of Tidore from his prison is not at all accounted for in the resolution of the romance plot. This evil Governor, later disguised as a prophetic Moor-priest in order to "advise" the King of Tidore, provides a vision of both the past and the future that contradicts the mood of the play's initial liberating exchange. He connects the transfer of Quisara to Armusia not to the sequence of liberating events I outlined above, but to the current subjection of the island and a future in which the island is also fully possessed by Europeans. He convinces the King of the danger Armusia represents in a speech that figures exchange as the opposite of liberation:

These men cam hether as my vision tels me, . . .
Their vessels like themselves, most miserable;
Made a long sute for traffique . . .
They had their sute, they landed, and too th'rate
Grew rich and powerfull, suckt the fat and freedom
Of this most blessed Isle, taught her to tremble;
Witness the Castle here, the Cittadell,
They have clapt upon the neck of your Tidore,

This happy town, till that she new these strangers . . .
Though you be pleas'd to glorifie that fortune,
And think these strangers Gods, take heed I say,
I find it but a handsome preparation,
A faire fac'd Prologue to a further mischiefe:
Marke but the end good King, the pin he shootes at
That was the man deliver'd ye, the mirrour,
Your Sister is his due, what's she, Your heire, sir?
And what's he a-kin then to? The Kingdome.
(4.1.44, 46–47, 48–54, 57–64)

Unlike Shakespeare's tragicomedies, there is no oracle or riddle in this play, only a false prophet, but one who nonetheless interrogates a formulation—the prosperous (re)unions—that plays like *Pericles* and *The Winter's Tale* might seem to take for granted. The Governor instead imagines a counter-tragicomic genre, a comic-tragedy in which the prologue is "faire fac'd" but the end is disastrous. Connecting the Portuguese hold on the island with the prosperous union, he interrogates the transfer of the things of value to the Portuguese and the embodiment of that value in Armusia. In the Governor's version of events the transfer of value is linked with the current subjection of the island as well as a future state in which the transfer of the island and all of its goods is complete.

It is not only the Governor's potentially untrustworthy history and prophecy that threatens the connection between exchange and liberty, but also Spanish poet and historian Bartolemeo de Argensola's history of this group of islands, published in 1609. According to Argensola, it is the King of Tidore, rather than the demonized ruler of Ternate, who links the islands' plenitude not with a tragicomic narrative but with their subjection: "we possess the most fruitful islands in Asia, only to purchase servitude and base subjection with their Product, converting this blessed bounty of Heaven into tribute paid to the ambition of intruding Tyrants."[43] In Argensola, the King's speech concludes, "in short, what is life worth without liberty." The transformation of the Governor's comic-tragedy into a tragicomedy, then, will depend on making the transfer of the value of the island's goods to Europeans compatible rather than incompatible with the liberation of the islands.

Like Elizabeth's letter, *The Island Princess*'s inversion of the potential comic-tragedy rehearsed by the Governor into tragicomedy depends on representing the island and its goods as valuable to Europeans while the King of Tidore speaks of liberation.[44] Transferring the critique of the island's subjection from the King of Tidore to the Governor of Ternate aids in this possibility. This transfer certainly makes the critique appear more dubious. But even more significant is that the placement of the critique and Armusia's resulting imprisonment within the context of the conflict among the islands themselves creates an opportunity to imagine the liberation of the goods and Armusia/the Europeans as part of the same process that resolves the conflict between the islands. The play can then counter the potential objection embodied in the Governor and his comic-tragedy, namely, the inability of the value of the island to appertain to Armusia and those he represents without coercion and subjection, precisely because the play links the freedom of Tidore with that of Armusia, making them allies who share a similar fate.

Moreover, I will argue that the play uses the conflict between the islands to imagine value created out of imprisonment. Imprisonment is in many ways ripe for employment in a tragicomic narrative. First, as in this chapter's epigraph from Cervantes, imprisonment makes apparent the inherent and grand value of liberty as its opposite: "there is no happiness on earth that can equal that of regaining one's lost liberty." Imprisonment also provides the opportunity for the captive to show bravery and honor, and for the redeemer to demonstrate—even increase—his worth. The value of the liberty for all those involved in the liberation potentially increases as a result of the former imprisonment. Imprisonment is thus ultimately fortunate or prosperous from the perspective of the end of the narrative. Finally, captivity narratives produce value that circulates among the various participants—captors, captives, liberators, etc. All of these possibilities abound in early modern discourses of captivity and all are put to use in the tragicomic narratives and dramatic structure of *The Island Princess*. Within this context, the language of redemption is used repeatedly and refunctioned over the course of the play as it mediates the development of discourses of free trade and freedom.

The tragicomic—that is, prosperous—potential in the play comes from the two imprisonments it stages. Put simply, imprisonment provides the necessary occasion for redemption—something it turns out Armusia needs even before he is imprisoned if the transfer of value to him is to be made appropriate. Early in the play, Armusia gains considerable value as a result of his redemption of the king, enacted by force, but enabled by his use of the merchant's disguise. The value Armusia seems to accrue in this exchange, however, is both reinforced and questioned by the Governor's comic-tragedy cited above. The Governor questions Armusia's motives precisely because of the reward he will receive for his actions. As I suggested above, by connecting the Portuguese hold on the island with the prosperous union in the final lines of his "prophecy," the Governor interrogates the transfer of the things of value to the Portuguese and the embodiment of that value in Armusia. Recall, his prophecy concludes, "That was the man deliver'd ye, the mirrour, / Your

Sister is his due, what's she, Your heire, sir? / And what's he a-kin then to? The Kingdome." "A-kin" is doubly resonant here: by becoming kin—that is, a relative through marriage—he is likened to, or even made commensurate with, the value of the island that would be transferred to him through his marriage to Quisara via the redemption of the King. But what the Governor's formulation also suggests is the elision of the transfer of value through Quisara, so that Armusia himself becomes the embodiment of the island and its "infinite value," which previously seemed to reside in Quisara—as well as the King. Referring to Armusia's rescue of him from the hands of the Governor of Tidore, the King says: "This, this man from the bowels of my sorrows / Has new begot my name, and once more made me" (2.6.137–38). In the King's tragicomic version of events, he is reborn, the product of Armusia's labors; thus loss leads to profitable recreation. According to the Governor's version of events, the King is not so much recreated but transformed, or subsumed, into Armusia. The question, then, is how does the play turn this imagined value transfer into an actuality that is not suspect, but is instead legitimate and the result of consent and even free trade? In other words, how does the play resolve the differences between the King's and the Governor's perspectives on Armusia's impending kinship with the King?

First, the play makes use of Armusia's imprisonment to legitimize his association with the king. In the play's early scenes, the nobility of the King's behavior is repeatedly contrasted to the Governor's ill treatment of him as a captive. The King thus accrues worth, what seems to be a kind of inalienable value, for his strength and refusal to beg for any form of relief. Armusia's imprisonment likens him to the King (the very King he redeemed earlier in the play), suggesting he is of similar value, actually "akin." This point is reinforced by the parallels between the two situations: Armusia himself is imprisoned by the King at the behest of the same Governor who imprisoned the King earlier in the play. Armusia thus occupies the place the King occupied before Armusia redeemed him.

Armusia gains legitimate value not only by being a prisoner, but also by being the King's prisoner. Though the play likens Armusia to the King, it also contrasts Armusia's nobility to the lack of nobility the King exhibits when he makes a prisoner of his own redeemer. While Armusia inhabits the King's previous position the King now occupies the Governor's position. Given that arguments in the period were made that to redeem prisoners in Barbary was to imitate Christ (as in the first epigraph to this chapter) and even to redeem the redeemer (since all Christians are part of Christ), to imprison a redeemer would seem blasphemous and debasing. Indeed, speaking of the King's ingratitude, Quisara likens him to a devalued coin:

How low and base thou lookst now that wert noble?
No figure of a King methinks shows on you,
No face of Majestie; foule swarth ingratitude
Has taken off thy sweetnesse . . .
Thou hast wrong'd thine own preserver, whose least merit
Pois'd with thy maine estate, thou canst not satisfie,
Nay put thy life in too, 'twill be too light still. (5.2.44–47, 52–54)

Like a clipped or sweated coin whose image or weight has been altered through illegitimate methods, the King is now outbalanced by Armusia, who has his former worth. Debased as a result of his faith in the Governor and his willingness to credit this false prophet, the King's value is transferred to Armusia, whose worth is now enhanced. Indeed, Armusia's compatriots counter the Governor's reading of Armusia's kinship with the island as suspect by insisting that they will redeem Armusia because "his life? why 'tis a thing worth all the Islands, / And they know will be rated at that value" (5.1.42–43). Early in the play, Quisara's first Portuguese suitor and rival of Armusia wishes that he "were of worth . . . / Of such a royall peece, a king" (1.2.42–43). This wish is partially granted to Armusia. While earlier in the play value seemed to be nonalienable and intrinsic, here the King's value is made alienable and transferable; it appears as something that can circulate. While the play does not focus on the transfer of goods themselves, except in Armusia's fantasy in which they throw themselves up freely, it does imagine the alienability of value through the tragicomic potential of captivity narratives in which the opposing states of imprisonment and liberation—held and not held—create the necessary conditions for alienability and circulation and for a state of freedom that, after imprisonment, is of an even higher value. Armusia's value is not just a reward he has earned, one that compensates for his earlier risk or sacrifice, but is dependent on the links among liberty, exchange, and transferability that frame his narrative of captivity as explicitly productive.

Moreover, the querying of Armusia's value produces a reevaluation that focuses not merely on demonstrating his worth, but on demonstrating the transferability, that is, alienability, of value itself. The play's early scenes seem primarily concerned with debating and establishing the worth of some of its main characters. For example, the first scene is focused on determining the worth of Quisara, the title character. In the second scene, the romantic dialogue between Quisara and her first Portuguese suitor, Ruy Dias, alters the terms of the previous more abstract discussion by making worth into a comparative issue. In the play's third scene, the discussion shifts from the relative worth of its two lovers to the worth of the Portuguese "discoverers" in relation to that of the island. This is the scene I mentioned earlier in which the island's pearls throw themselves up at the Portuguese discoverers. The convention of romance in which lovers of incommensurate worth must be made commensurate is applied here to the relationship between the Portuguese and the island's goods. But that commensurability is enabled, not through a universal equivalent, but by a transfer of value. Ania Loomba has argued that the Portuguese must demonstrate that they have something of worth to give in exchange for all of these objects.[45] But, rather than demonstrate an *a priori* worth, or provide objects of equal exchange, the play's rewriting of the conventions of romance emphasizes the transferability of value instead. It is not so much that Armusia and the other Portuguese are deserving of their new possessions; what matters is that the value of the possessions is transferable and can thus be re-embodied in the European characters. Armusia's life therefore is, or becomes, a "thing worth all the islands" in part because of the value that is transferred to him and that he accumulates—a value that then appears to be inherent and not derived from these other sources. What seems to be a question of deserving and value tout court is actually a question of the transferability of value. While *The Winter's Tale* is concerned with identifying the source of value and the means by which it is produced, *The Island Princess* sidesteps those questions by altering its initial concern about worth. The primary concerns of the play's opening scenes about whether one is worthy are, if not made irrelevant, at least rewritten by shifting the focus to questions about how value itself can circulate. It is not surprising, then, that the play first raises the questions of the free circulation of goods and the worth of the Portuguese in the image of rivers that throw up their pearls—an image that mystifies how the pearls would be transferred from the possession of the native inhabitants to the Portuguese and the means by which the pearls would otherwise be harvested. By shifting attention away from labor and toward liberation, the play imagines how value can be transferred and embodied not in those who perform the labor, but in those who possess its product.[46]

What we can see here is the beginning of a liberal discourse in which free becomes virtually synonymous with profit-bearing, even if who and what are free and traded are not entirely clear.[47] Who is free, or traded, or valuable: the king, the spices, Armusia, Quisara, the islands? Perhaps what circulates most in this play is the condition of transferability, such that all of the characteristics above are alienable, that is, they circulate from one character to another. As a result, the freedom or value of one character or set of objects seems to have bearing on that of another even if it is clearly the case that the opposite is more likely to be true. For example, the freedom of Armusia and the islands more likely might be negatively than positively correlated, but the condition of transferability that underlies the play enables the characteristics or qualities to circulate and become associated with more than one "character." Perhaps the play's underlying principle is that of redemption along with the related property of transferability.

Moreover, what looks like freedom—here redefined as the ability to be exchanged—is actually also the precondition for future prosperity.[48] The slavery to which the East India Company's President refers when he complains that the English must conform to Dutch trading practices and be subject to them as well, when inverted provides the very opportunity to transfer value. The play's tragicomedy works, then, because it employs redemption structurally in order to imagine value as transferable, thus imagining trade as independent of use value for its prosperity. To return to Mun, Indian wares have the same power to procure value and, I would add, they have this value precisely because they (can) circulate freely.

In the historical narrative cited earlier, in which David Middleton reports that his men are mistrusted because of the deceitful actions of Christian traders who have preceded him, the link between the tragicomic and freedom of trade is made even more explicit. When Middleton returns he discovers that his men have almost been imprisoned because of the comic-tragedy of the native inhabitants' relationship with the Portuguese and the Dutch: "for many years the Portugals and Hollanders have done as I have done, but in the ende they saw apparently they would have their country from them." But Middleton is relieved to report that when he returns the islanders begin to trust his motives: "wee became good friends and bought Spice apace: and I had bought my whole ships lading. Having an over-plus of stock left I thought I could not doe your Worships better service, then in laying out your money."[49] In *The Island Princess* the spices are left out of the resolution, but the narratives are similar. The islanders in Middleton's text are about to imprison a Christian because they falsely mistrust him, in this case because of the actions of other Christians who at first befriended them but in the end tried to take their country. Like Elizabeth's letter, Middleton's account and *The Island Princess* provide tragicomic narratives that counter the kind of comic-tragedy rehearsed by the Governor and "recorded" in Argensola's history. They do so by imagining alternative narratives to those of imprisonment and coercion, and specifically by using those narratives in order to produce more prosperous alternatives. The tragicomic structure thus can be employed in order to reject the colonial model and all of its costs in order to reform it into a model in which exchange is both prosperous and liberating.

The Island Princess and the dramatic genre of tragicomedy in general can go even one step further in this reformation through tragicomedy's dialectical dramatic structure. That structure is highlighted in the play's concluding gestures of liberation. At the urging of the disguised Governor, Armusia is offered the alternatives of death or conversion. He resists the latter profusely, slandering the islanders' gods and claiming ever greater faith and power for the Christian God. In the King's prior position (that of imprisonment), Armusia (and the value of the island by extension) are now in need of redemption. Practically, the play comes to resolution because other Portuguese characters destroy the town by force and reveal that the priest is actually the hated Governor of Ternata. But the play's full resolution also depends on the king's admitting he is half persuaded to be a Christian (as a result of the strength of Armusia's faith) and on the revelation of the Moor-Priest as the disguised Governor. Significantly, these transformations are simultaneous with the King's claim that the Governor kept the town and castle in which he was imprisoned in Ternata in a similar state of oppression:

His island we shall seize into our hands,
His father and himself have both usurp'd it,
And kept it by oppression; the Towne and Castle,
In which I lay myself most miserable,
Till my most honourable friend redeem'd me,
Signior Pyniero, I bestow on you. (5.5.78–83)

This quotation provides a clear example of the way the play uses the tragic potential to produce a prosperous conclusion, part of which depends on the transfer of the original site of imprisonment—Ternata—to Pyniero, the nephew of Quisara's first Portuguese suitor. The transfer of Ternata performs its transformation from a site of loss, imprisonment, and oppression to one of redemption and value in which the captivity of the King and that of Armusia are ultimately made productive.

Moreover, the prior act of redemption (Armusia's of the King) is offered almost, but not quite, as a causal explanation of the current transfer. The transfer of the island is thus doubly associated with redemption—the liberation of the island from oppression and the earlier liberation of the king. The latter is a point highlighted by the inclusion of a reminder of Armusia's prior act of redemption in a subordinate clause that is technically a non sequitur, but is made to seem connected to current action by its grammatical proximity. There are even further connections to the earlier acts of liberation in the play. The King's gestures here resemble Quisara's in the first act, but with a significant difference. She liberated her brother only to give *herself* away. He liberates the island only to give *the island* away. As a result of his gesture, everything is free. The freedom, at least of the island of Ternate, is paradoxically dependent on its transfer to the possession of another, but this point is elided by the representation of his gesture as generosity. The affective power of the lines, in fact, results from the King's double gesture: the freeing of the island from oppression and the bestowing of it, somewhat surprisingly, on the Portuguese Pyniero become one and the same powerful act. Finally, the King's gesture of generosity (combined with his willingness to contemplate the value of Christianity) restores his lost value and thus eliminates his debased condition which, like his inability to reward Armusia early in the play, would necessarily prevent him from feeling free. Thus, almost all of the play's acts of liberation are condensed into this final liberating transfer of Ternata.

The Island Princess appears to return all to its proper place. But what the play actually stages are productive transformations that rely on both the dialectics of tragicomedy and performative gestures like the king's multiple bestowals. While the play might not call much attention to its own theatricality, it nonetheless makes use of the potential productivity of the performative—the kind represented in the final scenes of *The Winter's Tale* and that I discussed in Chapter 3. The dialectics and the performative come together to transform potential harm into profit, and sites of imprisonment into sites—even evidence—of freedom and prosperity.

We can see how the play's tragicomic transformations work even more clearly by contrasting them with other earlier plays with which it is in dialogue. In Marlowe's *The Jew of Malta* and Shakespeare's *The Merchant of Venice*, transfers of wealth are coerced. In *The Island Princess*, value is free to circulate and its transfer is the very sign of liberation. In Marlowe's play the Turks ask of Barbaras, "Canst thou, as thou reportest make Malta ours?"[50] In return for this act of "liberation," they offer to make Barabas Governor. But rather than a liberating transformation, this play stays closely within the logic of revenge. Recall that in the opening scenes, Barabas and the play's other Jews are to redeem the Maltese from the Turks by paying long-overdue tribute. In the fifth act, after much death-filled revenge, Barabas enables the Turks to take over Malta. In the next scene, the now ex-Governor of Malta "offers" to gather up from his citizens "great sumes of money for [Barabas's] recompense" in exchange for Barabas's promise to set Malta free from the Turks (5.2.88). Barabas's schemes thus invert or correct the injustice of the opening scenes by making the Maltese act as their own form of redemption. They are made to pay their own tribute to the Turks, rather than forcing the Jews to do it for them, which was the original plan that launched Barabas's revenges. Even if we do not take into account that by play's end Barabas is dead and the Turks are captured for ransom, what we can see is the radical difference in the way Fletcher's tragicomic gestures of freedom and liberation are expansive. In contrast, in Marlowe's Malta all seems to collapse into itself, just as Barbaras literally falls into his own revenge p(l)ot.

Given the complex series of exchanges and transformations in *The Is-land Princess,* some summing up is in order: Armusia's liberation of the king of Tidore results in the King's re-creation symbolically as Armusia, who then embodies the island's value and whose own redemption is re-configured as the island's liberation. Thus the islands can simultane-ously be made valuable and liberated. The islands can then function imaginatively as valuable non-possessions for the English, who (unlike the Portuguese in the play) will not actually be in possession of the is-land in the most literal sense any time soon and who imagine themselves as liberating the islands through trade. The play's end thus inverts the Governor's prophecy into a tragicomedy that works by rejecting the colonial model in favor of one in which exchange is both prosperous and liberating. By bringing together the formal qualities of redemption (in which the tragedy averted provides the means for its own resolution and thus is prosperous) with its thematic ones (in which exchange, the transfer of possession, is fortunate, that is, liberating), the play prevents the disguised Governor's prophecy from becoming its truth. It does so by imagining redemption in a specifically economic form, in which trade is simultaneously free and valuable, that is, independent of use value and coercive possession.

In order to resolve the conflicts the play imagines between the islands, between the islands and the Europeans, and even among Europeans, the play creates tragicomedy out of imprisonment narratives in order to imagine both the creation of value and that value as something transfer-able, thus not requiring possession (that is, not requiring a proprietary claim). By addressing the conflicts among these various countries, the play also contributes to the development of discourses of free trade that would assuage concerns at home about the profitability of a trade in goods that are neither produced at home nor exclusively intended for use there.

The tragicomedy has further functions, especially in terms of imagin-ing free trade as prosperous. Jonathan Gil Harris has recently argued that trade between Christians and non-Christians is imagined ultimately as a zero-sum game, that is, if there are winners, there are losers.[51] I want to look at how tragicomedy circumvents this problem so that there can be, in the words of *The Winter's Tale*'s Paulina, "winners all." While it might seem that the King's debasement mirrors the fate of characters like Shylock in *The Merchant of Venice,* the play is far from over when Quis-ara makes her accusations against him, and his gestures of generosity more than redeem him. One still might argue that the prosperity of the ending, like that of *The Merchant of Venice,* depends on the losses of the Governor who is revealed to be a false and not a "pretious prophet," and who must give up his hold on Ternata. But the play avoids this problem in part by revealing that what the Governor "loses" here—that is, what he is forced to give up—was not rightfully his in the first place. Perhaps even more important, the play's tragicomic structure—particularly its tragicomic endings—work affectively to create the effect of surplus.[52] Through multiple acts of redemption (in the play's final moments) all becomes not only free, but also participant in a future prosperity. Quisara's previous suitor, Ruy Dias, who is figuratively imprisoned by his prior shame for his inability to rescue the King, is redeemed by the success of his efforts to free Armusia. The value of this redemption is made explicit as his comrades tell him in advance that Armusia's imprisonment provides him, Ruy Dias, with the opportunity to "redeem all" (5.1.57). Moreover, all of the characters participate in the play's end. Ruy Dias storms the town and gets to the castle in which Armusia is imprisoned. His nephew, Pyniero, captures the Moor-Priest and reveals him to be the Governor. The King releases Armusia. In lines that I mentioned above and will discuss further below, the King gives Quisara to Armusia and admits that he is "halfe perswaded" to be a Christian (5.5.65). Ruy Dias wishes the couple sweet and happy children, and Pyniero adds "and Kings at least" (5.5.71). Armusia asks to have his rash behavior (slandering the gods, and so on) excused. The rulers of the other islands give their blessings in a line that reinforces the connection between unity and prosperity: "your joy is ours" (74). The King then bestows Ternate to Pyniero and love to all. Armusia thanks Ruy Dias for his life, wife, and honor. The play concludes with the King's remarking on the end of "guns" and "hates," replaced through positive objects theoretically materialized by his performative speech: "joys, and triumphes, and universall gladnesse fly about us. / And know however subtill men dare cast, / And promise wrack, the gods give peace at last" (90–93).[53]

The play's end rewrites the previous imprisonments so that the capture of the Governor is enmeshed in several acts of generosity. Though a bit extreme, the play's ending, in its simultaneous bestowing of gifts and production of alliances, is not atypical for a tragicomic ending. Unlike The Merchant of Venice, which as I argued in Chapter 1 is not quite tragicomic, the play ends with a feeling of security and surplus that does not rely on magic, but is instead the product of the play's events. The tragicomic structure serves to make gains out of losses and works affectively to provide a feeling of security and permanence that results from having overcome so much trial, a feeling evidenced in the final lines cited above.[54]

The tragicomic within the play, then, has three primary functions. It rewrites the formula of the captivity narrative so that exchange can be thought of as liberation. In this way, it provides a model to understand how to make value out of imprisonment. But tragicomedy is also productive; it resolves the problem of enemies, especially enemies that hinder trade.

Even though there is still a residual enemy in this play, the play creates a feeling of security by reinforcing and highlighting the alliances that have been made, producing an imagined security that was hardly available given the complexity of trade relations in the Indies. The affective import of the genre is to create the feeling of friendly alliances that would allow trade and eliminate the additional, even prohibitive, expenditures necessary to maintaining forts and stock ships for war—the very costs that the English East India Company likened to slavery.

This affective quality is at the heart of tragicomedy's third function, which has to do with audience response. Much of the pleasure of tragicomedy lies not just in its characters' narrow escape from disaster but in the transformation of the potential disaster into something beneficial. More than relief, what tragicomedy offers is a surplus, as I have been arguing throughout this book. In *The Island Princess*, that surplus is the liberation of characters (and sometimes the countries they represent) that comes with the transfer of value. While the pleasure of the play, perhaps more than its politics, is what gets audience members to return to the theater, tragicomedies like this one—with its dual emphasis on liberation and profit (i.e., profit associated with liberation)—appeal to their audience's appreciation for profitable outcomes. In this tragicomedy, the particular pleasure is derived from the liberation of its characters along with a transfer of value that is not a redistribution, but is instead a means to benefit all parties involved, even if (or perhaps especially if) the greater material benefit accrues to the characters with whom audience members would most likely identify. Moreover, while the purpose of tragicomedy is foremost to entertain its audience, this play in particular seems invested in imagining a way to resolve the historical conflicts it represents among the islands of the East Indies and the countries competing for trade there that would make the trade possible and profitable. Though the play's explicit function is not to convince the inhabitants of the East Indies that it is safe to trade with England, nor to convince the English that this trade will benefit the commonwealth, the play's attempts to imagine resolutions to these conflicts contribute to the discourse of free trade and enhances its power by presenting a practical solution to the problems (not unlike the arguments made by the mercantilists and English East India Company) and providing its audience with the gratifying experience of watching their counterparts on the stage manage and participate in enterprises that imbue profit with the very pleasures of liberation.[55]

Productive Ambivalences

The play's tragicomic effects thus create security out of those very things that would threaten that security and gratification out of the additional material and ideal profits it imagines. Moreover, it even makes its own ambivalences productive. It is to these ambivalences that I turn now.

In her reading of the play, Ania Loomba insightfully points to the way that the play's ending rewrites the islands' histories, especially as represented by Argensola. Her focus is on the play as a fantasy in which native insurgencies are rewritten so that the "Muslim ruler literally gifts Ternate back to the Europeans."[56] After reading the early documents of the East India Company and its and other historical narratives of captivity, I would modify Loomba's insight. What the play emphasizes is not so much the fantasy of a willing colonial subject, but the possibility of imagining the islands and their goods as valuable without possessing them outright, that is, without colonial subjection.[57] To this end it might be important to note that the town of Ternata is in the end gifted not to the play's hero, Armusia, but to Pyniero, who is not a newcomer, but is the nephew of Armusia's rival-turned-ally and who in a sense has liberated the King by pulling off the Governor's disguise. As I understand the play's ending, though the value of the island is transferred, the islands themselves are and are not transferred. I write with some tentativeness, because the play's ending is strangely ambivalent. It is not only that Ternata is given to Ruy Dias's nephew and not Armusia, but also that the gift is Ternata and not Tidore. The fact that these are enemy islands suggests that their fates would be opposed rather than equated. The town and castle of Ternata are given to Pyniero (perhaps only to govern), but the status and possession of Tidore are left vague. Technically it is still in the hands of the King of Tidore, a fact that will remain unchanged as far as we know, regardless of the fact that Armusia will be marrying Quisara in a future imagined, but not performed, by the play. It might belong to his children, yes, but also hers, but that is only if the King has no heirs. This play is not about intergenerational restoration: Quisara is the King's sister, not his daughter. The play's end thus does not explicitly imagine the transfer of Tidore. This technicality rewrites the Governor's comic-tragic prophecy as partially a paranoid fantasy, at least from the perspective of Tidore.

My point here is not to argue for the ambivalence of the play's ending as ethical ambiguity, but as ambivalence that both accommodates and highlights a paradox—that the value of Tidore becomes transferable while the island is not in possession. I am not suggesting that the play counters the narrative in which the Europeans (read English) could profit from the islands. But I do think it writes against the strong colonialist narrative, not for ethical reasons, but for practical, profitable ones. As I argued earlier in my reading of Mun, the English need to reconceive the value of the islands' products as transferable, while the islands themselves are not literally incorporated into England. Perhaps "akin," which suggests resemblance but not identity, encapsulates that possibility in which the islands' value, but not the island, belongs to Armusia and could thus be seen as available to generate profit for the country he represents.

I conclude by exploring what might be the play's most surprising and productive ambivalence. Though Quisara converts to Christianity, the King who possesses and rules the island of Tidore does not. At the play's end, the King says: "you have *halfe* perswaded me to be a Christian" (5.5.65, emphasis added). The play represents his willingness, what I have been calling "free," ambivalently. The transformation of the King into Armusia and the transfer of value from the former to the latter then might be not only incomplete, but also not as smooth as it first appears.

In order to think through the significance of the King's ambivalence, it might be useful to reflect on the contrast between the "continual and orderly" transformation of money into goods into more money, which Mun articulates, and the violence by which those transfers and transformations occur in the play. Again, affectively the play and particularly the King's bestowing of gifts freely given (like Christ's blood) make the play feel as if the resolution is purely comic. But the ending literally depends on violence. It is not just that the imprisonments are necessary to the exchanges that lead to an idea of liberation as a reified, permanent state, but that the play's ending depends on the violent destruction of the town, which enables the Portuguese to get to the palace in which Armusia is held in order to liberate him. It is thus much more literally a tragic-comedy. My point is not so much that trade depends on violence to support it. I think it does, and I do not want to elide that point. But the play itself, as a tragicomedy, is more interested in representing the indirections and even violent interruptions necessary to produce the tragi-comic outcome from within the possible losses or tragedies.

I want to connect this insight to a similar point about the theories of value produced out of the specific necessities of the East Indies trade, then connect that point back to the question of genre. Mun speaks of the easy and orderly transformation of goods into money, but the reality was much more complicated. Indeed, it is the complexity of the trade and disruption of the smooth flows—the port-to-port trades, imports, and re-exports and the need to acquire Spanish New World silver—that resulted in the increased need for capital, which could be invested over longer periods of time. So money does not just go out and come back enhanced, as Mun elsewhere suggests.[58] It is the complexity of the trade and this need for capital that leads to the formation of joint-stock companies like the East India Company in the first place and then to theories of investment, both of which are the cornerstones of modern capitalism. The joint-stock companies enabled the pooling of resources of a greater number of investors in order to finance trades that required travel over long distances and profits that were temporally distant. These interruptions to the smooth process Mun describes were the very stimulus for the reconception of losses as expenditures, that is, as an investment in profits expected in the future.

The Island Princess might be a good play to remind us of the disruptions and interruptions of both the East India trade and tragicomedy, for it not only thematizes interruption of action (in part, through the imprisonments and concern with delay), but also makes interruption a formal component. *The Island Princess* is filled with interruptions. Characters often do not finish lines, usually because another character speaks before they can complete their own thoughts or statements. The lines, however, do not remain incomplete or unfinished; instead they are taken over and completed in another form by the interrupting character. They thus formally enact the transfer and transformations with which the play engages. Although these interruptions appear to provide alternatives or substitutions—another possible outcome—they actually enact the transformation of one alternative into the other through the transfer of the line from one speaker to another in the way that the tragicomedy seems to provide an alternative solution to the stark options offered by the Governor (for example, death or conversion). Moreover, most of the interruptions occur when the character's rhetoric gets overblown, carrying itself away into excess, but also into familiar territory. The interruptions often redirect the character's thoughts away from a familiar generic pattern.

The example of the King's ambivalence, to which I referred above, is a particularly interesting example of one of the play's interruptions. This one is noncharacteristic for being a sort of self-interruption, which is and is not about transformation itself. In this close-to-final speech, the King both gives the princess to Armusia and admits he is potentially transformed:

Take her friend,
You have half perswaded me to be a Christian,
And with her all the joys and all the blessings.
Why, what dreame have we dwelt in? (5.5.65–68)

Unlike the giving of Ternata to Ruy Dias's nephew, in which the mention of Armusia's rescue of the King is more causally related and apropos of the topic, here the king's admission that he is "halfe perswaded" to be a Christian is not technically thematically related. Moreover, the interrupting line does not have a grammatical relation to the syntax of the sentence it disrupts. Compare the mention of Armusia's rescue of the king in the midst of the gifting of Ternata, which is both a subordinate clause and at least thematically if not clearly causally linked. This admission of the king's half-persuasion is an interruption of his thought and the smooth transfer of Quisara from the King to Armusia, by a line that offers, only to take back, the possibility that the transformation (i.e., recreation) of the King and the island into Armusia is itself smooth. He is half-converted but also half not-converted, thus is and is not "akin." The transfers and transformations then might not be as smooth as they first appear.

Returning to the question of genre and generic development, we might say that the play presents tragicomedy, too, both as and not as the neatly packaged genre it appears to transform into in the hands of Fletcher and others. Perhaps it hangs onto or even reproduces its own mongrel, hodgepodge roots but in another form—that is, transformed. While all genres probably evolve over time, tragicomedy might be the genre that also foregrounds generic development precisely because it embeds the transformation of one genre into another within its own form and to some extent within each individual play. To connect this insight back to foreign trade I turn to Lyly's prologue to his tragicomic *Midas*: "Traffic and travel hath woven the nature of all nations into ours, and made this land like arras, full of device, which was broadcloth, full of workmanship. . . . If we present a mingle-mangle our fault is to be excused because the whole world has become a hodgepodge."[59] At first it seems that Lyly perceives foreign trade not as redemptive, as Elizabeth does, but as the source of the fall and the justification for the (theatrical) form that fall takes. However, he also scripts tragicomedy as a genre that formally reproduces England's perhaps too-free incorporation of the foreign—both its products and influences. Through a doubly embedded analogy, his rhetoric provides a nostalgic lament for the country's loss of transparent labor, but it also celebrates the reenvisioning of hodgepodge as arras—a tapestry with a story woven into it.[60]

My argument about tragicomedy is in agreement with his larger claim—that the generic development has a causal relation to trade—except that I want to argue that perhaps the re-Englishing of the Italianizing of the genre transforms the hodge-podge into something more dialectical and disjointed. A play like *The Island Princess,* with its repeated interruptions and redemptions of prisoners, enacts and marks such a generic shift. The interruptions, then, might be read as a redeployment of the genre's earlier forms, which nonetheless get put to use here not as interruptions per se, but as interruptions transformed into productive necessity, as in the case of the development of the joint stock. They exist then as interruptions and signs of the work of tragicomedy on the way to its end, work that does and does not hide the interruptions from view.

While the King says he is "half-converted" (perhaps a religious hybrid) and thus appears to welcome Christian principles, we would be much harder pressed to say, as critics do of *The Merchant of Venice*, that all has been converted to Christian use. Unlike Shylock, it is the King who closes the play, which he does with rhetoric of peace and unity. Both like and unlike Purchas's prophecy that all will be united under a singular Christianity, here the King of Tidore speaks of "gods" who "give peace at last." Why is the last line of a play that depends on the development of alliances and value of conversion a reference to the "gods" of Islam?[61] Significantly, the King retains his kingliness, his power over the world and words of the play—a power perhaps necessary to complete and legitimate the gesture in which he bestows Ternate on the Portuguese Pyniero. This play values distance and difference—not too much of it, but just enough for the transfer of this island's value to come not from coercion, but from a gift that comes from a subject whose seeming autonomy and freedom resemble that of value itself. Difference, we might say, is necessarily tolerated here. Unlike *The Merchant of Venice*, which depends on Shylock's simultaneous exclusion and conversion, and the *Jew of Malta*, which ends with the freedom of Malta but also the imprisonment of the Turkish prince and the death of the Jew, the ending of *The Island Princess* emphasizes redemptive alliance, the transformation of enmity into harmony.[62] This tragicomedy's redemption, even this model of tragicomedy itself, depends neither on a full incorporation nor exclusion, but a combination of both. The King speaks as if he is akin, but his difference is put to use to make the alliance and transfers more significant and valuable. In this way, though the play does not completely shy away from representing some of the costs of establishing a "free" trade, it ultimately makes use of all of those costs.

We thus could read the play as representing a utopian vision of trade that, as in Elizabeth's letter, makes friends out of enemies and allows profit to accrue without possession. But as I have argued, the play also recognizes the violence and interruptions that it represents as a necessary stepping-stone to these profitable resolutions. Even in this latter vision, the violence and interruptions are perhaps rendered as temporary rather than permanent conditions of the trade, an issue to which I will return in the Epilogue.

Chapter Five
Balance, Circulation, and Equity in the "Prosperous Voyage" of *The Renegado*

As I argued in the Introduction, profit was as troublesome to early modern thinkers as loss, and the mixing of two genres to produce a third kind makes tragicomedy a particularly effective form for addressing both problems simultaneously. All of the tragicomedies discussed in the preceding chapters, however, are much more exclusively focused on the problem of loss. In fact, as I have argued throughout the book, the solution tragicomedy offers to the problems of loss depends on transforming that loss into profit, and profit through its derivation in loss is legitimated, in some sense, prior to its appearance. But this chapter focuses on a play, Phillip Massinger's *The Renegado* (1623/4), whose need to redeem both loss and profit most fully challenges the capabilities of tragicomedy and also reveals how the developments of new economic theories were outgrowths of attempts to address these two interdependent problems.

While *The Renegado* is set in the pirate and market communities of Tunis, its only mercantile scenes are technically a result of its main (if not title) character, Vitelli's, use of a merchant disguise to penetrate the Islamic world of Tunis in order to rescue his sister, Paulina. She has been captured by the title character (the renegade, Grimaldi) and sold to the Tunisian viceroy. While conventional romance problems abound in the play's plot (a captured virgin and a forbidden love, for example), what frames and structures the play is a set of contradictory concerns about the outcome of new economic practices. On the one hand, the play represents ethical dilemmas that arise from the accumulation of too much profit. On the other hand, the play represents concerns about loss resulting from excessive consumption. The tension between these worries (about losses and profits) organizes the play at the thematic and formal levels.

These two worries are not so much opposed to one another as inextricably intertwined. In part, this interconnection develops from the play's location, Tunis, a market town in the Barbary States under Ottoman dominion. As other critics have argued, the play associates excess with the temptations of the Ottoman Empire, both with the overconsumption of goods that are imported from there (hence, loss) and, conversely, with the profits that can be accumulated there, especially if one "turns Turk."[1] Trade with the Ottoman Empire becomes associated with loss as well, because of the significant threat posed by the Barbary pirates operating primarily out of Algiers and Tunis. What has yet to be explored is the tension between these two undesired outcomes: too much profit and too much loss. Paradoxically, trade with the Ottoman Empire is of great concern because it can be a source of great profit as well as a source of great loss.

Because recent critics have focused justifiably on the concerns with the taint of trading with the infidel and the temptation to turn Turk to trade even more profitably, they have largely ignored the way that trading with the Ottoman Empire helps to raise, and even intensify, the contradictory nature of the problems that were being raised at home in England in regard to trade. As I have discussed in the preceding chapters, merchants needed to demonstrate that their activities ultimately increased the wealth of the commonwealth, rather than depleted it. Defending themselves against criticism that foreign trade drained the country of bullion, leading merchants argued that if net exports exceeded net imports, more bullion would return to the country than was leaving it.[2] But there was also great suspicion of profit for its own sake in the period, as demonstrated by the extensive discourse against usury and a variety of other economic practices that were deemed to be nonproductive—such as forestalling, regrating, and engrossing, all of which are about buying up products in order to resell them at a higher price, which was essentially the hope of merchants of foreign trade. These merchants then also had to demonstrate that profits were justified. Merchants engaged in overseas trade, as I suggested in the Introduction, were thus in the position of performing an unusual balancing act. They needed to show that their trade was profitable, but given that profit was likely to be suspect they had to find a way to disassociate profit from excess. They needed to show not only that such a profit was deserved, but that it was somehow *equitable*.

In this chapter, I argue that the newly developing balance of trade theory, which served as an explanation for the potential profitability of a foreign trade that also included the export of considerable amounts of money to purchase imports, is a particularly appropriate means of imagining profit as an equitable phenomenon. To put the case more strongly, the attempt to construe profit as equity might be not just a primary development of a "balance" of trade theory, but its raison d'être. This chapter's purpose is to demonstrate how the particularities of trade with the

Ottoman Empire, especially the difficulties of trade in Tunis, provide Massinger's tragicomic play with material that requires the exploration and resolution of some of the contradictions inherent to balance of trade theory. One could argue that *The Renegado* showcases the inventiveness of balance of trade theory, particularly the transformation of loss along with too much profit into profitable equity. As was my method in the preceding chapter, I hope to show how this tragicomedy's use of redemptive possibilities provides a means for resolving urgent tensions in new economic theories and practices. This "Tunisian" tragicomedy provides those means not by representing trade as a source of liberation or redemption as it was in the East Indies trade, but to represent trade, as it is figured in balance of trade theory, as redeemed. This redemption requires not only that trade needs to become disassociated from loss and excess, but that the tragicomic potential needs to transform trade's goal—profit—into an equitable phenomenon and the very sign or expression of trade itself.

Overbalance and Equity in Balance of Trade Theory

> And because the life of commerce and trade is money, whereof a greater scarcity is now found in this our kingdom than hath been in former times, we will and require you with all diligence and care to take into your considerations, what are the principal causes and occasions thereof, and by what means coin or bullion may be hereafter more plentifully brought into this kingdom; and how the same may be here kept and preserved from exportation unless it be only in cases necessary and profitable for the state?
>
> That to prevent an apparent consumption and confusion, which cannot otherwise be avoided, ye diligently observe the true balance of the trade of this kingdom, lest the importation of merchandize from foreign parts exceed the exportation of our own native commodities, and consider of some fitting courses to reduce the same to more equality, and to think upon the gain or loss that comes to our kingdom by the course of exchange now used by our merchants.
>
> —From James I, Instructions to the Commission on Trade *(1622)*

Balance of trade theory seems to be strikingly straightforward at first. The language of balance borrows from that of double-entry bookkeeping—the accounting system used by merchants to make sure debits equal credits and thus to verify that all expenditures and receipts are properly accounted for. Faced with the accusation that sending English coins and bullion out of the country to purchase goods abroad resulted in loss of English treasure and thus was responsible for the economic depression, leading merchants like Thomas Mun and Thomas Misselden argued for measuring net imports of foreign commodities against net exports, treating them like debits and credits. Misselden, long credited with coining the term "balance of trade," explains:

A merchant when he will informe himself how his Estate stateth, is said to take a Ballance of his Estate: wherein he collecteth and considereth all his wares, and monyes, and debts, as if hee would cast every thing into the scale to bee tried by waight: which is therefore in Merchants and accomptants terms, so called a Ballance of Accompt, or a Ballance of Trade. And to what end doth he this? Surely to try in what Estate he is . . . whether he hath got or lost.[3]

Extending the logic by analogy to the King and commonwealth, Misselden continues:

If hee will know the Estate of his Kingdome, Hee will compare the Gaine thereof with the expence; that is, the native commodities issued and sent out, with the Forraine Commoditie received in: and if it appeare that the forraine commodities doe exceed the native: either he must increase the native, or lessen the forraine, or else look for nothing else, but the decay of trade: and therein the loss of his revenue, and Impoverishing of his people.[4]

According to Misselden, then, a balance must be achieved for the well-being of the trade and the state by extension. Balance is the antidote to loss and impoverishment. As Misselden explains, the "remedy" to the "under-ballance of trade" (when foreign commodities exceed the native commodities exported) is "but to make our importations less and our exportations more."[5] The simple idea is to even out the accounts.

Because these writers were mostly arguing against those who claimed that trade was actually causing a drain on bullion and thus harming the state, much of the rhetoric is for moderation, especially, but not only, moderate consumption of foreign wares. Hence Misselden, blaming the twin problems of prodigality and poverty for the underbalance of trade, claims: "in the one there's too much: in the other there's too little: would God there were a good Medium in both."[6] Thus, moderation, balance, and equity became linked ideas. Since "balance" already had the connotations of "to counterpoise," "to compensate," "to be equal with," or even "to ponder," it would not be difficult for concepts of moderation to become associated with the new idea of a balance of trade as a way to communicate a reassuring state of affairs.[7]

But as the economic historian Joyce Appleby points out, balance was really a misnomer: what was really desired was a permanent imbalance.[8] Though the rhetoric suggested a desire to avoid any kind of excess, what merchants argued would benefit the commonwealth was, in fact, an excess of exports over imports of foreign wares, rather than an excess of imports over exports. Only an overbalance of trade, they argued, would provide long-term benefits for the nation. Crucially, what merchants and kings wanted was a benefit (not just a balance) and not simply a benefit derived from use-value—the bringing in of goods that would, as we might say, increase the standard of living. In fact, though all of these writers acquiesced to the idea of moderate consumption of foreign wares, importing goods was, in part, anathema to the theory that was developing, which insisted instead on exporting more products than were imported.

Emphasis on imbalance (i.e., overbalance) was a particularly salient feature in the writings of Thomas Mun, a director of the East India Company and leading member of James's newly formed commission on trade. As does Misselden, Mun likens the kingdom to a man who does "prosper and grow rich, who being possessed of revenues more or lesse, doth accordingly proportion his expences; whereby he may yearlie advance some maintenance for his posteritie." Mun argues:

So does it come to pass in those kingdoms which with great care and warinesse doe ever vent out more of their home commodities, than they import and use of forren wares; for so undoubtedly the remainder must return to them in treasure. But where a contrarie course is taken, through wantonnessee and riot; to overwaste both forren and domestike wares; there must the money of necessitie be exported, as the meanes to helpe to furnish such excesse, and so by the corruption of mens conditions and manners, manie rich countries are made exceeding poore, whilest the people thereof, too much affecting their owne enormities, doe lay the fault in something else.[9]

Going a step further in his logic than Misselden, Mun offers two possibilities here, neither of which is balance. One is underbalance, caused by moral defect and leading to a downward spiral into poverty. The other is overbalance, clearly the more desirable option—with it comes a remainder, treasure. Repeatedly when writers invoked a desire for the balance of trade, what was meant was an overbalance whose long-term benefit for the commonwealth was the return of more treasure. (The return of treasure is key; I will come back to this shortly.) If one were to stick strictly to the metaphor of balance, one would have to acknowledge that the scale would be tipped to one side.

But these writers did not abandon the rhetoric of balance. While Mun's defense of charges against the East India Company primarily functions to demonstrate that the importation of goods from the East Indies produces not a loss of treasure but a gain of it (primarily because those imports are reexported) his text also emphasizes the importance of restraint to avoid the "wantonnesse and riot" that leads to "over waste" of wares, which requires that money be exported to "furnish such excess." He concludes this admonition with a dual injunction: "industry to increase and frugalitie to maintain are the true watchmen of a kingdomes treasury."[10]

While his formulation, particularly its parallel construction, is evocative of balance, his point is not entirely about the moderation that balance might imply. What he promotes is an increase of production that is not balanced by a corresponding increase in consumption. He encourages moderation (maintenance as opposed to increase) on only one side of the equation. So, while one feels as if he has suggested balance, what he actually attempts to do is to encourage and legitimize profit, especially national profit.[11] What is key here, however, is that he does so precisely by encouraging moderation and evoking the idea of balance. He thus simultaneously addresses the primary pragmatic concern about loss and the ethical question of profit by making balance (or equivalence itself) the equivalent of profit. What we can see here is the way that overbalance (that is, profit) and the accumulation of treasure (even capital) was paradoxically understood also to be merely a steady state or safe state of equivalence that required, and was even equated with, the restraint that led to moderation. Thus overbalance and moderation appear to be compatible concepts. Indeed, it is the very notion of restraint that appears to make them so. The practical and straightforward point is that the nation's subjects should exercise restraint and thus not import more than is exported. But the theory also works more subtly to establish an association between balance and profit, such that a belief in and desire for both balance and overbalance can be held simultaneously. While the mercantilists' debate is known for producing an analytical discourse about the economy, what we can see here is how that discourse is not completely divorced from a series of ethical questions. In particular, this theory's emphasis on moderation readjusts the moral associations around profit from those of excess to those of balance.

Identifying overbalance with moderation seems fitting to an understanding of an economy of finite resources—a way to account for profit in a world that has not yet naturalized the concept of capital growth and where accumulation thus can be seen to result only from a corresponding drain elsewhere. Taking issue with profit therefore is not just a moral concern; profit, certainly unlimited self-generating profit, in some sense represents a system out of balance—one in which things are out of whack. Andrea Finkelstein argues that balance of trade theory develops from an understanding of the world as having limited goods and resources such that the gain of one country must necessarily result in the loss of another.[12] This is something of a balance sheet phenomenon, even if the end result is equivalence not at the national level but at the international one. The only way for one country to gain is if it exports more than it imports; all combined, the countries it trades with must be importing more from that one country than they are exporting; thus these other countries combined must be suffering from an underbalance of trade vis-à-vis this first country. Even though it might not have been a profound economic or moral problem to gain at the expense of other countries, especially Catholic and Muslim ones—in the words of *The Renegado*'s apprentice, it might be thought "a meritorious work" to "abuse a Turk in the sale of our commodities"—it goes against the very ideas of balance and moderation, which are both source and product of the balance of trade theory.[13] This theory is useful because it effectively calls overbalance "balance" and links profits to moderation, thus avoiding the recognition of loss elsewhere.

While balance of trade theory seems to resolve the problems of too much loss and profit simultaneously, it seems to beg some of its own fundamental questions. How does one make a profit not at the expense of another? Even more fundamentally, from where does that equitable profit come? If the point of overbalance is profit—the endless return of treasure—where does that profit come from in a world system of restraint and moderation without loss?[14] What we have here is not only an ethical problem in which someone's gain is someone else's loss. What we also have is a more conceptual problem: how can we have profit, pure and simple? While profit for us is a highly naturalized concept, largely disassociated from loss, the same was not at all the case in the early seventeenth century—not because of risk, but because the economy was not understood as something necessarily expanding or expansive. If the economic model is not based on the possibility of growth, all must be a zero sum game. One can profit at another's expense, but to do so is fundamentally disharmonious and perhaps ethically troubling.[15] In contrast, capitalism depends on a belief that even though resources might be fixed, capital as a whole can grow.[16] Thus one can benefit (i.e., accumulate capital) without ever having to subtract capital or ultimately resources from elsewhere. That is a fundamental difference between the understanding of a world that is under capitalism and a world that is not. What seems to be only a significant byproduct of the theory—that profit is equitable because it occurs in a world of moderation—is at the *heart* of the theory, which seeks to explain how to avoid a loss and legitimize profit, as well as how profit and capital accumulation are at all possible given limited resources.

For the state of equivalence to be fully reassuring, someone's gain must be nobody's loss. Similar to Finkelstein, Scott Shershow identifies "balance of trade" arguments, especially Mun's, with the restoring of a restricted economy (in which the central issue is scarcity and in which production, accumulation, and return are emphasized) "to the traditional image of a pernicious economy of loss."[17] Though Shershow's analysis shares with Finkelstein's an identification of a model of limited resources, it might also hint at a way not only to avoid loss, but to transform it and thus to get out of the fixed system in which gains on one side must equal losses on the other. Oddly, for a theory derived from the idea of a balance sheet—thus the metaphor of a balance, both of which are based on a momentary, static snapshot—balance of trade theory refocuses attention not on the store of money, but on the flow of money and goods. As economic historians have pointed out, this is one of the primary shifts in thinking about the economy that results from the mercantilists' debate. According to this theory, what is important is not just the initial outlay but what returns in the end; as I suggested in the book's Introduction, one can anticipate a different ending. Moreover, as I have been suggesting throughout this book, it is not just that the end is different than the beginning, but that the beginning transforms into a different ending. What matters most here is not just that one needs to wait until some later end point to balance the accounts, but the reason for doing so. Waiting until the end, or some later moment of reckoning to determine whether one has lost or gained requires monitoring the initial outlay of money as well as the continuous flow of money and goods. We can see how this works by looking at the criticism of balance as an idea to explain trade as profitable. Malynes, arguing against Misselden's idea that achieving a balance of trade will address the problem of bullion leaving the country, insists that a balance is only "a triall to find out whether he hath gained or lost, this is all a balance can doe."[18] It cannot show us "the difference of weight in the commerce of one kingdome with another."[19] Understanding the idea of balance as only a measure of a static moment, Malynes cannot imagine the increase of exports over imports as a sure way of enhancing the treasure of the kingdom, nor of escaping a fixed world in which the losses of one are the gains of another.[20]

The language of balance of trade theorists, by shifting attention away from static moments and toward the circulation and flow of money and goods, is particularly important because it provides for the possibility that while resources are necessarily limited, profits are not. When Mun, for example, argues that commercial outlays are not losses, he does so by showing how those outlays are productive:

For it is in the stock of the Kingdom as in the estates of private men, who having store of wares, doe not therefore say that they will not venture out or trade with their mony (for this were ridiculous) but do also turn that into wares, whereby they multiply their Mony, and so by a continual and orderly change of one into the other grow rich, and when they please turn all their estates into Treasure; for they that have wares cannot want mony.[21]

Wares and money, which are first only equated with each other, have the ability to valorize themselves through that very exchange in which they are initially only equated. Money is valuable because it can purchase wares; wares are valuable because they are convertible into money. This argument is tautological unless we recognize that money has value because it can be used to purchase commodities, which then can be sold for more money.[22] What we can see here is a kind of magical process, whereby the transformation of one thing into the other through continued circulation produces an excess, a profit by which treasure, even capital, is ultimately accumulated. Shifting the focus from the static store of money to the flow of commodities and money with them, the value originally advanced not only remains intact but also increases. In Marx's words, "it adds to itself a surplus-value, or is valorized. And this movement converts it into capital."[23] As Mun argues, "why should we then doubt that our monys sent out in trade, must not necessarily come back again in treasure; together with the great gains which it may procure in such manner as is before set down?"[24] Mercantilists did not just shift their attention from the store of money and goods to their flow, but also to the potentially unrestricted and equitable profits that developed as a result of transformative circulation.

These shifts in thinking about the flow of money and goods, which are crucial to the development of a notion of "investment," in which one expends money with the *expectation* of a profit, help to develop a theory of the economy and trade in which a static relationship between scarcity and abundance transmutes into a dynamic one between outlay and profit, but without shedding the idea of balance that loss and gain communicates. What I want to add to Shershow and Finkelstein's insights about the theory's relationship to a balance of loss and gain is the way that the theory tries to supersede a notion of a world of fixed goods and limited resources. When Mun describes the continuous circulation of money and wares, he most explicitly is trying to explain why sending out money does not lead to a drain in bullion. But his emphasis on continued and steady circulation on the one hand and (magical) transformations on the other allows him to present two opposing possibilities: moderation defined as a continual and orderly change and increase, as if they naturally cohere. This theory's emphasis on circulation imagines a creation of excess that can imagine an expanding economy, thus ultimately a world without losers.[25] The byproduct of a partially moral concern (profit at the expense of another's loss elsewhere) is the development of a theory of capital accumulation in which loss is not necessary. In contrast to Malynes's insistence on the limitations of balance and the scale for representing only a fixed moment, balance of trade theory emphasizes how continuous circulation transforms loss into productive expenditure so that accumulation no longer depends on or signifies the certainty of deaccumulation elsewhere. Even James, in his instructions to the newly formed commission on trade (cited in the epigraph) seems comfortable holding equality and profit in equipoise. Yet, that equipoise is itself the result of circulation that is productive.[26]

That productivity depends on the anticonsumptive logic of the theory's emphasis on circulation. While Mun speaks more than once about the usefulness of moderate consumption of foreign wares (that it keeps trade lively is his repeated refrain), the logic of mercantilist capitalist practices is anticonsumptive, which is not to say that it is necessarily opposed to pleasure or purchases. Instead it depends on repudiating the possibility that anything simply gets used up. Thus everything is transformed, transmuted, exchanged, or converted into something else in perpetual motion. In the economy Mun imagines and helps to produce, recirculation and re-employment are the rule. In place of the consumption of currency ("money sent out in trade") is the accumulation of capital ("come[s] back in treasure") that can be recirculated. Because nothing ever gets used up, there is no need for loss; there is endless productive capability (i.e., capital accumulation). And yet, the continued circulation of goods and money in which nothing is ever used up is also evocative of balance, of an even exchange that magically produces more. Most significant here is not just the simple idea that you need to trade to make a profit (nothing ventured, nothing gained), but that circulation itself somehow produces profit. Loss (or more precisely its reconfiguration), as I have been arguing throughout this study, is still necessary to get to an idea of profit, but the end result here is equity (no losers and earned profits) that is prosperous.

As I argued earlier, the reassuring notions of balance and moderation are transferred to the idea of profit whose own existence is explained by that of steady circulation and transformations. What we have at the same time, then, is a model of increase and accumulation that is commensurate with, rather than in contradiction to, balance, moderation, and equity. This theory has two primary implications: there are winners without losers, and profit or increase is not incompatible with a reassuring state of balance. What we might have here is an idealizing moment in which trade is actually imagined to produce a world without imbalances. On the one hand, mercantilism contains naïve optimism, but on the other it provides the foundation for the links among equity, equality, free trade, and profit, on which liberal and even neoliberal capitalism come to depend.

Though mercantilist theory depends on logical explanation and has come to be known, as I suggested above, for its analytical approach to the economy, what we can also see is how the theory, through its emphasis on the transformative powers of wares and money, also depends on a kind of magical thinking—a mystification that aligns it with, rather than differentiates it from, both the tragicomic theater and the religious discourse, which, as I have been arguing throughout the book, mercantilist discourse also refunctions to provide a rational explanation of the benefits of long-distance trade.[27]

But that refunctioning produces a theory that depends on two things in possible contradiction: circulation and restraint. The theory tries to accommodate these opposing ideas through the very notion of balance, but it is repeatedly on the verge of displacing one by the other, or favoring one over the other—hence, the bouncing back and forth in these texts between injunctions for moral behavior and arguments for profits. Similarly, though the theory imagines an economy of magical, endless circulation, that economy is nonetheless—even necessarily—grounded in restraint. Nothing is ever used up and value never dissipates because of endless transmutations and because one does not spend or expend unnecessarily. The mercantilist discourse thus deploys the magical idea of transformation for explicitly utilitarian ends in order to make everything purposeful and directed to feeding the system of productivity. Perhaps that utilitarian quality is what ultimately helps to mask the magical components and make the theory seem exclusively analytical. But the direct connection between restraint and circulation—the question of how restraint and endless circulation cooperate to imagine a world in which profit is first and foremost an expression of equity, that is, a world in which one need not fear loss (for worldly reasons) nor profit (for more spiritual ones)—remains unclear. The economic theory is insufficient to fully explain this phenomenon. For now, I will leave the question open in order to return to it at the end of the chapter after exploring how the specifically literary and theatrical deployment of tragicomic redemptions works to resolve this contradiction and thus to imagine a world in which restraint and endless circulation coexist.

Adverse Prosperity: Trade with the Ottoman Empire

Though balance of trade theory was developed in part specifically to address the concerns produced by the trade with the East Indies, especially the outflow of bullion to purchase goods, the Ottoman trade represented in Massinger's *The Renegado* provides a particularly interesting case study to test and explore the theory's associations among overbalance, circulation, and equity. Unlike the trade with the East Indies, in which English goods were not particularly vendible, trade with the Ottoman Empire included a significant export trade of English goods, especially cloth and tin, and a significant import trade. The development

of the East Indies trade around the Cape of Good Hope significantly reduced the import trade from the region, as the overland route via the
Levant was significantly more expensive and thus greatly diminished. If
anything, goods brought to England by the East India Company were by
the second decade of the seventeenth century reexported to the Ottoman Empire by the Levant Company. Thus, trade with the Ottoman
Empire—which included the purchase of currants and indigo for the
sale of cloth, tin, lead, and furs, as well as ginger, pepper, and cinnamon
from the East Indies—was not primarily considered a drain on the country's bullion.[28] Unlike East India Company merchants who had to explain how goods imported from elsewhere could be of value at home,
Levant Company merchants could actually claim that attaining a balanced trade in the region was a possibility.[29] In fact, by 1626 it was estimated that the Company's imports from and exports to the region were
equally heavy.[30]

Yet, given the possibilities for balance and the discourse about the
profitability of the Levant Company trade, the viability of the trade was
much more complicated than it first appears. While the Levant trade as
a whole was particularly profitable for the exchange of goods in both directions, piracy in the Barbary States continually threatened the English
trade not only in North Africa, but also in all of Turkey and the Levant;
all ships leaving the area had to cross the North African Mediterranean
and thus were subject to attack by the Barbary Corsairs. An estimated
466 English ships had been captured and their crews enslaved between
only 1609 and 1616.[31] Scholars estimate that 12,000 English subjects
were held in captivity in the Barbary States between 1600 and 1642. In
1625 alone, 4,500 were thought to be held.[32] Previous literary critics have
written of the extent of piracy in this region and its significance to the
literary and cultural imagination.[33] Pirates and their more legitimate
counterparts, privateers, were widespread on both sides, hindering trade
but also providing their countries with the funds needed to support
trades to other regions. They were a source of great fear, encroaching
ever closer to English waters, and were partially blamed for the loss of
bullion that plagued England in the early part of the seventeenth century. Both Mun and Misselden addressed the losses from piracy in their
tracts. Though previous critics have written insightfully about the association between piracy and economic loss, what they have not addressed
is the absoluteness of the threat piracy posed. It was not only the case
that certain ships were attacked and lost along with their goods and crew
(who might have been sold into slavery) but also that the entire trade
with the Ottoman Empire could be potentially halted. Thus, while on
the one hand, the trade in the region was extraordinarily profitable and
productive, there was also the possibility that the trade could become

entirely defunct.[34] Indeed, there were repeated threats by the Levant Company to remove their representatives and give up on the trade, because the losses seemed too great and it seemed almost impossible to conduct trade there at all. What is key here is that loss in the Ottoman trade is associated with total disruption or obstruction—the inability to circulate money and goods. Piracy threatened the whole system of circulation on which balance of trade and productivity depended. The Barbary States of Tripoli, Algiers, and Tunis, the last the setting for Massinger's *The Renegado*, thus provide an interesting proving ground to explore the crucial significance of circulation to balance of trade theory.

In the early years of the Company, a consul was established in Algiers with the hope of protecting the trade and even redeeming many of the English captives who had been sold into slavery.[35] But they had little positive effect, and consuls were recalled as even edicts from Constantinople ordering adherence to the capitulations, commercial agreements between Ottomans and foreign governments, were largely ignored.[36] As early as 1583, letters were sent to Turkey asking for increased assurance of the safety of English merchants and ships according to the earlier agreements, and threatening to give up the trade if it was not provided.[37] The ability to suppress the Barbary Corsairs was complicated by the fact that the Barbary States were under only nominal control of the Ottoman Empire; they maintained substantial autonomy. Thus, orders from Constantinople to cease attacking English ships often went unheeded and did little to solve the problem.[38] Interestingly, in 1616 the Pasha of Algiers asked the English ambassador to rein in English pirates who took two ships and sold their slaves and goods at Livorno. The Ambassador replied that he could not control them; they were "malefactors," that is, not operating as legitimate subjects on behalf of England. Reminding the pasha of attacks by the pirates of Algiers on English ships in recent years, he continues to argue that he cannot be called upon to "repair the damage," just as the pasha is not bound to answer for the pirates. The pasha interprets the disclaimer not as a straightforward acknowledgment of mutual powerlessness or lack of responsibility, but as a sign of revenge: "then you have taken our ships because we have took yours."[39] According to the Venetian ambassador, the incident was left unresolved even though the Pasha said they would punish the guilty if the English did the same. While it is unclear whether the instincts of the Pasha were correct and the frustrated English sought to recoup their losses—or at least make the Barbary States experience a similar, if not equivalent, form of frustration—what the incident suggests is a situation with the potential to spin out of control if the parties involved refused responsibility and instead sought to "resolve" tension through acts of revenge. In 1617, the company again spoke of relinquishing the trade altogether after they were threatened with a poll tax and when a principal English merchant, Garraway, was imprisoned and fined 10,000 pounds after importing goods to Constantinople that had been captured by a Maltese corsair from a Turkish ship.[40] Unfortunately, the original Turkish owner recognized the goods when Garraway tried to sell them. The ambassador was withdrawn, but only temporarily. James forced the company to appoint a new ambassador in 1619.[41]

But the corsairs continued to haunt and disrupt the trade. The years just preceding *The Renegado*'s first performance were marked by intense diplomatic and military efforts to salvage trade in the region. So severe was the threat that in 1620–21 a naval expedition, the only maritime operation of significance in James's reign, was sent to compel the Barbary States to repress the corsairs.[42] The Levant Company pledged to contribute 4000 pounds per annum for two years to this extraordinarily expensive military effort.[43] The crown made repeated attempts to raise money for these expeditions, arguing that their success would benefit the whole country. Many merchants argued that the decay of trade made them too broke to contribute, linking the various trade crises and suggesting that solving the problem in Barbary was made more difficult by slack trade elsewhere. Many documents nonetheless detail the high costs and repeated attempts to collect money that had been pledged. In fact, if the state papers are an accurate record, these matters completely dominated England's relationship with the Barbary States in these years.[44] Despite all of the money poured in, the expedition failed. In March 1621, the fleet, commanded by Sir Robert Mansell, "had done nothing, but negotiate with the pirates of Algiers for the liberation of some slaves."[45] According to A. C. Wood, the fleet failed to secure restitution of 150 ships and their crews captured during the past six years, or to destroy the Algerian ships in the harbor.[46]

In 1622, merchants of several companies in England agreed that captives lately taken should be redeemed by treaty; owing to the decay of trade, they claimed, it was not possible to raise additional funds for suppressing the pirates. Instead, they recommended sailing south in large fleets for protection. They claimed that failure of these methods would lead to the abandonment of trade with Turkey and the request for a letter of reprisal on the Grand Seignor's subjects.[47] But again diplomatic efforts were renewed. In the likely year of *The Renegado*'s first performance (1623) Sir Thomas Roe, the ambassador for England in Constantinople and thus the company's principal representative and chief negotiator, was ordered to demand of the Sultan that all English captives be set free and that all inhabitants of Tunis and Algiers cease further piracy.[48] This demand came yet again with a threat that included recalling all English merchants from Turkey and exacting satisfaction by force. The Sultan issued a firman ordering the enforcement of the capitulations and the return of English ships, slaves, and goods. Representatives from Tunis and Algiers were sent to Constantinople, and Roe made a formal agreement with them in March 1623. According to this agreement, England was permitted to maintain a consul at Algiers with authority over English subjects there and at Tunis. All English slaves were to be released; protection and good treatment were to be accorded to the subjects of England; and in all waters the ships were to treat each other in friendly fashion. In addition, eight hundred English prisoners were swapped for forty Algerians. The English also had to agree not to transport goods for enemies of the Turks. This latter point delayed the agreement's ratification in England, given the profits that would have to be forgone and the concern that the agreement would anger Spain. But the agreement was ratified and the company made another attempt to establish trade in Barbary.[49] A consul was reestablished in Tunis, although the trade there was little or none at all.[50] Pirate attacks did not end: some sources suggest that they were partially abated; others that they subsided not at all.[51] By 1624 there was talk again of ending trade with Algiers. In 1625, the Pasha imprisoned the consul and all other English subjects living there under the pretext that the English had seized some Algerian ships. According to Wood, efforts to trade in Barbary were most likely halted with just a few individuals operating on their own.

Putting together the pieces of this history, what we see are two very different pictures: in one, the trade is "balanced" (and thus profitable); in the other, it is nearly impossible to conduct. It is perhaps not so much that the trade in this region is filled with contradictions, but that conditions presented equally likely but opposing results. Thus, Wood's chapter on this period in the Levant Company's history is entitled "Prosperity and Adversity," and Michael J. Brown's history of Sir Thomas Roe's ambassadorship to Constantinople begins with a similar acknowledgment of potential for both difficulties and opportunities:

In theory, English merchants enjoyed extensive trading privileges in the eastern Mediterranean, so the negotiation of commercial treaties would not be of great importance. However, the exercise of those privileges was being severely jeopardized by the activities of the pirates of Algiers and Tunis, and stern representations needed to be made to persuade the sultan to restrain his unruly subjects.[52]

Perhaps even more unusual are the differing representations of not only what could happen, but also what did happen. On the one hand, one could say that the Levant trade doubled during the time that Roe was ambassador. On the other hand, the trade was understood as sufficiently loss-producing for the English to seriously consider putting a halt to it altogether. Misselden, for example, wrote that the "warres of the Pirats of Argier and Tunis hath robbed this common-wealth of an infinite value."[53] Was this a profitable trade or a loss-producing trade? I want to suggest that, paradoxically, this is not an either/or proposition, and that the trade was understood to be (and still was in these fairly recent histories) both. Both cases exist simultaneously, if also in tension with each other.

Before turning to *The Renegado*, I want to highlight a few salient features about the trade in the Ottoman Empire, how it relates to concerns about loss and profit and, by extension, how it highlights aspects of the developing balance of trade theories. The first is that the Ottoman trade could be profitable, but that the profits might never be realized (if ships were seized, if funds were used to redeem merchants and sailors who had been captured, and so on). This dichotomy mirrors what might be a more emotional or psychological aspect of the trade. Historical documents of the trade and even current histories of it seem to contain a considerable amount of both hope and despair. Treaties were renegotiated, orders were sent to suppress the pirates and make the trade safe, and yet nothing or almost nothing seemed to come of these agreements. This cycle of hope and disappointment would only enhance the already felt sense that trade with the Ottoman Empire was both a source of great gain and great loss. As a result, the Ottoman trade helps to (re)produce the current understanding of trade as loss-producing and profitable; it almost provides an allegory of the confusion about how loss is connected to profit. It is as if the problem of the Barbary pirates provides the pieces of the puzzle necessary to work out the relationship between loss and profit, but the pieces do not quite fit. As in the mercantilist theories, loss and profit co-exist, but in this trade they exist as two separate possibilities and not in a dynamic relation. In preceding chapters, I have argued that the theories of "investment" that develop from balance of trade theory depend on the transformation of loss, especially bullion sent out of the country, into expenditure. In contrast, loss and profit here are not put in dynamic relation to each other as they are in the balance of trade theory, and they are not put into dynamic relation precisely because the loss-version of events imagines loss not as productive expenditure but as the result of a halted trade in which circulation itself is prevented. Thus, it is not only that loss remains a problem, but also that both the source and legitimacy of profit (since it is not derived from transformed loss) are not firmly established.

Perhaps most important, the problems in the Barbary States raised the possibility of the very impossibility of trade. What if trade were simply halted? The impossibility of trade threatens the trade itself (i.e., exchange of goods) and the very idea of profitable circulation. The balance of trade arguments made in the mercantilists' texts try to reimagine a world with limited resources as a world in which endless circulation (not the "loss of infinite value") produces value and profit. Not only did the pirates threaten to disrupt trade and thus profits, but they also disrupted the circulation on which the entire theory of prosperity depended. It is not just that trade is necessary to make a profit, but that circulation itself is necessary, as I argued above, to imagine a profitable world economy, one that is not finite and has no losers.[54] While the problems and solutions addressed by the mercantilists do not map perfectly onto those of the Barbary/Ottoman trade, the latter is highly suggestive of the problems of imagining imbalance as balance, or of transforming impossibility into possibility. The potential absence of trade, I will argue below, thus provides an interesting proving ground for thinking about how circulation might resolve the contradictions in a theory that depends on reconciling overbalance with equity and infinite circulation with restraint.

These correlations produce a series of questions. Why stage a play about trade in a location where there effectively was no trade? Why pose questions about balance of trade—which is all about circulation and smooth, orderly flows—in a play located where trade for the English more or less does not exist and in a place whose subjects threaten to disrupt the entire trade of the region? To make the question more specific, why explore the two-pronged problem of illegitimate excess and possible loss in a location that stood for the potential impossibility of trade? Finally, what might emerge by posing these questions within a tragicomedy—that is, within a play whose narrative basis is in redemption—in the transformation of losses into profits? In other words, what tragicomically develops out of the inability to trade?

Locating Trade in *The Renegado*

On the one hand, we might say that Massinger's *The Renegado* begins with anything but the representation of the absence of trade. In the first scene, the play's hero, Vitelli, has an extended conversation with his apprentice, Gazet, about the wares he has brought with him from Venice. This first scene takes place in the market, with even the pirates coming to purchase wares, or more precisely to indulge in the benefits of the profits of their trade: according to Grimaldi, their profits enable (even entitle) them to consume at will. The very next scene, which focuses on the Basha of Aleppo's romantic overtures to the niece of the Ottoman Emperor and the play's heroine, Donusa, takes a fairly sudden turn when Donusa makes a startling request of her suitor. Bored with his insistence on romance conventions, she asks to be taken to the market so that she may survey its exotic commodities. The play thus places trade at its very center, making a point of demonstrating that trade will be the focus of its attention.

Yet to say that not a single commercial exchange takes place within the play would also be equally accurate.[55] The main character, Vitelli, is actually not a merchant; he has come to Tunis only to redeem his sister who has been captured by the renegade pirate, Grimaldi, and given to the viceroy of Tunis, Asambeg. Vitelli is only posing as a merchant. In the only scene that actually represents the mart in operation (in which Vitelli's apprentice is trying to sell wares), Gazet complains that the mart is "cold doings" and compares it unfavorably to the "stirrings" received by a "witch with a thrum cap / That sells ale underground to such as come / To know their fortunes in a dead vacation"; he imagines that her barely existing business exceeds his own by a factor of ten (1.3.25–29). Moreover, though Grimaldi, the renegade of the title, comes to the market to purchase wares, his actions are primarily disruptive; infuriated by Gazet's attempts to promote his wares, he threatens to "spoil" Gazet's market, thus disrupting what little traffic might occur (39). Gazet asks him to "hinder not the prospect of our shop" (1.3.77). When Grimaldi asks what he will do if he does not stop, Gazet answers, "Nothing, sir—but pray / Your worship to give me handsel" (that is, the first money taken by the merchant in the morning) (78–79). Powerless, Gazet replies that he can only do nothing, but after a pause adds that he can pray, not for divine patience or help, but for the market to resume and for money to exchange hands. Given that Gazet's only recourse is to pray to the renegado of the title, we can imagine that little is likely to come of such a supplication. Thus trade is at the play's center, and, alas, there is no trade in it at all. Yet I will argue that the play raises concerns about trade in precisely this way, that is, by representing trade as both all encompassing and as disrupted.

In the opening scene, however, the play seems less concerned with this tension between the dearth and centrality of trade than it is with representing the commercial as troubling for its lack of ethics. The play thus begins with what appears to be an even more fundamental concern. At first, it is not so much that trade or its disruption can cause problems, but that trade is itself a problem. The play opens as its hero Vitelli, disguised as a merchant, and his apprentice, Gazet, are setting up a shop to sell a variety of not so valuable *tsatskes*. In an opening dialogue that contains the play's only description of mercantile/retail practices (that is, if we don't include piratical practices), everything related to trade is ultimately debased:

. . . our wares,
Though brittle as a maidenhead at sixteen,

Are safe unladen; . . . without blemish;
And I have studied speeches for each piece
And, in a thrifty tone to sell them off,
Will swear by Mahomet and Termagant
That this is mistress to the great Duke of Florence,
That, niece to old King Pippin, and a third,
An Austrian princess by her Roman lip,
However my conscience tells me they are figures
Of Bawds and common courtesans in Venice. (1.1.2–4, 6–13)

Gazet's narrative begins like a conventional romance with a virgin ("brittle as a maidenhead") "safe unladen," whose purity is foregrounded in the absence of either crack or blemish (1.1.2–3). The tale imagines a "confluence of nations," like the markets of Tunis, and figures a journey in its representations of supposed subjects of worth (i.e., aristocracy) collected from Florence, Paris, and Austria (1.2.111). But his narrative is actually the story of a fall; for though the narrative brings us back home to Venice, that city of origin is the home of "bawds and common courtesans" (1.1.13). Virginity has turned out to be only a pretense or disguise, and Gazet's now debased "heroine" is only a whore of specious value. Inverting the traditional romance narrative in which a woman of apparent low birth turns out to be of high origins, this narrative's improper objects of desire (and of worship) are only wares whose originals are themselves of little worth. The images of noble figures worthy of respect turn out to be false idols guaranteed only by false oaths to "Mahomet." Moreover, the problem is not only the lack of authenticity of the objects being sold, but the practices of the merchant; when asked if he makes "no scruple of an oath," Gazet's reply foregrounds that a lack of ethics is fundamental to his trade: his indentures bind him only to "swear for his master's profit" (14, 15–16). He continues, "if it be lawful / In a Christian shopkeeper to cheat his father, / I cannot find but to abuse a Turk / In the sale of our commodities must be thought / A meritorious work" (19–23). The pun on "profit," like his willingness to swear by a Muslim prophet in order to cheat Turks, which he then represents as a means of achieving redemption (meritorious works were fundamental to Catholicism's redemptive practices), underscores the profound hypocrisy of his debased intentions and serves to undermine the whole enterprise in which profit is the goal. What the play needs—and what, I will argue, the tragicomic turn provides—is not the discovery of a princess of true worth as in the traditional romance, but the redemption of the economic practices that seem here to have instigated the fall.

Though the concerns here seem to be commonplace—cheating, misrepresentation, and theft—I want to argue that they stand in for developing economic practices, especially those relating to foreign trade, as a whole. Given that profit, as I argue above, is hard to understand in a world of limited resources except as a gain made at the expense of someone else's loss, it would be "natural" to represent profit as a result of unethical practices. Where else would the extra value that constitutes profit come from, if not from cheating?[56] Cheating and theft open the play as a guise or easier way to represent and understand potential discomfort with new economic practices, in which the desired effect, overbalance, appears to create a system out of whack, and whose redemption will then depend on restoring an idea of balance without giving up the idea of profit.

Excess and Balance in *The Renegado*

Indeed, concerns about balance permeate the entirety of the play. While the ostensible purpose of Vitelli's presence in Tunis is the redemption of his sister Paulina, the play's central plot problem becomes Vitelli's romantic and sexual relationship with the Muslim princess, Donusa, which is represented throughout the play as a relation of imbalance. They meet in the play's third scene when Donusa, who has just rejected not her suitor, Mustapha, but his performance of romance conventions, leaves the palace and the world of romance and instead comes in disguise to the market in order to be "though not a buyer, yet a looker on / Their [merchants'] strange commodities" (1.2.116–17).

The scene in which the lovers meet presents a variety of economic models whose potential and pitfalls the play will explore. Their meeting is framed by two opposing and extreme viewpoints on the relationships among the availability of resources, restraint, and consumption. In the first, Vitelli's Jesuit spiritual adviser, Francisco, who has spent much of his lines in the first scene encouraging Vitelli to be temperate and relinquish thoughts of revenge on Grimaldi, now somewhat gratuitously reminds Vitelli to beware the temptations of

. . . these Turkish dames [who]
(Like English mastiffs that increase their fierceness
By being chained up) from the restraint of freedom,
If lust once fire their blood from a fair object,
Will run a course the fiends themselves would shake at
To enjoy their wanton ends. (1.3.8–13)

Here Francisco worries that restraint and deprivation produce an overcompensation, a lack of control that manifests in an extreme overreaction. Vitelli, using a similar conceptual framework, then insists that he has too much woe to entertain thoughts of pleasure; his "base desires" are instead "strangle[d]" (1.3.19).

The pirate Grimaldi then enters, reveling in his excessive expenditures on pleasures, as if staging and even making an argument for exactly the kinds of indulgence that Francisco insists are fundamentally wrong, even sinful. Grimaldi, the renegade of the title, argues that the return for all of the hardships he endures on the seas is the ability to "wallow in / All sensual pleasures" (50–51). His excessive indulgence, however, comes not from prior restraint, but from the possibilities provided by a world with unlimited resources:

When this is spent, is not our ship the same,
Our courage, too, the same, to fetch in more?
The earth where it is fertilest returns not
More than three harvests while the glorious sun
Posts through the zodiac and makes up the year,
But the sea, which is our mother (that embraces
Both the rich Indies in her outstretched arms),
Yields every day a crop, if we dare reap it. (1.3.54–61)

Though he later acknowledges that his gains are like a sacrifice to Neptune, in this case paid by those who wish to traffic in the waters he patrols, his economic model is nonetheless of unlimited expenditure and consumption in a world—that of the sea—which is infinitely generative and thus in which loss is not transformed, but dismissed as insignificant. Everything can be consumed—that is, used up—but such consumption does not matter, because there is always more to supply him. He thus proclaims, "Let tradesmen think of thrift / And usurers hoard up. Let our expense / Be as our comings in are—without bounds" (62–64).[57] Rejecting the interdependent models of restraint and limited resources, Grimaldi imagines that both what he brings in and sends out are excessive, part of an unrestricted economy.[58] Though he is not exactly a prodigal who would end up in financial debt, his model is a good example of what balance of trade theory neither supports nor communicates. His model is not moderate, and it does not lead to profit or accumulation; instead it encourages a constant, unproductive circulation, a wash of intake and expenditure. While we might say he imagines a "balance," his habits and theory invoke anything but the kind of reassurance that was the goal of balance of trade theory. Grimaldi's practices (though not spiritual) are also not of this world, and his behavior, we are told immediately after, is tolerated by his employer, the viceroy of Tunis, only because the viceroy "receives profit / From the prizes he brings in, and that excuses whatever he commits" (1.3.93–95). This relationship provides a further explanation of Grimaldi's initial indifference to economic loss or religious repentance; indeed, the play figures his state as one of perverse redemption in which (illegitimate) profit counterbal-

ances his insolence, even pays the price of his sins. In a sense, he inverts
the logic of balance of trade theory: here profit is part of an equivalent
exchange, but the end result is an infinite cycle without bounds and
seemingly outside of anyone's control.[59]

Bringing Grimaldi back to earth, Gazet tries to reclaim the market for
the merchants Grimaldi had dismissed disparagingly: "Do you hear, sir?
/ We have paid for our ground" (1.3.74–75). Through a reminder of the
connection between fixed resources and current economic practices—
one must pay for the ground because of its limited availability—Gazet
admonishes Grimaldi for his lack of respect for the conventions of the
"legitimate" market. But its very legitimacy depends on drawing a fixed
line in the sand, one that imagines not a flow of goods and a world redeemed, but one in which having rights to the ground is clearly the result of someone else not having rights to the ground and in which things
certainly get used up rather than recirculated and self-valorized. What
we can see in all three of these negative models is the way that limits and
the absence of limits seem to produce less than desirable results: on the
one hand, the loss of self-control, integrity, and autonomy; on the other,
profits that are either limited and legitimate or the result of excessive expenditure and consumption. Both restriction and its absence lead to a
nongenerative cycle.

These negative models provide the lenses through which to view the
rest of the scene in which Vitelli meets Donusa, and she subsequently
falls in love with him. In contrast to the discrepant economies that frame
the scene of Vitelli's meeting with Donusa, Vitelli offers the model of a
perfectly balanced economy in the description of the first commodity he
hopes will attract Donusa. His looking-glass, he says, is

Steeled so exactly, neither taking from
Nor flattering the object it returns
To the beholder, that Narcissus might
(And never grow enamored of himself)
View his fair feature in it. (1.3.109–13)

In the language of the *Merchant of Venice*'s silver casket, one gets as much
as one deserves. Here, too, the mirror returns exactly what it receives,
with neither profit nor loss—a perfect balance of trade without excess or
restriction. Moreover, all of the objects that Vitelli describes have magical qualities that make them sources of reassurance, justice, and equity,
as if the wares themselves could counteract the concerns about excessive
circulation and consumption, or at least be symbolic of the very possibility of reassuring trade. Corinthian plates, for example, that usually conceal poison are instead so "innocent" and "faithful" that they fly into
pieces if venom is introduced, sparing their mistress and exposing the

traitor (1.3.122).[60] Similarly, in the lines cited above, the tragic story of Narcissus is reimagined, so that the glass's equity and fair judgment would have prevented Narcissus's literal and figurative fall. However, the encounter ends not with the reassurance that the objects reflect, but with an outrageous act on the part of Donusa. Smashing crystal glasses, she figuratively breaks the magical spell and disrupts the fantasy of equity and balance that Vitelli seems to offer in his representation of the wares.

The first act sets the stage for the rest of the play, which soon telescopes in on the difficulty of creating both balance out of loss and excess and a reassuring but unbounded profit. In Vitelli and Donusa's next scene, their roles are reversed: she seduces him not only with her beauty and position, but especially by offering him excessive quantities of valuable material objects in part to repay him for the glasses she has shattered at his shop. Even though the play contains no actual commercial transactions, it becomes obsessed with the impossibility of equivalent exchanges and proper returns. When Donusa seduces Vitelli, she repeatedly claims to be his "debtor," who will "make satisfaction / For wrongs unjustly offered" (2.4.78–79). She claims to have "injured [him] in some poor petty trifles," and offers to pay for "the trespass" (81–82). In the guise of compensating him for the glasses, she provides him with excessive "restitution" that includes "bags stuffed full of our imperial coin" and "gems for which the slavish Indian dives," as well as the possibility of being "possessed" of any gift "which is unbounded as the sultan's power" (2.4.83, 85, 89–90, 103). Though she is obsessed with making things right (that is, equitable), her response is to completely overcompensate for the initial injury, thus creating a potentially irresolvable imbalance.

Even the good Vitelli can now do is represented as indulgent beneficence. Thus, when Vitelli next meets his spiritual advisor, Francisco, he explains and perhaps justifies his glamorous transformation by claiming to have newly gained unbounded powers:

. . . There's nothing
That can fall in the compass of your wishes
(Though it were to redeem a thousand slaves
From the Turkish galleys, or at home to erect
Some pious work to shame all hospitals),
But I am master of the means. (2.6.30–35)

The inflated rhetoric of his offer to be the source of wish fulfillment, a fairy godmother that can rectify the scourge of trade, suggests that the benefit would be undermined by the source of his power. Francisco immediately admonishes him: "They steer not the right course, nor traffic well, / That seek a passage to reach heaven through hell" (2.6.45–46).

Vitelli's attempt to rescue prisoners and counterbalance the damage done by the Barbary Corsairs merely mirrors the perverse redemption of Grimaldi, whose profits, as I suggested earlier, serve to excuse his insolent behavior. Even the good deed, precisely what the English ambassador worked so hard to accomplish, is here canceled out by not only the source of the potential, but especially the Faustian excess and unboundedness of the ability.

Indeed, Vitelli is himself "overwhelmed" by Donusa's gift of unlimited abundance, to which she also adds the "tender of [her]self" (2.4.90, 101–2). His response is significantly twofold: he knows not how "like a royal merchant to return / [Her] great magnificence" (that is, what he should offer in return), and knows not how to "resist this battery" that makes his "flesh rebellious to [his] better part" (94–95, 109–110, 113). The encounter introduces two new and different, but interrelated, solutions to the problems of imbalance: effectively, Vitelli asks, how do I repay you, and how do I resist you? While the play uses language reminiscent of the complexities of an economy of gift exchange (loss of self-worth resulting from receiving more than can be returned), their exchange primarily emphasizes the impossibility of equivalent exchange within that context.

The play here highlights the limitations of the familiar gift economy model, raising questions of balance and suggesting the necessity of a different economic model—not one in which you gain honor and power by giving more in return (which leads to economic loss), but one which authorizes getting back more than you give and even makes doing so the fundamental goal. Reading this exchange between Donusa and Vitelli in context with the play's earlier emphasis on a discomfort with profit and lack of ethics in trade, I will argue that the play needs to imagine what Vitelli gives as generative of a legitimate profit. The play's resolution, then, depends not primarily on what Europeans can offer in return— Ania Loomba interestingly argues that they offer Christianity in exchange for all of the material goods they receive—but on using what they can offer in return (redemption) as a means to transform what one expends into a greater, but still reassuring, profit that would make the redemption of a thousand slaves a legitimate, rather than specious, affair.[61] It is in this regard that Vitelli's dual insistence on expenditure and resistance (how do I repay *and* resist you) and the complicated setting of Tunis are so important.

The Tunisian Challenge: Attempting Impossibilities

Vitelli's concern with his ability to repay Donusa is suggestive of the desire to eliminate the balance issues, to imagine a situation in which the flow from one side to another is merely an expression of a reassuring state of equivalence and mutuality in which nothing is disrupted—that is, in which neither balance nor circulation are disrupted. Vitelli's need to resist Donusa, however, suggests that part of the solution might be to restrain oneself so that no exchange ever takes place. But that would not provide balance; it would only provide stasis. There would be no trade, and of course there would be no play. How, then, can the restraint the play imagines provide the opportunity not to avoid economic and cultural exchange, but to imagine a situation in which the flows from one side to the other can be productive?

The answer might paradoxically lie in the play's representation of the ways that trade is disrupted or halted. By the fourth act, the earlier concerns about cheating and imbalance have transformed into more dire and potentially tragic forms of obstruction, paralleling the problems in Tunis I discussed above. Vitelli is imprisoned after his affair with Donusa, his "she-customer" has been revealed. The pirate Grimaldi has been cashiered by the Tunisian viceroy and thus prohibited from stealing; he falls quickly into a deep state of despair. As a result of Vitelli's imprisonment, Gazet, who had only recently been freed from his apprenticeship, now laments his inability to procure a coveted position at court. At the height of its problems the play represents commerce (legitimate or otherwise) as at a standstill. The play thus threatens tragic consequences not only in the figures of Vitelli and Donusa, who may be punished with death, but in the absence of economic and social possibility.

After the viceroy removes Grimaldi from his position and prevents him from stealing, the play represents his state as one of necessary religious despair and economic stagnation.[62] Furious with Grimaldi for his insolence and inability to take the ships and goods of Malta, the viceroy of Tunis fires him from his position, prohibits him from future piracy, and confiscates all of his goods. The play then emphasizes his transformation from a source and embodiment of uncontrolled expenditure, theft, and intake (i.e., an ungrounded infinite cycle), to one of impotence. Grimaldi's state of being defrocked—as Gazet puts it, "the miserable rogue must steal no more"—is associated with his own sense of despair, particularly his inability to qualify for redemption (3.2.43). He despairs, "though repentance / Could borrow all the glorious wings of grace, / My mountainous weight of sins would crack their pinions / And sink them to hell with me" (3.2.69–72). His wealth and means of acquiring more are taken away; the infinite cycle is replaced by despair and stagnation. In both cases, what the play emphasizes is a kind of stasis, defined by absence of movement and circulation. Linking despair and the disruption of commercial activity (even if the latter is piracy), the play imagines both as dead ends. Further equating the economic dead end with the spiritual dead end of despair, Grimaldi queries the relevance of seeking any remedy: "Why should I study a defense or comfort, / In whom black guilt and misery, if balanced, / I know not which would turn the scale? Look upward / I dare not" (3.2.61–64). Grimaldi has been reduced to a literal version of the state in which he put Gazet in the play's first act: doomed to seek assistance only where there is none. The balance he imagines (of two negatives) is now a sign not of reassurance, but of a state of stasis from which there appears to be no exit.

The other primary representation of obstruction, though more comic, is at least equally significant. Parallel to Grimaldi's despair is Gazet's lament over Vitelli's imprisonment as an obstruction to his personal success; he had only just finished negotiating a new position at court when their role as swindlers is revealed. Though Francisco calls it a "saving voyage," Gazet figures his near escape as lucky except for this one major loss of position: "Why sir, I had bought a place, / A place of credit, too, and had gone through with it, / I should have been made an eunuch" (4.1.150–52). While the pirate and merchant are both, in a sense, imprisoned, the disruption of trade is perhaps located most squarely in the impossibility embodied in the figure of the eunuch. Arguing that the play engages with conflicts between the interests of state and those of its free-trading servants, Jonathan Gil Harris insightfully reads the threat of castration as associated throughout the play with economic loss (like that of bullion flowing out of the country or lost when pirates attack ships) and even with the removal of money and merchandise from circulation. He argues that castration is a figure for wasteful hoarding, one of the targets of theorists like Mun and Misselden, who argued that expenditure was necessary to profit and that hoarding treasure is necessarily unproductive.[63] I want to take Harris's line of thinking one step further to argue that the castration anxiety in the play figures not just the loss of goods to piracy, or the taking of goods out of circulation that hoarding entails, but the very likely scenario in Tunis and by extension in the Levant trade as a whole: that there will be no circulation at all. While both Harris and Barbara Fuchs read the play's representations of castration as the emasculating threat of either competition with the Turks or the social mobility that comes from trade, respectively, I want to argue that the play's concern with impotence is not merely one that comes from occupying a position of inferiority and the loss that might come with it.[64] Not just emblematic of hoarding or competition, castration represents the fear of the very impossibility of trade; trade could be, in a sense, cut off. Thus when the play's one actual eunuch, Carazie, expresses surprise that Donusa would dote on a "haberdasher of small wares," Donusa's other servant reminds Carazie that he "hast none." He retorts, "if I had, I might have served the turn" (2.3.4, 5–7). His lack of "wares" is figured as an inability to participate in the exchange. Even more to the point, when Vitelli's freed apprentice Gazet learns that there is a position at court—that of the eunuch—whose main responsibilities include lying with women, he is eager to purchase that position. But the cost is high: Gazet offers up those things that make him a merchant and enable him to trade for this benefit. He exclaims, "I'll be an eunuch, though I sell my shop for't / And all my wares" (3.4.50–51). Though Gazet had earlier rebuked Grimaldi for hindering trade, Gazet imagines having to cede his previous trade altogether. The play here associates the costs of being a eunuch with the inability to trade and trade's disruption as well. What matters here is not that the eunuch is a figure for one who does not want to trade, but that he is a figure for the threat that trade could be completely obstructed and that nothing will circulate.

Such a disruption might be signaled by the unusual Italianate name of the play's actual eunuch, who is a servant to Donusa. Only a minor character, Carazie's significance exceeds his number of lines, precisely because he, despite his Italianate name, is the only English character in the play.[65] While "carazie" was not (as far as I have been able to discover) a seventeenth-century Italian word, John Florio defines the word "caratto" as "a fee which every man paies in Venice to Sainte Mark that obtaines any suite by law. Paying so much the hundred, it is called in Rome *la Sportula*."[66] "Sportula" is defined as "taken for money or meate distributed by Princes to the people as an almes." It was also money paid to the Pope or Saint Peter if a man obtained his suit by law. Finally, it is defined as "a little panier, mound, or basket."[67] In modern Italian, a "carato" is a jewel or a share in a business. Many of these meanings (except for the last definition of "sportula") associate the giving of something up (money mostly) with supporting the larger functioning of the community and guaranteeing one's place in it. "Caratto" is therefore simultaneously like and unlike the eunuch in the play; it functions more like Gazet's fantasy of the benefits afforded to the eunuch for the small portion paid.

Further strengthening the potential link between "caratto" and "Carazie" is the word "carazo," which is graphically closer to "Carazie" and appears specifically in the context of European trade with the Ottoman Empire. "Carazo" is the Venetian word for the "harach," a poll tax imposed on foreigners living in the Ottoman Empire and thus could be a related word, if not the same word, as "caratto," a likely possibility given the variances in Italian dialects in the early seventeenth century.[68] The carazo became a very contested issue in 1616 when the Ottoman government threatened to impose the tax on all French, English, Flemish, and Venetian merchants who had been living in Constantinople for more than one year.[69] The ambassadors of these countries mostly jointly (but also sometimes separately) contested the carazo, arguing that the capitulations exempted their merchants from this fee. Referring twice to its imposition as a form of tyranny, the Venetian ambassador insisted "that the matter of the carazo is most important."[70] Significant it must have been. It is discussed at least twenty times in dispatches between Venice and Constantinople in 1616 and 1617, many of which refer to its potential to harm trade. The two most extreme predictions of its effect come in the Venetian ambassador's report of his English counterpart's response. The latter threatens that he and all of his merchants will leave if the tax is not repealed. The English ambassador then tries to convince the French, Flemish, and Venetian ambassadors to do the same, that is, to advise their rulers not to keep an ambassador in Constantinople and not to permit their ships to come to its shores.[71] The Venetian ambassador, whose strategy is not as clearly stated in the documents, agrees that the carazo would compel merchants to abandon the trade. The replies he receives from Venice confirm that the carazo will either force Venice to abandon the mart or retaliate by imposing a similar burden on Turkish merchants in Venice.[72] As in the case of piracy, the carazo poses a threat to the possibility of smooth trade and maybe even all trade. Thus the carazo would produce the very opposite of Gazet's fantasy.

Embodying the disruption of trade in a eunuch named Carazie thus is significant for the way it imagines how what one gives up in order to participate in a commercial system could actually prevent the intended benefit from accruing, or even the entire system from functioning. Indeed, the whole joke of Gazet's desire to be a eunuch rests on the fact that the very things he gives up will prevent him from enjoying the profits for which he relinquished them. Not surprisingly, the play repeatedly figures this constitutive limitation as economic expenditure. Thus Carazie explains that the office can be purchased by "parting with / a precious stone or two" he knows "the price on't" (3.4.51–52). When only in the next scene Gazet laments the loss of such a great opportunity, he reiterates the idea: "I was glad to run away and carry / The price of my office with me" (4.1.155–56). What the play mocks here is loss that produces no return. In an inversion of balance of trade theory (in which loss is reconfigured as productive expenditure), the figure of the eunuch reconceives expenditure as loss that not only produces no return but also prevents the very possibility of it. Thus, in the figure of the eunuch the play connects the impossibility of trade (as the absence of circulation) to the impossibility of making a profit, of not seeing a return for one's expenditure.

Redemption, Restraint, and Tragicomedy

The tragic version of problems with balance of trade therefore is actually the absence of circulation. The potential absence of circulation represented in Tunis would make impossible the resolution of problems with either underbalance or overbalance. Locating the play in Tunis, where circulation is threatened, helps to highlight what is crucial to balance of trade theory. I am not just reading the problems of piracy for their own sake, then, but instead am trying to understand how the play tragicomically makes use of the problem of piracy in order to help resolve other problems conceptually—primarily those regarding imbalance, that is, the avoidance of loss and the simultaneous instantiation of an idea of profit without losers.

To this purpose, I return to modified versions of this chapter's initial questions. What tragicomically develops out of an inability to trade that is represented as an absence of circulation? How does tragicomedy, given its basis in a form of redemption that reimagines loss as potential profits, function in a play that insists that economic expenditure prevents its own purpose—the very possibility of transforming loss into profit?

Before turning to what I will argue is the play's vehicle for resolving its problems of imbalance and disrupted circulation, I want to look at what the play rejects as absolutely not the solution to its intertwined problems of legitimately reinstating the possibility of a profitable return and making sure that goods and money keep circulating. What the play rejects outright as useful to the resolution of its plot is any form of revenge. Francisco's first scene with Vitelli, for example, is preoccupied with repeatedly rebuking Vitelli for the blood-boiling revenge he wants to take on Grimaldi. Vitelli is not the only one Francisco tries to rein in. The virtuous Paulina wants to take revenge on Grimaldi, whose rape of her "gave a beginning / To all the miseries that since have followed." Resisting her means of plot generation, Francisco instead encourages her to forgive Grimaldi, because he has changed (5.2.77–78).

Even Grimaldi's initial solution to his state of despair is to take a form of revenge on himself. Reading from some of the best-known passages in Exodus, Grimaldi imagines that his best hope lies in making an equivalent exchange with those who have suffered on his behalf and by extension with the world that they comprise:

O with what willingness would I give up
My liberty to those that I have pillaged
And wish the numbers of my years, though wasted
In the most sordid slavery might equal
The rapines I have made; till with one voice

My patient sufferings might exact from
My cruel creditors a full remission,
An eye's loss with an eye, limb's with a limb.
A sad account . . . (4.1.53–61)[73]

He continues:

. . . To appease 'em
I would do a bloody justice on myself:
Pull out these eyes that guided me to ravish
Their sight from others; lop these legs that bore me
To barbarous violence; with this hand cut off
This instrument of wrong; till nought were left me
But this poor bleeding limbless trunk, which gladly
I would divide among them. (4.1.65–72)

Grimaldi's melodramatic dismemberment fantasy of self-revenge redu-
plicates, rather than resolves, the problems represented throughout the
play: here an even exchange or equal return is imagined as a form of dismemberment that would metaphorically reconstitute the crisis in Tunis
as at a standstill. These lines might also invoke a more current crisis—
the refusal on the part of the English ambassador to claim responsibility
for his pirates precisely because the Ottomans have not done so for the
Barbary Corsairs. Indeed revenge, especially in its Old Testament form,
is a kind of perverse form of gift economy in which the revenger's actions at a minimum must mirror in kind and amount what has been
done by the original offender. The notion of equity, which is endemic to
revenge, requires that this be so. Yet, as the genre of revenge tragedy
suggests, what revenge produces is intensified reduplication of the original set of problems and transgressions, therefore never productivity
(except for plot, of course).[74] The revenger enters into the original offender's world on the same terms; what results is annihilation, or at least
a cycle of destruction, a form of nonprosperous equity in which actions
intended to create an equal or greater loss follow upon each other's
heels until there is (almost) nothing left to lose. Revenge, the very opposite of sacrifice in which you give something up to benefit another, is
also counter to an economic model in which action is generative of profits, or institutes a self-generative cycle of profit production.

The play's insistent turn away from revenge provides the vehicle for a
tragicomically New Testament resolution in order to imagine an economy in which what one expends comes back, not in more destructive
form, but instead enhanced. After Vitelli succumbs to Donusa's temptations, Francisco notes that Vitelli is "lost" and "strangely metamor-
phosed" as the result of a "prosperous voyage" that he fears is not
"honest," and from which Vitelli must now "redeem" himself (2.6.1,

20–21, 3.2.20). He must repay the excess he has been given, which has paradoxically resulted in a loss, even two losses: the loss of self and the potential loss of wealth. Both of these losses are represented in the fear that he will have to overpay in return. How then to invert this situation so that what he extracts from the economic system of Tunis is a proper, but also prosperous return? What the play needs to do is to transmute the potential loss of money from obstructed trade and the unjustified excess of too much profit and consumption into legitimate profits. I will argue it does so by making getting more back than you give seem like a form of equity—even constituting getting more back as a form of equity.

Historically, the genre of romance negotiates the question of what is a worthy object of desire, thus already provides a model (and language) for resolving concerns regarding value and worth matched or unmatched, transforming incommensurate feelings and values into commensurate ones. Romance can contemplate potential losses resulting from engagement with the "other," be that "other" simply an object of desire or a potential commodity, or a representation of the temptations of difference. But what it might not negotiate is the possibility of future legitimate profits. I will argue that it is the "tragicomic" aspect of the theatrical form that performs this function. As I argued in the Introduction, tragicomedy works by making the tragedy averted the means for its own resolution. The work of this play's tragicomedy, then, is to resolve the crises of obstruction by making them vehicles for their own resolution and, as a result, transform all of the play's forms of excess into forms of profitable equity.

But how do those potential losses get turned into equivalences or even justified profits that appear to be equivalences? When Vitelli tries to detach himself from Donusa, he configures his act as returning what was given him as if he had overpaid for it, even though the problem was its excessive value for which he could not make restitution. He calls upon his religious faith to help him "express at what an overvalue I have purchased / The wanton treasure of your virgin bounties," and he configures returning the casket of jewels she gave him as "deliver[ing] back the price / And salary of your lust." (3.5.41–42, 48–49). He attempts to balance accounts and thus reclaim his lost integrity.

This balancing act inverts Grimaldi's desperate self-revenge fantasy (and the revenge fantasies of the play as a whole) by turning instead to possibilities for redemption. Indeed, just prior to this second visit with Donusa, Vitelli reassures the Jesuit, Francisco, that he will "redeem" himself (2.4.5). The vehicle for his redemption is his religious faith, which he calls upon to arm him and which he then clings to as his solace when he is discovered with Donusa and imprisoned: "What punishment / So'er I undergo, I am still a Christian" (3.5.95–96).[75]

Given the religious framework and themes of the play it is not surprising that redemption is a theme much harped on. But the play's insistent return to the theme of redemption is also motivated by the economic valences already present in the theological concept. Throughout the play, redemption is presented not only in economic terms, but also as an economic concept. For example, in the lines I cited earlier, the renegade Grimaldi imagines his redemption as the result of an equal number of good deeds that would balance his previous evil ones and thus would even out his account—that is, pay his "creditors" who would give him a "full remission" (4.1.59). Most literally, "redemption" means to "buy back," and Christian doctrine at least as far back as Anselm understood redemption in economic terms.[76] That redemption has an economic valence in the play in and of itself is not noteworthy. The more important question to ask is how is the idea of redemption, precisely because it understands the religious as economic, employed in the play? How do the processes and language of redemption make it available to negotiate the play's concerns with religious difference and the balance of trade as well?

In traditional accounts of redemption, excess is given to man by God, to whom man is always indebted; but God is also paid back in excess by Christ's death and suffering.[77] While in these accounts the economic language of redemption might have functioned to highlight the inappropriateness of economic gain in the earthly realm (as opposed to its propriety in relation to God's infiniteness), in the play redemption gets employed to legitimize and perhaps harness economic gain. Rather than devalue earthly gain, redemption revalues it. In fact, Grimaldi will redeem himself by acting as "a convoy for all merchants" and thus will be "thought worthy / To be reported to the world hereafter" (4.1.105–6). The merchants Grimaldi protects are now free to engage in their prosperous activities, which will be saved practically and ethically by Grimaldi's redemptive trajectory with which they are now associated. Reversing Catholic doctrine, in which renouncing worldly goods could lead to redemption, this tragicomedy employs religious redemption as both an alternative to revenge and as the virtuous guarantor of economic prosperity. Through an inversion in which the economic register borrows back its discourses of redemption from Christianity in order to accredit itself, this play most explicitly demonstrates how discourses of redemption can be productively recoded, in this case by equating redemption with the protection that makes trade not just profitable, but possible.

The pirate/renegade figure is thus turned into a primary focus of religious redemption and a source of legitimate profitability. His despair after the viceroy dismisses him and confiscates all of his goods, which

first took the form of a loss-producing equity (eye for an eye), is ultimately transformed into a form of prosperous equity. Reversing the
course of Marlowe's *The Jew of Malta* (which the play recalls when
Grimaldi's goods are confiscated in part because he praises the Knights
of Malta for having greater courage than the Ottoman Janisseries)—a
play that begins with attempts to redeem what is lost, but very quickly de-
volves into revenge—*The Renegado* repeatedly refuses revenge (which is
equity gone awry, an "eye for eye") for a more ethical and profitable redemption. In this recoding, the play makes use of the potential tragedy:
it moves through stagnating despair and imprisonment, employing redemption from those states as a vehicle for constituting uninhibited,
self-supporting circulation as permanent and always already linked to
worth.

Through its economic language, redemption can function to assimi-
late religious difference (through conversion) and integrate the economic, especially the excess of profit. Redemption, in part, can
legitimize the notion of excess by absorbing economic anxieties in its
very language. But it also nullifies those concerns by creating subjects
who are worthy of whatever profits they acquire or accumulate.[78] According to Catholic doctrine, man profits from God, but makes amends
by abandoning meed in the earthly sense, perhaps by giving alms.[79] The
abandonment of the economic is a way to redemption, to balance accounts with God. In this play (and perhaps in other tragicomedies) this
process is reversed—redemption enables participation in the economic
in the earthly realm. Man is made worthy and profit is thus not only legitimized, but also fundamental to a world in which reward is a sign of
one's worthiness. *The Renegado* therefore resolves some of the problems
that worried Bawd and Pander in Shakespeare and Wilkins's *Pericles*;
one does not have to repay God for ill-gotten and unbounded profits,
since those profits are associated with both the plenitude of God's grace
with which he redeems mankind and mankind's redeemed state
itself.[80] The excess of Grimaldi's unrestricted thieving economy is transformed into profit and made usable by the merchants Grimaldi originally cursed and defined himself against, but on whom he now stakes
his own salvation.

While Grimaldi focuses on compensating for past transgressions, it is
Vitelli, the play's primary protagonist, whom the play produces as the
model for the really worthy subject. This switch mirrors the confusion of
the title, which most literally refers to Grimaldi, the only actual renegade in the play. Vitelli, however, is the play's main character and his
conversion, which Donusa requests in order to save their lives, would be
the most potentially tragic outcome of the play's plot. Though he is
never tempted by this request, both Francisco and Gazet deem his rela-

tionship with Donusa and the wealth he acquires along with it, if not as a form of conversion, then at least as a transformation—one that serves as a sign that he has succumbed to temptation. While on the one hand Vitelli's redemption is configured in traditional terms that leave him indebted to God and subject to religious faith, his redemption is also particularly significant because it produces in him an ability to restrain himself.[81] The merchants' reassociation with restraint is key to the way that redemption works here to redeem profit itself. Likened twice to Ulysses and his men who resist the temptation of the siren (once by himself in 3.5 and then by the impressed viceroy in 4.3), Vitelli will put himself to the test without the aid of wax to stop his ears or ropes to tie himself to the mast.

. . . I will see and hear you [Donusa]
The trial, else, is nothing: nor the conquest
My temperance shall crown me with heareafter
Worthy to be remembered. Up, my virtue! (3.5.34–37)

While Grimaldi's redemption enables the circulation of goods and profit, Vitelli's redemption, which entails resisting Donusa (especially the overwhelming abundance of Ottoman wealth that she offers), focuses on his ability to restrain himself, which he claims as his own possession. When Francisco encourages him to "be still thyself," Vitelli replies, "Tis not in man / To change or alter me" (4.3.53–54). No longer possessed by Donusa's charms, he is self-possessed. If the play's romance and romance itself were devalued through its earlier associations (or conflation) with the mercantile (as in the play's opening scene), it is revalued as tragicomedy through the employment of redemption and restraint that serve to redeem the economic as well.

It is in this reassociation that the play makes use of the Tunisian location in order to tragicomically address and resolve the problems of loss and excess in a way that does not require putting a halt to circulation. Building on Keir Elam's reading of the eunuch figure in *Twelfth Night*, I want to argue that the play uses the eunuch, which symbolically represents the obstruction of trade, to provide a kind of inverse blueprint for tragicomically imagining restraint as a source of profitable redemption— one that imagines the restoration of the flow of goods and money as a means to legitimize and constitute the profit that such circulation generates. Tracing *Twelfth Night*'s debt to Terence's *Eunuchus*, Elam argues that the figure of the eunuch is not just a sign of frustration, or the inability to act. The pretense of the eunuch, he argues, is used to gain access (i.e., to women), thus to create possibilities where they did not exist before. As a result, "what looks like the neutralizing of male sexuality turns out instead to be a triumphant assertion of virility."[82] The theatrical figure of the eunuch is interesting because it paradoxically empowers the position of the impotent. The (impersonated) eunuch is a figure that inverts its own constitutive limitations and transforms those limitations into possibility. Similar to the counterfeit eunuch of Terence's play and *Twelfth Night* as well, this play's main character pretends to be a merchant in order to gain access to a woman, in this case his captured sister.[83] Transforming the eunuch as well as the defrocked pirate into restrained merchants, the play rewrites the threat of trade with Tunis—impotence and obstruction—as a kind of virility dependent on restraint: "up my virtue."[84] Impotence is thus transformed into its positive antitype; in Elam's terms, the inability to trade in Tunis, embodied in the figure of the impotent eunuch, is tragicomically transformed into a positive version of controlled circulation. Thus, Vitelli does not have to "strangle" his "base desires." In this model, money and goods can circulate productively, but not excessively, under the restrained control of the merchants and their advisors. The transformation of the eunuch into the restrained merchant kills two birds with one stone: it deactivates the threat of powerlessness associated with the absence of trade and circulation, opening up the opportunity for profit and not loss, while simultaneously imagining that profit as a sign of virtue.[85]

While restraint could be understood as a means to disavow the presence of commercial pressures and temptations, in the play it serves paradoxically to constitute economic transactions as profitable. The play's ending depends not only on Vitelli's restraint and Donusa's conversion, but also on Paulina's restraint and only her feigned willingness to submit to the viceroy's desires and to "turn Turk." Paulina pretends that she is willing to submit to the viceroy's desires in order to have access to Donusa and facilitate the escape that Francisco has planned, but what is repeatedly emphasized is that she restrains from such an act in reality.[86] Paulina's restraint enables the play to end with a revision of Gazet's opening narrative; there is a voyage home, but all of the returnees are worth more than they were on the outward leg of their journey. First, rather than destroy the blissful bower and its material temptations, Vitelli's "temperance" converts Donusa, who undergoes a complete transformation as a result.[87] The Europeans then take with them the converted Donusa and the Tunisians' "choicest jewels." (5.8.27). While earlier in the same act, "choicest jewel" referred figuratively to Donusa's faith and willingness to convert ("Willing she is, / I know, to wear it as the choicest jewel / On her fair forehead," 5.1.24–26), the jewel here is converted back to the literal, economic register that now also comes with the sanctification of a profit deserved by worthy Christians.[88] This is the "honest," "prosperous voyage," for which Francisco hoped he would be able to "rejoice" (2.6.20–21).

Restraint is important not only because it readjusts the moral associations around profit. The turn to restraint also creates the possibility for transforming the absence of trade into a version of controlled and profitable circulation, an equitable overbalance of trade that actually serves to merge trade and profit, making them synonymous with each other. As a result of their restraint, the play's subjects go home not only with their own goods and those of others as well, but also with their value enhanced. This enhancement is what begins to constitute profit as trade's purpose. The primary benefit of trade is no longer located in the use of goods that are exchanged, but instead becomes the enhancement or production of value—an enhancement in this case that develops out of tragicomically transforming threats to trade and potential losses into vehicles for two benefits that become linked: material profit and the increase of personal worth. Whereas in some of the texts I discuss in the preceding chapter trade is represented as redemptive because it repairs deficiencies in the availability of natural commodities, in this tragicomedy profit supplies the very place of that benefit. It is not only that profit, which was something of an embarrassing byproduct of trade whose real end was use, is remade as a legitimate end. Even more important is the way that redemption (from states of despair and dependence)—equated with uninhibited circulation (the redeemed pirate) and the worthy subject—serves to constitute profit (that is, an accumulation of value) as trade's purpose. Trade is now the very sign of productivity. We have thus come full circle from the concerns that usury, and even any trade for profit, is nongenerative and results in stagnation—concerns discussed in depth in Chapter 2. Equating balanced circulation, trade, and profitability serves to eliminate the negative associations with trade for exchange value rather than for use value.

While balance of trade theorists conceived of a legitimate and reassuring profit, this tragicomedy goes a step further, constituting profit as trade's raison d'etre, taking the first step toward naturalizing profit and thus effacing the need to ask about its source and the loss elsewhere that would be necessary to counterbalance it.[89] If profit is expected, proleptically anticipated from the beginning, loss elsewhere ceases to be a present concern. Shifting the focus from use value to exchange value and to a trade that is, in a sense, self-sustaining and self-generating clears the way for the generation of profits and ultimately capital accumulation.

Redemption does double work in the play: it addresses the religious anxiety, which is real in and of itself, while making religion (and religious difference)—by requiring redemption—a vehicle for resolving the economic problems in the play. While the plot resolution in part depends on Donusa's conversion to Christianity—an act that makes her as well as Vitelli a potential martyr, since she has given up trying to convert

Vitelli as a way to save both of their lives—I would argue that the focus on conversion is secondary in some sense. Its main function is to foreground the importance of redemption for both of the primary male "renegados"—Grimaldi and Vitelli. My reading revises earlier critics' focus on conversion, rather than on the related (but not identical) redemption, as the play's primary vehicle for resolution.[90] Redemption assuages anxiety about temptation and its potential to devalue the European subject and impinge on that subject's autonomy, represented (and gendered) throughout by the threats of castration, from which Gazet narrowly escapes.[91] It also transforms actual commercial losses ensuing from the obstruction of trade into seemingly moderate, legitimate profits, disarming ethical objections to the making of profits. The play's initial concerns with the balancing of accounts is resolved via the concept of "buying back" to both imagine and legitimize a profit that involves not simply an equation, but a transformation of subjects and cash flows, perhaps represented in the alteration of Donusa and her jewels. ("Investment," whose prior meanings were related to religious offices and clothing, means "to give capital another form.")[92] Moreover, through restraint, redemption cancels out both overbalance and obstruction, providing the enabling conditions (circulation) through which profit can be retroactively installed as the very definition, that is, the natural expectation and raison d'être, of trade. It paves the way for the emergence of the concept of "investing" (whose economic meaning was newly minted in English in the correspondence of the English East India Company in 1613) as a way to reconfigure and revalue expenditure as productive of a future profit. As a result, profit, rather than loss, as I have discussed earlier, becomes the expectation of expenditure. In fact, the definition of "to invest" is to employ money with the expectation of profit or interest (*OED*). As I quoted from Mun earlier, "why should we then doubt that our monys sent out in trade, must not necessarily come back again in treasure; together with the great gains."

While critics of *The Renegado* have argued that the play's voyage home is final and absolute and that the goods are taken out of circulation, I want to argue that the emphasis on redemptive restraint allows for a different possibility, one in which what is taken from Tunis is more like capital for future endeavors. Rather than distance themselves from the economic transactions of Tunis, as Barbara Fuchs argues, redemption enables them to imagine honest participation in trade. Fuchs argues that "redeemed Christians remain redeemed, and distance themselves from the play's transactions and hard bargainings" (65). But the play's ending, like that of *The Island Princess*, is more ambivalent. While on the level of plot it is true that all of the Christian characters escape from

Tunis, it is also true that the act of leaving is a sign or expression of Grimaldi's redemptive protection of merchants. He is the one who prepares and "steals" the ship—an act that he earlier defines as necessary to his salvation. Thus, while leaving might appear to be a way to distance themselves from the complexities of trade in the region, it is also an expression of the redemption of the economic—even part of what constitutes the trade itself as redeemed and possible.[93] We can read Grimaldi's aid to merchants as the inverse of Gazet's giving up of his stones to purchase a privilege, which will no longer be of use to him. Grimaldi's actual and imagined roles (as aid to merchants and the play's fleeing characters) suture the escape and the redemption of merchants to one another.

Moreover, the restraint that Grimaldi and Vitelli exhibit, rather than supporting or leading to submission, provides a secure ground for a form of autonomy that would enable subjects to extend themselves across geographical boundaries without the risk of succumbing to temptations—of women, religion, or goods themselves.[94] Whereas redemption in *The Island Princess* enabled the imagining of free subjects and free trade, *The Renegado* takes the next step and employs redemption tragicomically to imagine those who trade as also autonomous subjects. Perhaps to exercise restraint, then, is to purchase one's own redemption, not through alms given to others, but through self-control (a form of self-investment). That investment leads to two forms of profit: spiritual redemption and earthly gain that in this case accrues from the ability to engage in foreign trade as a sovereign subject—a subject not susceptible to the literal contamination by the foreign culture or figurative contamination of the gain itself. What we can see here, then, is how the appropriation of goods as one's desert and the autonomy of the subject develop as interdependent concepts in the context of a foreign trade that depends on restraint and uninhibited circulation. Whereas comedies like *Twelfth Night* and *The Merchant of Venice* foreclose foreign contact in order to create a safely insular but also static economy, this tragicomedy constitutes autonomous subjects as part of a global economic system.

As in *The Island Princess*, the affective quality of tragicomedy is important to the resolution's effects. Overcoming the obstacles of participating in the real and imagined world of Tunis, the profits taken seem earned rather than stolen, a collaborative effort that represents an opportunity that is neither piracy, theft, or impotence. The escape feels more like liberation than permanent distance. Perhaps it would be fair to say that liberation never feels like a dead end, only a beginning. One could argue that it is the beginning of a redeemed trade on different, more equitable and harmonious terms. Such an interpretation depends on whether one reads the removed wealth as signs of the possibility of trade or as its last moment.

Also difficult to determine is the play's position on whether the profits of the European characters are dependent on the loss of the Ottoman characters. Unlike *The Island Princess*, the play ends not with harmony, but with the deceived viceroy's receiving the news that all of the European characters, with the assistance of Grimaldi, have escaped along with the choicest jewels and those who guarded the ship stowed beneath. The viceroy blames his credulity, and rather than vow revenge, plans to go off to live and die in some cave alone. From the Christian perspective, what is taken might be a form of victory. But as I have been arguing, the refusal of revenge and the exercise of restraint make the profits feel equitable. One might even read the foregoing of revenge on the part of the Christian characters as a kind of sacrifice or loss that produces these future profits. Moreover, the viceroy imagines only his individual responsibility and isolation and not that of the empire. In fact, he imagines himself as having failed his master; thus his isolation might be read as a way to distance not the English from the Ottomans, but the viceroy from the Ottomans.

These readings interpret the end of the play as imagining a future in which trade between the Europeans and the Ottomans can proceed smoothly and profitably. But it is also possible to read the tension between the surface of the plot and the work of redemption as highlighting some of the contradictions that emerge from the attempt to imagine equitable profit in a world that has only begun to imagine the idea of capital growth. The jewels, the Turks stowed underneath the hatches, and the farewell cannon shot might then be neither exclusive signs of retreat nor a decimating victory, but signs instead of both future potential ("their sails spread forth") and the limits of the earth resources (5.8.28). Paradoxically, the ground must still be paid for; yet the potential for capital growth seems to be without limits. The honest, "prosperous voyage" home is thus suggestive of an economy not static (like that represented in the ending of *Twelfth Night*) but whose boundaries, though grounded in restraint, are potentially endless.

On the one hand, we have a utopian fantasy; on the other, the paying for ground and even restraint might serve as reminders that the socioeconomic system imagined might outgrow itself. I conclude by building on Fredric Jameson's suggestion that the romance has a necessarily utopian dimension.[95] In part, this book's objective has been to historicize the "utopian" or dialectical aspects of tragicomedy as partially a product of nascent capitalism. Might not the "utopian" dialectical dimensions of early modern English tragicomedy—which appear in the transformation of losses into profits—be a specifically historical "response" to nascent capitalist processes?[96]

It might be that tragicomedy develops from the vestiges of the romance form to transform utopian thinking into a form that accommodates capital. It thus makes sense that Marx would embrace the tragicomic form as the vehicle for doing away with, or getting beyond, capitalism into the not yet seeable. Marx's narratives use capitalism against itself. In his analysis it is not the averted tragedy that produces its own resolution but historical conflicts that are themselves productive. In Marx's historiography capitalism's bourgeoisie will ultimately bring into being its own gravediggers—the modern proletariat—and the growth of capitalism will lead not to the "end of history," but to socialism.[97] In the epilogue we will see how Webster's undoing of tragicomedy and denaturalizing of the economics it represents serve to demystify the workings of capital, especially the intrinsic productive power accorded to it in order to engage with the possibility that the system's own productivity might lead to its undoing.

Epilogue

Webster's The Devil's Law-Case, *the Limits of Tragicomic Redemption, and Tragicomedy's Afterlife*

> *Jesus Died for Somebody's Sins,*
> *But not Mine.*
>
> —Patti Smith, *"In Excelsis Deo"*

The main character of Webster's *The Devil's Law-Case* (c. 1617–19), the merchant Romelio, could be read as an embodiment of the productive power of capital discussed in this book. He trades as "generally" as the Hollanders do; he has money invested in the East Indies trade; he vents gold from mines in the West Indies; he thinks the nobility a "superstitious relique of time past."[1] Moreover, his wealth has far-reaching effects. Not only do his enterprises abroad prevent a glut of coins, they also make wealthy men of those who work for him: even his factors' and scriveners' wives are decked out in velvet and live in palaces. No miser or usurer, Romelio has wealth that travels the globe, produces more of itself, and even to some extent trickles down, seeping into the fabric of the mercantile world over which he seems to preside. As we are told in the play's opening line, he has "shewen a world of wealth" (1.1.1).

This capitalist's potential is quickly linked to that of the play's genre. In the opening scene, Romelio's requisite self-introduction concludes with a variation on the tragicomic formula that also links the genre explicitly to the economics of the East Indies trade: "for Silver, / Should I not send it packing to th'East Indies, / We should have a glut on't" (1.1.26-28). Like the mercantilists I discussed in the Introduction, Webster here presents a positive argument for money leaving the country. But whereas the economic theorists needed to defend themselves against the accusation that currency leaving the country was resulting in a shortage of money and wealth that inhibited the circulation of goods and currency at home, Romelio argues that the export of capital is not a loss, and is actually a solution to an inversion of the actual problem: an overwhelming glut of money. As I have been arguing throughout this book, tragicomedy works by making the averted tragedy the means for resolution and by transforming loss into profit. Romelio's claim for the benefits of his trade takes that formula to an extreme so that even the problem is transformed into its opposite.

In some ways *The Devil's Law-Case* seems relentlessly interested in the tragicomic formula. Sprinkled throughout the play are variations on the theme of turning loss into gain: Romelio fetches a "man to life, to make a new Will";[2] he imagines that he can "breed / Out of the death of two Noble men / The advancement of [his] house"; another of his plots is figured as an engine that will "weigh up [his] losses" (3.2.81, 3.3.20–22, 2.3.169). But the most explicitly tragicomic moment is one he does not plan and which backfires on him. The play's plot and tragicomic conclusion depend on Romelio's failed attempt at revenge. After his sister's two suitors fatally wound each other in a duel, Romelio goes in disguise to take his revenge against one of the almost-dead suitors, Contarino, whom Romelio opposed as a choice for his sister. Though the suitor would have died anyway, Romelio stabs him to be sure of his death and have his revenge satisfied. But instead of killing Contarino, this redundant act cures him. Like the flow of money to the East Indies, the flow of blood proves beneficial: the new incision cures the suitor by making a "free passage for the congealed blood" that delivers "putrifaction" in "abundance" (3.2.159, 160).[3] In both instances, the tragicomic is explicitly linked to an idea of improved circulation, compressing the importance of foreign trade and the flow of the nation's lifeblood—money—as the mercantilist writers themselves were to do.[4]

All of these elements argue for seeing *The Devil's Law-Case* as a model case for the links this book has established between tragicomedy and early modern economic practices. Yet the play repeatedly refuses the productive power of tragicomic formulations. As Walter Cohen astutely observes, Webster "exploits none of [tragicomedy's] conventional opportunities."[5] His "procedure is to heighten or exaggerate the traditional motifs of tragicomedy to the point where they self destruct."[6] While *The Devil's Law-Case* continually invokes the importance of fluidity and the freeing of passages, the plot proceeds by fits and starts. It is not only that the play appears disconnected and fragmented, but also that nothing in the play works as it is supposed to. The play does have a happy ending, but the "resolution" neither develops from nor bears the trace of the play's earlier losses. Nor is there any sense that surplus value has been produced. Though the play's potential climax and recognition scene is described as the fruit of a "heartie penitence" and worthy of a "spatious publike Theater," the spectacle of it all is for nought (4.1.106, 109). The lawyer presiding over this courtroom scene concludes his part of the trial by announcing that "my definitive sentence in this cause, / Is, I will give no sentence at all," and the scene ends when the sister's second suitor encapsulates the scene by calling it "A most confused practice, that takes end / In as bloody a tryall" (4.2.465–66, 643–44). Refusing to allow the generic conventions of tragicomedy to be productive at every turn, Webster represents even the family as a source of perverse degeneration rather than restoration.

Given the failure of tragicomedy to work here, I want to pose two primary questions. Why does this tragicomedy not function as it is supposed to, and what are the implications of this dysfunction for the productive power of capital and theater? The answer to these questions might lie in the exaggeration that Cohen notices and in the play's relationship to excess, both thematic and formal.[7] From the play's opening moments when Romelio invokes the tragicomic formula in order to explain that his expenditures to the East Indies prevent a glut of money at home, he links the tragicomic to an economic productivity so extreme that the result might be tragic excess, an overwhelming flood that could be destructive if it were not the case that the productivity simultaneously produces its own outlet. *The Devil's Law-Case* thus raises overflow and excess as productivity's tragicomic spectre. The tragicomic ending in turn might lead to a tragicomic reversal. In this way, the play simultaneously invokes the redemptive formula—nothing transforming into something—and the possibility that excess might turn that something back into nothing. In this way, productivity threatens to undo itself. In what follows, I explore how the play as a whole raises the questions of tragicomedy's limits by exploring productivity's excesses. Taking the tragicomic formula and the forms of economic productivity with which it is associated to the extreme, Webster, I argue, gives us a play that demystifies both as the economic ethic of productivity labors its own undoing. I thus provide a speculative exploration of the limits for the productive relations among tragicomedy, capital, and redemption. I conclude the book by looking at the way proponents of an expanding market in the twenty-first century reinvoke tragicomedy's redemptive logic to rein in the kinds of excesses Webster's play imagines precisely in order to allow capital to ceaselessly reproduce itself.

Tragicomedy Undone

Webster's play could serve as a case study for the limitations of capital's productivity and its relationship to tragicomedy: it explores what happens when the ethics of capitalist markets are let loose on the world with no restraint, examining this problem in relation to the power of tragicomic reversal to make losses productive. Toward the end of the second act, soon after Romelio has found out that he has had severe losses at sea, which are described as "infinite," he explains that he has lost "three goodly Carracks" (2.3.1, 37). In an attempt to explain the magnitude of such a loss, Romelio claims that "the very Spice in them, had they been shipwrackt heere upon our coast, would have made all our Sea a Drench" (2.3.39–40). A "drench" is a dose of medicine usually given to an animal and often made of spices, but is also a poisonous draught. Given the association with spices, the first meaning of "medicine" might be the most relevant, but given the associations the play makes between wounds and cures and excess and loss, the second meaning of "poison" resonates as well. On the one hand, the transformation of the entire sea into a salubrious drink seems tragicomic. Yet the spectre raised, as in the avoided glut of coins, is that the trade will harm those it is intended to benefit. Such a possibility is raised explicitly in the binary poison/cure and in the suggestion that the sea, rather than a vehicle for the transport of spices, is also a medium of drowning, the other meaning of "drench." Drowning, of course, was a very real danger of those who labored on the ships that transported spices to and from the East Indies.

Moreover, if the sea is reified into the commodity whose transport it enables—that is, if it is transformed from a sea into a cure made of spices—the result is the elimination of the sea as such. The trade in spice, then, is so excessive that it potentially takes over everything, even the means by which the trade in it is conducted and thus by which it can be made valuable at home. In this case, trade is imagined to have the potential to eliminate the "free passage" necessary to its own existence and thus to eliminate its own conditions of possibility. Here the tragicomic formula, in which loss produces profits, seems not just to reverse itself but actually to undo itself, such that the spice (the proceeds of the initial loss of coin) produces an excess that is yet more loss, creating the very glut threatened in the play's opening.[8] Loss here is imagined not only to be productive as in the tragicomic model, but also to be a potential sign of an ultimately destructive power inherent within productivity as well. Inverting the implications of the positive associations of productivity, Webster insightfully recognizes a glitch in the logic of endless productivity provided by the theories of circulation discussed in Chapter 5. The Devil's Law-Case invokes the idea that productivity itself will not likely be endless, and that it might have other unforeseen or disavowed costs.

Of course, Romelio is exaggerating. But his exaggeration is the point. His imagination of spice that transforms the sea matters in the play in a larger abstract way as well. What happens if trade, like the spice dumped into the sea, becomes the medium par excellence? What if the ethics of trade permeate everything?

Of particular importance to this study of the relationship between redemption, tragicomedy, and economic practices is the way that the play, by secularizing the notion of redemption and thus re-separating the economic from the religious, imagines the excessive productivity of the economic as its takeover of everything. Critics have certainly noticed the relentless secularism of the play's primary character, Romelio.[9] Unlike *The Renegado*, which is much dependent on a Jesuit for its plot resolution, Webster's play and its merchant, Romelio, repeatedly refuse the spiritual advice of the Capuchin. In addition, Romelio mocks and queries religious precepts, for example, on death and burial. After news of his losses, he responds that now he has nothing to fear. Such a response is anathema to the Capuchin, who worries that such presumption will lead to sin. It is not only within Romelio that such secularism seems to lay. When one of the surgeons suggests that "the hand of heaven" was at work in transforming Romelio's intent to kill into a cure, his analysis is undermined by the second surgeon's likening of the case to one in England in which a prisoner was cured of gout by being racked in the Tower (3.2.162, 164–65).

Perhaps the most significant example of such a demystification occurs in Romelio's description of his plan after his losses are revealed to him. Immediately after Romelio confesses not to fear future loss, he is told that the suitor his sister preferred made her the sole heir in his will. This information is what motivates Romelio to make sure that Contarino dies. (This is the action that saves Contarino.) He says he "must visit *Contarino*, upon that / Depends an Engine shall weigh up my losses, / Were they sunk as low as hell (2.3.168–70). Though in only the previous scene Romelio has rejected related religious principles, here religious redemption, as is typical within tragicomedy, is the vehicle through which he imagines the recuperation of his losses; they will be redeemed from "hell." What matters, however, is that religious redemption for Romelio is a vehicle; by that I mean *only* a vehicle in the literary sense. For Romelio, hell is only figurative and the idea of redemption becomes secular through its figurative use of hell. As a result, his tragicomic plan is demystified in both the strong and casual senses of that term: the practical aspects of the plan are disassociated from the magical formulation associated with religion in general and redemption in particular, and the real concerns are potentially laid bare. As a result, the hand of heaven everywhere is now replaced by the economic everywhere, which in turn has the potential to self-destruct from the very overreaching that its displacement of the religious suggests. Not just his plan, but also tragicom-

edy and the self-generating productivity of capital imagined by the mercantilists are demystified here.

My intention is not to suggest that Webster provides a moral tale in
which a turn away from religious principles or extraction of religion
leads to a (paradoxically) destructive upward spiral. Instead, the play's
drive toward secularity reveals the mystification at work in the triangulation of religious redemption, tragicomedy, and capital's productive energy. *The Devil's Law-Case*, then, is concerned not to demonstrate the
evils of a purely economic as opposed to a pure and purely religious
world, but to show both how the economic and the religious are deeply
imbricated and how the logic of economic productivity depends on religious principles that serve only to mystify the actual processes by which
capital is accumulated. This dependence is evidenced in the title, which
invokes a theological worldview only to subordinate that view to the secular authority of the law, both of which seem doomed by the connection.
Perhaps Webster glimpses throughout *The Devil's Law-Case* what Marx
would articulate two and a half centuries later: how deeply capitalism
shares its mystifications with religion in general and Christianity in particular, and how capitalism is likely to create its own gravediggers.[10]

Un-Brave New World: Discovering the East Indies in a Theater Without Wonder

What, then, are the implications of this demystification for the world of
the theater and its associations with productive power and capital? To
answer this question I turn to the play's engagement with spectacle. Unlike the other tragicomedies in this book, *The Devil's Law-Case* contains
no oracle or riddle, not even a false prophet. Instead what we have is a
lawsuit whose content is deemed by the plaintiff's lawyer to be worthy of
a "spatious publike Theater." (The theatrical connection is reinforced by
details that also highlight the economics of theater: for example, one of
the supposedly dead suitors pays a bribe both to gain entrance to the
hearing of the case and for a good vantage point.) The reason for the
lawyer's claim is the highly unusual, even unnatural, matter at its center.
Leonora, Romelio's mother, brings this suit in order to take revenge on
her son for his supposed murder of Contarino, who as we recall was one
of the suitors of Romelio's sister, Leonora's daughter. (We also recall
that Contarino is not actually dead, but Leonora is not aware of that
fact.) Leonora, too, was in love with this suitor of her daughter. In this
suit, Leonora accuses her own son of being a bastard, an accusation that
depends on publicly accusing herself of adultery. In a scene that is likely
in critical dialogue with the finale of *The Winter's Tale*, what is staged is
not a revivification of a wrongly accused mother and wife, but a court

case in which the mother accuses herself in order to disinherit her son and thus compound his previous losses, leaving him penniless.

Reversing *The Winter's Tale*'s trajectory from loss to profit and even, as I argued earlier, from loss to theatrical surplus value, this spectacle's goal is debasement not only of its characters, but perhaps of its own form as well. Prior to the hearing's commencement the clerk for the civil-lawyer presiding over the case says that Leonora has that "in her belly will drie up your inke" (4.1.1–2). The image suggests that the family is presented as a dead end rather than as a source of restoration and regeneration.[11] It also suggests that the spectacle the audience is about to witness will serve more as a form of punctuation, that is, a disruption to the plot, or even plotting itself.

Indeed, what the play serves up here is a whole lot of spectacle for nothing. This is so because her case depends on the claim that Romelio's actual father was a Spaniard, Don Crispiano, who was a friend of her husband's and who got her pregnant while her husband was away traveling. When a picture of Don Crispiano is brought into the court, the lawyer presiding over the case takes off his disguise and reveals himself to be that very same Crispiano, though—in a statement that recalls and inverts the aged statue of *The Winter's Tale*—he points out that the self represented in the picture was forty years younger. Having already removed himself from the case since he is a party to it (he had said his definitive sentence was that he would pronounce no sentence at all), he then exonerates himself by explaining that he could not be the father: he went to the East Indies four years before Romelio's conception and did not set foot in Europe until the present month.

But the scene does not end there. The other suitor, Ercole, also thought to be dead but actually living, reveals himself and accuses Romelio of having killed Contarino. But the only evidence for this is Leonora's word, and she is now discredited. In order to resolve the issue, a duel is planned between Romelio and Ercole. All that comes of the suit and the spectacle of the mother accusing herself of adultery is the plan of a duel to settle the death of the suitor thought to have died after fighting in a duel. While one suitor is revealed to be alive in this scene, the promised recognition of father and son is avoided. The reunion is thus no real reunion, the discovery is no real discovery, and the only revelation (that Romelio has killed Contarino) is actually false. The plot is repeatedly interrupted by the revelation of fictions. When fictions are revealed as such in other tragicomedies the revelation leads to resolution, but here the revelations all fall flat. The only actual crime the case exposes is the case itself, which turns out to be a false accusation. Moreover, the mother's revenge that prompts the suit and the duel that results from it are superfluous, since Contarino is not dead. Unlike *The*

Winter's Tale, whose spectacle functions to create value out of loss and to make the fact that Hermione is not dead theatrically valuable, here the fact that the suitors are not dead only makes the spectacle pointless. Similarly, when Leonora and the Capuchin later present a dumb show of coffins and winding sheets to Romelio just before his duel in order to "startle" him and make him "know whither [he] is going," Romelio only pretends to be penitent, a pretense that enables him to lock the Capuchin and his mother in a closet to allow him to duel uninhibited (5.4.117, 118). In lines that again are in stark contrast to the end of *The Winter's Tale*, Romelio only feigns to have been cured and redeemed by a miraculous spectacle: "O you have wrought a myracle, and melted / A heart of Adamant, you have compris'd/ In this dumbe Pageant, a right excellent forme / Of penitence" (5.4.138–41).

In *The Devil's Law-Case*, spectacle—bringing something into view, or making something materially present—has ultimately no purpose other than its own existence (as in the courtroom scene) or its purpose is anti-redemptive. In the courtroom scene in particular, the theater provides an excessive spectacle but one that has no value added—not, for example, the surplus value ascribed to Hermione's statue come to life, which redeems its audience like a disciplinary mint.[12] What we get in both of these scenes is spectacle without wonder.[13] If anything, these scenes are anti-wondrous; the potential for revelation to cause wonder is undermined and shown to be ineffectual, even spurious.

Through its insistence on secularity, *The Devil's Law-Case* removes the fiction of theater's surplus value. It leaves you only with the pleasure of viewing that which is not true, cannot be resolved, and cannot deliver anything like equity or justice. Perhaps because the spectacle is just spectacle—it offers no other end and no magical component—it does not call upon the audience to engage with a wondrous event, but instead offers only the perverse satisfaction of the absence of any resolution. In this way, Webster's tragicomedy might be, as Jonathan Dollimore suggests of Webster's tragedies, Brechtian in its intended effects on its audience.[14] *The Devil's Law-Case*, however, combines the detachment of Brechtian alienation with the pleasure of the excessive failures of the plot. Thus it offers a demystified theater, one that gives you everything at face value.

In order to connect this reading of the reduction of the theater's surplus value back to the economics of foreign trade, the other primary subject of this book, I want briefly to investigate the importance of foreign commerce and contact in this play. Unlike the other tragicomedies discussed in this book, *The Devil's Law-Case* takes place entirely at home in Naples. The economic world the play imagines, however, is global. Romelio has money in mines in the West Indies, and he sends money to the East Indies to conduct trade there. Battles with the Ottoman Empire are mentioned more than once. Though none of these locations is made into spectacle (that is, the foreign locations are not represented on the stage) each is relevant to the plot. Crispiano, who is crucial to the failure of Leonora's suit, has returned to Naples only in order to spy on Romelio because of his illicit activities in the West Indies' mines; Crispiano remembers distinctly that he was not in Naples when Romelio was conceived because it was 1571, the year of the celebrated sea battle of Lepanto, which was seen to mark the end of Ottoman expansion in Europe; and the marriage of Romelio's sister to Ercole (a Knight of Malta) is rushed at the play's beginning because of an impending battle with the Turks. In each of these cases, while the foreign economy, or scene, is not materialized in the play, it is to some extent made relevant to the domestic situation—domestic both in the sense of at home and of the family. These foreign scenes thus have an effect on the play and its movement, or lack of movement, even if from afar.

While all of these foreign locales have some relevance to the play, I want to argue that the East Indies occupy a special place, especially for the way the play imagines the relationship between theater and productive value. The East Indies is crucial to the plot in three ways. First, as I mentioned above, Crispiano cannot be Romelio's father because he was in the East Indies when Romelio was conceived. Moreover, Crispiano's fortuitous return *from* the East Indies to spy on Romelio leads to the non-recognition/recognition scene that disrupts Leonora's attempt at revenge. Finally, the play's resolution, such as it is, depends on the fact that one of the surgeons who witnessed Contarino's "miraculous" return to life convinces Leonora's waiting woman to tell the Capuchin that Contarino is still alive, thus ending the duel between Ercole and Romelio with which the play closes. That surgeon was supposed to be not at home in Naples, but in the East Indies. Romelio had hoped to "vent" him there in order to prevent the surgeon from speaking of his role in Contarino's death. But the surgeon does not go because of trouble with the Dutch there. If the surgeon had gone to the East Indies as he was supposed to, it is not entirely clear that the information about Contarino would be revealed at the necessary time. The East Indies thus functions as a place to exit/issue to, or to come back from. It operates as a kind of imaginative theatrical offstage, or space of discovery, a "material" source for the disruption of the play's revenge plot and for the play's more harmonious, if contrived and unsatisfying, resolution.

One could argue that all of the tragicomedies' endings are in some sense contrived, but in *The Winter's Tale* at least, as I argued at the end of Chapter 3, spectacle and theatrical surplus value overcompensate for that lack of credibility; indeed they produce surplus value out of that very poverty. The excessive spectacularity of *The Devil's Law-Case* (excessive because it has no value and produces no real profit) lacks wonder, but perhaps in the place of wonder it has the East Indies as a source, if not for value, then for the material of the play itself. It is not only money that flows to and from the East Indies, but characters as well. The East Indies, then, is not just a place to send money to or to bring money back from, but is a place that enables exits, entrances, and value to be supplied to the theater as well.

If the East Indies is represented as a figurative source for the play, and even a source for theatrical contrivance—a place where you can send characters that are in the way and retrieve characters that you need— might the East Indies also serve as a kind of funding source—even a kind of capital, symbolic or otherwise—for the theater? *The Devil's Law-Case* imagines the East Indies as providing stock for the play, that is, theatrical capital. This connection is only figurative, of course. But the use of the East Indies as a source for the play and perhaps a source for what replaces or prevents wonder might serve to remind the audience of the relationship between the institution of the theater (which often shared a financial structure—the joint-stock—with long-distance trading companies like the English East India Company) and the capital required to produce and reproduce theatrical properties. William Ingram has demonstrated convincingly how the theater came into being in relation to two economic laws. First, the Act of the Court of Common Council of 6 December 1574 levied a number of potential fees, licenses, bonds, and guarantees to be paid by those who housed plays in order to redistribute money ill spent on the unproductive and profligate pleasure of the theater to the more worthy support of those in need.[15] Given that the assessment of fees was in some sense dependent more on the worth of the establishment than on the profits of the play, providing a space for plays could be a risky business. As Ingram suggests, the risks resulting from the civic redistribution of wealth might have served as an incentive for the building of permanent playhouses in 1576. Ingram also suggests that the 1571 usury statute, which by limiting the practice of usury also tacitly sanctioned it, made possible and feasible a market for the borrowing and lending of money in London necessary to the emergence of permanent playhouses.[16] To overstate the case only slightly, the theater emerges in opposition to a civic attempt to redistribute necessities to the poorer commoners. The theater, then, abandons a model of charity in favor of a model of capital investment enabled by its more positive relation with the 1571 statute. This play might go a step further to connect the theater not just to laws that affected the money supply circulating at home, but to a larger global economy that needs to be reintegrated at home.

We thus could see capital as the replacement for wonder; indeed the play opens with the observation that Romelio has "*shewen* a world of wealth" (emphasis added). On the one hand, we could read the play as an exercise in what happens if we demystify theater, if we rob it of wonder and magic, and reveal just the capital that makes it work. Yet, as I have mentioned, there is also the sheer pleasure of watching the play not work. If the play is made out of an accumulation of events, a pile up of details, a congealed passage, all stripped bare of anything but their apparency, we are left with just a "confused practice," but one whose pleasures might provide a kind of value stripped of productivity—value not dependent on the transformation of loss into profit or the reproductive value transferred to and through heirs.

Crispiano's outlook might be useful in understanding the play's lack of productivity. He returns from the East Indies a very wealthy civil lawyer disguised as a merchant to find his son a prodigal who exceeds the "exhibition" allowed him—wenching, hunting, and so on (2.1.7).[17] Crispiano's objection, however, is atypical. He hopes that his son will only have more pleasure spending his allowance than Crispiano did getting it. If Crispiano's wishes were fulfilled in this way, he would not care if all his wealth "waste to as small an atomy as Flies / I'th Sunne" (2.1.24–25). Remember it is Crispiano's return from the East Indies that disrupts the court spectacle and leads to the pronouncement of a sentence that is no sentence and to an anti-revelation. His hope for his son's pleasure in the mere action of spending mirrors the pleasure that results from Webster's refusal to make everything, or even anything, work in the play's resolution and even in the play's construction. If the play provides something of a critique of the genre's, or even the theater's, ability to create surplus value out of its spectacles—where surplus value derives from the audience's wonder and their consequent desire to return and pay for repeated entrances—it on the other hand imagines pleasure. That pleasure, however, might be a commensurate exchange for the price paid for entrance, which in turn is the actual source for the theater's existence, or at least the existence of that day's performance. The theater's demystification—in the equation of payment and pleasure—then eliminates its potential to claim surplus value of either the material or ideal kind. The audience would get what it paid for and those who create the theater's effects would get paid for their visible labor as well—labor no longer concealed, or even congealed, in the theater's attempts to mask its own machinery.

Moreover, the pleasure the play affords is in the refusal to make reproductive power central even at the level of genre. Webster's play is filled with uneasy fits: from the difficulty of making plots work the way they are supposed to, to the difficulty of reintegrating profit, people, and products at home (people do not leave when they are supposed to and come back unexpectedly). These uneasy fits mirror the uneasy accommodation of theater to capital that the play imagines. If the economic is everywhere, it is also in some sense defused of the redemptive power to insist on its own reproduction—a defusion that returns to the theater some of its own power to provide pleasure with no need for a productive outlet. The play thus highlights the potential for productivity to undo itself and offers a model of pleasure without productivity in its place.

Tragicomedy's Afterlife

The argument of this book has been that tragicomic plays mediate between notions of redemption and newly developing economic practices, thus helping to explain how what seems like loss in the economic sphere could actually be a source of profit and productivity. The genre of tragicomedy persists on the stage in the later seventeenth century and beyond. My hope for this study of the early days of tragicomedy and its connection to global economics is that it helps to illuminate that later history and stimulate studies of it. But given the limitations of tragicomedy in the face of excess and demystification that a play like Webster's enacts, I want to conclude by looking briefly at the viability of tragicomedy outside of the literary domain and instead in the context of twenty-first century geoeconomic politics that seek either to rein in or make use of capitalism's excesses, or both. I do so in order to explore the way that the logic of redemption does and does not continue to negotiate the relationship between loss and profit, and does and does not enable economic forces to reproduce themselves without restraint or limitation.

I begin with an example that is most explicitly about transforming loss into literal profit. About ten months after Hurricane Katrina devastated New Orleans and many other cities along the Gulf Coast, a short piece entitled "Tragicommerce: How a Terrible News Event Made the Transition to Commodity" appeared in the Sunday *New York Times Magazine*. This article provides the history of the development of "Da Mayor in Your Pocket," a talking toy that repeats (mostly embarrassing) sound bites from an interview with New Orleans mayor C. Ray Nagin in the aftermath of the crisis.[18] The article, which has a playful (if not mocking) tone, calls attention to the transformation of the disaster and a news event relating to it into an object for consumption that, according to the product developer, "makes sense in a perverse, New Orleans kind of way." The author speculates that the mere "existence of such a thing offers relief as evidence that life goes on." I would add that it thus also offers evidence of the redemptive possibilities of this material (in both the strict and colloquial senses) world.[19] "Tragicommerce" is perhaps a fully secular version of redemption, one that takes the recoding that we see in early modern notions of "investment" and tragicomedy to its furthest extreme. The article, of course, does not link tragicomedy and commerce tout court but it, as does its neologism "tragicommerce," literalizes the productive relationship between (nonaverted) tragic events and their profitable outcomes. Loss and the representation of loss (in the mayor's comments) are tragicomically transformed into a literal profit. In its replacement of "comedy" by "commerce," the neologism "tragicommerce" semi-ironically raises the possibility that commerce is itself a form of redemption.

Even when tragicomedy is not explicitly invoked in the representation and exploration of current geopolitical events and concerns, this logic (in which the market is redemptive) is at work, or at least embedded, in the ways through which these events are understood, represented, or even enacted. I employ the following examples to explore the variety of ways in which the development of ideas about loss and productivity continue to depend on the tragicomic's redemptive processes. In particular, I am interested in the ways that redemption, tragicomic think, and capital triangulate in a global economy that would seemingly no longer need the idea of redemption to provide a model for transforming loss into profit—a need, as I have argued throughout this book, that emerged in the early years of England's participation in a global economy.

Many current violent conflicts, especially those waged or supported by the West in general and the United States in particular, are represented/marketed as an especially secular and economic form of redemption—the universalizing and proselytizing spread of freedom, democracy, and market values as they are linked in neoliberalism. I turn first to a problem that is on the surface at the furthest remove from the explicitly economic concerns that are this book's focus but which, because of its ironic tone, helps to illuminate the logical connection between neoliberalism and redemption. A headline in the satiric *Onion*'s *Top Ten Stories of 2006* issue reads, "Israel Bombs Anti-Semitism out of Lebanon."[20] In satiric mode, the article proceeds to quote interviews with victims who claim to have seen the light and to have given up their hatred for Jews and the state of Israel after losing homes, family members, and limbs. Though satiric (and admittedly also insensitive), the article highlights an aspect of this particular conflict along with the logic that underlies so much of current geopolitical violence: the idea that violence is not only ultimately redeemed by the positive, prosperous, beneficial outcome it produces (as might be the case in Fletcher's *The Island Princess* or Massinger's *The Renegado*) but also that violence is the very means, even the only means, to achieve a state of redemption.

In his study of the relationship between religion and capital markets, *Confidence Games: Money and Markets in a World Without Redemption*, Mark C. Taylor, for example, argues that the United States represents the threat of other countries as an evil in order to provide the "opportunity for America to redeem itself."[21] In *Formations of the Secular*, Talal Asad argues that the violence is understood as a means to redemption. He argues that liberalism justifies itself as a force fighting an encroaching jungle that threatens to overwhelm the enlightened space it occupies and represents. The forces of liberalism then must attack the jungle to keep it back. Distinguishing the violence of enlightenment from that of the jungle itself, liberalism claims the right to use violence precisely when it redeems the world.[22] As President George W. Bush said in a press conference in April 2004, "freedom is the Almighty's gift to every man and woman in this world. As the greatest power on earth we [the Unites States] have an obligation to help the spread of freedom." In Asad's more critical terms, liberal politics "must dominate the unredeemed world—if not by reason then alas by force—in order to survive."[23] The logic of redemption is thus employed to counter an encroaching jungle that must be beaten back not just to preserve the space that liberalism occupies, but especially to spread neoliberalism everywhere in order to make sure that the market manifests its global destiny. This attempt to spread neoliberal ideas is based on a messianic vision of the end of history that depends on an idea of redemption in the loose sense—that is, a saving of the world through the spread of a particular set of ideas—and in which loss is thought to produce a financial profit. Out of violence comes the redeemed and market-oriented (if not fully capitalist) state.

Destruction is thus deemed ultimately productive as a way of spreading liberal democracy in which "market exchange is an ethic in itself, capable of acting as a guide to all human action" and in which the market is considered a morally superior form of political economy and a paradigm for understanding and structuring social life, including politics.[24] Self-interest, profit, and individualism are thus reformed as both ends and means: they are goals and guiding principles as well. Profit, though, has in some sense dropped out of this conversation in the most explicit sense because fundamental to the ideology of neoliberalism is that the market ethic needs to be and is everywhere (geographically and within all domains of social existence). The market and the principles that support it are then understood to constitute the benefit, since the principles of the market are understood to be those that will best guide humanity. Literal financial profit thus drops out of the equation because it is paradoxically masked by its replacement with the ethic that supports it and is also the self-evident goal. Given profit's self-evidence, redemption serves not to help imagine profit's possibility in the face of loss, as it did in the early modern period. Instead, the existence of the market and its goals everywhere is imagined to be the state of redemption.

In this vision of neoliberalism, there is no limit to the productively re-demptive power of the market, no chance that the sea will turn into the poisonous, rather than salving, drench imagined in *The Devil's Law-Case*. Yet even supporters of a "free" market economy must contend with the reality of the market's negative consequences: from global warming and oil spills to the displacement of workers from their home countries. I conclude with examples of the ways that participants in the market con-tinue to depend on the logic of redemption to rein in not the market's forces, but its potentially negative consequences.

A recent *New York Times* article on the "carbon-neutral" phenomenon, in which individuals and corporations put money into others' projects that would offset the amount of greenhouse gases their own activities produce, is accompanied by an illustration of a man on his knees, hands clasped in prayers, tears running down his face. His confessor holds a bag of money he has just received from the penitent, who says, "Forgive me for I have S.U.V.'d." The confessor says, "Go thy way. Thy sins are off-set." Framing the top of the illustration is a banner with the motto, "re-pentance and redemption"; in the background the offending vehicle is driving away leaving clouds of pollution in its wake.[25] According to the article, environmentalists are in disagreement about the neutrality and effectiveness of these offsets. The president of an environmental grant-making group likens the worst of the program to the Roman Catholic Church's sale of indulgences before the Protestant Reformation. The ar-ticle's author, Andrew Revkin, sums up the environmentalists' disap-proval by saying that the programs are "easy on the sacrifice and big on the consumerism"—hence, the illustration's emphasis on confession and redemption. The problem, however, is not only that consumption and sacrifice take place in unequal amounts; it is the distribution that matters. Combining the idea of Roman Catholic indulgences with the logic of Christ's sacrifice, carbon-neutral offsets work by having "sinners" pay someone else to sacrifice for them. Rather than Christ's purchasing our sins through an overabundance of God's mercy, we pay someone else to redeem us so that we can, in effect, keep on sinning. Moreover, the terms of the market, like investment (terms that, as I have argued throughout this study, have developed through a reforming and refunc-tioning of Christian ideas of redemption), now dictate the relationship between sacrifice and redemption. While "Da Mayor in Your Pocket" might be a benign example of how one person's loss is transformed into profit reaped elsewhere, programs like the carbon-neutral scheme give us insight into the potential tragedies that await us when an unstoppable market can displace pain and suffering elsewhere. That market does not threaten the environment alone. Corporate globalization has displaced hundreds of millions of migrant workers whose only chance for legitimacy, in the United States at least, depends on the realization that their underpaid labor is necessary to the market's unimpeded progress. Without their participation in that progress, those who are already citizens might have to sacrifice for themselves.

While the ostensible purpose of the carbon neutral program and immigration reform is to rein in the market (even the immigration debate is framed as an attempt to prevent abuses), the real purpose, of course, is to allow some to continue their current practices without guilt and to stave off environmental disaster for individual societies or the globe as a whole. While the latter might be a worthwhile goal, these kinds of programs and reforms also allow for twenty-first-century commercial (business and consumption) practices to go on uninterrupted. People can run their corporations, fly to their meetings, and live the lifestyle that centuries of productivity have brought into being, while doing their part (or some part) to make certain that all of the "spice" they import or consume does not turn the sea into a drench.

A similar phenomenon has emerged in what has come to be called the "fourth sector," organizations dedicated to traditional commercial goals and noncommercial benefits—what one *New York Times* writer, Stephanie Strom, refers to as "social *purpose* and financial *promise*."[26] This article is interestingly titled, "Make Money, Save the World: Businesses and Nonprofits are Spawning Corporate Hybrids." The mixed corporate genre to which they refer also takes different forms: some are more like the carbon-neutral programs in that profits are diverted to "good" ends, but the means by which those profits are made remain unexamined. Others are more experimental, trying to do both things at once. These companies try to make money through products and services that benefit the community, what one entrepreneur explains as "embedding social responsibility in everything we do." The former still only brings market logic to the fulfillment of social responsibility. The latter does not, but it remains unclear the extent to which the market as it is can accommodate these changes. The real change would be to let the social values alter the market, but as the article suggests, that proves to be very difficult. That which is in the market seems to need to behave according to its overriding principles. Thus the majority of these corporate/socially responsible hybrids, like the neoliberal programs they are intended to partially rein in, imagine the market and its forces to have a role in the creation of a better world.

All of these examples partially beg a question that I raised in the outset of this section: if the recoding of Christian redemption served to facilitate the development of capitalism at a very specific historical juncture, why does tragicomic/redemption think still persist in the era of late-capital globalization? A full answer to this question would require a fuller consideration of the history of secularization and the force of theology within it, as well as a history of capitalism. That would lead to the beginning of another book, rather than the end of the present one. But I will speculate here briefly on an answer to this important question. A partial answer might lie in the affective pull of the possibility of redemption, especially in a world that seems simultaneously to be increasingly secular and increasingly religious in its orientation. A more economic answer might lie in the persistence of worries about loss: if loss is inherent to a late capitalism that threatens with excess as much as early forms of capitalism threatened with scarcity, redemption's transformative powers still have a role to play. An even more specific answer might be found in both the aim of neoliberal thinkers and those who understand the market as socially responsible without insisting that the market itself is social responsibility par excellence, as neoliberalists do. As I suggested above, the point of these programs and projects is to allow the market to continue to grow as if that growth is without legitimate opposition or negative consequences. In my reading of Webster's *The Devil's Law-Case*, I argued that the separation of the economic from the religious, which results from the secularization of redemption, serves to highlight the dangers of productivity as the economic takes over everything in its path. I therefore suggest that neoliberal thinkers and corporate directors redeploy redemption in the late twentieth and early twenty-first centuries, not as the early mercantilists and joint-stock companies did—to explain how loss could produce profit—but to reimagine excess not only not as loss-producing, but as the result of a triumph against potentially antimarket forces and as the material that constitutes and defines our ever-expanding world economy. Redemption thus eliminates opposition.

This reimagination succeeds in part because what remains unquestioned in neoliberal thought, the carbon-neutral programs, the fourth-sector hybrids that attempt to do good deeds with their profits, and even to some extent in proposed immigration reform legislation, is the goal of productivity itself. Such programs merely accommodate us and our world to the reach and logic of the market. These programs create the opportunity for the market to overreach even as they seek to prevent certain of its negative excesses. The limits of the tragicomic model, in which loss is continuously made productive and transformed into profits—limits glimpsed in the antiproductive effects of the excess of capitalism in *The Devil's Law-Case*—are through these programs ceaselessly stretched. The tragicomic redemptions they enact enable the market economy to remain unquestioned. Such programs defer the day we might be called to account. But the way of neoliberalism, which provides market rather than politically and socially equitable solutions to global, environmental, and humanitarian problems, only seeks to eliminate the dialectical struggle between the forces of the market and those who bare its costs.

In the structure of dialectical struggle is the possibility for managing or even negotiating current socioeconomic problems as well as producing as yet unimagined alternatives. In the Introduction, I argued that tragicomic redemption has dialectical potential: the presence of comic and tragic elements allows for productive contradictions; moreover, as opposed to comedy, tragicomedy provides a more dialectical model that imagines extension rather than contraction and allows the plays to engage with problems, rather than circumvent or simply transform them. While the comedies I discuss in the first chapter fail to imagine expansion and productivity because they are not dialectical, it might be the case that tragicomedies, in their dialectical form, contain the potential (as does *The Devil's Law-Case*) to imagine the undoing of capitalism's insistence on a narrative of productivity. These more recent examples of the deployment of tragicomic logic suggest that the dialectical narrative structure, which is a potential of the tragicomic, can also be what the tragicomic narrative represses, especially when its outcome—productivity—remains unquestioned and even becomes the purpose of future deployments of the narrative. Perhaps, then, we need to investigate the effects of socioeconomic theory and practice that privilege productivity so as not to limit the potential for the kinds of transformations that dialectical struggle can produce. Turning our attention elsewhere—perhaps to distribution and even to consumption—might yield another scene of possibility—one that might make for a different and perhaps better, more equitable world.

Notes

Introduction

1. Flynn and Giráldez argue that global trade begins in 1571, the year the city of Manila was founded, thus the first time that there was a direct trade link between America and Asia, and therefore when all "important populated continents began to exchange products continuously . . . and in values sufficient to generate crucial impacts on all trading partners." Dennis Flynn and Arturo Giráldez, "Born with a 'Silver Spoon': The Origin of World Trade in 1571," in *Metals and Monies in an Emerging Global Economy,* ed. Flynn and Giráldez (Brookfield, Vt.: Variorum, 1997), 259–79.

2. John Lyly, *Midas,* ed. David Bevington (Manchester: Manchester University Press, 2000), Prologue in Paul's (13–15, 20–22).

3. An arras is a tapestry that has a story woven into it.

4. The shortage of bullion was a condition of Europe since at least the late Middle Ages, but it was a new problem for England. In *Money and Its Use in Medieval Europe,* Peter Spufford compares England in the Middle Ages to an oil-producing nation, "an island well supplied with money, because of its wool, even when the rest of Europe was suffering from a bullion shortage." In fact, he analogizes the flow of silver *to* England in the Middle Ages to the flow of silver sent to the East *by* the English East India Company in the seventeenth century—the very outflow defended by East India Company merchants participating in these debates (Cambridge: Cambridge University Press, 1988), 388–90.

5. For discussions of the East India Company's reliance on imports and re-exports rather than English exports, see K. N. Chaudhuri, *The English East India Company: The Study of an Early Joint-Stock Company, 1600–1640* (New York: August Kelley, 1965), and Robert Brenner, *Merchants and Revolution: Commercial Change, Political Conflict, and London's Overseas Traders, 1550–1653* (Princeton, N.J.: Princeton University Press, 1993). For a more extensive discussion of the complexities of England's trade with the East Indies, see Chapter 4.

6. Thomas Mun, *England's Treasure by Forraign Trade* (1664), Reprints of Economic History Classics (Oxford: Basil Blackwell, 1928), 14. Though published in 1664, the text was written between 1623 and 1628.

7. Mark Blaug, ed., *The Early Mercantilists: Thomas Mun (1571–1641), Edward Misselden (1608–1634), Gerard de Malynes (1586–1623)* (Aldershot, England: Elgar, 1991), xi.

8. The primary participants in these debates—Gerald Malynes, a master of assay

at the mint, Edward Misselden, a member first of the Merchant Adventurers and later of the English East India Company, and Thomas Mun, a director of the East India Company—would not have considered themselves of the same school of thought, however. On the contrary, they were often in disagreement with each other. This was especially the case for Malynes. At the heart of the debate was the question of whether the wealth of the country depended on keeping money within the kingdom. For insightful discussions of the terms and impact of these debates, see Joyce Appleby, *Economic Thought and Ideology in Seventeenth-Century England* (Princeton, N.J.: Princeton University Press, 1978); Mary Poovey, *A History of the Modern Fact: Problems of Knowledge in the Sciences of Wealth and Society* (Chicago: University of Chicago Press, 1998); Andrea Finkelstein, *Harmony and Balance: An Intellectual History of Seventeenth-Century English Economic Thought* (Ann Arbor: University of Michigan Press, 2000); and Jonathan Gil Harris, *Sick Economies: Drama, Mercantilism, and Disease in Shakespeare's England* (Philadelphia: University of Pennsylvania Press, 2004).

9. See Thomas Mun, *A Discourse of Trade from England unto the East-Indies: Answering to diverse Objections which are usually made against the same* (London, 1621); Thomas Mun, *England's Treasure*; and Edward Misselden, *The Circle of Commerce. Or the Balance of Trade, in defence of free trade: Opposed to Malynes Little Fish and his Great Whale, and poized against them in the Scale* (London, 1623).

10. This theory is, in fact, considered wrong by modern economists because it does not take into account the effect of an increased money supply—primarily a raise in domestic prices and thus imports. Its account of the actual flows of the economy is thus only partial. Modern economists have been somewhat bemused by this error: "How anyone could ever have thought that a permanent balance of trade surplus should be beneficial to a nation has been a source of discussion ever since." Blaug, *Early Mercantilists*, ix.

11. Joyce Oldham Appleby explains that these theories made a significant break with the past by "joining the discrete acts of buying and selling to a single commercial process." As a result, the effects of gold and silver leaving England "could only be gauged in reference to an explanation of the entire movement of trade." As Appleby points out, "balance of trade" is thus a misnomer. *Economic Thought and Ideology*, 48. For discussions of "balance" as a misnomer, see also Mary Poovey, *A History of the Modern Fact*, and Andrea Finkelstein, *Harmony and Balance*. For a further discussion of the importance of balance of trade arguments, see Chapter 5.

12. The sale of these goods within England would not fully address the problem since the main concern in these debates was not the profitability of the East India Company, but the benefit of the nation.

13. Mun, *England's Treasure*, 16.

14. Joyce Appleby explains that according to Mun it "was not treasure, that nations should seek, but earnings, the residual credits that remain as a kind of sedimentary deposit from the flow of trade" (*Economic Thought*, 39). She argues that Mun made money the passive servant of commodities; it would follow goods. While I do not disagree entirely with her assessment, what I would want to add is that money is also active. What matters is not the static store of money, but as I argue below, the continual and orderly transformation of money and goods into one another.

15. Here is Mun: "why should we then doubt that our monys sent out in trade, must not necessarily come back again in treasure; together with the

great gains which it may procure in such manner as is before set down." *England's Treasure*, 19.

16. Without the logic of transformation, Mun's theory would be somewhat tautological. Money is valuable because it can purchase wares; wares are valuable because they can be converted into money. In effect, Mun theorizes an early version of Marx's "General Formula for Capital." Mun's anthropomorphic and idolatrous language seems strikingly similar to Marx's; perhaps it would be more historically accurate to say that Marx's language recalls Mun's. But there is a significant difference between them. What is usually understood to be figurative and even ironic in Marx—his prosopopoeial animations of commodities—is offered in these earlier texts with a straight face. In other words, for Marx, transformation is a means of representing the "mystified" way that exchange elides how capital (i.e., unpaid labor as surplus value) is actually produced. Karl Marx, *Capital: A Critique of Political Economy*, vol. 1, trans. Ben Fowkes (New York: Vintage, 1976), 247–57.

17. For an expanded discussion of the significance of the emergence of the commercial usage of "investment" in this context, see my "Transformations of Value and the Production of 'Investment' in the Early History of the English East India Company." *Journal of Medieval and Early Modern Studies* 34, no. 3 (2004): 611–41.

18. Original Correspondence of the English East India Company, India Office Records, vol. 2, 255, 251, 262 (emphases added).

Moreover, The *Oxford Dictionary of English Etymology* explains the etymological connection between "investment" and clothing (vestments) by highlighting their shared transformative possibilities: to "invest" is to give "the capital another 'form.'" It is transformability that enables (or is necessary to) an economic system in which profit is the result of the outlay of money (and not of the labor that actually adds value). While the logic of investment initially depends on these seemingly legible transformations, the outcome is the naturalization of profit as expenditure's heir. *Oxford Dictionary of English Etymology*, ed. C. T. Onions (Oxford: Oxford University Press, 1969).

19. The refinement of my understanding of the temporal dimensions of Mun's theory is indebted to conversations with Zachary Lesser.

20. *Sir Philip Sidney*, ed. Katherine Duncan-Jones (Oxford: Oxford University Press, 1989), 244. Sidney allows for the possibility that it could be done with discretion, as did the ancients once or twice; these were "recounted with space of time, not represented in one moment," 244.

The term "tragicomedy" was first used by Plautus in his prologue to *Amphitruo*. Worrying that the audience might frown upon hearing that the play is a tragedy, the speaker of the prologue, who is also a god, offers to change it to a comedy, but with all the lines the same. Acknowledging the absurdity of such a change, he offers instead to make the play mixed, a tragicomedy. According to the speaker, it cannot be a comedy alone if kings and gods appear. Here, as in Sidney, the objection is to propriety. Cited in the introduction to John Fletcher, *The Faithful Shepherdess*, ed. Florence Ada Kirk (New York: Garland, 1980), xxxiv.

21. One of the reasons that these recuperative efforts take the form of emphasizing the political potential of these plays is because the tragicomic form, as Walter Cohen explains, is "designed to effect reconciliation following a period of serious conflict." "Prerevolutionary Drama," in *The Politics of Tragicomedy: Shakespeare and After*, ed. Gordon McMullan and Jonathan Hope (London: Routledge, 1992), 127. The form thus has a tendency to appear depoliticizing. In his

discussion of the "utopian imagination" in both Shakespeare's romances and comedies, Kiernan Ryan tries to recuperate "wish-fulfillment" as more political, that is, as a form of critical utopia. "Shakespearean Comedy and Romance: The Utopian Imagination" in *Shakespeare's Romances: Contemporary Critical Essays*, ed. Alison Thorne (New York: Palgrave, 2003), 27–52. Offering a different perspective on the politics of the genre, Zachary Lesser argues that tragicomedy's popularity might be due in part to the way its mixed form "relied on the same kind of paradoxical mixture" that Stuart society used "to prevent debates from becoming unbridgeable divides." "Tragical-Comical-Pastoral-Colonial: Economic Sovereignty, Globalization, and the Form of Tragicomedy," *ELH* 74.4 (winter, 2007).

22. *Literary Criticism: Plato to Dryden*, trans. Allan Gilbert (Detroit: Wayne State University Press, 1962), 507. Guarini was primarily defending his pastoral tragicomedy, *Il Pastor Fido*, against accusations that it was amoral, unnatural, and that it violated Aristotelian principles. The primary critic was Giason Denores. In 1605 Cardinal Bellarmino informed Guarini that he had done "as much harm to morals as Luther and Calvin had done to religion." *Three Renaissance Pastorals*, ed. Elizabeth Donno (Binghamton, N.Y.: Medieval and Renaissance Texts and Studies, 1993), xx.

23. Mimi Dixon, "Tragicomic Recognition: Medieval Miracles and Shakespearean Romance," in *Renaissance Tragicomedy: Explorations in Genre and Politics*, ed. Nancy Maguire (New York: AMS Press, 1987), 60. There is no single agreed upon definition of tragicomedy either in Renaissance texts or in current critical discussion of the subject. Barbara Mowat usefully identifies three related models of tragicomedy operating in the Renaissance. In the first, the dramatic "kinds" are freely mixed, what Sidney referred to as a mongrel. The second is a tragedy with a happy or double ending, or plays of tragic sorrow that yield to delight and joy. The third is Guarini's model; while the basic structure is comic, it includes persons of high rank; it has near deaths, but avoids actual ones. In this model tragicomedy prepares its audience by juxtaposing the grave and farcical in its opening scenes, and keeps its audience in suspense throughout as to how a credible miracle will lead to a happy ending. Guarini argues that this form of tragicomedy is "reasonable, properly proportioned, and . . . legitimate according to the rules of Aristotle." Barbara Mowat, "Shakespearean Tragicomedy" in *Renaissance Tragicomedy*, 81–82. Guarini, 512, 530. This is the model most closely followed by Beaumont and Fletcher, who are the English Renaissance playwrights usually credited with making stage tragicomedy popular. The difference between the second and third model is the extent to which the two kinds are kept largely separate (the second model) or the forms are mixed and the comic resolution is prepared for (the third model). As will become clear in my discussion below, what is primarily important in this third type of tragicomedy is the dialectical relationship between the two genres.

Given these multiple models, it is not always clear to which categories certain plays belong. For example, Barbara Mowat and Walter Cohen both refer to Shakespeare's problem comedies as tragicomedies. Some critics include Shakespeare's "romances" and some do not. My primary concern is neither to determine what plays really are tragicomedies, nor to develop a precise definition. Instead, my interest, as will shortly become clear, is to explore why tragicomedy is a genre "useful" for representing economic concerns, especially those related to foreign trade.

Complicating matters further is the dominance of Shakespeare studies and the convention of referring to Shakespeare's tragicomedies as "romances." There is no single definition of romance in the period either. The narrative romance is usually characterized by deferrals and by the interlacing of multiple plot strands. Shakespeare's tragicomedies have been called "romances" because of their use of magical, miraculous elements and related improbable events. I would argue, however, that their mixture of tragic and comedic elements and the specific relationship that exists between them is what links these plays together at a more fundamental level. Neither the category of "romance" or "tragicomedy" was included in the first folio. For recent discussions of tragicomedy in the early modern period, see *Renaissance Tragicomedy* and *The Politics of Tragicomedy*. See also Verna Foster, *The Name and Nature of Tragicomedy* (Aldershot, England: Ashgate, 2004); Robert Henke, *Pastoral Transformations: Italian Tragicomedy and Shakespeare's Late Plays* (Newark: University of Delaware Press, 1997); Marvin Herrick, *Tragicomedy: Its Origin and Development in Italy, France, and England* (Urbana: Illinois University Press, 1955); David L. Hirst, *Tragicomedy* (London: Methuen, 1984). For a discussion of genre theory in the Renaissance, see Rosalie Colie, *The Resources of Kind: Genre Theory in the Renaissance*, ed. Barbara Lewalski (Berkeley: University of California Press, 1973).

24. To my knowledge, no published work has considered the connection between the generic foundation of tragicomedy and its economic concerns. Most critical accounts of the political aspects of Shakespeare's "romances" as a genre (that is, his tragicomedies) focus on issues of court and aristocracy, such as the succession, and the politics of the (royal) family and its relationship to the constitution of patriarchal authority. See, for example, Leonard Tennenhouse, *Power on Display: The Politics of Shakespeare's Genres* (New York: Methuen, 1986) and David Bergeron, *Shakespeare's Romances and the Royal Family* (Lawrence: Kansas University Press, 1985). Even discussions of *The Tempest* that focus on the New World are more interested in the power relations of colonial practices than on economic practices. Similarly, critics of non-Shakespearean tragicomedy have focused on issues that are "political" in the stricter sense of the term, that is, about issues of government. (I separate the discussion of Shakespearean and non-Shakespearean because the criticism is usually on one or the other. As a result, Shakespeare's tragicomedies are now by convention referred to as either romances or problem plays and are rarely thought of alongside other tragicomedies or even as tragicomedies.) Such emphases, while useful, do not provide much explanation of either economic concerns raised in the plays or the relationship between the genre and questions of shifting economic relations. There are a few critics who have thought about *The Winter's Tale*'s representations of economics or political economy (see Chapter 3). Critics of tragicomedies that have "colonial" mercantile contexts have also discussed how these plays raise concerns about the risks of foreign trade, but they have been less focused on the economic practices themselves. See, for example, Ania Loomba, "'Break her Will and Bruise no Bone Sir': Colonial and Sexual Mastery in Fletcher's *The Island Princess*," *Journal for Early Modern Cultural Studies* 2.1 (2001): 68-108; and Shankar Raman, *Framing "India": The Colonial Imaginary in Early Modern Culture* (Stanford: Stanford University Press, 2001). Zachary Lesser's book-in-progress is an exception. This book explores how the formal structure of tragicomedy encodes political questions and conflicts of early Stuart society, and it contains a chapter that focuses on tragicomedy and the naturalization of laws of commerce.

25. Romance and tragicomedy were often linked in the early modern period.

I am not making an argument for them as totally distinct. Instead, I want to highlight what is distinctive to tragicomedy. Some romances are also tragicomedies, but all romances are not necessarily so.

26. Susanne Langer argues that tragedy averted is essential to tragicomedy in *Feeling and Form: A Theory of Art* (New York: Scribner, 1953), 363. Of course, this requirement was important to Guarini as well, who argued that the moderation that was necessary to tragicomedy would allow near deaths, but not actual ones. This idea was picked up by Fletcher and included in his address to the reader in the publication of his *The Faithfull Shepheardesse*: "a tragic-comedie is not so called in respect of mirth and killings but in respect it wants deaths, which is inough to make it no tragedie, yet brings some neere it, which is inough to make it no comedie." It is not surprising that Fletcher paraphrases Guarini here, since this play is very much in dialogue with Guarini's *Il Pastor Fido*, the play for which Guarini wrote his defense. John Fletcher, *The Faithfull Shepheardesse* (London, 1609). Of course, not all tragicomedies stick to this requirement; Shakespeare's *The Winter's Tale*, of course, contains one "resurrection" but also two additional deaths.

It might not be the case that all Renaissance tragicomedies follow the formula of producing a prosperous conclusion out of the averted tragedy exactly, but nonetheless this relationship between tragedy and comedy is at the root of the genre. I am here building on Mimi Dixon's formulation of the central paradox of tragicomedy. Emphasizing the importance of recognition and recognition scenes to tragicomedy, Dixon argues that tragicomedy involves a reenvisioning. The moment of recognition results in a redefinition—for example, crucifixion as divine comedy. As a result, pain itself can be creative. I want to make an even stronger case: it is not just that the recognition results in redefinition, but that the tragic component and the conflict that develops from it produce a prosperous return. Thus, while Dixon is interested in looking at genre as formal potential in order to free genre from history, in this project I am particularly interested in exploring how formal potential is historical. Mimi Dixon, "Tragicomic Recognition: Medieval Miracles and Shakespearean Romance," in *Renaissance Tragicomedy*, 56. Gordon McMullan recognizes a similar, though not identical, structure in his reading of *The Two Noble Kinsmen*. He says that the character Palamon (when he says that nothing could buy dear love, but the loss of it) recognizes "the paradox that the vehicle of [the new genre's] regenerative teleology is dispersal, dissemination, and loss." In his formulation, however, there is no transformation, only an equivalent return. *The Politics of Unease in the Plays of John Fletcher* (Amherst: University of Massachusetts Press, 1994), 261.

27. Even some tragicomedies that seem to be structured by obstacles ultimately form themselves around loss and its transformation. For example, Beaumont and Fletcher's *A King and No King* seems to be structured by the obstacle family ties present to the king's love for his supposed sister. But his repudiation of her results in the representation of her as a lost thing, which ultimately produces a resolution that returns her inheritance to her while accommodating his desire. Francis Beaumont and John Fletcher, *A King and No King* (London, 1619).

28. Loomba, " 'Break Her Will, and Bruise no Bone Sir,' " 101. Jonathan Gil Harris's book is also more concerned with the formation of the nation in its relation to the foreign and the global. Thus, he is interested in romance's attention to alterity: "romance's projections and erasures of alterity also offered mercantilist writers and early modern playwrights narrative strategies with which

to imagine the commercial nation as well as its transactions with foreign bodies within an overarching global system." His focus is more on the thematic concerns shared between romance and these plays; my study is more interested in the narrative arc of tragicomedy—the way its formal structure is useful to addressing concerns with overseas trade. He, too, is interested in generic hybrids (though he excludes Shakespeare's romances from this category). *Sick Economies*, 24.

29. I mean "rematerialize" in its double sense: that which is lost reappears not only along with a gain, but as gain. Moreover, the significance of "rematerialize" is that it also calls attention to the reappearance of the loss itself that is, with traces of the loss still visible, or even reproduced in other forms.

30. *The Works of John Webster*, vol. 2, ed., David Gunby et al. (Cambridge: Cambridge University Press, 2003) 1.1. 26–28.

31. Compare Thomas Mun, who argues that it is safe to send money out by pointing to the benefits of trade for the merchants of Tuscany: "We see that the current of Merchandize which carries away their treasure, becomes a flowing stream to fill them again in a greater measure with mony" (*England's Treasure*, 18).

32. Saint Anselm, (1033–1109) *Cur Deus Homo (Why God Became Man)*, trans. Sidney Norton Deane (Chicago: Open Court Publishing, 1903), Book One, Chapter XII, "Whether it were proper for God to put away sins by compassion alone, without any payment of debt." Debora Shuger argues that Anselm's doctrine of redemption passed into Reformation doctrine largely unchanged. See *The Renaissance Bible: Scholarship, Sacrifice, and Subjectivity* (Berkeley: University of California Press, 1994). Jaroslav Pelikan also explains that Anselm's definition of the atonement as an act of satisfaction (i.e., the price of mankind's sins) rendered by the death of Christ to the violated justice of God was the common property of Roman Catholics and Protestants. Socinus, writing in the late sixteenth century, challenged this doctrine on the basis that it was vulgar and that it suggested that God would not or could not forgive sins by sheer mercy. *The Reformation of Church and Dogma (1300–1700)*, vol. 4 (Chicago: University of Chicago Press, 1984), 324–25. The debate evidently strengthened defenses of Anselm's definition of the satisfaction, which continued to be the "dominant metaphor of the redemption for the Lutheran dogmaticians." According to Pelikan, "the Reformation and its aftermath had, if anything, intensified the hold of the metaphor of satisfaction on the Western doctrine of the atonement" (359–60). One significant difference in Reformation doctrine was that the death of Christ provided satisfaction only for the elect and not necessarily for all humanity.

33. *Cur Deus Homo*, Book 2, Chapter XIV, "How his death outweighs the number and greatness of our sins."

34. Outlining the paradox of the relationship between Christianity and Judaism, Peter Stallybrass argues that even though Christianity is itself founded on the language of pawnbroking—Christ is the pawn who redeems Christian souls—Christianity then disavows (and thus purifies) its own economics by displacing certain economic practices (for example, commodification and exchange value) onto Jews. "The Value of Culture and the Disavowal of Things" in *The Culture of Capital: Properties, Cities, and Knowledge in Early Modern England*, ed. Henry Turner (New York: Routledge, 2002), 282. My emphasis in this study is not on the disavowal of the economics of redemption, but on the recoding of them. This recoding in many cases requires not a disavowal, but an engagement

with economic practices and explicitly an engagement with the possibilities for both loss and profit.

35. "A SERMON PREACHED before the KINGS MAIESTIE, at White-hall, on Monday, the XXV of December, A. D. MDCIX. being CHRIST-MASSE day," in *Sermons by the Right Honorable and Reverend Father in God, Lancelot Andrewes, late Lord Bishop of Winchester* (London, 1629), 29.

36. George Lawson, *Theo-politica, or, A body of divinity containing the rules of the special government of God, according to which, he orders the immortal and intellectual creatures, angels, and men, to their final and eternal estate: being a method of those saving truths, which are contained in the Canon of the Holy Scripture, and abridged in those words of our Saviour Jesus Christ, which were the ground and foundation of those apostolical creeds and forms of confessions, related by the ancients, and, in particular, by Irenæus, and Tertullian* (London, 1659), 100.

37. *The workes of the reuerend and faithfull seruant af Iesus Christ M. Richard Greenham, minister and preacher of the Word of God collected into one volume: reuised, corrected, and published, for the further building of all such as loue the truth, and desire to know the power of godlinesse* (London, 1612), 34.

38. The phrase "restricted economy" is from Bataille's distinction between a general or unrestricted economy and a restricted one. Bataille develops his idea of the general economy from Mauss' analysis of the gift. A general economy is one of sacrifice and surplus, excessive giving. The distinguishing feature of a restricted economy (e.g., capitalism) is scarcity. *The Accursed Share: An Essay on General Economy*, 3 vols., trans. R. Hurley (New York: Zone Books, 1991) and *Visions of Excess: Selected Writings, 1927–1939*, ed. A. Stoekl, trans. A. Stoekl et al. (Minneapolis: University of Minnesota Press, 1985), 116–29. For a very insightful reading of early modern English anxieties about losses and returns that critically employs Bataille's concepts of restricted and general economies, see Scott Shershow, *The Work and The Gift* (Chicago: University of Chicago Press, 2005). As I hope is clear, I am not championing capitalism and its productive potential, but highlighting instead some of its mystifications and locating a potential source for them in Christian doctrine.

39. I would like to add one qualification to my description of contemporary capitalism: while we expect profits to be the result of investment, recent crises (e.g., Enron, the stock market decline, the questionable morality of stock options for senior executives) have led to outcries against certain "excessive" forms of profit-making, but not the notion of profit itself.

40. Of course, usury and profit-making/investing are not identical practices. But given that the East India Company, in whose letters the commercial usage of "invest" first appears, was founded as a joint-stock precisely so that it could function as an accumulation of capital, that is, as investors, and not as individual merchants acting on their own behalf, suggests that the injunction would certainly apply here as well. As I have argued elsewhere, the joint-stock functioned to separate investors from laborers and thus would make its "venturers" renamed today as "investors" more like than unlike usurers, who make money from their money, rather than from their labor. On the joint-stock as an accumulation of capital, see K. N. Chaudhuri, *The English East India Company*. On the development of joint-stock companies in the period, see also *Select Charters of Trading Compaies, A.D. 1530–1707*, ed. Cecil T. Carr (New York: Burt Franklin, 1913); and W. R. Scott, *Constitution and Finance of English, Scottish, and Irish Joint-Stock Companies to 1721* (Cambridge: Cambridge University Press, 1910–12).

41. My point here is not simply that the model of redemption legitimizes

profit, but that it simultaneously theorizes profit, that is, accounts for its possibility, while legitimizing it.

42. Tragicomedy might also address concerns about too much profit, by formally encoding moderation. In his defense of tragicomedy, Guarini argues that tragicomedy is the mingling of tragic and comic pleasure, which does not allow "hearers to fall into excessive tragic melancholy or comic relaxation." Later in the same paragraph he complains that in contrast, both tragedy and comedy "are at fault because they go to excess" ("Compendium," 512). Thus, the tragicomedy itself as theorized is intended as a corrective to generic excess.

43. See Jeffrey Knapp for an argument against the Renaissance theater as a secular theater. He argues, "English theology and ecclesiology shaped the drama at a fundamental level, in helping to determine the conceptualization of the player and the playwright as professions, and of the theater as in institution." *Shakespeare's Tribe: Church, Nation, and Theater in Renaissance England* (Chicago: University of Chicago Press, 2002), 9. I am arguing that the theater is only partially secularized as it absorbs and refunctions Christian discourses and earlier forms of Christian drama. The result is neither a fully secular theater nor a fully Christian theater.

44. John Parker, "God Among Thieves: Marx's Christological Theory of Value and the Literature of the English Reformation" (Ph.D. diss., University of Pennsylvania, 1999); Stallybrass, "The Value of Culture."

45. *OED.* Prior to the Middle Ages, "adventure" referred primarily to chance or blows of fate. In the courtly romances of the Middle Ages, adventure becomes something actively sought out and glorified. For a discussion of shifts in the ideology of adventure, see Michael Nerlich, *Ideology of Adventure: Studies in Modern Consciousness, 1100–1750* (Minneapolis: University of Minnesota Press, 1987). Nerlich identifies the first occurrence of merchants calling themselves adventurers in England in 1443. He argues that the term gains "world-historical importance in England, where it was the proud professional designation for long-distance merchants whose trade was especially risky" (58). For a further discussion of the differences between "venturing" and investing," see my "Transformations of Value," especially pp. 632–33.

46. I am grateful to Joanna Cheethem for her insights about the differences between the economic theory and the religious discourses in this regard.

47. Scott Shershow, "Shakespeare Beyond Shakespeare," in *Marxist Shakespeares*, ed. Jean Howard and Scott Shershow (London: Routledge, 2001), 259. Luke 6:35.

48. Part of the difference between the two versions might depend on mankind's point of identification. The biblical injunction to lend with the intention of losing all depends on Christ as point of identification or model. Man falls and forsakes all; Christ expends, and man profits. In theories of investment, man would be more like man, that is, benefiting from the expenditure. The economic theory, in a sense, collapses man and Christ into one, except, of course, in cases in which there is also a lender and a surety. See Chapter 1, especially the discussion of *The Merchant of Venice.*

49. In Mun's argument, there is a certainty that money will turn into, even produce, more money. Over time, then, the actual process of transformation would cease to be visible.

50. On the relationship between discourses against usury and concerns about the poor, see Norman Jones, *God and the Moneylenders: Usury and Law in Early*

Modern England (Oxford: Basil Blackwell, 1989). On usury and the expropriation of the value of labor, see Scott Shershow, *The Work and the Gift*, 148.

51. Max Weber, *The Protestant Ethic and the Spirit of Capitalism*, trans. Talcott Parsons (London: George Allen and Unwin, 1930).

A number of critics and historians have also argued that the debates over economic policy in the 1620s were unique in that they focused on the economic as a separate, secular domain. Joyce Appleby, for example, claims that "it is the differentiation of things economic from their social context that truly distinguished the writings of the so-called mercantilist period" (*Economic Thought*), 26. Similarly, in tracing the difference between the discussions that led to the usury statute of 1571 and that of 1624, Norman Jones emphasizes how secular the arguments became, focused not on moral and religious questions, but on those of practical economics. For example, he cites Francis Bacon's point that there will only be borrowing if there is profit and if there is no borrowing there will be a whole host of inconveniences (*God and the Moneylenders*, 18). While I largely agree with both Appleby's and Jones's assessments, I would argue that the secularity of economic arguments in the period is also partially the result of the recoding of religious discourse and thus that these arguments are not entirely separate from religious doctrine nor free from the constraints of the moral economy.

52. One might notice, however, that earlier tragicomedies tend to be more of a mix and later ones depend more on a dynamic relationship. It would be possible to venture an argument that this development has something to do with the kinds of questions that begin to occupy the early modern stage.

53. This book thus participates in a developing conversation about "historical formalism," a recent movement in literary theory interested in reclaiming form and genre as historical, that is, viewing the historicity of texts through the lens of genre. For discussions of historical formalism, see *Renaissance Literature and Its Formal Engagements*, ed. Mark David Rasmussen (New York: Palgrave, 2002); and also Ellen Rooney, "Form and Contentment," *Modern Language Quarterly* 61 (2000): 17–40. For some very helpful discussions of the relationship between early modern generic and historical developments, see Stephen Cohen, "Between Form and Culture: New Historicism and the Promise of a Historical Formalism," in *Renaissance Literature*, 17–41; Jean Howard, "Shakespeare, Geography and the Work of Genre on the Early Modern Stage," *Modern Language Quarterly* 64, no. 3 (2003): 299–322; and "Gender on the Periphery," in *Shakespeare and the Mediterranean: The Proceedings of the Seventh World Shakespeare Congress, Valencia 2001*, ed. Tom Clayton, Susan Brock, and Vicente Fores Lopes (Newark: University of Delaware Press, 2004), 344–62. For a foundational text on the historicity of genre, see Fredric Jameson, *The Political Unconscious: Narrative as a Socially Symbolic Act* (Ithaca, N.Y.: Cornell University Press, 1981).

54. "Shakespearean tragicomedy" is not a precisely accurate term for *Pericles*, since it was most likely the product of a collaborative effort between Shakespeare and Wilkins.

55. For a detailed discussion on how theories of "investment" appropriate profits so that they accrue to capital and not to labor, see my "Transformations of Value," especially pp. 625–32.

56. Two qualifications are important: the history is not only in the form, it is also in thematic content. Second, the plays are not only historically distant;

they do speak to many of our own historical concerns, as I have noted throughout.

Chapter 1. Stasis and Insularity in The Merchant of Venice *and* Twelfth Night

1. This is the case even though the economic plot in which Antonio borrows money from Shylock is initiated by the romantic plot, Bassanio's pursuit of Portia, which is in itself an economic plot. The play then inverts the hierarchical relationship between the romantic and economic plots, making the bond the focus of the play.

2. *Twelfth Night,* of course, raises issues related to social mobility, and Feste repeatedly "begs" for coins, but the world of the play insists that it is untouched by these socioeconomic concerns.

3. William Shakespeare, *The Comical History of the Merchant of Venice, Or Otherwise Called the Jew of Venice* in *The Norton Shakespeare,* ed. Stephen Greenblatt et al. (New York: Norton, 1997), 1.1.15–17, 20–22. All further references are cited in the text.

4. Critics have underscored how in this moment, as well as in the later casket scene, Bassanio's plans emphasize risk. Antonio has to shoot—that is, venture forth—another arrow just as the inscription on the lead casket says, "Who chooseth me must give and hazard all he hath" (2.7.9). But even though he does have to "adventure both" arrows, Bassanio's plan works to transform that risk into an expenditure that becomes a means of redemption. In fact, Basssanio presents the plan as not risky for Antonio. Since Bassanio will watch this arrow, the worst that can happen is that he does not find the first. At a minimum, he will at least return the second arrow. The first is merely sunk costs. It is unclear exactly how the analogy fully translates to this situation, that is, how he would return the second arrow to Antonio if he does not win over Portia.

5. Initially the play represents the tragic potential of trade as a primary concern, but as the play continues it adds the concern about the ethics of profit in the character of the usurer, Shylock. Critics have tended to focus on the latter problem, ignoring to some extent the former. I want to argue that the two concerns coexist and that in some sense the former problem is displaced onto the latter. One critic who focuses more on the losses of the ships is Phyllis Rackin, "The Impact of Global Trade in *The Merchant of Venice,*" *Shakespeare-Jahrbuch* 138 (2002): 73–88.

6. See especially Lars Engle, " 'Thrift Is Blessing': Exchange and Explanation in *The Merchant of Venice,*" *Shakespeare Quarterly* 37 (1986): 20–37; Karen Newman, "Portia's Ring: Unruly Women and Structures of Exchange in *The Merchant of Venice,*" *Shakespeare Quarterly* 38 (1987): 19–33; and Marc Shell, *Money, Language, and Thought: Literary and Philosophical Economies from the Medieval to the Modern Era* (Berkeley: University of California Press, 1982), 47–83.

7. See the Introduction. Saint Anselm, (1033–1109) *Cur Deus Homo (Why God Became Man)*, trans. Sidney Norton Deane (Chicago: Open Court Publishing Co., 1903).

8. In fact, given its source in the model of loss and redemption, the pound of flesh fuses the connection between Antonio's potential losses and Bassanio's arrow strategy.

9. Stallybrass's focus is not the play, however, but Christianity's own discomfort with its economic and Jewish origins, though these are not the same thing.

In fact, what Stallybrass argues is that Christianity attempts to free itself from an economics based on exchange value and commodification by displacing those practices onto Jews and thus disavowing them. "The Value of Culture and the Disavowal of Things" in *The Culture of Capital: Properties, Cities, and Knowledge in Early Modern England*, ed. Henry Turner (New York: Routledge, 2002), 275–92.

10. Recent critics of *The Merchant of Venice* have pointed to the play's inability to resolve its economic conflicts but few have connected this inability back to genre. Phyllis Rackin, for example, argues that the end of the play leaves us with the same ambivalence regarding trade with which the play begins—both fear and desire, "The Impact of Global Trade," 87. Walter Cohen, one of the only critics to link this inability back to questions of genre, argues that the play's "central design [fails] to provide a completely satisfying resolution to the dilemmas raised in the course of the action." "*The Merchant of Venice* and the Possibilities of Historical Criticism," *English Literary History* 49 (1982), 775. Cohen is arguing against Lawrence Danson's thesis that the play transforms conflicts into harmonies through both incorporation and transcendence. Cohen focuses on the tension between the play's utopian tendencies (e.g., a society without exploitation) and its critical representation of usurious practice in order to read the play largely as a response to a conflict between two modes of production whose merit is in part its refusal to resolve all through transcendence. My concern with form has less to do with the play's ability to resolve a conflict between two modes of production than it does with the tension in the play between the two genres it incorporates and the play's resulting inability to imagine a world that can accommodate new economic practices.

11. Scott Shershow argues that the play shares with capitalism the ruse of loss with return. I will return to this point in greater depth below. Scott Shershow, "Shakespeare Beyond Shakespeare," in *Marxist Shakespeares*, ed. Jean Howard and Scott Shershow (London: Routledge, 2001), 259–60.

12. See Chapter 4 for a discussion of the way that trade was represented as producing mutual advantage.

13. It is the yielding of the religious to the economic that I argue helps to enable the tragicomic fortunate narrative to develop in Shakespeare's tragicomedies, *Pericles* and *The Winter's Tale*.

14. In fact, all of the play's economies fail to work the way that they are supposed to: all Antonio's ships miscarry; Portia defies her father's will by helping Bassanio choose the right casket and thus gain access to her inheritance; the usurer refuses to take money/interest as repayment of a debt.

15. For a discussion of early modern debates about the satisfaction and Socinus's role in them, see Debora Shuger, *The Renaissance Bible: Scholarship, Sacrifice, and Subjectivity* (Berkeley: University of California Press, 1994).

16. George Lawson, *Theo-politica, or, A body of divinity containing the rules of the special government of God, according to which, he orders the immortal and intellectual creatures, angels, and men, to their final and eternal estate: being a method of those saving truths, which are contained in the Canon of the Holy Scripture, and abridged in those words of our Saviour Jesus Christ, which were the ground and foundation of those apostolical creeds and forms of confessions, related by the ancients, and, in particular, by Irenæus, and Tertullian* (London, 1659), 100.

17. *The workes of the reuerend and faithfull seruant af Iesus Christ M. Richard Greenham, minister and preacher of the Word of God collected into one volume: reuised, cor-*

rected, and published, for the further building of all such as loue the truth, and desire to know the power of godlinesse (London, 1612), 34.

18. *OED*, def. 3. The first example the *OED* gives of this latter definition is from Bacon's 1605 Advancement of Learning. II. 48b: "As money will fetch all other commodities, so this knowledge is that which should purchase all the rest.

19. Harry Berger, Jr., "Marriage and Mercifixion in *The Merchant of Venice*: The Casket Scene Revisited," *Shakespeare Quarterly* 32 (1981): 155–62.

20. Roma Gill, "Introduction," *The Jew of Malta*, ed. Roma Gill (Oxford: Oxford University Press, 1995), xiii.

21. Christopher Marlowe, *The Jew of Malta*, ed. David Bevington (Manchester: Manchester University Press, 1997), 1.2.91.

22. Ibid., 1.2.97–100. See John, 11.50. After this moment, Jesus no longer went about publicly, but instead left the region for the country bordering on the desert.

23. Ibid., 1.2.116.

24. Ibid., 1.2.103.

25. Ibid., 1.2.104–5.

26. Perhaps Shakespeare's play, even more than Marlowe's, depends on a variation of scapegoat logic. These things can only reappear if Shylock is gone, which is not quite the same as having him be blamed and still present. The rest of the play resolves itself almost entirely without him.

27. At the news of the Duke's partial pardon, Shylock complained, "you take my life/ When you do take the means whereby I live" (4.1.371–72). These are lines Marx famously cites when he explains the threat capital poses to the worker—that of taking away his access to the means of subsistence. *Capital*, 618, fn. 30.

28. Scott Shershow, "Shakespeare Beyond Shakespeare," 259–60.

29. I am thus agreeing with and building on Walter Cohen's insight that the play is not merely an instance of "ironic demystification," "Possibilities of Historical Criticism," 774–75.

30. The dependence on a transfer of funds and scapegoat logic might also help the play to take a detour around the contradictions in the doctrine of redemption by partially ignoring the fact that the price to be paid gets paid elsewhere, that is, by someone who is not one of the fold. Of course, the play undermines even this reading, by making part of the price the price to become part of the fold.

31. Revenge tragedy itself might be an unexpected stepping-stone to tragicomedy. The end of *The Jew of Malta*, for example, ends with the death of Barabas, the imprisonment of the Turks and thus the end of the threat they have posed, and finally with an emphasis on the liberation of Malta. But there is still a considerable amount of loss left unaccounted. See Chapter 5 for a discussion of how tragicomedy serves to imagine profit without loss elsewhere precisely by turning away from revenge.

32. See the discussion of balance of trade theory and *The Renegado* in Chapter 5 to see how circulation combined with a tragicomic turn away from revenge allow for a notion of profit without loss elsewhere.

33. I am thus partially disagreeing with critics who would locate capitalist energy more in Antonio than in Shylock. While I agree that Shakespeare might be trying to imagine a capitalist system in which loss produces return, it is the exclusion of Shylock and the scapegoat logic in general that partially prevents such a possibility, even if Shylock's discourse is more associated with hoarding than with

circulation. Michael Ferber, "The Ideology of *The Merchant of Venice*," *English Literary Renaissance* 20 (1990): 447–48. Ferber's argument anticipates my own, but I think that what Shakespeare's tragicomedies ultimately imagine is not sacrifice and risk, but a system in which the expected result is that loss will transform into profit. See also Walter Cohen's "*The Merchant of Venice* and the Possibilities of Historical Criticism." Richard Halpern, in contrast, argues that Shylock embodies capital in *Shakespeare Among the Moderns* (Ithaca: Cornell University Press, 1997), 159–226.

34. Even these discussions tend to be focused less on specific economic concerns and processes than on the social conflict that emerges from class tensions.

35. Eric Mallin notes that the play provides a parody of tragicomedy. I will return to this point later. *Inscribing the Time: Shakespeare and the End of Elizabethan England* (Berkeley: University of California Press, 1995), 169.

36. Though using the double name "Viola/Cesario" and double pronouns "s/he" or "him/her" is somewhat cumbersome, I will do so throughout in order to hold onto the complexity of the gendered identity of this character.

37. Stephen Orgel, *Impersonations: The Performance of Gender in Shakespeare's England* (Cambridge: Cambridge University Press, 1996); Keir Elam, "The Fertile Eunuch: *Twelfth Night*, Early Modern Intercourse, and the Fruits of Castration," *Shakespeare Quarterly* 47 (1996): 1–36.

38. Orgel, *Impersonations*, 54.

39. Elam, "The Fertile Eunuch," 2.

40. Ibid., 11.

41. See the Introduction.

42. William Shakespeare, *Twelfth Night. The Arden Shakespeare*, ed. J. M. Lothian and T. W. Craik (London: Routledge, 1975), (1.2.47–56). All further references are cited in the text.

43. The *OED* cites the first economic usage of "investment" in 1613, but it might have had some currency earlier. John Florio's 1598 Italian-English Dictionary provides the following definitions of the verb "investire": "to invest, to install, to cloth, to enrobe, to put in possession. Also, to charge upon an enemie. Also, to laie out or emploie ones money upon any bargaine for advantage." *A Worlde of Wordes, or Most copious, and exact dictionarie in Italian and English* (London, 1598), 190. Though this entry only provides evidence of the usage in Italian, it would suggest the possibility to an English reader of extending the usage to the economic.

44. Ann Rosalind Jones and Peter Stallybrass, *Renaissance Clothing and the Materials of Memory* (Cambridge: Cambridge University Press, 2000), especially 17–33. They argue that "men and women of every class stored up wealth in clothes." In those instances, clothing is less like an investment. As I explain in the Introduction, the idea of investment originates along with economic theory that emphasizes not the importance of storing up wealth, but of circulating money in order to generate profits and ultimately capital.

45. On the importance of negative trade imbalances to early economic theory see the Introduction. I will return to the concern about the emptying of coffers later in the chapter.

46. K. N. Chaudhuri, *The English East India Company: The Study of an Early Joint-Stock Company, 1600–1640* (New York: August Kelley, 1965); F. J. Fisher, "London's Export Trade in the Early Seventeenth Century," in *The Growth of English Overseas Trade in the Seventeenth and Eighteenth Centuries*, ed. W. E. Minchinton

(London: Methuen, 1969); see also Patricia Fumerton, *Cultural Aesthetics: Renaissance Literature and the Practice of Social Ornament* (Chicago: University of Chicago Press, 1991), especially 169–206.

47. Chandra Mukerji, *From Graven Images: Patterns of Modern Materialism* (New York: Columbia University Press, 1983).

48. Joan Thirsk, *Economic Policy and Projects: The Development of a Consumer Society in Early Modern England* (Oxford: Oxford University Press, 1978).

49. See *Letters Received by the East India Company from its servants in the East. Transcribed from the "Original Correspondence" Series of the India Office Records*, ed. W. Foster, vol. 1 (London: Sampson Low, Marston & Company, 1896–1902), 18; and K. N. Chaudhuri, *The English East India Company*, 41.

50. "Investment," *Oxford Dictionary of English Etymology*, ed. T. F. Hoad (Oxford: Oxford University Press, 1986).

51. See my "Transformations of Value and the Production of 'Investment' in the Early History of the English East India Company," *Journal of Medieval and Early Modern Studies* 34, no. 3 (2004): 611–41.

52. On the importance of the transformative power of clothing, wares, and money to the developing notion of commercial "investment," see my "Transforming Investments," especially 612–18.

53. As far as I know, only Elam mentions it, but he does not discuss it. No other critic as far as I know has been attentive to it.

54. I am not arguing that loss disappears from the play entirely. The play continues to register these losses, but the characters do not.

55. *Inscribing the Time*, 167.

56. Elam, "The Fertile Eunuch," 2.

57. Stephen Booth, "*Twelfth Night* 1.1: The Audience as Malvolio," in *Shakespeare's "Rough Magic": Essays in Honor of C. L. Barber*, Peter Erickson and Coppelia Kahn, ed., (Newark: University of Delaware Press, 1985), 149–67.

58. Cristina Malcomson, "'What You Will': Social Mobility and Gender in *Twelfth Night*," in *The Matter of Difference: Materialist Feminist Criticism of Shakespeare*, ed. Valerie Wayne (Ithaca, N.Y.: Cornell University Press, 1991), 50.

59. Elam, "The Fertile Eunuch," 31–32.

60. David Kastan, "*All's Well That Ends Well* and the Limits of Comedy," *ELH* 52 (1985): 576.

61. At first, it seems that the play and particularly Viola's plan is about transforming limitations into their fortunate potential (the tragicomic), but the comedic takes over and the play continues along the lines of wish-fulfillment, in which the reality principle merely gives way to the pleasure principle.

62. A reading of the play's engagement with questions of identity and ontology would distract from the main argument of the book and the chapter. I have pursued these connections elsewhere, however. In "Material Dispossessions and Counterfeit Investments: The Economies of *Twelfth Night*," I explore how the play's disavowals manifest in its representation of counterfeits, the relationship between subjects and objects, and in the play's imagination of autonomous subjects. *Money and The Age of Shakespeare: Essays in New Economic Criticism*, ed. Linda Woodbridge (New York: Palgrave, 2003), 113–127.

63. *Inscribing the Time*, 169.

64. Both the *Arden* and the *Norton* editions list Antonio, the other sea venturer to whom I refer here, as a captain, a position that would make the parallel between Sebastian's and Viola's interactions even stronger. Since the play does not explicitly refer to him as a captain, I will refer to him throughout as a sea ven-

turer. Since he seems to be held responsible for not returning money that was stolen from Orsino's ships (a point I will discuss below) he might have very well have been the ship's captain, however.

65. The practice of paying for one's release from imprisonment was common not necessarily for those who committed ordinary crimes within a country, but for foreigners who were captured, especially foreign merchants and pirates. For an extended discussion of the redemption of prisoners in these contexts, see Chapter 4.

66. On the importance of recompense in the play, see Camille Slights, "The Principle of Recompense in *Twelfth Night*," *Modern Language Review* 77 (1982): 537–46.

67. Given the connection between "fallen" and "apprehended" united in this unusual use of "lapsed," and Antonio's previous refusal to repay what he stole, we might conclude that the purse already contains the idea of refuted redemption even before Viola/Cesario is unable to return it.

68. Piracy was, however, a serious concern for those engaged in overseas trade. At the turn of the century both the Mediterranean and Irish Seas were menaced by pirates. According to Kris Lane, the period from 1568–85 was also one of unmitigated piracy by the English and that from 1585–1603 of privateering by them in the Caribbean. *Pillaging the Empire: Piracy in the Americas 1500–1700* (New York: M. E. Sharpe, 1998).

69. For further discussions of piracy's disruptive potential, see Chapter 5.

70. As I mentioned earlier, this trade imbalance was often blamed on the unpopularity of wool cloth, thus providing a further connection between Viola's purchase of clothing and the exchange of the purse. See the Introduction as well as Chapters 4 and 5 for more detailed discussions of concerns about the balance of trade and the development of the idea of a balance of trade. See also Chaudhuri, *The English East India Company*; Fisher, "London's Export Trade"; Thirsk, *Economic Policy and Projects*.

71. C. E. Challis, *The Tudor Coinage* (Manchester: Manchester University Press, 1978), especially 274–99; John Craig, *The Mint: A History of the London Mint from A.D. 287 to 1948* (Cambridge: Cambridge University Press, 1953); Sir Albert Feavearyear, *The Pound Sterling: A History of English Money* (Oxford: Oxford University Press, 1963).

72. Gerard Malynes, *Saint George for England, Allegorically Described* (London, 1601), 42. For a further discussion of Malynes's text and its relationship to the representation of usury in *The Merchant of Venice*, see Jonathan Gil Harris, *Sick Economies: Drama, Mercantilism, and Disease in Shakespeare's England* (Philadelphia: University of Pennsylvania Press, 2004), especially 57–62.

73. I'm building here on Jonathan Goldberg's observation that Malvolio ends up in possession of Viola's clothing. "Textual Properties," *Shakespeare Quarterly* 37 (1986): 213–17.

74. Jones and Stallybrass, *Renaissance Clothing*, 199.

75. The deferred ending will depend not only on locating Malvolio, but also "entreating him to a peace," which is unlikely since Malvolio's final lines invoke a revenge plot, not a tragicomedy or even a comedy.

76. The purse as obstacle and nonobstacle might be emblematic of the relationship between piracy and trade. In its illegitimate form piracy was a risk and obstacle to overseas mercantilist ventures, but its legitimate form, privateering, financed much of Elizabeth's investment in the Levant Company, out of which the East India Company was formed. For the complex relationship between

trade and piracy, see Barbara Fuchs's *Mimesis and Empire: The New World, Islam, and European Identities* (Cambridge: Cambridge University Press, 2001).

77. This combination might help to explain why so many directors choose to end the play with Viola in women's clothing and Antonio pardoned and liberated from his imprisonment.

78. I am not arguing that a profit-producing world is necessarily a better world. Instead, I am interested in demonstrating how the play's formal limitations prevent it from fully imagining the potential for profits to which it also alludes. For a discussion of the ways that tragicomedy, productivity, and the forces of capitalism potentially outdo and thus undo themselves, see the Epilogue— both the reading of Webster's *The Devil's Law-Case* and the analysis of the persistence of tragicomic/redemption think in neoliberal ideals and late global capitalism.

Chapter 2. The Voyage Out

1. Saint Anselm (1033–1109), *Cur Deus Homo (Why God Became Man)*, trans. Sidney Norton Deane (Chicago: Open Court Publishing, 1903). See the Introduction for a discussion of Anselm's influence on the early modern understanding of the economics of redemption.

2. The traditional romance engagement with good and evil is thus rewritten in an economic form borrowed from Anselm's model in order to engage with economic problems themselves. It might not so much be the case then that Protestantism and capitalism are linked in precisely the ways Weber suggests, but that the religious model was necessary or available to explore how capitalism itself works. The utopian dimension of early modern tragicomedy might then itself be a historical product of the workings of capital. I will discuss the latter point in greater detail in Chapter 5. Max Weber, *The Protestant Ethic and the Spirit of Capitalism*, trans. Talcott Parsons (London: George Allen and Unwin, 1930).

For discussions of the opposition of good and evil in the romance, see Northrop Frye, *Anatomy of Criticism: Four Essays* (Princeton, N.J.: Princeton University Press, 1975). For a Marxist analysis of the genre of romance see Fredric Jameson, *The Political Unconscious* (Ithaca, N.Y.: Cornell University Press, 1982).

3. For example, in his article on incest and eating in the play, Anthony J. Lewis suggests that the easiest way for English audiences of the seventeenth century to comprehend the ghastliness of sexual abuse is via the more familiar horrors of hunger, disease, and the sicknesses attendant on gluttony. But I would like to suggest that given that almost all of the problems in the many worlds Pericles visits are economic, that incest (or sexual transgression, in general) is not the play's primary concern. To the extent that the play is concerned with sexual transgression—incest and prostitution—both are rendered as explicitly economic problems about, and caused by, the exchange of women. " 'I Feed on Mother's Flesh': Incest and Eating in *Pericles*," *Essays in Literature* (1988): 147–63.

One exception is Braden Cormack whose recent essay, while not primarily about the economic, provides a reading of the economic undercurrents of Pericles' actions during his first visit to Tharsus. This article, though more about geographic than economic expansion, shares a similar interest in the extension of boundaries. His essay focuses on the extension of authority beyond national boundaries, especially those hard-to-define boundaries of the sea. He reads *Pericles* within the context of contested disputes to sovereign proprietorship of the sea, arguing that Pericles "reinvents his national identity as an imperial or transnational identity." "Marginal Waters: *Pericles* and the Idea of Jurisdiction" in *Literature, Mapping, and the Politics of Space in Early Modern Britain*, ed. Andrew Gordon and Bernhard Klein (Cambridge: Cambridge University Press, 2001).

In her essay on property rights in *Pericles*, Constance Jordan argues that incest is an image of Pericles' own desire for absolute rule that violates the rights of the people and is all consuming rather than generative. She argues that Pericles' feeding the people of Tharsus with corn is a sign of tyrant reform and Pericles' understanding of limited *dominium*. Her reading of property is focused less on economic practices and more on the relationship between absolute rule and theories of ownership. "Eating the Mother: Property and Propriety in Pericles," in *Creative Imitation: New Essays on Renaissance Literature in Honor of Thomas Greene* (Binghamton, N.Y.: Binghamton University Press, 1992), 331–54.

4. See Aristotle, *The Politics*, trans. Sir Ernest Barker (Oxford: Oxford University Press, 1995), book 1, especially chapters 8–10 on the art of acquisition. For a discussion of the Aristotelian understanding of usury in early modern England, see also David Hawkes, *Idols of the Marketplace: Idolatry and Commodity Fetishism in English Literature, 1580–1680* (New York: Palgrave Macmillan, 2001).

5. *Aristotles Politiques, or Discourses of gouernment. Translated out of Greeke into French, with expositions taken out of the best authours, specially out of Aristotle himselfe, and out of Plato, conferred together where occasion of matter treated of by them both doth offer it selfe: the obseruations and reasons whereof are illustrated and confirmed by innumerable examples, both old and new, gathered out of the most renowmed empires, kingdomes, seignories, and commonweals that euer haue bene, and wherof the knowledge could be had in writing, or by faythfull report, concerning the beginning, proceeding, and excellencie of ciuile gouernment. By Loys Le Roy, called Regius. Translated out of French into English* (London, 1598), 49.

6. Aristotle, *Politics*, 1258a35.

7. Eric Spencer, "Taking Excess, Exceeding Account: Aristotle Meets *The Merchant of Venice*," in *Money and the Age of Shakespeare: Essays in New Economic Criticism*, ed. Linda Woodbridge (New York: Palgrave Macmillan, 2003), 148–49, emphasis in original. The relationship between money, usury, and reproduction has been the focus of much current critical debate. See, for example, Marc Shell, *Money, Language, and Thought: Literary and Philosophic Economies from the Medieval to the Modern Era* (Berkeley: University of California Press, 1982).

8. Aristotle, *Politics*, 1258a35. The 1598 translation also opposes the natural practices of necessary nourishment to both usury and engrossing: "but the other which engroseth and selleth commodities, worthly blamed, because it is not agreeable to Nature, but rather to the end one might gaine and encroch upon another. Above all the rest, Usurie deserveth to bee hated, for that by it menne gaine and profite by money, not for that intent and purpose for which it was ordained, namely, for the exchaunging of commodities; but for the augmenting of it selfe: which hath procured in the name of, to witte, issue or engendring: because thinges engendred, are like the engendrers; and Usurie is naught else but money begotten of money: in so much, that amongst all the meanes of getting, this is most contrarie to Nature." *Aristotles Politiques*, 49. Engrossing was a term for the much vilified practice of buying up all of a commodity, or as much as one could, in order to gain a monopoly and thus "regrate" it at a much higher price.

9. For Aristotle, then, productivity requires that the product is not identical to the material that produces it. Interestingly, the root of "proletarian" in Latin,

"proletarius," is a Roman citizen of the lowest class under the Servian constitution, one who served the state not with his property but only with his offspring, from "proles," offspring, and "proletus," provided with offspring. These connections are noteworthy given the relationships between interest and offspring and between economic productivity and reproduction in early modern thought.

10. Interestingly, "labour," which might be related etymologically to *labare*, "to slip," extends its meaning in the sixteenth century from "to work or toil," to "the travail of childbirth." All three meanings are relevant here to the sin of incest as it relates to reproduction and commerce.

11. All citations are from the Arden Shakespeare *Pericles*, ed. Suzanne Gossett (London: Thomson Learning, 2004), (1.1.65–68). All further references are cited in the text.

12. This correlation is original to the play, that is, it is not existent in the sources. While the riddle in Thomas Twyne's *The Patterne of Painefull Adventures*, a primary source for the play, does include the idea of feeding on mother's flesh, the famine at Tharsus is not represented in related terms. *The patterne of painful aduentures Containing the most excellent, pleasant, and variable historie of the strange accidents that befell vnto Prince Apollonius, the Lady Lucina his wife, and Tharsia his daughter. Wherein the vncertaintie of this world, and the fickle state of mans life are liuely described.* (London, 1576, reprinted 1594, 1607). Nor is the connection as tight in Wilkins's prose romance, *The Painful Adventures of Pericles* (1608). In this later text, so "ravenous" is the "mouth of famine" that all "tendernesse between the mother and the children" is exiled, but cannibalism is not threatened. *The painfull aduentures of Pericles prince of Tyre Being the true history of the play of Pericles, as it was lately presented by the worthy and ancient poet Iohn Gower* (London, 1608), 25. This prose romance is thought to be a record of Wilkins's memory of the play, of which he was most likely a significant collaborator. See the Oxford/Norton textual note to the play. Wilkins's text seems to be a mix of the play and of Twyne's text, the most immediate prose source for the play.

13. In Tharsus this threat is generationally inverted: there the threat is that mothers will feed off of the flesh of their children.

14. The belief referred to in the riddle is that the viper eats its way out of its mother's body. Thus, the difference between the viper's feeding on mother's flesh and the natural kind (in which the engendered sustains itself with what is residual) is that the viper eats what is presumably necessary to the mother's own existence— a form of extreme ingratitude that is not a kind labor. Ingratitude, as I will discuss below, becomes a thematic concern of the play.

15. While the scenes in the play I have already discussed do not explicitly represent economic activity based on profit rather than need, it will soon become clear that the play is moving precisely in that direction and that the inversion of Aristotle in the riddle lays the groundwork for imagining exchanges for profit as productive rather than as stagnant. When "balance of trade" mercantilists argued that it was ultimately a good thing to send money out of the country in order to participate in foreign trade they, like the play, did so in part by naturalizing profit and the flow of money and goods that produced it: "The sum of all that hath been spoken, concerning the enriching of the Kingdom, and the encrease of our treasure by commerce with strangers, is briefly thus. . . . Let Princes oppress, Lawyers extort, Usurers bite, Prodigals wast, and lastly let Merchants carry out what mony they shall have occasion to use in traffique. Yet all these actions can work no other effects in the course of trade than is declared in this discourse. For so much Treasure only will be brought in or carried out of a

Commonwealth, as the Forraign Trade doth over or under balance in value. And this must come to pass by a Necessity beyond all resistance. So that all other courses. . . . [are] in the end not only fruitless but also hurtful: they are like to violent flouds which bear down their banks, and suddenly remain dry again for want of waters." Thomas Mun, *England's Treasure by Forraign Trade* (1664) *Reprints of Economic History Classics* (Oxford: Basil Blackwell, 1928), 87–88. Though published in 1664, the text was written in the 1620s.

16. Ironically, though Pericles travels to find a wife, she is too internally focused (like the love of Sebastian and Viola perhaps). As I will discuss below, though the play's episodic travels rework its original internal focus, it does so only to return home, that is, for Pericles to return to his own daughter, though now in a legitimized relation that will parallel her hyperlegitimized form of profit-making.

17. While there are marriages in the play, the drive toward marriage is not at all central to the play as the concern with exogamy would suggest. Thus the initial focus on incest, as I have suggested above, is more figurative than literal.

18. See the Introduction for a detailed discussion of how tragicomedy depends on transforming averted tragedy into resolution.

19. For a discussion of concerns about domestic production, see Joan Thirsk, *Economic Policy and Projects: The Development of a Consumer Society in Early Modern England* (Oxford: Oxford University Press, 1989). For further discussion of concerns about money leaving the country and the balance of trade arguments that developed to address them, see the Introduction and Chapter 5.

20. For an insightful discussion of "consumption" in early modern England, see Jonathan Gil Harris, *Sick Economies: Drama, Mercantilism and Disease in Shakespeare's England* (Philadelphia: University of Pennsylvania Press, 2004), especially chapter 7.

21. Quoted in B. E. Supple, *Commercial Crisis and Change in England, 1600–1642* (Cambridge: Cambridge University Press, 1959), 31. Supple notes that grain imports to London by aliens alone in 1609 were over 40,000 quarters, 31, fn. 3.

22. Ibid., 12–13.

23. *Seventeenth Century Economic Documents*, ed. Joan Thirsk and J. P. Cooper (Oxford: Clarendon Press, 1972), 459–69. Edward Misselden also recommended the statutes of employment as a way to keep coin from leaving the country. *Free Trade, or the Meanes to Make Trade Florish: Wherein, the Causes of the Decay of Trade in the Kingdome, are Discovered: And the Remedies aloso to Remoove the Same, are Represented* (London, 1622), 103. According to Jacob Viner, the statute of employments had been inoperative for most of the latter part of the sixteenth century. Jacob Viner, *Studies in the Theory of International Trade* (New York: Harper and Bros., 1937).

24. Jonathan Gil Harris insightfully explores how early modern economic writing represents the foreign as pathological, as a threat to the health of the economy. He argues that the foreign is in a sense scapegoated in order to privilege, even naturalize, the global economy. *Sick Economies*.

25. One could say the play's model of "character development" is actually one of "character accumulation." At play's end, Pericles acquires the cities with which he comes into contact, but throughout the play he acquires the conditions of other characters.

26. In Wilkins's *Painful Adventures of Pericles* (1608), the comparison of rich men to whales is preceded by a comparison of the "sea to brokers and usurers,

who seem faire and look lovely until they have got men into their clutches, when one tumbles them and an other tosses them, but seldome leaving until they have suncke them" (32).

27. This fantasy inverts and also literalizes that of Tharsus in which poverty is figuratively excoriated.

28. Scott Shershow demonstrates how this displacement begins to occur in the early modern period, as well as how it still exists in political discussions and legislation concerning work and charity. See his *The Work and the Gift* (Chicago: University of Chicago Press, 2005), especially pages 147–48 and 115–35. For a discussion of the uses to which representations of the beggar were put in early modern England, see William Carroll, *Fat King, Lean Beggar: Representations of Poverty in the Age of Shakespeare* (Ithaca, N.Y.: Cornell University Press, 1996).

In his discussion of the benefits of foreign trade, Edward Misselden blames any underbalance of trade on both poverty and prodigality, which he represents as opposite sides of the same coin. He admonishes against both idleness and excess and concludes the discussion by lamenting the losses that accrue as a result of the idle poor who could be put to work just in London alone. He thus argues against charity as a form of static expenditure. *The Circle of Commerce. Or the Balance of Trade, in defence of free trade: Opposed to Malynes Little Fish and his Great Whale, and poized against them in the Scale* (London, 1623), sigs. Ff–Ff4.

29. In place of "repair my fortunes," *The Norton Shakespeare* reads "repair my losses" (scene 5, 157).

30. The play thus provides an alternative to the amoral usurers and brokers of Wilkins's prose version of Pericles' painful adventures. The armor is useful in this regard, because it both represents a borrowing and something that is his own, which he can then use to profit. That it was ever a borrowing becomes subordinated to the use to which it is put. Rather than remain in debt, he becomes a man of much credit. At the level of plot, the armor gives him something of his own to use to participate in the tournament and ultimately to benefit from his contact with the foreign kingdom of Pentapolis.

31. I say "temporarily" because these problems will resurface in the play's final locale—the brothel of Mytilene.

32. We will see a similar use of the comedic obstacle in *The Winter's Tale*, but there the comedic obstacle has tragic possibilities and also real power; it is not pretense, and it is the means by which the play's tragic potential is converted into prosperity. See Chapter 3.

33. The armor, itself a lost object, rematerializes as credit. Pericles goes into debt in order to obtain the armor he needs to win Thaisa in the tournament and produce a profit. The armor is thus its own collateral; it is the sign of his creditworthiness and what that credit allows him to borrow in order to produce a future profit. Perhaps the collapsing of the two into each other represents the mystification of capital's relation to the capitalist, as does the replacement of class difference by Pericles' material accumulations.

34. See act 3, scene 3, 18–26 discussed above as well as act 1, scene 4, 99–104. Pericles' is a loan to be repaid, but only if his fortunes improve. It is this risk-free. Pericles nonetheless defaults, and either he or the play completely forgets about the fishermen to whom Pericles is indebted. Shakespeare's Coriolanus has a similar lapse of memory when it comes to remembering the poor who come to his assistance.

35. Marina is purchased by the brothel's servant from the pirates, who "rescued" her from being killed by Dionysa's servant (himself an impoverished slave

offered money and freedom to counter his conscience). Thus real commercial profits are associated with what the play represents as the worst of transgressions: murder and pandering. Marina is literally "displaced" to the brothel as a result of Dionysa's bad faith and repudiation of charitable obligation.

36. The most literal meaning of "commodity" here is profit or advantage. Interestingly, though, the first example the *OED* gives of "commodity" as "something in which one deals or trades" is from Thomas Dekker's *The Belman of London* (London, 1608). The line cited is, "The whore is called the commodity."

37. Of course, the condition for quitting early is having an estate to rely on. It is also worth noting that there is no model for repentance here.

38. Of course, credit, then as now, could refer to one's personal reputation and to the belief in one's ability to repay a monetary debt. On credit in early modern England, see Craig Muldrew, *The Economy of Obligation* (New York: Palgrave Macmillan, 1998).

39. See Anselm, *Cur Deus Homo*, especially book one, chapters VI, XI, XII, XIII, and XXII.

40. Paradoxically, Aristotle's primary concerns with usury and trade for financial benefit are stagnation, on the one hand, and infinite accumulation, on the other.

41. Of course, these were not the only ways to seek salvation, but they were the most literal ways to purchase it.

42. I believe that part of the complexity here results from the fact that Anselm's economic understanding of the redemption of mankind as a whole passed into the Reformation largely unchanged, but the individual's relation to salvation and grace had changed enormously. Grace was no longer something one could earn; one could only demonstrate having already received God's grace. The distinction is crucial, if confusing. In Reformation doctrine, it is unclear how much one needs (to do) in order to have God's grace precisely because God's grace, which is infinite, is not something one can earn. Yet, given these terms, Aristotle's distinction (which some thinkers, for example, Perkins, tried to reconcile with Reformation doctrine) between a finite need that is morally sound and a corrupt form of infinite acquisition loses some of its meaning precisely because no amount of "profit" can seem to be properly earned.

43. The highs and lows, gains and losses, of the play are primarily initiated by the sea, long associated with the "fortunes" of romance and by the seventeenth century a frequent actual and imagined source of economic risk, loss, and potential gain.

44. Marina is excluded from Tharsus only to be the source of good profits, that is, virtuous accumulation in the brothel scenes in Mytilene, coincidentally one of the places where Aristotle set up a school.

45. Adapting from Wilkins, the Norton/Oxford edition adds, "I came here meaning but to pay the price, / A piece of gold for thy virginity; Here's twenty to relieve thine honesty" (19, 124–26).

46. Such a possibility is underscored in the potential parody of redemption her activities offer: Bawd speculates that she could make a "puritan of the devil" and that she is likely to "undo a whole generation." (4.5.17–18, 13). Rather than differentiate Marina from the Tharsians who are responsible for her dislocation to the brothel in the first place, Bawd's worries liken her to them. My point is not to argue that the play's commercial profits are now justified through association with her virtues, or that her virtues are devalued for their association with

the coins they procure, but to demonstrate the way that the play paradoxically makes both readings possible and perhaps even interdependent.

Chapter 3. Poverty, Surplus Value, and Theatrical Investment in The Winter's Tale

1. All citations of *The Winter's Tale* are from *The Norton Shakespeare*, ed. Stephen Greenblatt et al. (New York: Norton, 1997), 2873–953. Etymologically, "to re-create" means "to restore or refresh." Given that "recreation" could also mean nourishment in the seventeenth century, the play could be said to be addressing similar thematic concerns to those of *Pericles*.

2. To "re-create" means not only to create again, but also to create something new.

3. The primary theorization of tragicomedy in the early modern period was Giambattista Guarini's "The Compendium of Tragicomic Poetry" (1599) in *Literary Criticism: Plato to Dryden*, trans. Allan Gilbert (Detroit, Mich.: Wayne State University Press, 1962). For a more detailed discussion of tragicomedy and its productive contradictions, see the Introduction.

4. See especially Michael Bristol, "In Search of the Bear: Spatiotemporal Form and the Heterogeneity of Economies in *The Winter's Tale*," *Shakespeare Quarterly* 42.2 (1991): 145–67; Stanley Cavell, "Recounting Gains, Showing Losses: Reading *The Winter's Tale*," in his *Disowning Knowledge in Six Plays of Shakespeare* (Cambridge: Cambridge University Press, 1987), 193–221; and Barbara Correll, "Scene Stealers: Autolycus, *The Winter's Tale* and Economic Criticism," in *Money and the Age of Shakespeare*, ed. Linda Woodbridge (New York: Palgrave, 2003), 53–65.

5. Though we might be tempted to imagine Bohemia and Sicilia as similarly endowed with resources, especially given the oft-quoted "twinned lambs" speech, this scene makes clear that Bohemia is marked by its relative insufficiency.

6. The above reading is, of course, dependent on theories of gift exchange. What I am interested in here, however, is exploring not primarily how gifts, debt, and repayment structure power relationships, but how unrepayable debt is reconceived as a form of loss that can be transformed into profits later. On the gift, see Marcel Mauss's seminal *The Gift: The Form and Reason for Exchange in Archaic Societies*, trans. W. D. Halls (New York: Norton, 1990). For a critique of the gift, see Jacques Derrida, *Given Time*, vol. 1, *Counterfeit Money*, trans. Peggy Kamuf (Chicago: University of Chicago Press, 1992). For a discussion of the interdependence of work and the gift, see Scott Shershow, *The Work and the Gift* (Chicago: University of Chicago Press, 2005).

7. For an insightful psychoanalytic reading of these relationships, see Janet Adelman, *Suffocating Mothers: Fantasies of Maternal Origin in Shakespeare's Plays, Hamlet to The Tempest* (New York: Routledge, 1992).

8. Contrary to other critics, I would say that the problem of having an heir is not the play's primary issue; it is vehicle rather than tenor. For critics who read the play as focused on the issue of finding an heir, see Leonard Tennenhouse, *Power on Display* (New York: Routledge, 2005); and David Bergeron, *Shakespeare's Romances and the Royal Family* (Lawrence: University Press of Kansas, 1985).

9. Critics have noted before that the play's thematic exchanges are between loss and redemption. I want to take that observation seriously to think about why the play is so focused on these exchanges given the way the play is satu-

rated with economic language. Stanley Cavell, for example, describes his experience of reading the play and of the play itself as being "engulfed by economic terms." Yet he dismisses what I will argue is their primary significance, by shifting attention away from the play's notions of paying back toward the play's telling and recounting. As will become clear, my own reading, though its emphasis is very different, is indebted to Cavell's. See his "Recounting Gains, Showing Losses."

10. Cranmer's 1545(9) *Book of Common Prayer*, following Tyndale, translates what was usually "forgive us our debts as we also forgive our debtors," as "Forgive our trespasses as we forgive those who trespass against us," which, as John Parker and Peter Stallybrass following him suggest, says something about Protestant discomfort with the economics of Christianity as well as about shifting notions of property. See John Parker, "God Among Thieves: Marx's Christological Theory of Value and the Literature of the English Reformation" (Ph.D. diss., University of Pennsylvania, 1999); and Peter Stallybrass, "The Value of Culture and the Disavowal of Things," in *The Culture of Capital: Properties, Cities, and Knowledge in Early Modern England*, ed. Henry Turner (New York: Routledge, 2002). Leontes' Lord, while he uses "trespass," seems to hold on to the notion of debt in "paid down." For a discussion of the economics of redemption in the early modern period, see the Introduction.

11. Compare the moral deficit in the account of Bawd and Pander in *Pericles* discussed in Chapter 2.

12. Guarini argues that tragicomedy does not allow "hearers to fall into excessive tragic melancholy or comic relaxation." In contrast, both tragedy and comedy "are at fault because they go to excess" ("Compendium," 512).

13. To clarify a point about the economics of Christian redemption: the Fall is fortunate for mankind in general, but Christ (like Leontes above) overpays.

14. This line is perhaps inverted in the Lord's later suggestion that Leontes has "indeed paid down / More penitence than done trespass."

15. In contrast to the double meanings of fardel, *poena* in Latin (etymologically related to penitence) is money paid as atonement, or more generally, a fine, penalty, punishment, hardship, or loss.

16. Compare the fardel and the prosperous resolution it produces to the things in *Twelfth Night* that are not returned, and thus are signs of the inability to imagine a profitable resolution. See Chapter 1.

17. The situation of the clown and his father is later referred to with the malapropism "preposterous estate" (5.2.131–32). In the play's primary source, Robert Greene's narrative romance, *Pandosto*, the gold found with Fawnia (i.e., the Perdita equivalent) allows the shepherd to shift from a "mercenary shepherd" to one who owns his own land and sheep. See Stanley Wells, *"Perymedes the Blacksmith" and "Pandosto" by Robert Greene, a Critical Edition* (New York: Garland, 1988). The text is very specific about this change in status. At first, the shepherd and his wife "lay up" the money and jewels so they are not spied. But then "when it [the babe] grew to ripe yeeres, that it was about seven years olde, the shepheard left keeping of other mens sheepe, and with the money he found in the purse, he bought him the lease of a pretty frame, and got a small flocke of sheepe, which when Fawnia. . . . came to the age of ten yeres, hee set her to keepe" (41). He then purchases more land "intending after his death to give it to his daughter" (42). What is striking about the differences in the two texts is that in *Pandosto* these changes in status are articulated in relation to the daughter, but they are more for her benefit than they are an advantage she

herself provides. The gold that is found with her is in *Pandosto* employed as her own inheritance—which in some sense is, of course, what it ought to be, or already was. In contrast, in the play there is no mention of this specific change of status from mercenary to owner. Instead, the emphasis is purely on the increase in wealth that results from the discovery of Perdita. This value is represented, as I will discuss below, in the spices that they will purchase for the sheep-shearing festival. The relationship between wage-labor and owner (i.e., raised in the shift from mercenary to owner) does not disappear in the play; instead it reappears in the relationship between Autolycus and the shepherd family, as I will argue below, with the effect of making more explicit the relationships among capitalist investment, foreign exchange, and wage labor.

To further contextualize the greater emphasis on the shift in the shepherd's status to owner, it might be worth reflecting on Fletcher's address to the reader in the publication of his pastoral tragicomedy, *The Faithfull Shepheardesse*. In explaining and justifying the genre, Fletcher reminds his readers that the shepherd according to "all the ancient Poets and modern" is "the owners of flockes and not hyerlings." In order to be worthy of pastoral representation, one must not be a mercenary. John Fletcher, *The Faithfull Shepheardesse* (London, 1609). In *Pandosto*, Greene makes his shepherd become worthy. In the play, one could argue that class status is not taken for granted, but emphasized as the result of tragicomedy itself and the economic processes it represents.

18. Bristol, "In Search of the Bear," 166.

19. Ibid. As will become clearer below, I do not fully agree with Bristol's assessment that time is crucial. Moreover, while the early mercantilists did sometimes mention that their profits were justified because of the long duration of their ventures, their more theoretical explanations of value production are not particularly engaged with questions of time.

20. While Leontes does repent daily, it is Paulina who keeps him from remarrying. He even wants to marry his own daughter immediately upon seeing her and, of course, before her true identity is revealed. Paulina has to remind him of his wife and the oracle.

21. For a more detailed discussion of the way that "investment" was theorized in relation to these accusations, see the Introduction and my article, "Transformations of Value and the Production of 'Investment' in the Early History of the English East India Company," *Journal of Medieval and Early Modern Studies* 34, no. 3 (2004): 611–41.

22. See especially his *England's Treasure by Forraign Trade* (1664) (Oxford: Basil Blackwell, 1928), 16. Though published in 1664, the text was written in the 1620s.

23. Moreover, value accumulates to the expenditure itself, which seemingly "labors," rather than to those who work (or even to those who take risks). For more on how theories of "investment" appropriate profits so that they accrue to capital and not to labor, see my "Transformations of Value."

24. Greene, *Pandosto*, 61.

25. To "nurse" means to nurture or restore as well as to promote growth or development, thus is connected to "re-creation" and "investment." *OED*.

26. My understanding of the link between the theological and the magical in the theory of investment is indebted to Marx's analysis of the commodity, especially the section on commodity fetishism. Karl Marx, *Capital: A Critique of Political Economy*, vol. 1, trans. Ben Fowkes (New York: Vintage, 1976), 163–77. For a discussion of Marx's use of the language of theology in his analysis of the com-

modity, see John Parker, "What a Piece of Work Is Man: Shakespearean Drama as Marxian Fetish, the Fetish as Sacramental Sublime," *Journal of Medieval and Early Modern Studies* 34, no. 3 (2004): 643–72.

27. I am indebted to David Glimp for this insight.

28. This question is, in a sense, one of the primary questions Marx asks in *Capital*: How is value created by capital itself?

29. Currants were a primary import of the Levant Company. According to J. Theodore Bent, a quarrel between the Venetians and England concerning the duty on currants was the origin of England's trade in the East (i.e., the Levant). See "The English in the Levant," *English Historical Review* 5 (1890): 654–64. In 1628, the Venetian ambassador remarked that "men have been said to hang themselves because they have not enough money to buy them [currants] on certain popular festivals." *Calendar of State Papers Venetian 1628–29*, 553. Cited in Robert Brenner, *Merchants and Revolution: Commercial Change, Political Conflict, and London's Overseas Traders, 1550–1653* (Princeton, N.J.: Princeton University Press, 1993).

30. On masterless men, see A. L. Beier, *Masterless Men: The Vagrancy Problem in England 1540–1640* (London: Methuen, 1985); Paul Slack, *Poverty and Policy in Tudor and Stuart England* (London: Longman, 1988); Richard Halpern, *The Poetics of Primitive Accumulation: English Renaissance Culture and the Genealogy of Capital* (Ithaca, N.Y.: Cornell University Press, 1991); and William C. Carroll, *Fat King, Lean Beggar: Representations of Poverty in the Age of Shakespeare* (Ithaca, N.Y.: Cornell University Press, 1996).

31. Thomas More, *Utopia*, ed. Robert M. Adams (New York: Norton, 1975).

32. Marx, *Capital*, vol. 1, 874–75.

33. Service, in contrast, is an unprofitable occupation, meaning that it is not productive of capital. As a result, when Camillo says he wants to return to Sicilia, Polixenes objects because Camillo has created the need which he fills; if he leaves, the loss will be greater than if Camillo had never served him. In effect, his leaving will "wipe out" what he has added in the past, leaving a bigger hole behind him (4.2.8). Whatever value service provides (rather than produces) is embodied in Camillo himself; it is thus neither transferable, nor alienable.

34. Perhaps this is an early example of what Marx describes as the necessity of surplus population. See *Capital*, vol. 1, chapter 25.

35. This reading is dependent on Bristol's arguments about the festival and its food as partial payment to the sheep-shearing laborers.

36. As a result, I both agree and disagree with Barbara Correll's reading of Autolycus as the definitive capitalist. He is both capitalism's agent and its surplus population. See "Scene Stealers."

37. How is it that capital "employed" not only reproduces itself, but also expands? While this surplus value seems to accrue to and belong to the expenditure itself, the value, as Marx has argued, actually comes from un(der)paid labor.

38. The collapse of commodity and added value is comically registered in the dual resonances of "boot": both a covering for the foot (perhaps they change shoes) and "advantage, making good, remedy," hence, profit.

39. In *Pandosto*, the play's primary source, there is much greater focus on the problem of the marriage as an end in itself, rather than as vehicle for the resolution of other aspects of the plot. And though *Pandosto* ends with ambassadors rejoicing that "those kingdoms which through enmite had long time been dis-

severed should now through perpetual amitie be united and reconciled," the story ends tragically (91). Pandosto (the Leontes character) reflects on his prior betrayal of his friend and the actual death of his wife, and in despair kills himself. Thus, there is no redemption and none of the profits that proliferate at the play's end. There is also no Autolycus figure at all; I would argue, however, that Autolycus is drawn partially out of the shepherd whose poverty is relieved by the gold sent out with the abandoned babe.

40. Correll, "Scene Stealers," 58.

41. Ibid., 60.

42. Correll is drawing a distinction between the aristocratic family romance and the thieving (i.e., capitalist) activities of Autolycus. My point is that they become increasingly inseparable.

43. The marketing of Autolycus's skill as a peddler of ballads underscores the commercial value inherent in them: "he sings several tunes faster than you'll tell money. He utters them as he had eaten ballads." (4.4.185). The ballad is interesting for a number of reasons: it is a low form of musical poetry and also a mixed genre, not because it could often contain the story of a reversal of fortunes, but because it combines art with news; the ballad was a means of communicating stories with some pretence to truth and currency. Moreover, the ballad, especially in the play, is an artistic form that is itself a ware—a literally profitable medium.

44. A burden could also be an oracle, deriving from its relation to "onus" and "mass," that is, the lifting up of a voice or utterance. *OED*.

45. Guarini, "Compendium," 512.

46. In the play, Apollo is not the source of Autolycus's ballads, but of the oracle, which foretells future prosperity.

47. In the play's penultimate scene, Autolycus is still a loose strand. Significantly, the problem is not represented as his poverty, but as whether he will amend his ways. The play offers, however, only a parodic solution. He asks for pardon from the clown and shepherd; his virtue and value will thus be guaranteed by the "swearing" of the clown—a "gentleman born" "these four hours," newly made and, I might add, newly made on Autolycus's own account (5.2.120, 122, 140). The authenticity of Autolycus's own (self) redemption (that is, his buying back) and thus the creation of value within the play are therefore rendered unstable by the specious guarantees of the play's circular self-valorizations. (He is the guarantee for those who guarantee him.) Value created is perhaps no more than ciphers standing in the "rich place[s]" of these unstable conversions. His preposterous redemption calls attention to the ways that loss only seemingly has been fully converted. In the language of the play, only the "outside of poverty" has been exchanged. The "real," material transformations must take place elsewhere, or at least without Autolycus's aid.

48. That is, it must be one genre or another.

49. In his lines we hear a revised echo of the shepherd's son's assessment of his father's situation: "If the sins of your youth are forgiven you, you are well to live. / Gold all gold."

50. *Sir Philip Sidney*, ed. Katherine Duncan-Jones (Oxford: Oxford University Press, 1989), 244.

51. The problem with exchange has been defined as one of incommensurability since Aristotle, on whom Marx builds. But rather than simply disavow the need for exchange, the play rematerializes it in the nonaristocratic characters.

52. In other words, you cannot trespass on territory that is united with your own.

53. Though I disagree with Cavell here, I am nonetheless building on his reading. To "relish" means to taste. Etymologically, it also invokes the idea of a remainder.

54. Howard Felperin, *Shakespearean Romance* (Princeton, N.J.: Princeton University Press, 1972).

55. For the implications of these kinds of performative speech, see Judith Butler's discussion of Austin in *Gender Trouble: Feminism and the Subversion of Identity* (New York: Routledge, 1990).

56. The latter usage occurs in Leontes' punning dialogue with Mamillius: "Thy mother plays, and I / Play too; but so disgraced a part, whose issue / Will hiss me to the grave" (1.2.188–90). Of course, this play contains that most famous issue—"pursued by a bear" (stage direction at 3.3.57).

Chapter 4. Captivity and "Free" Trade

1. Michael Neill, "'Material Flames': The Space of Mercantile Fantasy in John Fletcher's *The Island Princess*," *Renaissance Drama* 27 (1999): 19–31. It would be naïve to believe that the English had no imperialistic objectives, forts, or desire to put the native inhabitants under their "protection." But understanding the company's emphasis on a set of more strictly mercantile objectives, as I will argue below, is crucial to understanding how and why discourses of free trade develop out of this trade.

2. Samuel Purchas, *Hakluytus Posthumus or Purchas his Pilgrimes*, vol. 1 (Glasgow: MacLehose and Sons, 1905–7), 50. This work was published in its entirety in 1625, but sections were printed in pamphlet form in the early 1620s.

3. Ibid.

4. "An Answer to the Hollanders Declaration, Concerning the Occurrents of the East India," 1622. *Hakluytus Posthumus*, vol. 5, 158.

5. While English discourse about the Indies is not free from such a technique, I think there is a substantial difference in England's early intentions in the Indies. Though there were aristocratic investors in the company, the discourse surrounding these voyages is much more focused on profit and merchandise than honor and country. For discussion of the class composition of investors in the company see Robert Brenner, *Merchants and Revolution: Commercial Change, Political Conflict, and London's Overseas Traders, 1550–1653* (Princeton, N.J.: Princeton University Press, 1993), and K. N. Chaudhuri, *The English East India Company: The Study of an Early Joint-Stock Company, 1600–1640* (New York: August Kelley, 1965).

On the Black Legend, see William Maltby, *The Black Legend in England: The Development of Anti-Spanish Sentiment, 1558–1660* (Durham, N.C.: Duke University Press, 1971). See also the more recent Maria DeGuzman, *Spain's Long Shadow: The Black Legend, Off-whiteness, and Anglo-American Empire* (Minneapolis: University of Minnesota Press, 2005).

6. Original Correspondence of the English East India Company, India Office Records, vol. 3, 286, July 16, 1615.

7. Ibid., vol. 5, 610, February 14. 1618. Also cited in Chaudhuri, *The English East India*, 57.

8. While the early letters from factors in the Indies back to the company ex-

press some hope for the sale of English goods, that optimism is not long lasting. Later letters and documents indicate that the company was primarily interested in importing and re-exporting. See K. N. Chaudhuri for a detailed history of the early years of the English East India Company. In *Merchants and Revolutions,* Robert Brenner also argues against the traditional account that new trade routes were developed to find markets for woolen cloths. As does Chaudhuri, Brenner argues instead that these trades concentrated on imports and were also important to the reexport market.

9. I am not arguing that none of these goods was ever consumed in England. Instead, the significant point is that the solving of one problem (not draining England's resources) could create another (no benefit for the nation). If the goods are resold in England, there might be profit for the company, but not an increase in bullion for the nation. In fact, there was considerable discussion about the dangers of excessive expenditure on imported goods in general and goods from the Indies in particular. I discuss this in more detail in my article, "Transformations of Value and the Production of 'Investment' in the Early History of the English East India Company," *Journal of Medieval and Early Modern Studies* 34, no. 3 (2004): 611–41. See also Jonathan Gil Harris's book, especially his chapter on consumption, which provides an extensive discussion of the debate about the importation and use of foreign wares. *Sick Economies: Drama, Mercantilism, and Disease in Shakespeare's England* (Philadelphia: University of Pennsylvania Press, 2004).

10. The notion of a favorable balance of trade was just being made in this period, again, as a result of the bullion-intensive trade with the Indies. I believe that the argument for a favorable balance of trade needs to be made for the reasons I have outlined above—because the trade required so much outflow of bullion to be profitable and the trade was unique in that profit was its primary benefit as opposed to use. See the Introduction and Chapter 5 for further discussions of the significance of the newly developing balance of trade argument and the conditions under which it was developed.

11. *A Discourse of Trade From England unto the East-Indies* (1621) (New York: Facsimile Text Society, 1930), 26, emphasis added.

12. See the Introduction for an extended discussion of the development of the concept of "investment" within this context.

13. For an insightful discussion of Fletcher and Massinger's *The Sea Voyage* in relation to these other kinds of discourses of free trade, see Zachary Lesser, "Tragical-Comical-Pastoral-Colonial: Economic Sovereignty, Globalization, and the Form of Tragicomedy," *ELH* 74, no. 4 (Winter 2007).

14. *Hakluytus Posthumus*, vol. 1, 10.

15. Ibid., 56.

16. Neill, "Material Flames," 104. In a reading of a similar passage by Misselden, Jonathan Gil Harris highlights the mercantilists' emphasis on the significance of the trade between nations. *Sick Economies,* 7. Harris also provides a useful historical discussion of the trope of trade as a source of unification and friendship.

17. George Birdwood, and William Foster, eds., *The First Letter Book of the East India Company 1600–1619* (1892; London: Bernard Quartich, 1965), 19–21.

18. Ibid., 19.

19. One of the earliest printed documents of the East India trade makes clear that European claims to the islands, like those the Portuguese are accused of making here, could prevent the English from establishing trade. The document includes a letter from the King of Ternata to the King of England explaining that

he would like to trade with the English, but is prevented by the Dutch, who made it a precondition of their willingness to help Ternata withstand the Portuguese. In other words, the English were prevented from trading with Ternata because of a preceding conflict between not only Ternata and one European nation, but between two other European nations. See Henry Middleton, *The Last East-Indian Voyage Containing much varietie of the state of the seuerall kingdomes where they haue traded: with the letters of three seuerall Kings to the Kings Maiestie of England, begun by one of the voyage: since continued out of the faithfull obseruations of them that are come home* (London, 1606). I will discuss these letters below.

20. Elizabeth's and Mun's texts also share a belief in the benefit of a lack of natural wealth to the production of industry itself. Of the distinction between natural and artificial wealth Mun says, "so doth it [natural wealth] make the people careless, proud and given to all excesses; whereas the second doth enforceth vigilancy, literature, arts and policy." Interestingly, this passage is the only citation of Mun in Marx's *Capital.* It appears in a discussion of the dependence of surplus value on the worker having "extra" time (over and above what is necessary to his subsistence) in order to "perform unpaid labor for other people." *England's Treasure by Forraign Trade* (1664) (Oxford: Basil Blackwell, 1928), 81–82. Though published in 1664, the text was written between 1623 and 1628. *Capital,* 649. I mention this connection here, since at stake in all three arguments is the relationship among the alienability of value—of either products or the worker's labor—freedom, and prosperity.

21. Here is Mun: "For it is in the stock of the Kingdom as in the estates of private men, who having store of wares, doe not therefore say that they will not venture out or trade with their mony (for this were ridiculous) but do also turn that into wares, whereby they multiply their Mony, and so by a continual and orderly change of one into the other grow rich, and when they please turn all their estates into Treasure; for they that have wares cannot want mony." Thomas Mun, *England's Treasure,* 16. See also the Introduction and Chapter 5 for further discussion of the idea of transformation to the developing concepts of investment and balance of trade.

22. John Fletcher, *The Island Princess,* in George Williams, ed., *The Dramatic Works in the Beaumont and Fletcher Canon,* vol. 5 (Cambridge: Cambridge University Press, 1966), 1.3. 140–42, 145–50. All further references are cited in the text.

23. As critics have pointed out, the play's only explicit reference to the mercantile comes in Armusia's use of merchant's habits to disguise himself when he frees the King. The play's initiating offer, however, links redemption and exchange. Given that the context for the play is the Portuguese colonization of the island, trade is certainly the unspoken subtext. As I will suggest below, that subtext is brought even closer to the surface by the way that the play's conflicts develop along lines similar to those of merchant captivity narratives.

24. Even though the debt might initially seem to lead to more, rather than less, subjection, paradoxically, it is the very position of debt that enables the imagination of a future freedom that is more highly valued. I will discuss this point in greater depth below in a reading of the tragicomic potential of the play's later plot lines relating to Armusia's captivity.

25. Marcel Mauss, *The Gift: The Form and Reason for Exchange in Archaic Societies,* trans. W. D. Halls (New York: Norton, 1990).

26. In his recent book, Robert Markley is also interested in the implications of noncolonial European trade in the Far East. Though his focus is primarily the Restoration and eighteenth century, the book opens with attention to the

early years of the English East India Company. Building on the work of historians such as Kenneth Pomeranz—who argues that China and not Europe is the economic engine for the early modern world and thus that Western Europe's primacy in later centuries is not the necessary conclusion of seventeenth century developments—Markley puts greater emphasis on the resistance and power of rulers in the East Indies. *The Far East and the English Imagination, 1600–1730* (Cambridge: Cambridge University Press, 2006).

Though I largely agree with the premises of the historians that Markley cites —Pomeranz, Frank, and Chaudhuri, for example—an in depth engagement with them is beyond the scope of this book as a whole and this chapter in particular. My concern is to explain how certain capitalist practices developed in England at this time because of the particular complexities of conducting trade with the East Indies. To be clear, I am not arguing that the case of England (or even Western Europe) is exceptional, nor that England provided the most fertile soil for capitalist development as a result of seeds that were sown in the early part of the seventeenth century.

27. For discussions of captivity narratives in the period, see Linda Colley, *Captives: Britain, Empire, and the World: 1600–1850* (New York: Pantheon, 2002); Daniel Vitkus, ed., *Piracy, Slavery, and Redemption: Barbary Captivity Narratives from Early Modern England* (New York, Columbia University Press, 2001); and Barbara Fuchs, *Mimesis and Empire: The New World, Islam, and European Identities* (Cambridge: Cambridge University Press, 2001), 154–63.

28. One might even conjecture that the resurgence of the medieval romance in the Renaissance had something to do with the reintroduction of the kinds of cross-cultural contacts and conflicts brought about by the crusades within the context of new modes of foreign trade. As I will explore below, those new forms of trade had an effect on the new genres.

29. *The first Englishmen in India: letters and narratives of sundry Elizabethans, written by themselves*, ed. J. Courtenay Locke (New York: AMS Press, 1970), 83. This text is reprinted from *Hakluytus Posthumus*, vol. 10, 165ff.

30. *Ibid.*, 89.

31. Richard Hakluyt, *Voyages and Discoveries The Principal Navigations, Voyages, Traffiques and Discoveries of the English Nation*, ed. Jack Beeching (London: Penguin, 1972), 168.

32. Ibid., 171.

33. *Hakluytus Posthumus*, vol. 5, 165, dated 1622.

34. Ibid., 167.

35. Ibid., 167–68.

36. Henry Middleton, *The last East-Indian Voyage* (1606), K3v, K4r.

37. *Original Correspondence*, vol. 8, 1029, January 11, 1622. According to the terms of the Dutch-Anglo accord, the two companies were to contribute equally to the defense against the Spanish and the Portuguese. The English would get one third of the trade of the Spice Islands, and the pepper trade of Java was to be shared equally. See Chaudhuri, *The English East India Company*, 50, and *Hakluytus Posthumus*, vol. 10, 507–8. According to the explanation of the events leading up to the torture and execution of Englishmen at Amboyna in 1622, the English complained that the Dutch spent lavishly and unnecessarily on building of forts that the English then had to support. *Hakluytus Posthumus*, vol. 10, 508. The Dutch also continued to capture English ships, more ships than the English captured of theirs. Chaudhuri, *The English East India Company*, 60–62.

38. Most of this section of the chapter was written in 2004 and 2005, when the

parallels to current events—the revelation of torture and humiliation of prisoners at Abu Ghraib and Guantanamo Bay—were much in my mind. On July 16, 2005, the *New York Times* reported that the United States Court of Appeals for the District of Columbia Circuit had decided the day before that the military could resume war crimes trials of terrorism suspects at Guantanamo Bay, overturning a judge's decision of the year before. The current judge argued that the Geneva conventions do not "create judicially enforceable rights." Neil A. Lewis, "Ruling Lets U.S. Restart Trial at Guantánamo Bay." On this same day, closer to home, at an air force base in Goldsboro, North Carolina, federal immigration officials posed as members of the Occupational Safety and Health Administration. They posted fliers telling immigrant workers of a mandatory safety meeting; when the workers arrived they were arrested. The justification of the sting operation was the "very serious vulnerability when there are illegal aliens working at . . . sensitive work sites in the U.S." Most of those arrested were from Mexico, Honduras, El Salvador, and Ukraine. Steven Greenhouse, "Immigration Sting Puts 2 U.S. Agencies at Odds." I mention these events here because I think they represent both the implications and the limits of connections that were first being made among freedom, trade, captivity, and even labor in the seventeenth century. Given the heightened debates about immigration in 2006, we can also see how the implications of these terms' interdependency has spread to issues regarding not only the ability to be free to sell one's labor, but even to be considered legal to sell one's labor.

39. *Hakluytus Posthumus*, vol. 3, 108–9. Dated 1610.

40. Armusia and the other Europeans there are all Portuguese, but as Shankar Raman persuasively argues, it is possible to read Armusia as representative of the English newcomers. *Framing "India": The Colonial Imaginary in Early Modern Culture* (Stanford, Calif.: Stanford University Press, 2001). See also note 44 below.

41. The play thus makes more explicit what is only implicit when the islands of Ternate and Tidore make simultaneous trade and protection agreements in the correspondence cited above.

42. Quisara's previous suitor is still plotting against Armusia. But the suitor's concerns are pushed to the margins of the plot and quickly represented as nonthreatening given that his nephew, with whom he entrusts his revenge, hopes to dissuade the suitor from this dishonorable action.

43. Bartholomew Leonardo de Argensola, *The Discovery and Conquest of the Maluco and Philipine Islands*, trans. John Stevens (London, 1708), 41. This text was published in Spanish in 1609. In Argensola's history, as in the play, the King of Tidore's speech emphasizes liberty. But liberty in Argensola's version of the speech is the means to glory and safety and can be purchased not with goods, but only with war that will throw off the European yoke. While the play repeatedly emphasizes redemption—that is, purchasing the subject back—what Argensola emphasizes is the way the islanders have purchased subjection. In his account quoted above, goods purchase that subjection.

Argensola's history was written to celebrate the 1606 fall of Ternate to Spanish forces. This context further complicates the question of the text's veracity. For a discussion of other issues surrounding the fictionality of Argensola's account, see John Villiers, "'A truthful pen and an impartial spirit': Bartolome Leonardo de Argensola and the Conquista de las Islas Malucas," *Renaissance Studies* 17 (2003): 449–73.

44. My use of "European" here is a bit imprecise. In the play, all of the European characters are Portuguese. The question of whether or not the Portuguese

are stand-ins for the English is a complicated one and has been carefully addressed by recent critics of the play. Shankar Raman argues that the newcomer, Armusia, represents the English (maybe even Sir Francis Drake) who are newer to the East Indian trade and are in competition with the Portuguese. He also explores Armusia's newcomer status to consider the class differences among the nobler adventurers and those with more purely mercantile interests. *Framing "India": The Colonial Imaginary in Early Modern Culture* (Stanford, Calif.: Stanford University Press, 2001). In contrast, Michael Neill argues that the conflict represented in the play is between the Dutch and the Portuguese. Ania Loomba, whose insightful reading also provides useful historical information about the Moluccas, explores the tensions among the different islands and relations among the Dutch, English, and Portuguese. "'Break Her Will and Bruise No Bone Sir': Colonial and Sexual Mastery in Fletcher's *The Island Princess*," *Journal for Early Modern Cultural Studies* 2.1 (2001): 68–108.

My focus here is less on the political conflicts among European nations vying for control of the East Indies trade and more on the economic problems raised by a trade that develops out of that competition. My reading of the play sees the Portuguese characters as a way to imagine a different possibility for the English and is indebted to these three insightful analyses.

45. This argument was the focus of a paper delivered at the Group for Early Modern Cultural Studies Conference in New Orleans, November 2000. Loomba argues that the play raises questions of worth because the Europeans do not have anything of worth to offer the islands in exchange for their goods. In her reading, the play balances the books when the heathens convert. They gain a God when they lose their wealth, and thus the play justifies economic plunder

46. For a more detailed discussion of the way that the tragicomic form can mystify the need for labor to transform loss into profit and create the surplus value that enables capital investment, see the penultimate section of Chapter 3. See also my "Transformations of Value, " especially 625-632.

47. It is not only that value circulates and is transferable, but also that the very transferability of value becomes paradoxically the means by which value can accumulate. In Marx's terms, capital is self-accumulating.

48. This argument could be further developed by looking at the development of the slave trade later in the seventeenth century, which is beyond the scope of this book. However, I would like to point to a striking example of this connection, namely Frederick Douglass's autobiography. One of the main components of the way Douglass imagines the state of being free is being able to sell one's own labor. In other words, for Douglass, to be free is to be able to alienate one's own labor. Marx, of course, develops a strong critique of this kind of conceptual link. He demonstrates that the ability to sell one's labor only appears to be a form of freedom and is the ruse by which exploitation appears as freedom under capitalism. A recent study of slavery and globalization (much closer to Douglass than to Marx on this point) argues that the distinction between exploitation and slavery is that in the latter one is not free to sell his or her labor. Kevin Bales, *Understanding Global Slavery: A Reader* (Berkeley: University of California Press, 2005). Frederick Douglass, *Narrative of the Life of Frederick Douglass, An American Slave, Written by Himself*, ed. David Blight (Boston: Bedford/St. Martin's Press, 2003).

49. *Hakluytus Posthumus*, vol. 5, 108–9.

50. Christopher Marlowe, *The Jew of Malta*, ed. David Bevington (Manchester:

Manchester University Press, 1997), 5.1.85. All further references are cited in the text.

51. Harris, *Sick Economies*, especially 6–7.

52. In contrast, *The Merchant of Venice*, represents what Shylock gives up as a loss, regardless of whether we think the play is sympathetic to his loss or not.

53. As in the finale of *The Winter's Tale*, (some) separations have been overcome and the affective mood has become seemingly "universal," as all of the main Portuguese characters—Ruy Dias, Armusia, and Pyniero—have a hand in the final redemption.

54. Moreover, when the play is in its tragic heights, the characters—the Governor and Armusia especially—can only imagine resolutions that depend on stark alternatives: e.g., conversion or death. But this tragicomic ending proposes solutions that are seemingly not as binary.

55. Though, as I said above, the play's explicit function is neither to convince the inhabitants of the East Indies that is safe to trade with England, nor is it to convince the population of England that this trade will benefit the commonwealth, the question of whether the trade will benefit England, more than that of whether the trade is beneficial for the East Indies, is a framing concern of the play. What I have been arguing throughout this chapter, however, is that the discourses of free trade developing in this period, which are necessary to understanding the trade as profitable for the English, develop within the context of imagining the trade as free and beneficial for the inhabitants of the Indies as well.

56. Loomba, "Colonial and Sexual Mastery," 89.

57. I am not disagreeing with Loomba's reading as much as building on it. I believe the English East India Company's economic methods and discourses developed into a form of imperialism that does not require physical coercion and ultimately produces a liberal discourse in which the state of freedom requires participation in such trade practices.

58. "Why should we then doubt that our monys sent out in trade, must not necessarily come back again in treasure; together with the great gains which it may procure in such manner as is before set down." Mun, *England's Treasure*, 19.

59. John Lyly, *Midas*, ed. David Bevington (Manchester: Manchester University Press, 2000), Prologue in Paul's (13–15, 20–22).

60. We might also take note that the fall from broadcloth to arras is a peculiar one, one that mirrors the antitheatrical complaint that theater encourages the shift from labor to idleness. But we might also read Lyly's prologue as also conventionally disingenuous, or perhaps more tragicomic than it first appears: from simple broadcloth to an elaborate arras, a tapestry that has woven into it a story, might this fall be productive? In this analogy, art displaces use and work. But perhaps even more important for a prologue to a tragicomedy (and one that represents the ultimate satisfaction of the desire for gold as a man's ironic undoing) is that it understands international traffic as the source for the transformation of England as plain product into a rich fabric, through an analogy to the transformation of England's primary export into a luxurious, richly textured story. Foreign trade is partly a fall; but it is also through this integration of the foreign that a transformation of labor into the luxury of art occurs.

61. The play represents Muslims as polytheistic.

62. One could object that the Governor of Ternate is the excluded element here. I do not disagree, but the play deemphasizes his role by making him a clear villain, whose revenge is not an attempt to seek justice, given that the play's plot

begins with the attempt to right his initial wrong—the capture and imprisonment of the King of Tidore. His imprisonment at the end is only the appropriate replacement of the King; in contrast, the imprisonment of Armusia, who redeemed the King, was the inverse of justice done at the Governor's behest. Moreover, even though the Governor, one enemy is imprisoned, the play still emphasizes the importance of alliance for trade, something only given lip service in the earlier *Merchant of Venice*.

Chapter 5. Balance, Circulation, and Equity in the "Prosperous Voyage" of The Renegado

1. See Barbara Fuchs, *Mimesis and Empire: The New World, Islam, and European Identities* (Cambridge: Cambridge University Press, 2001), 118–38; Jonathan Gil Harris, *Sick Economies: Drama, Mercantilism, and Disease in Shakespeare's England* (Philadelphia: University of Pennsylvania Press, 2004), 136–62. For discussions of representations of England's relationship with the Ottoman Empire, see Nabil Matar, *Turks, Moors, and Englishmen in the Age of Discovery* (Cambridge: Cambridge University Press, 1998); also his *Britain and Barbary 1589–1689* (Gainesville: University of Florida Press, 2005); and Daniel Vitkus, *Turning Turk: English Theater and the Multicultural Mediterranean, 1570-1630* (New York: Palgrave Macmillan, 2003). See also the work of Early Modern Ottoman historian, Daniel Goffman, especially *Britons in the Ottoman Empire, 1642–1660* (Seattle: University of Washington Press, 1998) and *The Ottoman Empire and Early Modern Europe* (Cambridge: Cambridge University Press, 2002).

2. See also Jonathan Gil Harris, *Sick Economies*, for a discussion of the play's engagement with concerns about loss of bullion. His chapter ultimately focuses on the conflicts between the interests of states and those of its "free-trading" merchants.

3. Edward Misselden, *The Circle of Commerce. Or the Balance of Trade, in defence of free trade: Opposed to Malynes Little Fish and his Great Whale, and poized against them in the Scale* (London, 1623), sig. Ee3v. As Andrea Finkelstein points out, Francis Bacon actually gave the theory its name in a private memorandum of 1616, "Advice to Villiers." But since the term did not appear in print until Bacon's 1625 *Essays*, Misselden is usually credited with the term. See her *Harmony and Balance: An Intellectual History of Seventeenth-Century English Economic Thought* (Ann Arbor: University of Michigan Press, 2000), 89–90.

4. Edward Misselden, *The Circle of Commerce*, sig. Ff.

5. Ibid., sig. Ff2v.

6. Ibid., sig. Ffv.

7. *Oxford English Dictionary*.

8. Joyce Appleby, *Economic Thought and Ideology in Seventeenth-Century England* (Princeton, N.J.: Princeton University Press, 1978), 38. See also Andrea Finkelstein, *Harmony and Balance*, 90.

9. Thomas Mun, *A Discourse of Trade from England unto the East-Indies: Answering to diverse Objections which are usually made against the same* (London, 1621), sigs. B1–B1v.

10. Ibid., sig. Bv.

11. One way that Mun sidesteps the question of legitimacy is by repeatedly representing the merchant's efforts and thus his profits as being not self-serving (a charge laid by Malynes) but instead working in the service of the common-

wealth. Moreover, while he gives precise figures for the enormous rates of profit, he is careful always to refer to those profits as accruing to (some abstract notion of) the nation ("the Common-wealth of Christendome"), rather than individual merchants. The merchant's profit is almost completely elided from the text except for a brief refutation of the excessiveness of such profits: the merchant's "time of forebearance" is long and his money spent in the employment of the nation's subjects is great. See especially sigs. C2v–C3 for these refutations. For other justifications of merchants' profits as belonging to their trade because the private wealth is linked to the common-wealth, see Edward Misselden, *The Circle of Commerce*, sig. D.

12. *Harmony and Balance*, 89 passim.

13. Even if one could get around the moral objection to benefiting at the expense of another country (and the discourse is always about the country's benefit not the company or merchants), one could still worry about being on the wrong side of the balance sheet. That concern is largely what prompted these debates in the first place.

Philip Massinger, *The Renegado*, in Daniel Vitkus, ed., *Three Turk Plays from Early Modern England* (New York: Columbia University Press, 2000), 1.1.23. All further references are cited in the text.

14. This question takes some of the questions that I argue *The Winter's Tale* explores and extends them by placing them within a more global context.

15. As Finkelstein insightfully demonstrates, one of the theory's contradictions is that it requires individuals to behave ethically and not value their well-being over that of the members of the commonwealth of the whole, but then it has no difficulty accommodating the idea that one country's (i.e., England's) well-being is of greater value than that of not only other countries, but of what we would now call the international community as a whole. *Harmony and Balance*, 84.

16. Of course, critics of capitalism, Marx being the most famous, have demonstrated that capital growth does depend on exploitation elsewhere. In his analysis of nineteenth-century European (especially English) economies, Marx focused on the exploitation of the working class—the long hours and underpaid labor even of children. Much of current analysis focuses on the way such conditions have been transferred to the Third World or to the immigrant population within the West. The latter has made strange bedfellows of capitalism's strongest supporters and supporters of immigrants' rights in the 2006–7 debates on immigration reform in the United States.

17. Scott Shershow, "Shakespeare Beyond Shakespeare," in *Marxist Shakespeares*, ed. Jean Howard and Scott Shershow (London: Routledge, 2001), 251. Shershow is building on Bataille's opposition between a restricted economy and a general economy concerned with surplus; the latter emphasizes "gifts, sacrifices, and reckless expenditures without the prospect of loss with return or reserve" (246).

18. Gerard Malynes, *The Center of the Circle of Commerce, Or, A Refutation of a Treatise, Intituled the Circle of Commerce, or the Balance of Trade, Lately Published by E.M.* (London, 1623), 55. For a discussion of Gerard Malynes's objections to the use of the metaphor of the scale and to double-entry bookkeeping as conjectural because they required the stopping of time and thus provided "an accurate representation of commerce only to be effacing the work performed by the system itself," see Mary Poovey, *A History of the Modern Fact: Problems of Knowledge in the Sciences of Wealth and Society* (Chicago: University of Chicago Press, 1998), 76–78.

19. Gerard Malynes, *The Center of the Circle of Commerce*, 56.

20. Malynes has two arguments against the certainty of the benefit of increasing exports. First, they might benefit the merchant and not the commonwealth. Second, the only way to make sure money does not leave the country is to make sure it is not undervalued.

21. Thomas Mun, *England's Treasure by Forraign Trade* (1664) (Oxford: Basil Blackwell, 1928), 16. Though published in 1664, the text was written between 1623 and 1628.

22. This is in essence a noncritical, early version of Marx's "General Formula for Capital." Karl Marx, *Capital: A Critique of Political Economy*, vol. 1, trans. Ben Fowkes (New York: Vintage, 1976), 247–57.

23. Ibid., 252.

24. Mun, *England's Treasure*, 19.

25. Fundamental to capitalism is the notion of investment in which one sends money out in the expectation of a profit. Different from venturing, investing's definition is not based on an equal chance of gain or loss, but on the expectation of a profit. Perhaps we have here some of the roots of capitalism, particularly its notions of justice and equity. Under capitalism one is paid the value of one's labor—a seemingly fair deal, yet the end result is profit. How these two opposing facts (like those evident in Mun's description of the transformation of money into wares) can exist simultaneously is at the heart of Marx's examination of capitalism and the critique of exploitation with which he is most famously associated. For Marx, the only way for the value of commodities to increase is through labor. If labor increases the value, the commodities' new value would equal its own value plus that of the labor. For money to turn into more money, then, some of labor's value must remain unpaid. Unpaid labor is thus the source of surplus value and capital accumulation. In Marx's analysis, there is still a balance in which the gain of one is the loss of the other. Proponents of capitalism instead argue for a world of continued increase in which there are no losers. Such is the basis, for example, of the largely discredited "trickle down" theories of the Reagan administration—invented by the appositely named Dr. Laffer. For further discussions of wages, capital, and investment, see my "Transformations of Value and the Production of 'Investment' in the Early History of the English East India Company," *Journal of Medieval and Early Modern Studies* 34, no. 3 (2004), especially 625–32.

26. *Seventeenth Century Economic Documents*, ed. Joan Thirsk and J. P. Cooper (Oxford: Clarendon Press, 1972), 16–23.

27. For a discussion of the mystification that takes place in assigning transformative powers to wares and money in both Mun's and Marx's accounts, see my "Transforming Investments," especially 615–18.

28. The company also imported dates, raisins, lemons, oranges, olives, almonds, and ostrich feathers from the Barbary States.

29. In 1592 the Turkey Company and Venice Company were given a new charter as the Levant Company. The Company's trade covered "Turkey," that is, the Ottoman Empire, including North Africa and the Levant (the Eastern Mediterranean).

30. A. C. Wood, *A History of the Levant Company* (London: Frank Cass, 1964), 42. According to Wood, Sir Thomas Roe, the ambassador to the Ottoman Empire, thus also the chief representative of the company there, estimated an export of 250,000 pounds per annum to Turkey.

31. Michael J. Brown, *Itinerant Ambassador: The Life of Sir Thomas Roe* (Lexington: University of Kentucky Press, 1970), 138.

32. Linda Colley, *Captives: Britain, Empire, and the World, 1600–1850* (New York: Pantheon, 2002), 43–44; Samuel Chew, *The Crescent and the Rose: Islam and England during the Renaissance* (New York: Oxford University Press, 1937), 368.

33. See Fuchs, *Mimesis and Empire;* Harris, *Sick Economies;* Nabil Matar, *Turks, Moors, and Englishmen in the Age of Discovery* and *Britain and Barbary 1589–1689;* Daniel Vitkus, *Turning Turk; Piracy Slavery, and Redemption;* and Daniel Vitkus, ed., *Barbary Captivity Narratives From Early Modern England,* with an introduction by Nabil Matar (New York: Columbia University Press, 2001).

34. According to Alfred C. Wood, the trade was prosperous and expanding from 1605 to 1645. *A History of the Levant Company,* 42.

35. Consuls made major decisions for the company and were responsible for collecting customs. They were also responsible for making sure the capitulations were followed. For more information on the responsibilities of consuls, see Wood, *A History of the Levant Company,* 217–21.

36. Much of this history depends on Wood, *A History of the Levant Company,* especially 59–64. See also M. Epstein, *An Early History of the Levant Company* (New York: Augustus M. Kelley, 1968), first published in 1908.

37. Richard Hakluyt, *The Principal Navigations, Voyages, Traffiques and Discoveries of the English Nation* (Glasgow: James Maclehose and Sons, 1904), vol. 5, 263–65. In 1579, the Sultan granted permission to trade and protection for three English merchants. Elizabeth replied, requesting open access for all English merchants. She argued that doing so would bring great English commodities to Turkey, thus ending both necessity and the loss resulting from having to buy them at higher costs elsewhere. This letter is both more deferential than the one sent to initiate trade with the kings of the East Indies and more focused not just on use value, but on the importance of avoiding loss. In 1580, an agreement was made extending the privileges granted to the three English merchants to all Englishmen (183–89).

38. While the situation might seem unusual, it is perhaps not all that different from twenty-first century geopolitics: the attempts to hold Lebanon responsible for the actions of Hezbollah, for example. Of course, the Barbary States were actually separate geographical states.

39. *Calendar of State Papers Venetian, 1600–1640,* vol. 14, 1615–17, p. 352.

40. I will discuss the poll tax in greater depth below.

41. Wood, *A History of the Levant Company,* 50.

42. David Loades, *England's Maritime Empire: Seapower, Commerce, and Policy, 1490–1690* (New York: Longman, 2000), 152.

43. Wood, *A History of the Levant Company,* 61.

44. *Calendar of State Papers, Domestic Series of the Reign of James I, 1619–1623* (London: 1857–1872) vol. 3: 11, 12, 15, 20, 41, 172, 177, 185, 190, 230, 233, 242, 250, 255, 259, 287, 291, 296, 298, 300, 302, 317, 324, 335, 347, 348, 357, 380, 387, 405, 409, 422, 441, 463, 490, 554.

45. Ibid., 233.

46. Wood, *A History of the Levant Company,* 61.

47. *Calendar of State Papers, Domestic Series of the Reign of James I, 1619–1623,* 393.

48. The play makes reference to the new sultan, Murad IV, who came to power in 1623. The ambassador to Constantinople was both representative of the crown and the company. He was chosen by the English monarch, but in consul-

tation with the company. The company was responsible for the salary of the ambassador and all of his costs, including gifts made to Ottoman rulers.

49. This history of Roe's negotiations is taken from Wood, *A History of the Levant Company*, 61–64; and Brown, *Itinerant Ambassador*, 139–64.

50. Wood, *A History of the Levant Company*, 62.

51. The former is Brown, *Itinerant Ambassador*; the latter is Wood, *A History of the Levant Company*.

52. Brown, *Itinerant Ambassador*, 119.

53. Edward Misselden, *Free Trade, or the Meanes to Make Trade Florish: Wherein, the Causes of the Decay of Trade in the Kingdome, are Discovered: And the Remedies also to Remoove the Same, are Represented* (London, 1622), sig. C1v.

54. In addition to disrupting circulation, piracy—because it is based on theft—is fundamentally about profiting from another's loss. It thus threatens the very idea of capitalist prosperity, which is theoretically victimless.

55. That trade is at the play's center is something of a critical consensus. Differentiating the play from its sources in Cervantes, Barbara Fuchs asserts that "Massinger places the emphasis squarely on commerce." *Mimesis and Empire*, 134. Though critics have explored the significance of piracy in the play in great detail, none have noted the ways that trade is actually absent. The play places an emphasis not only on commerce, but also on its disruption.

56. I am building here on Scott Shershow's insights into the relationship between the representation of thievery and cheating on the one hand, and the processes by which capital accrues on the other, especially in Ben Jonson's plays. See his "Idols of the Marketplace: Rethinking the Economic Determination of Renaissance Drama," *Renaissance Drama* 26 (1995): 1–27.

57. We might say that Grimaldi "protests too much" in his attempt to distinguish himself from merchants. While piracy was a disruptive threat to overseas trade, in its legitimate form—privateering—piracy was crucial to the accumulation of capital necessary for the expansion of England's mercantile overseas activity. As both Barbara Fuchs and Jonathan Gil Harris point out, privateering profits were crucial in providing the much needed capital for the English East India Company, for example. See Fuchs, *Mimesis and Empire*, and Harris, *Sick Economies*.

58. The phrase "unrestricted economy" is from Bataille's distinction between a general or unrestricted economy and a restricted one. Bataille develops his idea of the general economy from Mauss's analysis of the gift. A general economy is one of sacrifice and surplus, excessive giving. The distinguishing feature of a restricted economy (e.g., capitalism) is scarcity. *The Accursed Share: An Essay on General Economy*, 3 vols., trans. R. Hurley (New York: Zone Books, 1991) and *Visions of Excess: Selected Writings, 1927–1939*, ed. A. Stoekl, trans. A. Stoekl et al. (Minneapolis: University of Minnesota Press, 1985), 116–29. For an insightful reading of early modern English anxieties about losses and returns that employs Bataille's concepts of restricted and general economies to argue that anxieties about trade are displaced by a fantasy of generosity, see Scott Shershow, "Shakespeare Beyond Shakespeare," 245–64.

59. It might be useful to compare Grimaldi's imagined economy to that of Marina's in *Pericles*. As I argue in Chapter 2, she produces an economy in which unlimited accumulation is the sign of virtue. Interestingly, she does so by inverting the economy for which she is intended, one to which she was brought by pirates. Reading these two plays together might allow us to see the ways that *Pericles*

might be raising economic issues regarding piracy and its role in the disruption and development of overseas trade.

60. My reading of the reassuring qualities of the wares develops from the insights of Denys Vanrenen, "Vitelli: The Apple of Donusa's Eye," unpublished manuscript.

61. Loomba's argument is insightful and has explanatory power for the play and some of the anxieties it represents regarding English relations with the Ottoman Empire. But it does not literally address the economic concerns, which would be unrelieved by the export of religion and not more wares. Moreover, lack of interest in English exports was not a primary problem in England's trade with the Ottoman Empire as it was in the trade with the East Indies. Instead, the problems, as I outlined above, were primarily with the potential and actual disruption of the trade due to piracy. The concern of English merchants, then, was not only with having something symbolically to give (as Loomba argues) or economically to sell, but also and especially wanting to sell more than they buy or, even more interestingly, getting back more than they expend. That is actually the inverse of the gift economy, in which the desired position is that of economic loss. Less interested in honor or power for power's sake, the aim of capital expenditure is, as Mun puts it, for money to come back enhanced. That is ultimately what develops out of balance of trade theory. What I am interested in here is the benefit of raising these issues in a play set where circulation itself might be impossible.

Ania Loomba made this argument most specifically in a paper presented at the Group for Early Modern Cultural Studies Conference in New Orleans, Louisiana in 2001. See also her "'Delicious Traffick': Alterity and Exchange on Early Modern Stages" *Shakespeare Survey* 52 (1999): 201–14, and "'Break her Will and Bruise no Bone Sir': Colonial and Sexual Mastery in Fletcher's *The Island Princess*," *Journal for Early Modern Cultural Studies* 2, no. 1 (2001): 68–108.

62. While it might seem that the disruption of the activity of a Barbary pirate would allow for more economic activity, it might be the case that Grimaldi's activities also too closely mirrored the activities of the English pirates whose attacks were a great source of income for England. As I mentioned above, Fuchs reminds us that much of the funding for the East India Company came from the revenue of privateers, and Harris argues that Asambeg's profits from Grimaldi's activities were reminiscent of the ways that the crown prospered from its privateers. See *Mimesis and Empire*, and *Sick Economies*, respectively.

63. Harris, *Sick Economies*, 157–60.

64. Ibid. Fuchs, *Mimesis and Empire*, 134–37.

65. It seems fairly unusual to have one English character in the play. The characters in most plays representing foreign trade have Spanish, Portuguese, Italian, or—as in the case of *The Sea Voyage*—French characters. Usually, there are groups of characters from different countries.

66. John Florio, *A Worlde of wordes, or Most copious, and exact dictionarie in Italian and English* (London, 1598), E6v.

67. Ibid., Kk4v.

68. "Carazo" and "harach" are cross-listed in the indexes for the *Calendar of State Papers Venetian*.

69. *Calendar of State Papers Venetian*, vol. 14, 289.

70. Ibid., 289, 301, 310.

71. Ibid., 310–12.

72. Ibid., 346.

73. Exodus 21:23–24 and 22:1–3.

74. For discussions of Renaissance revenge tragedy, see Fredson Bowers, *Elizabeth Revenge Tragedy, 1587–1642* (Gloucester, Mass.: Peter Smith, 1959); Eleanor Prosser, *Hamlet and Revenge* (Stanford, Calif.: Stanford University Press, 1967); Michael Neill, "Remembrance and Revenge: Hamlet, Macbeth, and the Tempest" in Ian Donaldson, ed., *Jonson and Shakespeare* (Atlantic Highlands, N.J.: Humanities Press, 1983), 35–56; Stephen Kerrigan, *Revenge Tragedy* (Oxford: Oxford University Press, 1996); and Rene Girard, "Hamlet's Dull Revenge," in *Shakespeare and the Question of Theory,* ed. Patricia Parker and Geoffrey Hartman (New York: Methuen, 1985), 280–302. While none of these critics writes about the economics of revenge specifically, Girard characterizes revenge as unproductive mimesis.

75. Religion has a complex role in the play. On the one hand, it is the structuring opposition of difference in the play; it provides the primary conflict—that between Muslims and Christians—expressed through a relationship of incommensurable desire and exchange. But religion also provides a moral framework for this play. The repeated answer to the problem of this opposition and its temptations (conversion, castration, wealth, goods, women) is to exercise restraint by relying on, or turning to, religious faith—the proper one, that is. To put it another way, religion in the play functions not just as an external source of conflict, but as an explicit moral framework, one that protects virtue and provides the means to counter temptations. What is odd here (though perhaps not quite paradoxical) is that religious faith produces the very opposition and its consequent temptations from which it then also serves as protection. By giving us two similar opposites, "evil" can be transformed into "good," and that conversion can then be put to use in the working through of economic concerns—the possibilities of loss as well as the ethical questions about the making of profits.

76. Saint Anselm, *Cur Deus Homo (Why God Became Man)*, trans. Sidney Norton Deane (Chicago: Open Court Publishing, 1903).

77. Ibid.

78. In this way, though the play's Christian characters on the surface espouse Catholic doctrine (Grimaldi asks, "can good deeds redeem me," 4.1. 96), the play justifies profit not by meritorious good deeds, but sees good works (according to Reformation doctrine and particularly Calvinist doctrine) as a sign of deserving. See R. H. Tawney, *Religion and the Rise of Capitalism* (Gloucester, Mass.: Harcourt Brace, 1962). Tawney explains that the ideal for Calvin "is a society which seeks wealth with the sober gravity of men who are conscious at once of disciplining their own characters by patient labor, and of devoting themselves to a service acceptable by God" (105). In this ideal society, "good works are not a way of attaining salvation, but they are indispensable as a proof that salvation has been attained" (109). Moreover, "the Christian must conduct his business with a high seriousness, as in itself a kind of religion" (111).

79. James Simpson, "Spirituality and Economics in Passus 1–7 of the B Text," *Yearbook of Langland Studies* 1 (1987): 83–103.

80. See Chapter 2 for a discussion of the parodic treatment of these worries in *Pericles*.

81. Vitelli's own initial remarks about his redemption are conventionally economic: "I grant to have mastered / The rebel appetite of flesh and blood / Was far above my strength and still owe for it / To that great power that lent it" (4.3.26–29).

82. Keir Elam, "The Fertile Eunuch: *Twelfth Night,* Early Modern Intercourse,

and the Fruits of Castration," *Shakespeare Quarterly* 47 (1996): 11. His reading is not about this historical situation, nor is it about trade.

83. While this play does not have a character who pretends to be a eunuch, the fates of all of the primary Venetian male figures (the defrocked pirate, the almost castrated apprentice, the disguised and then exposed merchant) excepting only the Jesuit, beg to be read in relation to the English eunuch, Carazie.

84. I am building here on Fuchs's insight that the play "replaces the model of Grimaldi, the renegade pirate, with that of the successful merchant." She argues that the merchant can trade without changing allegiances and thus has more fluidity and is less reviled, but that his excessive aspirations might cost him his masculinity. *Mimesis and Empire*, 136. My reading differs from hers in that it reads the limitation—that is, restraint—as transformable into positive productivity.

85. Recognizing this significance of the figure of the eunuch to obstructed trade helps to contextualize the play's early associations between restraint and overexpenditure.

86. Paulina has a charm that keeps her safe from rape as long as she is herself unwilling. Rather than reading this as just a plot necessity, I would suggest that it helps to keep in the foreground her active refusal of the viceroy's interest. The fact that the relic she wears will only protect her from coercion but not from succumbing to temptation, a fact of which the audience is repeatedly reminded, serves to highlight both her restraint and her autonomy.

87. After Vitelli baptizes her she claims, "I am another woman" (5.3.121).

88. Paulina is the agent of this theft as well, so it might also be the case that the "choicest jewels" figuratively contain within them her magical relic (the source of protection from Muslim desires) transformed or converted into an economic profit.

89. While trade and exchange were considered highly natural in the early part of the seventeenth century, profit was only becoming so. Joyce Appleby argues that the personal drive for gain as a natural, ineradicable prompter of human action gradually became integrated into new economic theories. Her subsequent discussion is focused on the ways that laws attempted to accommodate these naturalized behaviors by not encouraging theft. For example, laws that instituted high customs on imports and thus would encourage sneaking goods into the country were considered unproductive. My point is much less about the way the system accommodated the behaviors it was beginning to recognize as natural and is more about understanding how the economic practices and theories that developed in relation to them functioned to naturalize their own objectives—in this case, profit. Appleby, *Economic Thought and Ideology*, 93–95.

90. For discussions of conversion, see Loomba, "Delicious Traffick," Jonathan Burton, "English Anxiety and the Muslim Power of Conversion: Five Perspectives on 'Turning Turk' in Early Modern Texts," *Journal for Early Modern Cultural Studies* 2 (2002): 35–67; and Patricia Parker, "Preposterous Conversions: Turning Turk, and its 'Pauline Rerighting.'" *Journal for Early Modern Cultural Studies* 2 (2002): 1–34.

91. It is also significant that these losses are associated with the one character in the play who is connected with any form of labor and thus might actually be a productive, but exploited force, in the economy, the shadow-side of the profits the play justifies. Gazet's association with the shadow-side of capitalist profits might then partially undermine the play's profitable narratives.

92. *Oxford Dictionary of English Etymology*, ed. C. T. Onions (Oxford: Clarendon Press, 1969).

93. Jonathan Gil Harris reads the escape as consonant with Misselden's view of "free trade" in which the treasure is free from Turkish enemies, *Sick Economies*, 160–61. My emphasis falls less on the Turks as competition and more on the way the play uses the problems presented by the Turkish corsairs as a means to resolve problems within balance of trade theory itself.

94. This possibility develops in part because the idea of restraint disassociates indulgence and excess from profit by communicating the autonomy of the redeemed and restrained subject, who is then, by definition, anything but obstructed. (In order to exercise restraint, one must already be in a position of autonomy and control.)

95. Fredric Jameson, *The Political Unconscious: Narrative as a Socially Symbolic Act* (Ithaca, N.Y.: Cornell University Press, 1981).

96. I am not arguing that tragicomedy and the utopian dialectic make their first appearances in response to capitalist processes, but that this particular instantiation of tragicomedy becomes useful for this purpose.

97. See Karl Marx and Frederick Engels, *The Communist Manifesto: A Modern Edition*, introduction by Eric Hobsbawm (New York: Verso, 1998). Francis Fukuyama argues, incorrectly I think, that the expanse of liberal capitalism constitutes the end of history, that is, the absence of contradictions necessary for radical systemic change. *The End of History and the Last Man* (New York: Free Press, 1992).

Epilogue

Note to epigraph: Patti Smith, "In Excelsis Deo." Written by Patti Smith © 1975 Linda Music. Used by Permission. All Rights Reserved.

1. *The Works of John Webster*, vol. 2, ed. David Gunby et al. (Cambridge: Cambridge University Press, 2003), 1.1.7, 37. The full title of the play is *The Devil's Law-Case. Or, When Women Goe to Law, The Devill is Full of Businesse*. All further references are cited in the text.

2. This formula is tragicomic because Romelio actually wants the man to die. Here he fetches a man to life, which would be contrary to his purpose, only in order for his temporary existence to be profitable to him in the future.

3. Whereas in other tragicomedies, for example, *The Tempest* and *The Renegado*, redemption is the preferred alternative to revenge, in this play the revenge and the redemption are one and the same. But they are not confused with each other as they are in Shylock's grief in *The Merchant of Venice*. Instead, this play demonstrates—perhaps even parodies—the genre's insistence that such a shift from revenge to redemption ought to occur and will also be productive. Of course, in this play, the redemption is kept a secret; the revenge that did not work and thus never actually took place produces only more failed attempts at revenge. Redemption, then, is not a conscious alternative but merely what happens after the attempts at revenge keep failing.

4. Most editors date the play's performance sometime between 1617 and 1619. It would thus predate the mercantilists' primary debate. The play was first published in 1623 in the middle of that debate.

5. Walter Cohen, "Pre-revolutionary Drama" in *The Politics of Tragicomedy: Shakespeare and After*, ed. Gordon McMullan and Jonathan Hope (London: Routledge, 1992), 135.

6. Ibid.

7. Though Cohen has written insightfully about the theater and the economy, his analysis here has different concerns. His reading of the play is part of a survey of tragicomedy that attempts to counter readings of tragicomedy that read the genre as apolitical or backwards from the revolution. For an interesting reading of the relationship between class and family dynamics in the play, see Aspasia Velissariou, "Class and Gender Destabilization in Webster's *The Devil's Law-Case*," *Cahiers Élisabéthains* 63 (2003): 71–88.

8. For a discussion of the ways the English East India Company needed to configure money sent out of the country to purchase spices not as loss, but as potentially profitable expenditure, see the Introduction and Chapter 4.

9. See, for example, Lee Bliss, *The World's Perspective: John Webster and the Jacobean Drama* (Piscataway, N.J.: Rutgers University Press, 1983), especially 181–85.

10. See Karl Marx, *Capital: A Critique of Political Economy*, vol. 1, trans. Ben Fowkes (New York: Vintage, 1976); and Karl Marx and Frederick Engels, *The Communist Manifesto: A Modern Edition*, intro. Eric Hobsbawm (New York: Verso, 1998). For a discussion of the theology of Marx's analysis, see John Parker, "What a Piece of Work Is Man: Shakespearean Drama as Marxian Fetish, the Fetish as Sacramental Sublime," *Journal of Medieval and Early Modern Studies* 34, no. 3 (2004): 643–72.

11. Such a reading is supported by many of the details of the domestic plot. For example, the mother figure accuses herself of adultery to get revenge on her son, who would become what the clown in *The Winter's Tale* might call a bastard newly made; in the words of the court, she will labor her son's undoing. The sister whose troubled marriage negotiations get the plot rolling agrees to pretend that she is pregnant by one of the supposedly dead suitors in order to claim her brother's soon-to-be-born bastard child, whom he conceived with a nun. Lee Bliss understands the representation of the failure of the family as a way of critiquing the "relentless pursuit of solely private ends" (*World's Perspective*, 181). I read the play as less moralistic and more interested in revealing and debunking the myth of the family as a source of restoration, as a way to make all things right.

12. For a reading of the statue as surplus value, see the final section of Chapter 3.

13. On wonder in Shakespeare's plays, see T. G. Bishop, *Shakespeare and the Theater of Wonder* (Cambridge: Cambridge University Press, 1996).

14. Jonathan Dollimore, *Radical Tragedy: Religion, Ideology, and Power in the Drama of Shakespeare and His Contemporaries* (Durham, N.C.: Duke University Press, 2004), especially 64–67.

15. William Ingram, *The Business of Playing: The Beginnings of the Adult Professional Theater in Elizabethan London* (Ithaca, N.Y.: Cornell University Press, 1992), especially 115–49.

16. William Ingram, "The Economics of Playing," in *A New History of Early English Drama*, ed. John Cox and David Kastan (New York: Columbia University Press, 1997), p. 315.

17. The word "exhibition" is interesting here for the way it combines showing and the spending necessary to one's living.

18. Rob Walker, "Tragicommerce: How a Terrible News Event Made the Transition to Commodity," *New York Times Magazine*, 25 June 2006, 22.

19. I refer both to the possibility of making a commercial profit and the idea that life in this world is what matters.

20. *The Onion*, 42, no. 51 (21–27 December 2006), 9.

21. Mark C. Taylor, *Confidence Games: Money and Markets in a World Without Redemption* (Chicago: University of Chicago Press, 2004), 211.

22. Talal Asad, *Formations of the Secular: Christianity, Islam, Modernity* (Stanford, Calif.: Stanford University Press, 2003), 61.

23. Asad is clear to explain that the similarity of these projects to Christian redemption makes them neither necessarily Christian nor religious; there is no place in secular redemptive politics he argues for "the idea of a redeemer saving a sinner through *his* submission to suffering." *Formations of the Secular*, 61–62.

24. P. Treanor, "Neoliberalism, Origins, Theory, and Definition," http://web.inter.nl.net/users/Paul.treanor/neoliberalism.html, cited in David Harvey, *A Brief History of Neoliberalism* (Oxford: Oxford University Press, 2005), 3. The literature on neoliberalism is extensive. In addition to Harvey, see Michael A. Peters, *Poststructuralism, Marxism, and Neoliberalism: Between Theory and Politics* (Lanham, Md.: Rowman & Littlefield, 2001) for a discussion of neoliberalism and political theory; and Aihwa Ong, *Neoliberalism as Exception: Mutations in Citizenship and Sovereignty* (Durham, N.C.: Duke University Press, 2006) for an anthropological approach.

25. Andrew Revkin, "Carbon Neutral Is Hip, But Is It Green?" *New York Times*, 29 April 2007.

26. *New York Times*, 6 May 2007, 1, 8 (emphasis added).

Bibliography

Adelman, Janet. *Suffocating Mothers: Fantasies of Maternal Origin in Shakespeare's Plays, Hamlet to the Tempest.* New York: Routledge, 1992.

Agamben, Giorgio. *The Coming Community.* Trans. Michael Hardt. Minneapolis: University of Minnesota Press.

Agnew, Jean-Christophe. *Worlds Apart: The Market and the Theater in Anglo-American Thought, 1550–1750.* Cambridge: Cambridge University Press, 1988.

Althusser, Louis, and Etienne Balibar. *Reading Capital.* Trans. Ben Brewster. London: Verso, 1997.

Anderson, Judith. *Translating Investments: Metaphor and the Dynamic of Cultural Change in Tudor-Stuart England.* New York: Fordham University Press, 2005.

Andrewes, Lancelot. "A SERMON PREACHED before the KINGS MAIESTIE, at White-hall, on Monday, the XXV. of December, A. D. MDCIX. being CHRIST-MASSE day." *Sermons by the Right Honorable and Reverend Father in God, Lancelot Andrewes, late Lord Bishop of Winchester.* London, 1629.

Annand, William. *Fides Catholica, or, The Doctrine of the Catholick Church: In Eighteen Grand Ordinances.* London, 1661.

Anselm. *Cur Deus Homo (Why God Became Man).* Trans. Sidney Norton Deane. Chicago: Open Court Publishing, 1903.

Appleby, Joyce Oldham. *Economic Thought and Ideology in Seventeenth-Century England.* Princeton, N.J.: Princeton University Press, 1978.

Argensola, Bartholomew Leonardo de. *The Discovery and Conquest of the Maluco and Philipine Islands.* Trans. John Stevens. London: 1708.

Aristotle. *The Politics.* Trans. Sir Ernest Barker. Oxford: Oxford University Press, 1995.

Aristotles politiques, or Discourses of gouernment. Translated out of Greeke into French, with expositions taken out of the best authours, specially out of Aristotle himselfe, and out of Plato, conferred together where occasion of matter treated of by them both doth offer it selfe: the obseruations and reasons whereof are illustrated and confirmed by innumerable examples, both old and new, gathered out of the most renowmed empires, king-domes, seignories, and commonweals that euer haue bene, and wherof the knowledge could be had in writing, or by fayethfull report, concerning the beginning, proceeding, and excellencie of ciuile gouernment. By Loys Le Roy, called Regius. Translated out of French into English (London, 1598).

Asad, Talal. *Formations of the Secular: Christianity, Islam, Modernity.* Stanford: Stanford University Press, 2003.

Bales, Kelvin. *Understanding Global Slavery: A Reader.* Berkeley: University of California Press, 2005.

Barbour, Richmond. *Before Orientalism: London's Theater of the East, 1576–1626.* Cambridge: Cambridge University Press, 2003.

Bartels, Emily. *Spectacles of Strangeness: Imperialism, Alienation, and Marlowe.* Philadelphia: University of Pennsylvania Press, 1991.

Bataille, Georges. *Visions of Excess: Selected Writings, 1927–1939.* Ed. A. Stoekl. Trans. A. Stoekl et al. Minneapolis: University of Minnesota Press, 1985.

———. *The Accursed Share: An Essay on General Economy.* 3 vols. Trans. R. Hurley. New York: Zone Books, 1991.

Beaumont, Francis, and John Fletcher. *A King and No King.* London, 1619.

Beier, A. L. *Masterless Men: The Vagrancy Problem in England 1540–1640.* London: Methuen, 1985.

Bent, J. Theodore. "The English in the Levant." *English Historical Review* 5 (1890): 654–64.

Berger, Harry. "Marriage and Mercifixion in *The Merchant of Venice*: The Casket Scene Revisited." *Shakespeare Quarterly* 32 (1981): 155–62.

Bergeron, David. *Shakespeare's Romances and the Royal Family.* Lawrence: University Press of Kansas, 1985.

Birdwood, George, and William Foster, eds. *The First Letter Book of the East India Company, 1600–1619.* London: Bernard Quartich, 1965.

Bishop, T. G. *Shakespeare and the Theater of Wonder.* Cambridge: Cambridge University Press, 1996.

Blaug, Mark, ed.. *The Early Mercantilists: Thomas Mun (1571–1641), Edward Misselden (1608–1634), Gerard de Malynes (1586–1623).* Aldershot, Hants.: Elgar, 1991.

Bliss, Lee. *The World's Perspective: John Webster and the Jacobean Drama.* Piscataway, N.J.: Rutgers University Press, 1983.

Booth, Stephen. "*Twelfth Night* 1.1: The Audience as Malvolio." In *Shakespeare's "Rough Magic": Essays in Honor of C. L. Barber.* Ed. Peter Erickson and Coppelia Kahn. Newark: University of Delaware Press, 1985, 149–67.

Bowers, Fredson. *Elizabeth Revenge Tragedy, 1587–1642.* Gloucester, Mass.: Peter Smith, 1959.

Braudel, Fernand. *Civilization and Capitalism, 15th-18th Century, Vol. I: The Structure of Everyday Life.* Berkeley: University of California Press, 1992.

Brenner, Robert. *Merchants and Revolution: Commercial Change, Political Conflict, and London's Overseas Traders, 1550–1653.* Princeton, N.J.: Princeton University Press, 1993.

Bristol, Michael. "In Search of the Bear: Spatiotemporal Form and the Heterogeneity of Economies in *The Winter's Tale*." *Shakespeare Quarterly* 42, no. 2 (1991): 145–67.

Brown, Michael J. *Itinerant Ambassador: The Life of Sir Thomas Roe.* Lexington: University of Kentucky Press, 1970.

Bruster, Douglas. *Drama and the Market in the Age of Shakespeare.* Cambridge: Cambridge University Press, 2005.

Burton, Jonathan. "English Anxiety and the Muslim Power of Conversion: Five Perspectives on 'Turning Turk' in Early Modern Texts." *Journal for Early Modern Cultural Studies* 2 (2002): 35–67.

Butler, Judith. *Gender Trouble: Feminism and the Subversion of Identity.* New York: Routledge, 1990.

Calendar of State Papers, Domestic Series of the Reign of James I, 1619–1623.

Calendar of State Papers Venetian, 1600–1640.

Carr, Cecil, ed. *Select Charters of Trading Companies, A.D. 1530–1707.* New York: Burt Franklin, 1913.

Carroll, William C. *Fat King, Lean Beggar: Representations of Poverty in the Age of Shakespeare.* Ithaca, N.Y.: Cornell University Press, 1996.

Cavell, Stanley. "Recounting Gains, Showing Losses: Reading *The Winter's Tale.*" *Disowning Knowledge in Six Plays of Shakespeare.* Cambridge: Cambridge University Press, 1987. 193–221.

Challis, C. E. *The Tudor Coinage.* Manchester: Manchester University Press, 1978.

Chaudhuri, K. N. *The English East India Company: The Study of an Early Joint-Stock Company 1600–1640.* New York: August Kelley, 1965.

———. *Asia Before Europe: Economy and Civilisation of the Indian Ocean from the Rise of Islam to 1750.* Cambridge: Cambridge University Press, 1990.

Chew, Samuel. *The Crescent and the Rose: Islam and England During the Renaissance.* New York: Oxford University Press, 1937.

Cohen, Stephen. "Between Form and Culture: New Historicism and the Promise of a Historical Formalism." In *Renaissance Literature and Its Formal Engagements.* Ed. Mark Rasmussen. New York: Palgrave, 2002. 17–41.

Cohen, Walter. *Drama of a Nation: Public Theater in Renaissance England and Spain.* Ithaca, N.Y.: Cornell University Press, 1985.

———. "*The Merchant of Venice* and the Possibilities of Historical Criticism." *English Literary History* 49 (1982): 765–89.

———. "Prerevolutionary Drama." In *The Politics of Tragicomedy: Shakespeare and After.* Ed. Gordon McMullan and Jonathan Hope. London: Routledge, 1992. 122–51.

Coleman, D. C., ed. *Revisions in Mercantilism.* London: Methuen, 1969.

Colie, Rosalie. *The Resources of Kind: Genre Theory in the Renaissance.* Ed. Barbara Lewalski. Berkeley: University of California Press, 1973.

Colley, Linda. *Captives: Britain, Empire, and the World: 1600–1850.* New York: Pantheon, 2002.

Cormack, Braden. "Marginal Waters: *Pericles* and the Idea of Jurisdiction." In *Literature, Mapping, and the Politics of Space in Early Modern Britain.* Ed. Andrew Gordon and Bernhard Klein. Cambridge: Cambridge University Press, 2001. 155–80.

Correll, Barbara. "Scene Stealers: Autolycus, *The Winter's Tale* and Economic Criticism." In *Money and the Age of Shakespeare: Essays in New Economic Criticism.* Ed. Linda Woodbridge. New York: Palgrave Macmillan, 2003. 53–67.

Craig, John. *The Mint: A History of the London Mint from A.D. 287 to 1948.* Cambridge: Cambridge University Press, 1953.

DeGuzman, Maria. *Spain's Long Shadow: The Black Legend, Off-whiteness, and Anglo-American Empire.* Minneapolis: University of Minnesota Press, 2005.

Derrida, Jacques. *Given Time, Vol. 1, Counterfeit Money.* Trans. Peggy Kamuf. Chicago: University of Chicago Press, 1992.

Dixon, Mimi. "Tragicomic Recognition: Medieval Miracles and Shakespearean Romance." In *Renaissance Tragicomedy.* Ed. Nancy Maguire. New York: AMS Press, 1987.

Dollimore, Jonathan. *Radical Tragedy: Religion, Ideology, and Power in the Drama of Shakespeare and His Contemporaries.* Durham, N.C.: Duke University Press, 2004.

Donno, Elizabeth, ed. *Three Renaissance Pastorals*. Binghamton, N.Y.: Medieval and Renaissance Texts and Studies, 1993.

Elam, Keir. "The Fertile Eunuch: *Twelfth Night,* Early Modern Intercourse, and the Fruits of Castration." *Shakespeare Quarterly* 47 (1996): 1–36.

Engle, Lars. *Shakespearean Pragmatism: Market of His Time*. Chicago: University of Chicago Press, 1993.

———. "'Thrift Is Blessing': Exchange and Explanation in *The Merchant of Venice.*" *Shakespeare Quarterly* 37 (1986): 20–37.

Epstein, M. *An Early History of the Levant Company.* New York: Augustus M. Kelley, 1968.

Feaveryear, Sir Albert. *The Pound Sterling: A History of English Money.* Oxford: Oxford University Press, 1963.

Felperin, Howard. *Shakespearean Romance.* Princeton, N.J.: Princeton University Press, 1972.

Ferber, M. "The Ideology of *The Merchant of Venice.*" *English Literary Renaissance* 20 (1990): 431–64.

Ferguson, Margaret. *Dido's Daughters: Literacy, Gender, and Empire in Early Modern England and France.* Chicago: University of Chicago Press, 2003.

Finkelstein, Andrea. *Harmony and Balance: An Intellectual History of Seventeenth-Century English Economic Thought.* Ann Arbor: University of Michigan Press, 2000.

Fisher, F. J. "London's Export Trade in the Early Seventeenth Century." In *The Growth of English Overseas Trade in the Seventeenth and Eighteenth Centuries.* Ed. W. E. Minchinton. London: Methuen, 1969.

Fletcher, John. *The Faithfull Shepheardesse.* London, 1609.

———. *The Island Princess. The Dramatic Works in the Beaumont and Fletcher Canon.* Ed. George Williams. Vol. 5. Cambridge: Cambridge University Press, 1966. 539–643.

Florio, John. *A Worlde of wordes, or Most copious, and exact dictionarie in Italian and English.* London, 1598.

Forman, Valerie. "Material Dispossessions and Counterfeit Investments: The Economies of *Twelfth Night.*" In *Money and the Age of Shakespeare: Essays in New Economic Criticism.* Ed. Linda Woodbridge. New York: Palgrave, 2003. 113–27.

———. "Transformations of Value and the Production of 'Investment' in the Early History of the English East India Company." *Journal of Medieval and Early Modern Studies* 34 (2004): 611–41.

Foster, Verna. *The Name and Nature of Tragicomedy.* Aldershot, England: Ashgate, 2004.

Foster, W., ed. *Letters Received by the East India Company from its Servants in the East.* Transcribed from the "Original Correspondence" Series of the India Office Records. 6 vols., 1618–41. London: Sampson Low, Marston & Company, 1896–1902.

Frye, Northrop. *Anatomy of Criticism: Four Essays.* Princeton, N.J.: Princeton University Press, 1975.

Fuchs, Barbara. *Mimesis and Empire: The New World, Islam, and European Identities.* Cambridge: Cambridge University Press, 2001.

Fukuyama, Francis. *The End of History and the Last Man.* New York: Free Press, 1992.

Fumerton, Patricia. *Cultural Aesthetics: Renaissance Literature and the Practice of Social Ornament.* Chicago: University of Chicago Press, 1991.

Gill, Roma. "Introduction." *The Jew of Malta.* By William Shakespeare. Ed. Roma Gill. Oxford: Oxford University Press, 1995. ix–xii.

Gillies, John. *Shakespeare and the Geography of Difference.* Cambridge: Cambridge University Press, 1992.

Girard, René. "Hamlet's Dull Revenge." In *Shakespeare and the Question of Theory.* Ed. Patricia Parker and Geoffrey Hartman. New York: Methuen, 1985. 280–302.

Goffman, Daniel. *Britons in the Ottoman Empire, 1642–1660.* Seattle: University of Washington Press, 1998.

———. *The Ottoman Empire and Early Modern Europe.* Cambridge: Cambridge University Press, 2002.

Goldberg, Jonathan. "Textual Properties." *Shakespeare Quarterly* 37 (1986): 213–17.

Greene, Robert. *Perymedes the Blacksmith and Pandosto.* Ed. Stanley Wells. New York: Garland, 1988.

Greene, Roland. *Unrequited Requests: Love and Empire in the Colonial Americas.* Chicago: Chicago University Press, 1999.

Greenham, Richard. *The workes of the reuerend and faithfull seruant af Iesus Christ M. Richard Greenham, minister and preacher of the Word of God collected into one volume: reuised, corrected, and published, for the further building of all such as loue the truth, and desire to know the power of godlinesse.* London, 1612.

Greenhouse, Steven. "Immigration Sting Puts 2 U.S. Agencies at Odds." New York Times. 16 July 2005.

Guarini, Giambattista. *The Compendium of Tragicomic Poetry.* In *Literary Criticism: Plato to Dryden.* Trans. Allan Gilbert. Detroit, Mich.: Wayne State University Press, 1962. 504–33.

———. *Il Pastor Fido. Three Renaissance Pastorals,* Ed. Elizabeth Donno. Binghamton, N.Y.: Medieval and Renaissance Texts and Studies, 1993.

Hakluyt, Richard. *Voyages and Discoveries: The Principal Navigations, Voyages, Traffiques and Discoveries of the English Nation.* Ed. Jack Beeching. London: Penguin, 1972.

Halpern, Richard. *The Poetics of Primitive Accumulation: English Renaissance Culture and the Genealogy of Capital.* Ithaca, N.Y.: Cornell University Press, 1991.

———. *Shakespeare Among the Moderns.* Ithaca, N.Y.: Cornell University Press, 1997.

Harris, Jonathan Gil. *Sick Economies: Drama, Mercantilism, and Disease in Shakespeare's England.* Philadelphia: University of Pennsylvania Press, 2004.

Harte, N. B. "State Control of Dress and Social Change in Pre-Industrial England." In *Trade, Government, and Economy in Pre-Industrial England: Essays Presented to F. J. Fisher.* Ed. D. C. Coleman and A. H. John. London: Weidenfeld and Nicolson, 1976. 132–65.

Harvey, David. *A Brief History of Neoliberalism.* Oxford: Oxford University Press, 2005.

Hawkes, David. *Idols of the Marketplace: Idolatry and Commodity Fetishism in English Literature, 1580–1680.* New York: Palgrave Macmillan, 2001.

Heckscher, Eli. *Mercantilism.* Trans. Mendel Shapiro. 2 vols. London: Allen and Unwin, 1955.

Henke, Robert. *Pastoral Transformations: Italian Tragicomedy and Shakespeare's Late Plays.* Newark: University of Delaware Press, 1997.

Herrick, Marvin. *Tragicomedy: Its Origin and Development in Italy, France, and England.* Urbana: Illinois University Press, 1955.

Hirst, David L. *Tragicomedy.* London: Methuen, 1984.

Hope, Jonathan, and Gordon McMullan, eds. *The Politics of Tragicomedy: Shakespeare and After.* London: Routledge, 1992.

Howard, Jean. "Gender on the Periphery." In *Shakespeare and the Mediterranean: The Proceedings of the Seventh World Shakespeare Congress, Valencia 2001.* Ed. Tom Clayton, Susan Brock, and Vicente Fores Lopes. Newark: University of Delaware Press, 2004. 344–62.

———. "Shakespeare, Geography, and the Work of Genre on the Early Modern Stage." *Modern Language Quarterly* 64, no. 3 (2003): 299–322.

Ingram, William. *The Business of Playing: The Beginnings of the Adult Professional Theater in Elizabethan London.* Ithaca, N.Y.: Cornell University Press, 1992.

———. "The Economics of Playing." In *A New History of Early English Drama.* Ed. John Cox and David Kastan. New York: Columbia University Press, 1997. 313–27.

"Israel Bombs Anti-Semitism Out of Lebanon." *The Onion* 42, no. 51 (21–27 December 2006), 9.

Jameson, Fredric. *The Political Unconscious: Narrative as a Socially Symbolic Act.* Ithaca, N.Y.: Cornell University Press, 1981.

Jones, Ann Rosalind, and Peter Stallybrass. *Renaissance Clothing and the Materials of Memory.* Cambridge: Cambridge University Press, 2000.

Jones, Norman. *God and the Moneylenders: Usury and Law in Early Modern England.* Oxford: Basil Blackwell, 1989.

Jordan, Constance. "Eating the Mother: Property and Propriety in Pericles." *Creative Imitation: New Essays on Renaissance Literature in Honor of Thomas Greene.* Binghamton, N.Y.: Binghamton University Press, 1992. 331–54.

Kastan, David. "*All's Well That Ends Well* and the Limits of Comedy." *ELH* 52 (1985): 575–89.

Kerrigan, Stephen. *Revenge Tragedy.* Oxford: Oxford University Press, 1996.

Knapp, Jeffrey. *Shakespeare's Tribe: Church, Nation, and Theater in Renaissance England.* Chicago: University of Chicago Press, 2002.

Kopytoff, Igor. "The Cultural Biography of Things: Commoditization as Process." In *The Social Life of Things: Commodities in Cultural Perspective.* Ed. Arjun Appadurai. Cambridge: Cambridge University Press, 1986. 64–91.

Korda, Natasha. *Shakespeare's Domestic Economies: Gender and Property in Early Modern England.* Philadelphia: University of Pennsylvania Press, 2002.

Lane, Kris. *Pillaging the Empire: Piracy in the Americas, 1500–1700.* New York: M. E. Sharpe, 1998.

Langer, Susanne. *Feeling and Form: A Theory of Art.* New York: Scribner, 1953.

Lawson, George. *Theo-politica, or, A body of divinity containing the rules of the special government of God, according to which, he orders the immortal and intellectual creatures, angels, and men, to their final and eternal estate : being a method of those saving truths, which are contained in the Canon of the Holy Scripture, and abridged in those words of our Saviour Jesus Christ, which were the ground and foundation of those apostolical creeds and forms of confessions, related by the ancients, and, in particular, by Irenæus, and Tertullian.* London, 1659.

Lesser, Zachary. "Tragical-Comical-Pastoral-Colonial: Economic Sovereignty, Globalization, and the Form of Tragicomedy." *ELH* 74, no. 4 (2007).

Lewis, Anthony. "'I Feed on Mother's Flesh': Incest and Eating in Pericles." *Essays in Literature* (1988): 147–63.

Lewis, Neil A. "Ruling Lets U.S. Restart Trial at Guantánamo Bay." *New York Times*. 16 July 2005.

Loades, David. *England's Maritime Empire: Seapower, Commerce, and Policy, 1490–1690.* New York: Longman, 2000.

Locke, John Courtenay, ed. *The First Englishmen in India: Letters and Narratives of Sundry Elizabethans, written by themselves.* New York: AMS Press, 1970.

Loomba, Ania. "'Break Her Will and Bruise No Bone Sir': Colonial and Sexual Mastery in Fletcher's *The Island Princess.*" *Journal for Early Modern Cultural Studies* 2, no. 1 (2001): 68–108.

———. "'Delicious Traffick': Alterity and Exchange on Early Modern Stages." *Shakespeare Survey* 52 (1999): 201–14.

Lyly, John. *Midas.* Ed. David Bevington. Manchester: Manchester University Press, 2000.

Maguire, Nancy Klein, ed. *Renaissance Tragicomedy: Explorations in Genre and Politics.* New York: AMS Press, 1987.

Malcomson, Cristina. "'What you Will': Social Mobility and Gender in *Twelfth Night.*" *The Matter of Difference: Materialist Feminist Criticism of Shakespeare.* Ed. Valerie Wayne. Ithaca, N.Y.: Cornell University Press, 1991. 29–58.

Mallin, Eric. *Inscribing the Time: Shakespeare and the End of Elizabethan England.* Berkeley: University of California Press, 1995.

Maltby, William. *The Black Legend in England: The Development of Anti-Spanish Sentiment, 1558–1660.* Durham, N.C.: Duke University Press, 1971.

Malynes, Gerard. *The Center of the Circle of Commerce, Or, A Refutation of a Treatise, Intituled the Circle of Commerce, or the Balance of Trade, Lately Published by E.M.* London, 1623.

———. *Saint George for England, Allegorically Described.* London, 1601.

Markley, Robert. *The Far East and the English Imagination, 1600-1730.* Cambridge: Cambridge University Press, 2006.

Marlowe, Christopher. *The Jew of Malta.* Ed. David Bevington. Manchester: Manchester University Press, 1997.

Marx, Karl. *Capital: A Critique of Political Economy.* Vol. 1. Trans. Ben Fowkes. New York: Vintage, 1976.

———. *Grundrisse.* Trans. Martin Nicolaus. London: Penguin, 1973.

Marx, Karl, and Frederick Engels. *The Communist Manifesto: A Modern Edition.* Intro. Eric Hobsbawm. New York: Verso, 1998.

Massinger, Philip. *The Renegado. Three Turk Plays from Early Modern England.* Ed. Daniel Vitkus. New York: Columbia University Press, 2000.

Matar, Nabil. *Britain and Barbary, 1589–1689.* Gainesville: University of Florida Press, 2005.

———. *Turks, Moors, and Englishmen in the Age of Discovery.* Cambridge: Cambridge University Press, 1998.

Mauss, Marcel. *The Gift: The Form and Reason for Exchange in Archaic Societies.* Trans. W. D. Halls. New York: Norton, 1990.

McMullan, Gordon. *The Politics of Unease in the Plays of John Fletcher.* Amherst: University of Massachusetts Press, 1994.

Minchinton, W. E. "Introduction." *The Growth of English Overseas Trade in the Seventeenth and Eighteenth Centuries.* Ed. W. E. Minchinton. London: Methuen, 1969.

Middleton, Henry. *The last East-Indian voyage Containing much varietie of the state of the seuerall kingdomes where they haue traded: with the letters of three seuerall Kings to the Kings Maiestie of England, begun by one of the voyage: since continued out of the faithfull obseruations of them that are come home.* London, 1606.

Misselden, Edward. *Free Trade, or the Meanes to Make Trade Florish: Wherein, the Causes of the Decay of Trade in the Kingdome, are Discovered: And the Remedies also to Remoove the Same, are Represented.* London, 1622.

———. *The Circle of Commerce. Or the Balance of Trade, in defence of free trade: Opposed to Malynes Little Fish and his Great Whale, and poized against them in the Scale.* London, 1623.

More, Thomas. *Utopia.* Ed. Robert M. Adams. New York: Norton, 1975.

Mowat, Barbara. "Shakespearean Tragicomedy." In *Renaissance Tragicomedy: Explorations in Genre and Politics.* Ed. Nancy Maguire. New York: AMS Press, 1987.

Mukerji, Chandra. *From Graven Images: Patterns of Modern Materialism.* New York: Columbia University Press, 1983.

Muldrew, Craig. *The Economy of Obligation: The Culture of Credit and Social Relations in Early Modern England.* New York: Palgrave Macmillan, 1998.

Mun, Thomas. *A Discourse of Trade from England unto the East-Indies: Answering to diverse Objections which are usually made against the same.* London, 1621.

———. *England's Treasure by Forraign Trade, Or, The Balance of our Forraign Trade is the Rule of our Treasure* (1664). Oxford: Basil Blackwell, 1928.

Neill, Michael. "'Material Flames': The Space of Mercantile Fantasy in John Fletcher's *The Island Princess.*" *Renaissance Drama* 27 (1999): 19–31.

———. "Remembrance and Revenge: Hamlet, Macbeth and the Tempest." In *Jonson and Shakespeare.* Ed. Ian Donaldson. Atlantic Highlands, N.J.: Humanities Press, 1983.

Nerlich, Michael. *Ideology of Adventure: Studies in Modern Consciousness, 1100–1750.* Minneapolis: University of Minnesota Press, 1987.

Newman, Karen. "Portia's Ring: Unruly Women and Structures of Exchange in *The Merchant of Venice.*" *Shakespeare Quarterly* 38 (1987): 19–33.

Ong, Aihwa. *Neoliberalism as Exception: Mutations in Citizenship and Sovereignty.* Durham, N.C.: Duke University Press, 2006.

Onions, C. T., ed. *Oxford Dictionary of English Etymology.* Oxford: Clarendon Press, 1969.

Orgel, Stephen. *Impersonations: The Performance of Gender in Shakespeare's England.* Cambridge: Cambridge University Press, 1996.

Original Correspondence of The English East India Company, India Office Records.

Parker, John. "God Among Thieves: Marx's Christological Theory of Value and the Literature of the English Reformation." Ph.D. diss., University of Pennsylvania, 1999.

———. "What a Piece of Work Is Man: Shakespearean Drama as Marxian Fetish, the Fetish as Sacramental Sublime." *Journal of Medieval and Early Modern Studies* 34, no. 3 (2004): 643–72.

Parker, Patricia. "Preposterous Conversions: Turning Turk, and Its 'Pauline' Rewriting." *Journal for Early Modern Cultural Studies* 2 (2002): 1–34.

Pelikan, Jaroslav. *Reformation of Church and Dogma, 1300–1700.* Chicago: University of Chicago Press, 1984.

Peters, Michael A. *Poststructuralism, Marxism, and Neoliberalism: Between Theory and Politics.* Lanham, Md.: Rowman & Littlefield, 2001.

Pietz, William. "The Problem of the Fetish, II: The Origin of the Fetish." *RES* 13 (1987): 23–45.

Poovey, Mary. *A History of the Modern Fact: Problems of Knowledge in the Sciences of Wealth and Society.* Chicago: University of Chicago Press, 1998.

Prosser, Eleanor. *Hamlet and Revenge.* Stanford: Stanford University Press, 1967.

Purchas, Samuel. *Hakluytus Posthumus or Purchas his Pilgrimes.* 20 vols. Glasgow: MacLehose and Sons, 1905–7.

Rackin, Phyllis. "The Impact of Global Trade in *The Merchant of Venice.*" *Shakespeare-Jahrbuch* 138 (2002): 73–88.

Raman, Shankar. *Framing "India": The Colonial Imaginary in Early Modern Culture.* Stanford: Stanford University Press, 2001.

Rasmussen, Mark David, ed. *Renaissance Literature and Its Formal Engagements.* New York: Palgrave, 2002.

Revkin, Andrew. "Carbon Neutral Is Hip, But Is It Green?" *New York Times.* 29 April 2007.

Robertson, Kellie. *The Laborer's Two Bodies: Labor and the "Work" of the Text in Medieval Britain, 1350–1500.* New York: Palgrave Macmillan, 2006.

Rooney, Ellen. "Form and Contentment." *Modern Language Quarterly* 61 (2000): 17–40.

Ryan, Kiernan. "Shakespearean Comedy and Romance: The Utopian Imagination." In *Shakespeare's Romances: Contemporary Critical Essays.* Ed. Alison Thorne. New York: Palgrave Macmillan, 2003. 27–52.

Scott, W. R. *Constitution and Finance of English, Scottish, and Irish Joint-Stock Companies to 1721.* Cambridge: Cambridge University Press, 1910–12.

Shakespeare, William. *The Comical History of the Merchant of Venice, Or Otherwise Called the Jew of Venice. The Norton Shakespeare.* Ed. Stephen Greenblatt et al. New York: Norton, 1997. 1081–145.

———. *Measure for Measure. The Norton Shakespeare.* Ed. Stephen Greenblatt et al. New York: Norton, 1997. 2021–90.

———. *Pericles. The Arden Shakespeare.* Ed. Suzanne Gossett. London: Thomson Learning, 2004.

———. *The Tempest. The Norton Shakespeare.* Ed. Stephen Greenblatt et al. New York: Norton, 1997. 3047–107.

———. *Twelfth Night, The Arden Shakespeare.* Ed. J. M. Lothian and T. W. Craik. London: Routledge, 1975.

———. *The Winter's Tale. The Norton Shakespeare.* Ed. Stephen Greenblatt et al. New York: Norton, 1997. 2873–953.

Shell, Marc. *Money, Language, and Thought: Literary and Philosophical Economies from the Medieval to the Modern Era.* Berkeley: University of California Press, 1982.

Shershow, Scott. "Idols of the Marketplace: Rethinking the Economic Determination of Renaissance Drama." *Renaissance Drama* 26 (1995): 1–27.

———. *The Work and The Gift.* Chicago: University of Chicago Press, 2005.

Shuger, Debora. *The Renaissance Bible: Scholarship, Sacrifice, and Subjectivity.* Berkeley: University of California Press, 1994.

Sidney, Philip. *Sir Philip Sidney.* Ed. Katherine Duncan-Jones. Oxford: Oxford University Press, 1989.

Simpson, James. "Spirituality and Economics in Passus 1-7 of the B Text." *Yearbook of Langland Studies* 1 (1987): 83–103.

Slack, Paul. *Poverty and Policy in Tudor and Stuart England.* London: Longman, 1988.

Slights, Camille. "The Principle of Recompense in *Twelfth Night.*" *Modern Language Review* 77 (1982): 537–46.

Sommerville, John. *The Secularization of Early Modern England: From Religious Culture to Religious Faith.* Oxford: Oxford University Press, 1992.

Spencer, Eric. "Taking Excess, Exceeding Account: Aristotle Meets *The Merchant of Venice.*" In *Money and the Age of Shakespeare: Essays in New Economic Criticism.* Ed. Linda Woodbridge. New York: Palgrave Macmillan, 2003. 143–58.

Spufford, Peter. *Money and Its Use in Medieval Europe.* Cambridge: Cambridge University Press, 1988.

Stallybrass, Peter. "Marx's Coat." In *Border Fetishisms: Material Objects in Unstable Spaces.* Ed. Patricia Spyer. New York: Routledge, 1998. 183–207.

———. "The Value of Culture and the Disavowal of Things." In *The Culture of Capital: Properties, Cities, and Knowledge in Early Modern England.* Ed. Henry Turner. New York: Routledge, 2002. 275–92.

———. "Worn Worlds: Clothes and Identity on the Renaissance Stage." In *Subject and Object in Renaissance Culture.* Ed. Margreta de Grazia, Maureen Quilligan, and Peter Stallybrass. Cambridge: Cambridge University Press, 1996. 289–320.

Strohm, Stephanie. "Make Money, Save the World: Businesses and Nonprofits are Spawning Corporate Hybrids." *New York Times,* 6 May 2007.

Supple, B. E. *Commercial Crisis and Change in England, 1600–1642.* Cambridge: Cambridge University Press, 1959.

Tawney, R. H. *Religion and the Rise of Capitalism.* Gloucester, Mass.: Harcourt Brace, 1962.

Taylor, Mark C. *Confidence Games: Money and Markets in a World Without Redemption.* Chicago: University of Chicago Press, 2004.

Tennenhouse, Leonard. *Power on Display: The Politics of Shakespeare's Genres.* New York: Methuen, 1986.

Thirsk, Joan. *Economic Policy and Projects: The Development of a Consumer Society in Early Modern England.* Oxford: Oxford University Press, 1978.

Thirsk, Joan, and J. P. Cooper, eds. *Seventeenth Century Economic Documents.* Oxford: Clarendon Press, 1972.

Turner, Henry, ed. *The Culture of Capital: Properties, Cities, and Knowledge in Early Modern England.* New York: Routledge, 2002.

Twyne, Thomas. *The patterne of painefull aduentures Containing the most excellent, pleasant, and variable historie of the strange accidents that befell vnto Prince Apollonius, the Lady Lucina his wife, and Tharsia his daughter. Wherein the vncertaintie of this world, and the fickle state of mans life are liuely described.* London, 1576, reprinted 1594, 1607.

Vanrenen, Denys. "Vitelli: The Apple of Donusa's Eye." Unpublished manuscript.

Velissariou, Aspasia. "Class and Gender Destabilization in Webster's *The Devil's Law-Case.*" *Cahiers Élisabéthains* 63 (2003): 71–88.

Villiers, John. "'A Truthful Pen and an Impartial Spirit': Bartolome Leonardo de Argensola and the Conquista de las Islas Malucas." *Renaissance Studies* 17 (2003): 449–73.

Viner, Jacob. *Studies in the Theory of International Trade.* New York: Harper and Bros., 1937.

———. *Religious Thought and Economic Society.* Ed. Jacques Melitz and Donald Winch. Durham, N.C.: Duke University Press, 1978.

Vitkus, Daniel. *Turning Turk: English Theater and the Multicultural Mediterranean, 1570–1630.* New York: Palgrave Macmillan, 2003.

Vitkus, Daniel, ed. *Barbary Captivity Narratives from Early Modern England.* New York: Columbia University Press, 2001.

————. *Piracy, Slavery, and Redemption: Barbary Captivity Narratives from Early Modern England.* New York: Columbia University Press, 2001.

Walker, Rob. "Tragicommerce: How a Terrible News Event Made the Transition to Commodity." *New York Times Magazine.* 25 June 2006, 22.

Weber, Max. *The Protestant Ethic and the Spirit of Capitalism.* Trans. Talcott Parsons. London: George Allen and Unwin, 1930.

Webster, John. *The Devil's Law-Case. Or, When Women Go to Law, the Devil is Full of Business. The Works of John Webster.* Vol. 2. Ed. David Gunby et al. Cambridge: Cambridge University Press, 2003.

Wilkins, George. *The painfull aduentures of Pericles prince of Tyre Being the true history of the play of Pericles, as it was lately presented by the worthy and ancient poet Iohn Gower.* London, 1608.

Williams, Raymond. *Keywords: A Vocabulary of Culture and Society.* Oxford: Oxford University Press, 1976.

Wood, A. C. *A History of the Levant Company.* London: Frank Cass, 1964.

Woodbridge, Linda. *Vagrancy, Homelessness, and English Renaissance Literature.* Urbana: University of Illinois Press, 2001.

Žižek, Slavoj. *The Sublime Object of Ideology.* London: Verso, 1989.

Index

Abu Ghraib, 236n.38

accumulation, 64; of capital, 152, 154–55, 181, 241n.25; infinite, 79–84, 243–44n.59. *See also* balance of trade theory; capitalism; investment; Marx, Karl; mercantilism; trade, overseas

Adam and Eve, 7

Adelman, Janet, 227n.7

Amboyna, 235n.37

Amphitruo (Plautus), 207n.20

Andrewes, Lancelot, 12

Anselm, Saint, 11, 15, 19, 20, 33, 38, 74, 79, 83, 177, 221nn.1, 2, 226n.42. See also *Why God Became Man* (*Cur Deus Homo*)

anti-Semitism, 47, 198

Appleby, Joyce, 149, 205n.8, 206nn.11, 14, 214n.51, 246n.89

Argensola, Bartolomeo de, 135, 138, 140

Aristotle, 79, 80, 81, 232n.51; on usury and unnatural breeding, 66, 67; on usury and stagnation, 67, 73

Asad, Talal, 199

autonomous subjects, 179, 181, 183

balance of trade theory: 5, 14, 15, 147–56, 223n.15, 233n.15; and benefit of the commonwealth, 149–51; and capitalism, 151, 152, 155, 184; compatibility of overbalance and moderation in, 151–52, 155; consumption in, 149–51, 155; definition of, 4; emphasis on flow and

circulation of goods and money, 4–6, 153–56, 189; and equity, 147–54, 156, 184; imbalance in, 149–51, 156, 162; imports and exports in, 148–51, 153, 155; link of moderation, balance, and equity in, 149–52, 155–56, 162; loss and profit in, 3–6, 151–52, 154–56; and the Ottoman Empire, 156–62, 247n.93; and *The Renegado*, 21, 148, 166–70, 173, 174, 177; restraint in, 151, 152, 156, 162; return of treasure in, 5, 150–56; as a theory of a world of fixed resources, unlimited growth, and no imbalances, 151–55, 162, 165. *See also* bullion, drain of; investment; Malynes, Gerard; mercantilism; Misselden, Edward; Mun, Thomas; trade, overseas

Bales, Kevin, 237n.48

ballads, 102–4, 106–8

Barbary States (Algiers, Tripoli, and Tunis), 158–61, trade with, 147–57, 162; in *The Renegado*, 21, 146, 162, 169, 172–75, 179–81, 183. *See also* piracy, in the Barbary States

Bataille, Georges, 212n.38, 240n.17, 243n.58

Beaumont, John: and John Fletcher, 210n.27

beggars: in *Pericles*, 75–78

Beier, A. L., 230n.30

Bent, J. Theodore, 230n.29

Berger, Harry, Jr., 41

Bible: Geneva, 15; King James, 11, 12; New
Testament, 37, 40, 175; Old Testament,
37, 40, 44, 45, 175
black legend, 115
Blaug, Mark, 205n.4
Bergeron, David, 209n.24, 227n.8
body politic, 118
Book of Common Prayer, The (Cranmer),
228n.10
Booth, Stephen, 53
Bowers, Fredson, 245n.74
Brechtian alienation, 193
Brenner, Robert, 205n.5, 230n.29,
232nn.5, 8
Bristol, Michael, 94–95, 99, 227n.4,
230n.35
brothels. *See* prostitution
Brown, Michael, J., 160, 242n.31,
243nn.51, 52
bullion: drain of, 1, 3–5, 11, 13, 57–58,
72–73, 95, 108, 116–17, 142, 147–49,
154–57, 186–89, 205nn.4, 5. *See also*
balance of trade theory; investment;
trade, overseas
Burton, Jonathan, 246n.90
Bush, George W., 199
Butler, Judith, 232n.55

capital, 95, 96, 99, 100, 102, 106, 142, 151,
155, 182; accumulation of, 152, 154–55,
181, 241n.25; casualties of, 99;
demystification of, 22; growth and
equity, 184, reproduction of, 188, 197;
as replacement for wonder, 195, 196;
self-generating potential of, 15; and
theater, 195, 197. *See also* capitalism;
global economy; investment; Marx,
Karl; surplus value
Capital. See Marx, Karl
capitalism, 23, 73, 76, 80, 199, 243n.54;
and balance of trade theory, 151, 152,
155, 184; demystifications of, 185;
ethics of, 188–90; and equity, 241n.25;
excesses of, 22, 197, 200–203;
limitations of, 203; roots of, 241n.25;
ruse of, 44; mystifications of, 191,
225n.33; and productivity, 44–45, 186,
188, 203; and redemption, 88, 197–203
(*see* economics of Christian
redemption); as a system of growth,
151–52; and tragicomedy, 87–88, 98,

108, 184–85, 188–90, 198. *See also*
capital; global economy; investment;
labor; Marx, Karl; surplus value
captivity, 21, 118, 121; in *The Island
Princess*, 21, 121–24, 128–29, 131; in the
Barbary States, 157–59; productivity in
The Island Princess, 131–36, 139. *See also*
captivity narratives; prisoners
captivity narratives, 114, 121, 124–28;
redemption and profit linked in,
125–28; and mercantile activity, 125–28.
See also captivity; prisoners
carbon-neutral offsets, 200–202
Carroll, William, 225n.28, 230n.30
Catholicism: and economics, 21. *See also*
Christian redemption, pre-Reformation
Cavell, Stanley, 97, 107, 227n.4, 227–28n.9
Cervantes, Miguel, 131, 243n.55
Challis, C. E., 220n.71
charity, 20, 64, 65, 67, 69–74, 77, 79
Chaudhuri, K. N., 205n.5, 218n.46,
219n.49, 220n.70, 232nn.5, 7, 8,
234n.26, 235–36n.37
Cheetham, Joanna, 213n.46
Chew, Samuel, 242n.32
Christian redemption, 7, 12, 31, 200; and
capitalism, 88, 132, 201–2; changes
under Reformation doctrine, 81;
contradictions of, 36–38, 41–42; in *The
Devil's Law-Case*, 22, 188, 193; differences
from economic discourses, 14–16; and
economic discourses and practices,
11–18, 19, 64, 74, 78, 113, 177 (*see also*
economics of Christian redemption);
fortunate fall (*felix culpa*), 1, 15, 33; in
The Merchant of Venice, 27–28; materiality
of, 87; in *Pericles*, 64, 74, 78, 81–84; pre-
Reformation, 64, 164, 177, 178, 245n.78;
and prosperity, 8–10; in *The Renegado*, 21,
164, 166, 169, 170, 175–79, 181–82,
245n.75; the satisfaction, 11–14;
satisfaction as revenge, 35–36, 41;
secularization/refunctioning of as
economic, 14, 64, 74, 78, 83, 88, 93,
97–98, 104, 107, 190–91, 214n.51,
216n.13; secularization of (twenty-first
century), 198, 202; and tragicomedy, 7–8,
11, 14, 16–18, 56, 113 (*see also specific
plays*); triangulation with capitalism and
tragicomedy, 97–98, 188, 190–91, 197,
198. *See also* Adam and Eve; Redemption

circulation of money and goods, 4–5, 36;
in *The Renegado*, 165–69, 171, 173–74,
180; obstructed, 60–62, 158, 161–62,
170–74, 180, 243n.54; uninhibited,
182–84. *See also* accumulation; balance
of trade theory; capital; exchange
class conflict, 75–79
class difference, 70–71, 75–78
cloth, decline in sale of, 3; and
"investment," 207n.18, 50–52; and the
East Indies trade, 51; in *Twelfth Night*,
50–55, 58–60
coercion, 114–16, 120–21, 126–28, 135,
140; in *The Island Princess*, 123, 129–31,
136, 142; refusal of, 114–16, 120–21,
127–28. *See also* colonialism
Cohen, Walter, 187, 188, 207n.21, 208n.23,
216n.10, 217n.29, 217–18n.33
Colie, Rosalie, 209n.23
Colley, Linda, 235n.27, 242n.32
colonialism, 21; English refusal in the East
Indies, 114–16, 120–21, 128–29, 135,
140–42, 145; resistance to in *The Island
Princess*, 21, 138, 141–42
comedy, 27–28, 32, 38, 48, 59; closure in,
10, 78, 114; conventions inverted,
67–68; generic limitations for
imagining foreign trade as profitable,
8–10, 17, 19, 27–28, 32, 38, 54–55,
60–63, 78, 114; marriage plot in, 38–39,
44, 46; parody of comedic obstacle,
77–78; in relation to tragicomedy, 7, 8,
10, 28, 32, 38, 52–55, 59–63. See also
The Merchant of Venice; Twelfth Night
Comedy of Errors, The (Shakespeare), 61
comic-tragedy, 130, 131, 135, 141
commerce: as a form of redemption
(twenty-first century), 198–201. *See also*
capitalism; East Indies trade; English
East India Company; global economy;
global trade; investment; Levant
Company; mercantilism; Ottoman
trade; trade, overseas;
commodification, 100, 103, 105, 189, 197
commodity, 102, 107, 120, 162, 231n.43;
definition of, 225–26n.36
commonwealth, economic benefit of, 117,
140, 149–51, 159, 206n.12, 13
Communist Manifesto, The (Engels and
Marx), 247n.97; and tragicomedy, 185
competition, economic: 21; with the

Dutch in the East Indies trade, 21,
124–28, 135, 194
confession, 200
consumerism, 200. *See also* consumption
consumption, 165–67, 197, 201, 203; in
balance of trade theory, 149–51, 155; in
Pericles, 66–70, 72–73, 78;
transformation of excess and
consumption into legitimate profit, 21,
169, 176, 178, 180–82
conversion: in *The Island Princess*, 136, 137,
139, 142–45; in *The Merchant of Venice*,
39–42, 46; in *The Renegado*, 147, 169,
178–82, 245n.75
Cormack, Braden, 221n.3
Correll, Barbara, 101, 227n.4, 230n.36
Craig, John, 220n.71
Cranmer, Thomas: *The Book of Common
Prayer*, 228n.10
credit, 77, 225n.33; in *Pericles*, 80–83
cross-dressing, 48, 49, 52

debt, 77–78, 123–24; and sin, 11; in *The
Merchant of Venice*, 28–32, 40–41; as
opposed to begging in *Pericles*, 77–78; in
The Winter's Tale, 88–89, 91, 97
DeGuzman, Maria, 232n.5
democracy, 198
Derrida, Jacques, 227n.6
deserving, 13
Devil's Law-Case, The (Webster), 200, 202,
203, 221n.78; absence of restraint in,
189; capital, productive power of, in,
186, 188; capital, productive power and
its relation to tragicomedy, in, 188–90;
demystification of capital in; 22,
190–91; demystification of productivity
in, 22, 188–94, 196; East Indies in,
186–89, 192, 194–96; economics of
redemption in, 188, 190–91, 197; ethics
of trade in, 187–89; excessive (tragic)
productivity in, 22, 188–91, 197; family
in, 22, 187–88, 190–92, 194, 196; global
economy in, 186–87, 189, 193–96;
perversion in, 22, 192, 193; pleasure of,
193, 196–97; redemption in, 22, 188,
193; revenge in, 22, 187, 191, 192, 194;
secularization of redemption in,
190–91; theater, economics of, in, 191,
194–96; theater/spectacle in, 22, 188,
191–94, 196; tragicomic formula in,

The Devil's Law-Case (*cont.*)
    10–11, 186–87, 190; and tragicomic
    productivity, limitations of, 22, 187–93,
    196–97; triangulation of religious
    redemption, tragicomedy, and capital
    in, 188, 190–91; and *The Winter's Tale*,
    191–95
distribution, 203; unequal, 75–78
Dixon, Mimi, 7, 210n.26
Dollimore, Jonathan, 193
Donaldson, Ian, 245n.74
Douglass, Frederick, 237–38n.48
Drake, Francis, 125, 236n.44

East Indies trade (English), 3–6, 11, 20,
    21, 114–18; and balance of trade
    arguments, 3–6, 117, 156–57, 233n.10;
    coercion in, 114–16, 120–21, 126–28,
    135, 140; coercion/subjection, refusal
    in, 114–16, 120–21, 127–28;
    competition with Dutch, 124–28, 135,
    194; conflict among East Indies islands
    in, 121, 126, 129–31, 136, 138, 140,
    236n.41; conflict between Europeans
    and inhabitants of the East Indies in,
    126, 128–29, 135, 140; in *The Devil's
    Law-Case*, 186–89, 192, 194–96; free
    trade in, 114–18, 120–21, 127–28, 135,
    140; imports, 116; in *The Island
    Princess*, 121–24; liberation in, 118,
    120–21; mercantile as opposed to
    colonial objectives, 114–18;
    multilateral trade, 116–17, 142;
    national benefit of, 117, 140;
    opposition to Dutch, Portuguese, and
    Spanish practices, 114–16, 120,
    128–29, 135, 140; and outflow of
    bullion, 3, 11, 116–17, 142, 156–57,
    205n.4; reexports, 3, 116–17, 120–21;
    rejection of colonial models of
    possession, 114–18, 120–21, 141–42,
    145; sale of English cloth, 3, 51; as
    source of redemption, 113–14, 119–21;
    as space of theatrical discovery,
    194–96; and theories of investment,
    3–6, 212n.40; theorizing profitability
    of, 115–17, 120–21, 140; tragicomic
    effects of, 119–21, 128; and value,
    alienability of, 117, 121. *See also*
    English East India Company;
    investment; *The Island Princess*

economics of Christian redemption: 8–18,
    19, 31–32, 36–38, 43, 55, 64, 109, 113,
    177; *in The Devil's Law-Case*, 188,
    190–91, 197; in *The Jew of Malta*, 42–44,
    137, 145; in *The Merchant of Venice*, 19,
    27–44, 47; in *Pericles*, 64, 80–84; in *The
    Renegado*, 21, 148, 171, 177–80;
    secularization/refunctioning of as
    economic, 14, 64, 74, 78, 83, 88, 93,
    97–98, 104, 107, 190–91, 214n.51,
    216n.13; and tragicomedy, 11, 16–20,
    46, 64, 78, 88; in *The Winter's Tale*, 88,
    90–93, 95–98, 104, 107. *See also*
    Christian redemption; economic
    theory; economies; investment; nothing
economic theory, general: and dramatic
    genres, 2, 23–24, 87–88, 103; recoding
    of, 14, 16, 21; theater's participation in,
    2; and tragicomedy, 2, 6, 9–11, 13,
    16–21, 23–24, 27–28, 49, 52, 64–65, 68,
    73–74, 77–79, 86–90, 92–98, 107, 109,
    113, 119–21, 128, 130, 135–37, 140,
    146, 187, 197, 198. *See also* balance of
    trade theory; commerce; East Indies
    trade; economics of Christian
    redemption; economies; global
    economy; investment; trade, overseas
economies: dynamic, 17, 19–20, 64, 68,
    72–74, 154, 184, 233n.11; insular and
    static, 10, 19, 27, 42, 45–46, 60–68,
    71–74, 183, 238n.62; insular and static
    in *The Merchant of Venice*, 27, 42, 45–46,
    183, 238n.62; insular and static in
    Pericles, 65–74; insular and static in
    Twelfth Night, 27, 60–65, 183; restricted,
    13, 40, 152–53, 240n.17; unrestricted,
    243n.58; models in *The Renegado*,
    165–75; models in *The Winter's Tale*, 93,
    96–98, 104, 107. *See also* balance of
    trade theory; commerce; East Indies
    trade; economic theory; global
    economy; investment; trade, overseas
Elam, Keir, 49, 52, 179–80, 219n.53, 53
Elizabeth I: circulating letter to the Kings
    of the East Indies, 119–21, 124, 128,
    130, 135, 144, 145, 234n.20; and trade
    with Ottoman Empire, 242n.37
enclosure of land, 99
Engels, Frederick. See *The Communist
    Manifesto*
Engle, Lars, 215n.6

English East India Company, 3–4, 17, 150, 182, 195, 220n.76, first voyage, 1, 119; documents of, 5–6, 21, 119, 141. *See also* East Indies trade

engrossing, 147

Epstein, Mortimer, 242n.36

equity, 120, 155, 163, 203; and balance of trade theory, 147–49, 152–54, 156, 184; and capitalism, 184, 193, 241n.25; in *The Renegado*, 21, 148, 167–68, 170, 175, 176, 178, 181–84

eunuchs: and trade in *The Renegado*, 21, 170–74, 179–80, 182, 183, 246n.83; in *Twelfth Night*, 48–49, 52

Eunuchus (Terence), 49, 80

exchange, 129; in *The Island Princess*, 122–24, 129, 133, 135; and liberation in *The Island Princess*, 122–24, 128–30, 136–37, 139; incommensurate exchange and balance in *The Renegado*, 165–71, 174–76, 182. *See also* circulation of money and goods

exchange-value, 181

exogamy, 68, 72

expansion: economic, 10–11, 13, 19, 36, 107, 114, 153–54, 203; failure of, 22, 46, 203; geographic, 10, 19; in *Pericles*, 19, 64–69, 73–74, 78, 79, 81

expenditures, concerns about, 3, 161, 205n.4 (*see also* loss transformed into profit); and unlimited resources, 166–67. *See also* balance of trade theory; bullion, drain of; investment

exports, 99; and balance of trade theory, 148–51, 153, 155; in relation to imports, 3–4; in the Ottoman trade, 156–57, 244n.61. *See also* reexports

Faithfull Shepheardesse, The (Fletcher), 210n.26, 229n.17

family, 22, 187–88, 190–92, 194, 196

fardel, 94, 100, 101, 103–5

Ferber, Michael, 46

Feveryear, Sir Albert, 220n.71

Finkelstein, Andrea, 151–54, 206n.8, 206n.11

Fisher, F. J., 218n.46, 220n.70

Fitch, Ralph, 125, 127, 128

Fletcher John, 144, 210n.26. See also Beaumont, John; *The Faithfull Shepheardesse; The Island Princess*

Florio, John, 172, 218n.43

Flynn, Dennis, 205n.1

foreign trade. *See* East Indies trade; English East India Company; global economy; investment; Levant Company; Ottoman trade; trade, overseas

foreigners, 2, 58, 60–61, 68–69, 144; in *Pericles*, 70–74, 78, 84. *See also* intercultural contact

forestalling, 147

formalism, historical, 18, 23–24, 32, 63, 214n.53

fortunate fall (*felix culpa*), 1, 6–7, 15, 33, 94. *See also* Christian redemption; economics of Christian redemption

Foster, Verna, 209n.23

fourth sector organizations, 201, 202

Fox, John, 125, 127, 128

free trade, 114–18, 120–21, 127–28, 135, 138, 140, 155, 183, 238n.55, 247n.93; in *The Island Princess*, 21, 122–24, 129, 132–34, 136–38, 145; and tragicomedy, 117–18, 121, 128, 130, 135–37, 140. *See also* colonialism, English refusal in the East Indies; freedom; liberation

freedom, 114, 118; in *The Island Princess*, 21, 128, 129, 134–37, 142; and labor, 236n.38; and overseas trade, 127; and prosperity, 114, and prosperity in *The Island Princess*, 124, 128, 133, 134, 137–40; and redemption (twenty-first century), 198, 199; and trade, 121. *See also* free trade; liberation; redemption, of prisoners

Frye, Northrop, 221n.2

Fuchs, Barbara, 182, 220n.76, 235n.27, 239n.1, 242n.33, 243nn.55, 57, 244n.62, 246n.84

Fumerton, Patricia, 218n.46

genre: crossbreeding and hybrids of, 1, 20, 27, 39, 42, 46, 103; and economic/material practices and theories, 1–2, 18, 23–24, 32, 55, 87–88, 103 (*see also specific genres*); experimentation with, 2; generic flexibility, 18; limitations of (*see specific genres*); shifts and transformations of, 23–24, 85–87, 100–103, 107, 144, 146,

genre (*cont.*)
203. *See also* comedy; comic-tragedy; revenge comedy; revenge tragedy; romance; tragedy; tragicomedy *and specific plays*
gift economy, 88, 124, 139, 169, 175, 243n.58, 244n.61; in *The Merchant of Venice*, 38, 41, 44–47. *See also* Mauss, Marcel
Gill, Roma, 217n.20
Giráldez, Arturo, 205n.1
Girard, Rene, 245n.74
global economy, 1, 107, 195, 205n.1; and autonomous subjects, 183, 247n.94; in *The Devil's Law-Case*, 186–87, 189, 193–96; limited resources and uninhibited circulation in, 182–84; and profit, 152; and redemption (twenty-first century), 197–203; and theater, 195; and tragicomedy, 187, 197, 198; triangulated with redemption and tragicomedy, 197–203; unlimited resources and expenditure in, 166–67; without imbalances, 151–55. *See also* East Indies trade; globalization; global trade; trade, overseas
globalization, 116
global trade, 94–98; equity in, 120; mutuality of, 118; as source of liberation, 114; as source of redemption, 113–14, 119, 144; and theories of investment, 3–6; unifying effects of, 118–19, 145. *See also* East Indies trade; global economy; globalization; investment; Levant Company; mercantilism; Ottoman trade; trade, overseas
Goffman, Daniel, 239n.1
Goldberg, Jonathan, 220n.73
grace, 20
Greene, Robert, 96. See also *Pandosto: The Triumph of Time*
Greenham, Richard, 12–13, 37–38, 43
Guantanamo Bay, 236n.38
Guarini, Giambattista: "The Compendium of Tragicomic Poetry," 7, 8, 92, 103, 108, 213n.42, 227n.3, 231n.45; *Il Pastor Fido*, 210n.26

Hakluyt, Richard, 125, 242n.37
Hakluytus Posthumus or Purchas his Pilgrimes (Purchas), 114, 115, 118–19, 145

Halpern, Richard, 218n.33, 230n.30
Harris, Jonathan Gil, 9, 138, 171, 224nn.20, 24, 233nn.9, 16, 239nn.1, 2, 242n.33, 243n.57, 244n.62, 247n.93
heirs, 89–94, 101
Henke, Robert, 209n.23
Herrick, Marvin, 209n.23
Hirst, David, 209n.23
Hope, Jonathan, 6
Hurricane Katrina, 197, 200
hybrids, corporate, 201

immigration, 236n.38, 240n.16; reform, 201, 202
imports, 98–99, 116; in balance of trade theory, 148–51, 153, 155; as a drain on bullion, 1, 3–4, 11, 13, 57–58, 72–73, 95, 108, 116–17, 142, 147–49, 154–57, 186–89, 205nn.4, 5; by the East India Company, 116–17, 142; by the Levant Company, 23, 230n.29, 241n.28; in relation to exports, 3–4
incest: as opposite of expansion, 65–68; in *Pericles*, 19, 65–72, 78, 79, 81; and unnatural breeding/usury in *Pericles*, 66–68
individualism, 199
indulgences, 200
Ingram, William, 195
intercultural contact: 2, 60–61, 68–69, 144. *See also* East Indies trade; foreigners; Ottoman trade; piracy, in the Barbary States
investment: 2, 23, 44–45, 49–52, 154–55, 161, 183, 195, 198, 200, 207n.18; and Christian redemption, 13–18, 88 (*see also* economics of Christian redemption); definitions of, 5, 13, 50–52, 182, 218n.43; in early modern theaters, 195, 197; and East Indies trade, 3–6, 212n.40; investing as opposed to venturing, 95–97; noncommercial definitions of, 50, 241n.25; as theft, 101–2; theorizations of, 3–6, 51–52, 142–43; and tragicomedy, 9–11, 16–18, 23–24, 52, 88, 198; in *Twelfth Night*, 50–52, 61; usage in the correspondence of the English East India Company, 5–6, 182; in *The Winter's Tale*, 20, 88, 94–98, 101. *See also* balance of trade theory; bullion,

drain of; capitalism; East Indies trade; English East India Company; expenditure; mercantilism; trade, overseas

Island Princess, The (Fletcher), 114, 121, 125, 182–84, 198; captivity in, 21, 121–24, 128–29, 131–36, 39; colonial model, rejection of, in, 21, 138, 141–42; conflict among East Indies islands (Ternate and Tidore) in, 121, 129–31, 136, 138; coercion and subjection in, 123, 129–31, 136, 142; conflict between Portuguese and inhabitants of the East Indies in, 121–22, 129–30, 136, 138; conversion in, 136, 137, 139, 142–45; East Indies trade in, 121–24; exchange in, 122–24, 129, 133, 135, 139; free trade in, 21, 123, 132–34, 137–38, 145; freedom in, 21, 128, 129, 134–37, 142; freedom and prosperity in, 124, 128, 133, 134, 137–40; interruptions in, 143–45; liberation in, 21, 136; liberation and exchange in, 122–24, 128, 129–30, 136–37, 139; profit in, 21, 124, 132, 134–35, 137, 138, 140–42, 145; redemption, general, in, 21, 131, 135, 136, 139, 145; redemption of prisoners in, 121–24, 128, 129, 131–33, 136, 139; trade as source of redemption/ liberation in, 122–24, 129, 136–38; tragicomic liberation in, 128, 130, 135, 136–37, 140; tragicomic productivity in, 128, 131–40, 144; value in, 21, 124, 129, 138; value, alienability/ transferability of, in, 129–38, 140, 142, 144, 145
issue: in *The Winter's Tale*, 87, 103, 108

James I, 126; commission on trade, 3–4, 73, 148, 150, 155
Jameson, Fredric, 184
Jew of Malta, The (Marlowe), 178, 217n.31; economics of redemption in, 42–44, 137, 145; revenge in, 42–43, 137, 145; rewritten in *The Merchant of Venice*, 43–44; scapegoat logic in, 43–44
joint-stock companies, 16, 142–44, 195, 202, 212n.40. *See also* English East India Company
Jones, Ann Rosalind, 50, 59

Jones, Norman, 213n.50, 214n.51
Jordan, Constance, 221n.3

Kastan, David, 54
Kerrigan, Stephen, 245n.74
King and No King (Beaumont and Fletcher), 210n.27
King of Ternate (historical), 126
King of Tidore (historical), 130
Knapp, Jeffrey, 213n.43

labor: 16, 22–23, 134, 144, 201, 223n.10, 234n.20, 240n.16; and freedom, 236n.38; in *Pericles*, 75–78; reproduction of, 99; as opposed to idleness, 75–78; value of, obscured, 22, 45, 99–102, 106, 109, 241n.25; visible, 196; wage labor, 100; in *The Winter's Tale*, 20, 88, 100–102, 106, 109. *See also* surplus value
Lane, Kris, 220n.68
Langer, Susanne, 210n.26
Lawson, George, 212n.36, 37
Lepanto, battle of, 194
Lesser, Zachary, 207n.19, 208n.21, 209n.24, 233n.13
Levant, 21, 157. *See also* Ottoman Empire
Levant Company: 3, 17, 21, 157–60, 220n.76, 241n.29; imports by, 23, 230n.29, 241n.28. *See also* Ottoman trade
Lewis, Anthony J., 221n.3
Lewis, Neil A., 236n.38
liberalism, 155, 199
liberation, 114, 118, 120–21; in the East Indies trade, 118, 120–21; in *The Island Princess*, 21, 122–24, 128–30, 136–37, 139; trade as source of, 114, 122–24, 129, 136–38; and tragicomedy, 114, 128, 130, 135–37, 140
Loades, David, 242n.42
Loomba, Ania, 9, 134, 141, 169, 209n.24, 236n.44, 246n.90
Lopez, Dr., 42
loss: disavowal in *The Merchant of Venice*, 47; in *The Merchant of Venice*, 28–30, 31, 33–36, 38, 40, 47; not transformed into profit, 196; in Ottoman trade, 147, 157–58, 160–62; productivity of, 1, 4–6, 15, 88–98, 113, 187, 153–54, 197–200, 203; and profit, 1, 5, 11, 14–18, 161; and profit in *The Renegado*, 146–47, 173,

loss (*cont.*)
174, 181–82, 184–85; resulting from
overseas trade, 3–6, 11, 28, 57–58, 72–73,
95, 116–17, 142, 147–49, 151–57, 186–89,
205n.4 (*see also* balance of trade theory;
bullion, drain of; mercantilism);
transformation of, 1, 4, 22, 38, 49, 52, 182,
187 (*see also* investment); transformed into
profit in *Pericles*, 64, 65, 68, 72–74, 77–78,
83–84; transformed into profit in *The
Winter's Tale*, 85–103, 106; in *Twelfth Night*,
9–10, 48–49, 52, 57; in *Twelfth Night*,
disavowed, 9–10, 19, 47, 53–55, 58–63; in
The Winter's Tale, 85–93, 95, 98, 100; in *The
Winter's Tale*, rematerialized, 92–94;
without return, 173. *See also* economics of
Christian redemption
Lyly, John. See *Midas*

Maguire, Nancy, 208–9n.23
Malcomson, Cristina, 53
Mallin, Eric, 53, 55, 218n.35
Malta: expulsion of Jews, 42. See also *The
Jew of Malta*
Maltby, William, 232n.5
Malynes, Gerard, 58, 153, 154, 205–6n.8,
240n.11
Mansell, Sir Robert, 159
market: as an ethic in itself, 199, 201; free
market, 200; redemptive qualities of
(twenty-first century), 198–203; in *The
Renegado*, 21, 146, 152, 162–64, 166–67,
171, 177–80; unlimited productive
power of, 200; values of, 198; tragic
consequences of, 200–202. *See also*
capitalism; commerce; neoliberalism;
trade, overseas
Markley, Robert, 234n.26
Marlowe, Christopher, 42. See also *The Jew
of Malta*
marriage plot, 38–39, 44, 46, 77–78
Marx, Karl, 99, 102, 191, 217n.27, 229n.26,
230nn.28, 34, 37, 232n.51, 234n.20,
237n.47, 247n.97; on capitalism's
mystifications, 241n.27; on exploitation,
240n.16, 241n.25; "General Formula for
Capital," 154, 207n.16, 241n.22; and
tragicomedy, 185
masterless persons, 98, 99
Massinger, Philip, 9, 21, 217n.32. See also
The Renegado

Matar, Nabil, 239n.1, 242n.33
Mauss, Marcel, 124, 212n.38, 227n.6,
243n.58. *See also* gift economy
McMullan, Gordon, 6, 210n.26
mercantilism: 4, 16, 17, 78, 95, 114, 140,
146, 147–55, 161, 162, 186–87, 202,
205n.8, 223n.15; and redemption,
13–16, 32; moral questions in, 151–52,
154–56; and refunctioning of religious
discourse, 78, 156 (*see also* Christian
redemption; economics of Christian
redemption); and tragicomic theater,
156. *See also* balance of trade theory;
investment; Malynes, Gerard;
Misselden, Edward; Mun, Thomas;
trade, overseas
Merchant of Venice, The (Shakespeare), 20,
83, 107, 137–39, 145, 167, 238n.52;
Christianity in, 30–33, 45; comedic
conventions of, 27, 32, 38, 44–47; debt
in, 28–32, 40–41; disavowal of profit in,
45–47; and economics of Christian
redemption, 19, 27–44, 47; as generic
hybrid, 27, 39, 42, 46; generic
limitations of, 32, 38, 45–47; gift in, 38,
41, 44–47; insular and static economies
in, 27, 42, 45–46, 183, 238n.62; loss in,
28–31, 33–36, 38, 40; loss, disavowal of,
47; marriage plot in, 38–39, 44, 46;
mercy in, 36–43; miraculous
productivity in, 44–46; the pound of
flesh in, 19, 27, 29–40, 46; religious
conversion in, 39–42, 46; religious
difference and conflict in, 30–32,
34–36; revenge in, 33–36, 38, 43, 46; as
revenge comedy, 43, 45; revenge and
elimination of trade in, 33, 35–36; as
rewriting of *The Jew of Malta*, 43–44; risk
in, 215n.4; scapegoat logic in, 45–47,
62; tragic consequences of trade in,
28–30, 32–35, 38, 43–44, 48; tragicomic
potential of, 27, 33, 35–36, 38, 40; usury
in, 30, 45
mercy, 36–43
Merchant Adventurers, 3
Midas (Lyly), 2; foreign trade in, 2,
238n.60; intercultural contact in, 2, 144
Middleton, David, 128–29, 135
Middleton, Henry, 233n.19
Midsummer Night's Dream, A (Shakespeare), 8
Mincinton, M. E., 218n.46

Misselden, Edward, 247n.93; and balance of trade, 4, 148–50, 153, 157, 161, 171, 205–6n.8, 224n.23, 225n.28, 233n.16

Money. *See* bullion, drain of; capital; circulation of money and goods; expenditure; investment

More, Thomas, 99

Mowat, Barbara, 208n.23

Mukerji, Chandra, 219n.47

Muldrew, Craig, 226n.38

Mun, Thomas, 234n.20, 241n.25; and balance of trade, 4–5, 95, 117, 142, 148, 150–55, 157, 171, 182, 205–6n.8, 206n.15, 223n.15, 229n.22, 240n.11, 241n.27; balance of trade and power of Indian wares, 119, 120, 128, 135, 141; and dynamic economies, 17, 154, 233n.11; and increase of treasure, 211n.31, 244n.61; and productivity, 15, 206n.9. *See also* balance of trade theory; mercantilism

Murad IV, 242–43n.48

mystery cycle plays, 7–8

Nagin, C. Ray, 197

nation: imagination of, 210n.28. *See also* commonwealth

Neill, Michael, 114, 119, 236n.44, 245n.74

neoliberalism, 155, 198, 199, 201, 202; and redemption, 199–200

Nerlich, Michael, 213n.45

Newman, Karen, 215n.6

nothing, 13, 16, 37–39, 42, 43; in *The Winter's Tale*, 89–91, 92, 97. *See also* economics of Christian redemption; investment

oracle: as model for redemption, 8, 85–86, 88–90, 92, 97, 104

Orgel, Stephen, 49

Othello (Shakespeare), 61

Ottoman Empire, 21, 146, 194; temptations of, 147, 165, 176, 178–79, 183. See also Levant Company; Ottoman trade; piracy, in the Barbary States; *The Renegado*

Ottoman trade: and balance of trade theory, 156–62, 247n.93; exports in, 156–57, 244n.61; and English pirates, 158, 175; imports in, 156–57; poll tax in, 159, 172–74; in relation to East Indies trade, 156–57; as source of both loss and profit simultaneously, 147, 157–58, 160–62; and temptation to turn Turk, 147; Barbary pirates and the potential to completely halt Ottoman trade, 157–62, 180. *See also* Barbary States; Levant Company; piracy, in the Barbary States; *The Renegado*

Painful Adventures of Pericles, The (Wilkins), 107, 223n.12, 224n.26, 225n.30

Pandosto: The Triumph of Time (Greene), 96, 107, 230n.37

Parker, Andrew, 200

Parker, John, 14, 228n.10, 229n.26

Parker, Patricia, 246n.90

Pelikan, Jaroslav, 211n.32

performativity and performative speech, 108, 137, 138

Pericles (Shakespeare and Wilkins), 85, 97, 107, 130, 178; begging and borrowing in, 75–78; charity in, 20, 64, 65, 67, 69–74, 77, 79; Christian model of redemption in, 64, 74, 78, 81–84; Christian redemption, refunctioned as economic and secular in, 64, 78, 83, 216n.13; class conflict in, 75–79; class difference in, 70–71, 75–78; consumption of too many foreign goods in, 72–73; credit in, 80–83; distribution, unequal in, 75–78; dynamic/nonstatic economies in, 19–20, 64, 68, 72–74; economic concerns, centrality of, 65, 84; economies, insular in, 65–68, 71–74; economics of redemption in, 78, 80–84; economic problems separated from moral problems, 79, 83; episodic structure of, 65, 72, 78, 85; exogamy in, 68, 72; expansion, geographical and economic in, 19, 64–69, 73–74, 78, 79, 81; expansion as opposite of incest in, 65–68; incest in, 19, 65–72, 78, 79, 81; incest and unnatural breeding in, 66–68; infinite accumulation in, 64, 79–84, 243–44n.59; inversion of comedic conventions in, 67–68; losses transformed into profits in, 64, 65, 68, 72–74, 77–78, 83–84; piracy in, 243–44n.59; poverty in, 68, 70–72, 75–78; productivity in, 68–69, 73–74,

Pericles (cont.)
   78; profit making, ethical objections to,
   79–82; prostitution in, 68, 79–83;
   redemption in, 68, 69, 74, 80–82, 84;
   relationship to foreigners and foreign
   economies in, 70–74, 78, 84; scarcity and
   plenitude in, 65, 68–75, 79; self-
   consumption in, 66–71, 78; stagnation in,
   69–70, 72, 84; tragicomic economics in,
   68, 73–74, 77–79; tragicomic redemption
   in, 74, 82; tragicomic transformations in,
   77–78; usury in, 66–67, 74
perversion, 22, 192, 193
piracy, 21, 57–58, 243–44n.59; and balance
   of trade theory, 157–62; in the Barbary
   States, 21, 157–62, 169, 174, 175; Barbary
   pirates as threat to system of circulation
   of goods, 158, 161–62, 173, 180, 243n.54;
   Barbary pirates in *The Renegado*, 21, 57,
   146, 162, 163, 166–67, 170, 171, 174–75,
   177; English, 158, 175; as funding source
   for trade, 157; as obstruction to trade,
   157–62; in *Twelfth Night*, 57–58, 61
pleasure, 22, 193, 196–97
Politics (Aristotle), 66, 67. *See also* Usury
poll tax (*carazo*), 159, 172–74
Poovey, Mary, 206nn. 8, 11
postcolonialism, 116
pound of flesh: in *The Merchant of Venice*,
   19, 27, 29–40, 46
poverty, 20, 22, 73, 149, 150, 195; in
   Pericles, 68, 70–72, 75–78; in *The Winter's
   Tale*, 96, 97, 100, 104–6. *See also* beggars;
   scarcity
primitive accumulation, 99
*Principal Navigations, Voyages, Traffiques and
   Discoveries of the English Nation, The*
   (Hakluyt), 125, 242n.37
prisoners: redemption of, 21, 114, 121–24,
   128, 129, 131–33, 136, 139, 165; in
   Twelfth Night, 60–62. *See also* captivity;
   captivity narratives
productivity, 4–6, 15, 93; of circulation,
   153–56; and capitalism, 203; dangers of,
   201–2; in *The Devil's Law-Case*, 22,
   187–91, 197; demystification of, 22, 185,
   190–91; excessive, 22, 46; insistence on,
   22, 202–3; lack of, 66, 67, 73, 181;
   and/or loss, 1, 4–6, 88–98, 153–54; in
   The Merchant of Venice, 44–46; narrative
   of, 2; in *Pericles*, 68–69, 73–74, 78;

significance of, 3; trade as sign of, 181;
   and tragicomedy, 2, 8, 22, 68, 86–89,
   94, 97, 98, 102, 103, 107–8, 113, 128,
   131, 133, 135–40, 144, 187–90, 192,
   193, 194, 196–97, 203; tragicomic
   limitations in *The Devil's Law-Case*, 22,
   187–90, 192, 193, 196–97. *See also*
   investment; loss; profit; prosperity
profit, 21, 125–28, 199; disavowal of, 28–32,
   40–41; disavowal in *Twelfth Night*, 9–10,
   19, 47, 53–55, 58–63; in East Indies trade,
   115–17, 120–21, 140; ethical objections
   to, 79–83, 147, 152, 163–65, 169; global,
   152; in *The Island Princess*, 21, 124, 132,
   134–35, 137, 138, 140–42, 145;
   justifications of, 13–14, 78, 146, 161;
   legitimate, 21, 169, 176, 178, 180–82; loss
   transformed into, 1, 5, 11, 14–18, 49, 52,
   85–103, 106, 151–52, 154–56, 161; losses
   transformed into in *Pericles*, 64, 65, 68,
   72–74, 77–78, 83–84; redemption of in
   The Renegado, 21, 166, 167, 169, 176–83;
   in *The Renegado*, 21, 146–47, 152, 163–65,
   169, 173–78, 180–85; and revenge, 40; as
   synonym for and raison d'être of trade,
   181–82; unlimited, 153; in *The Winter's
   Tale*, 85–103, 106; without capital growth,
   151–52. *See also* balance of trade theory;
   investment; productivity; prosperity
proletarian, 222n.9
prosperity, 13, 114; and Christian
   redemption, 8–10 (*see* economics of
   Christian redemption) and freedom,
   114; and freedom in *The Island Princess*,
   124, 128, 133, 134, 137, 138–39, 140; in
   The Renegado, 175–76, 177–78, 180–84.
   See also balance of trade theory;
   investment; productivity; profit
Prosser, Eleanor, 245n.74
prostitution, 68, 79–83
Protestant doctrine, 37. *See also* Christian
   redemption; Reformation (Protestant)
Purchas, Samuel, 114, 115, 118–19

Rackin, Phyllis, 215n.5, 216n.10
Raman, Shankar, 209n.24, 236n.40,
   236n.44
re-creation, 86–87, 91, 93, 132, 138;
   theatrical, 20, 22, 86–88, 104–9, 188,
   191–94, 196; and tragicomedy, 89–90
redemption, 7, 197; and art, 104–8, 144; and

capitalism, 89–90; commerce as a form of, 198–201; in *The Devil's Law-Case*, 22; economics of (*see* economics of Christian redemption); and freedom (twenty-first century), 198, 199; and geopolitics (twenty-first century), 196–99; and global economics (twenty-first century), 197–203; in *The Island Princess*, 21, 131, 135, 136, 139, 145; and neoliberalism, 199–200; in *The Merchant of Venice*, 29, 109; and neoliberalism, 199–200; in *Pericles*, 68, 69, 74, 80–82, 84; of prisoners, 21, 114, 124–28, 165; of prisoners in *The Island Princess*, 121–24, 128, 129, 131–33, 136, 139; of profit, 21, 166, 167, 169, 176–83; religious redemption reconfigured as economic redemption in *The Winter's Tale*, 93, 96–98, 104, 107; and revenge, 34–38, 46; trade as source of, 113–14, 119–21, 144; trade as source in *The Island Princess*, 122–24, 129, 136–38; and tragicomedy, 74, 82, 98, 117, 121, 148, 156, 164, 174, 176–79, 181, 183–84; triangulation with capitalism and tragicomedy, 97–98, 188, 190–91, 197–203; in *Twelfth Night*, 48–50, 52, 55, 61; failed in *Twelfth Night*, 56–59, 61–62; and violence, 198–99; in *The Winter's Tale*, 8, 20, 85–90, 92–95, 97, 104–8. *See also* Anselm, Saint; Christian redemption; economics of Christian redemption

reexports, 3, 78, 116–17, 120–21. *See also* exports

Reformation (Protestant), 11, 16, 81, 211n.32. *See also* Protestant doctrine

regrating, 147

religious difference: in *The Merchant of Venice*, 30–32, 34–36; in *The Renegado*, 176, 184, 245n.75. *See also* conversion

renegades, 163, 166, 170–71, 177–79, 182

Renegado, The (Massinger), 156, 158, 159, 190, 198; absence/disruption of trade in, 162–63, 170–74, 176, 177, 180; alternatives to revenge in, 21, 175–77, 184; ambivalence about romance conventions in, 9, 162–64, 165, 179; balance and incommensurate exchange in, 165–71, 174–76, 182; and balance of trade theory, 21, 148, 166–70, 173, 174, 177; castration and disrupted trade in, 21, 170–74, 179–80, 182, 183, 246n.83;

centrality of trade in, 162–63; circulation of goods, in, 165–69, 171, 173–74, 180; conversion in, 147, 169, 178–82, 245n.75; economic models in, 165–69, 174–75; economics of redemption in, 21, 148, 171, 177–80; economic stagnation in, 170–74; equity in, 21, 148, 167–68, 170, 175, 176, 178, 181–84; illegitimate/unethical trade/profit in, 152, 163–65, 169; importance of location in Barbary States, 21, 146, 162, 169, 172–75, 179–81, 183; loss and profit in, 21, 146–47, 169, 173, 174, 176, 178, 180–82, 184–85; markets and merchants in, 21, 146, 152, 162–64, 166–67, 171, 177–80; piracy in, 21, 146, 162, 163, 166–67, 170, 171, 174–75, 177; prosperous return in, 175–78, 180–84; redemption of economic gain in, 166, 167, 169, 177–79, 183; redemption, religious, in, 21, 164, 166, 169, 170, 175–79, 181–82, 245n.75; refusal of revenge in, 165, 174–75, 178; religious conflict in, 176, 184, 245n.75; renegades in, 163, 166, 170–71, 177–79, 182; restraint in, 165, 166, 169, 170, 179–84; temptations of Ottoman Empire in, 147, 165, 176, 178–79, 183; tragicomic redemption of trade, 148, 162, 164, 174, 176–81, 183–84; tragicomedy, affective qualities of, 183–84; world of limited resources and uninhibited circulation in, 166–67, 182–84

repentance, 200; in *The Winter's Tale*, 20, 85–86, 89, 91–97

reproduction, 89, 108; of capital, 188, 197; of labor force, 99. *See also* incest

restraint, 189; in balance of trade theory, 151, 152, 156, 162; in *The Renegado*, 165, 166, 169, 170, 179–84

revenge: alternatives to, 21, 175–77, 184; in *The Devil's Law-Case*, 22, 187, 191, 192, 194; and elimination of trade, 33, 35–36; In *The Jew of Malta*, 42–43, 137, 145; in *The Merchant of Venice*, 19, 33–36, 38, 43, 45, 46; as opposed to sacrifice, 175; and redemption, 34–38, 46; refusal in *The Renegado*, 165, 174–75, 178; in *Twelfth Night*, 62; and the satisfaction, 35–36, 41; unprofitability of, 40. *See also* revenge comedy; revenge tragedy revenge comedy, 19, 43, 45. *See also* revenge

revenge tragedy, 19, 42–43, 175, 245n.74. *See also* revenge

risk, 95–97; vs. transformation, 9

Roe, Sir Thomas, 116, 159–60, 242n.30

romance (genre), 7, 20, 101–2, 107, 124, 134, 146, 184; ambivalence about, 9, 162–65, 179; tragicomedies categorized as, 6, 208–9n.23, 209n.24; tragicomedy, opposed to, 7, 9, 96, 102, 107, 208–9n.23, 209n.25

Ryan, Kiernan, 207–8n.21

sacrifice, 175, 200, 201

scapegoat: in *The Merchant of Venice*, 45–47, 62; in *Twelfth Night*, 62

scarcity, 65, 68–75, 79

Sea Voyage, The (Fletcher and Massinger), 233n.13, 244n.65

secularization, 14, 202; of Christian redemption, 14, 64, 74, 78, 83, 88, 93, 97–98, 104, 107, 190–91, 198, 202, 214nn.51, 52, 216n.13; of the theater, 193

Shakespeare, William: historicity of plays, 23–24; movement from comedy to tragicomedy, 19–20, 23–24, 107; tragicomedies categorized as romances, 6, 208–9n.23, 209n.24. See also *The Merchant of Venice*; *A Midsummer Night's Dream*; *Pericles*; *The Tempest*; *Twelfth Night*; *The Winter's Tale*

Shell, Marc, 215n.6, 222n.7

Shershow, Scott, 15, 44, 76–77, 152–54, 212n.38, 213n.50, 216n.11, 227n.6, 243nn.56, 58

Shuger, Debora, 211n.32, 216n.15

Sidney, Philip, 6, 106

Simpson, James, 245n.79

sin, original, 11. *See also* Christian redemption; redemption

Slack, Paul, 230n.30

slavery, 127, 135, 140, 237n.48; in the Barbary States, 157–60, 169

Slights, Camille, 220n.66

Smith, Patti, 186

social mobility, 47, 52, 63

social responsibility, 201

Socinus, Faustus, 36–37, 211n.32

spectacle. *See* theatrical re-creation/spectacle

Spencer, Eric, 66

spices, 3, 51, 94, 99, 116. See also East Indies trade; English East India Company; imports; Levant Company

Spufford, Peter, 3

Stallybrass, Peter, 14, 32, 50, 59, 211n.34, 228n.10

statutes of employment, 73

Strom, Stephanie, 201

Supple, B. E., 224n.21

surplus value, 20, 98–102, 241n.25; theatrical, 187, 192–96; in *The Winter's Tale*, 20, 98–102, 104–8. *See also* capital; capitalism; labor; Marx, Karl

Taylor, Mark C., 199

Tawney, R. H., 245n.78

Tempest, The, 209n.24

Tennenhouse, Leonard, 209n.24, 227n.8

theater: companies, 16; demsytification of, 22, 191–94, 196; economics of, 191, 195–97; and East Indies trade as space of discovery, 194–96; and economics, 2, 104–8, 194–97 (*see also* tragicomedy; *specific plays*); and global economy, 195; emergence of permanent playhouses, 195; secularization of, 193

theatrical re-creation/spectacle: and capital, 195, 197; in *The Devil's Law-Case*, 22, 188, 191–94, 196; demystified, 22, 191–94, 196; and surplus value, 187, 192–96; and tragicomedy, 17, 89–90; in *The Winter's Tale*, 20, 86–88, 104–9. *See also* productivity; theater; tragicomedy

theft, 98–103, 106–8; as investment, 101–2

Thirsk, Joan, 219n.48, 220n.70, 224n.19

trade, free. *See* free trade

trade, overseas: 19–22, 51, 114, 146–56; in the Barbary States, 147–57, 162; and Christian redemption, 11–19, 64, 74, 78, 113, 177 (*see also* economics of Christian redemption); and comedy, 8–10, 17, 19, 27–28, 32, 38, 60, 78, 114; decay of cloth trade, 3, 51, 159; equity in, 120, 147, 148, 149, 152–56, 163, 184, 203; ethics of, 187–89; and freedom, 127; James I's committee on, 3–4, 73, 148, 150, 155; and liberation, 118, 120–21; loss from drain of bullion, 1, 3–4, 11, 13, 28, 57–58, 72–73, 95, 116–17, 142, 147–49, 154–57, 186–89,

205n.4; multilateral, 116–17, 142; mutuality of, 118; national benefit of, 117, 140; redeemed, 21, 73–74, 148, 164, 174, 176–79, 181, 183–84; as source of redemption, 89–90, 113–14, 119–21, 197–203; as a source of redemption in *The Island Princess,* 122–24, 129, 136–38; tragic consequences of, 28, 48, 200–202; tragic consequences in *The Merchant of Venice,* 28–30, 32–36, 38, 43–44, 48; in *The Renegado,* 21, 146, 152, 162–80, 182, 183; in *Twelfth Night,* 57–58, 60, 62; and tragicomedy, 1–2, 9–11, 13, 16–18, 78, 88, 113, 119, 146, 148, 162, 164, 174, 176–81, 183–84, 238n.60 (*see also* economic theories and practices *and specific plays*); unfair trade practices, 127; unifying effects of, 118–19, 145; in *The Winter's Tale,* 94–98; of wool, 23, 51, 98–99. *See also* balance of trade theory; commerce; consumption; East India trade; economic theory; economies; English East India Company; exchange; expenditure; exports; free trade; global economy; global trade; imports; investment; Levant Company; loss; market; mercantilism; Ottoman trade; piracy; productivity; profit; prosperity

tragedy, 33; opposed to tragicomedy, 7; of trade, 28–30, 32–35, 38, 43–44, 48, 200–202

tragicomedy, 176; aesthetics of, 92; affective qualities of, 183–84; and capitalism, 87, 98, 108, 184–85, 198; demystified, 190–91, 197; critical history of, 6–7, 17; depoliticization in, 6; dialectical qualities of, 8, 10, 19, 63, 68, 107, 109, 135, 137, 144, 184, 203; and dynamic relationships, 19–20, 63; and economic theory and practices, 2, 6, 9–11, 13, 16–20, 23–24, 27–28, 49, 52, 64–65, 68, 73–74, 77–79, 86–90, 92–98, 107, 109, 113, 117–21, 128, 130, 135–37, 140, 146, 187, 197, 198 (*see also* tragicomedy, productivity of); epistemological effects of, 17; and free trade, 117–18, 121, 128, 130, 135–37, 140; formal properties of, 7–11, 78, 86–90, 92, 94, 103, 108, 186, 187, 190, 231n.45; generic tension in, 1, 18; generic transformations in, 77–78,

102, 103, 107, 144, 146, 203; and incorporation of foreign, 144; and liberation, 114, 128, 130, 135–37, 140; limitations of, 22, 187–93, 196–97, 202–3; in Marx, 185, and medieval drama, 7; mystifications of, 156; and narrative romance, 6–7, 9, 208–9n.23, 209nn.24, 25; as opposed to comedy, 7, 8, 10, 28, 32, 38, 52–55, 59–63, 78–79; as opposed to romance, 7, 9, 96, 102, 107, 208–9n.23, 209n.25; as opposed to tragedy, 7; potential for, 27, 33, 35–36, 38, 40, 48–49, 52, 54–55, 60, 63, 87; productivity of, 22, 62, 86–89, 94, 97, 98, 102, 103, 107–8, 113, 128, 131, 133, 135–40, 144, 187–90, 192–94, 196–97, 203; productivity, refusal and limits, of, 40, 187–90, 192, 193, 196–97; and prosperous transformations, 7–8, 46, 103, 135, 146; and re-creation, 86–87, 89–90; and redemption, 7–8, 11, 14–18, 56, 74, 82, 98, 108, 113, 117, 121, 148, 156, 164, 174, 176–79, 181, 183–84 (*see also specific plays*); roots in other genres, 7–8; and spectacle/theatrical re-creation, 17, 22, 86–90, 104–9, 188, 191–94, 196; theater as, 104–8; as a third kind, 7–8; theories of, 7–11, 87, 103, 106, 108; triangulation with capitalism and redemption, 97–98, 188, 190–91, 197–203; yielding of religious to economic in, 64, 78, 83, 88, 93, 96–98, 104, 107, 216n.13. See also *The Devil's Law-Case, The Island Princess, Pericles, The Renegado, The Winter's Tale*

tragicommerce, 197–98

trespass, 92, 101, 106

trickle-down theory, 241n.25

Tunis. *See* Barbary States

Twelfth Night, 83, 104, 105, 107, 179–80, 184; Antonio's purse in, 56–58, 61–62; clothing in, 50–55, 58–60; cross-dressing in, 48, 49, 52; and comedic conventions, 27–28, 48, 59; and comedic conventions, limitations of, 28, 52–55, 59–63; comedic closure and static economy in, 60–63; economic practices in, 27, 47, 49–50, 56–57, 60–63; economic practice, absence of critical discussion of, 47; eunuch in, 48–49, 52; as hybrid between tragicomedy and romantic comedy,

Twelfth Night (*cont.*)
9–10, 27, 54–55, 62; insular and static economy in, 27, 60–65, 183; investment in, 50–52, 61; loss in, 9–10, 48–49, 57; loss and/or profit disavowed in, 9–10, 19, 47, 53–55, 58–63; loss transformed into profit in, 49, 52; material contexts, suppression of, 47, 50, 52–55, 58–63; overseas trade in, 57–58, 60, 62; piracy in, 57–58, 61; redemption in, 48–50, 52, 55, 61; redemption, failed in, 56–59, 61–62; scapegoat in, 62; sea venturers in, 55–56, 60–61; social mobility in, 47, 52, 63; tragicomic potential in, 48–49, 52, 54–55, 60, 63
Twyne, Thomas, 223n.12

Utopia (More), 99
utopia: and capitalism, 22, 184–85
use-value, 116, 120, 150, 181
usury, 13–16, 66, 96, 103, 108, 147, 166, 195; in Aristotle, 66, 67, 73; lack of productivity of, 66, 67, 73, 181; in *The Merchant of Venice*, 30, 45; in *Pericles*, 66–67, 74

value: alienability of, 21, 117, 121; alienability/transferability in *The Island Princess*, 129–38, 140, 142, 144, 145; expropriation of, 16; in *The Island Princess*, 124, 129, 138; of labor, 22, 45, 100–102, 106, 109, 196, 241n.25; surplus value, 20, 98–102, 104–8, 241n.25; surplus value and theatrical re-creation/spectacle, 187, 192–96; in *The Winter's Tale*, 20, 87–109. *See also* exchange-value; use-value
Vanrenen, Denys, 244n.60
venturing: definition of, 14; opposed to investing, 95–97; in *Twelfth Night*, 10, 55–56, 60–61
Villiers, John, 237n.43
violence: geopolitical, 198; as a means to redemption, 198–99
Vitkus, Daniel, 235n.27, 239n.1, 242n.33

wealth. *See* accumulation; balance of trade theory; investment
Weber, Max, 16, 221n.2

Webster, John: tragedies, 193. See also *The Devil's Law-Case*
West Indies, 186, 193, 194
Wilkins, George, 223n.12. See also *The Painful Adventures of Pericles; Pericles*
Why God Became Man (Anselm), 11, 15, 19, 20, 33, 38, 74, 79, 83, 177, 221nn.1, 2, 226n.42; secularization of (*see* Christian redemption); vulgarization of, 41
Winter's Tale, The: 22, 24, 130, 134, 137, 138, 238n.53, 240n.14; comedic obstacle in, 100, 225n.32; crossbreeding of genres in, 20, 103; death in, 86, 108, 210n.26; debt in, 88–89, 91, 97; and *The Devil's Law-Case*, 191–95; economic disparity in, 88–89, 91; economic practices in, 93–98; economics of redemption in, 86, 88, 90–93, 95–98, 107; genres, shifts and transformations of, 85–87, 100–103, 107; generic and economic connections in, 87–88, 103; heirs in, 89–94, 101; "issue" in, 87, 103, 108; investment, economic, in, 20, 88, 94–98, 101; investment as theft, 101–2; labor in, 20, 88, 99–102, 106, 109; loss in, 85–93, 95, 98, 100; loss transformed into profit in, 85–88, 92–94, 99–103, 106; nothing in, 89–92, 97; oracle in, 8, 85–86, 88–90, 92, 97, 104; and overseas/global trade, 94–98; poverty in, 96, 97, 100, 104–6; re-creation in, 86–87, 89–91, 93; redemption in, 8, 20, 85–88, 92–95, 98, 104; redemption and art in, 104–8; religious redemption reconfigured as economic redemption in, 88, 93, 96–98, 104, 107, 216n.13; repentance in, 20, 85–86, 89, 91–97; surplus value in, 98–102, 104–8; theatrical spectacle and profit in, 20, 86–90, 104–9; tragicomedy and economics in, 88, 98; tragicomic productivity in, 86–90, 94, 98, 102, 103, 107–8; tragicomic theater in, 104–8; value depletion in, 89–92, 94; value production in, 20, 87–89, 91–109
wonder, absence of, 193, 195, 196
Wood, A. C., 159, 160, 241–42n.30, 242nn.34, 35, 36, 41, 43, 46, 243nn.50, 51

Acknowledgments

It is a great pleasure to thank in print the many people who enriched the experience of writing this book and the years in which it was written. Without the conversations, suggestions, and encouragement of many colleagues this would have been a very different book. At my MLA interview, Beth Robertson first asked me if redemption might be relevant to the economics of early modern England. She is still asking me provocative questions. Peter Stallybrass encouraged me to follow my instincts on the importance of "investment" to early modern drama and economic practices—advice that proved critical to the ultimate direction of the project. Katherine Eggert—department chair, senior colleague, and friend—has supported me unstintingly in all of her roles. She also read the entire manuscript and helped to shape it in too many ways to list here. David Glimp arrived at Colorado when the book was already in its final stages, but he helped me to see my work in different ways and thus to get excited about it anew. I also want to thank Elizabeth Hanson, one of the readers for the University of Pennsylvania Press, for her careful reading of my manuscript. Her insights and suggestions not only led to a better book, but also made the revision process an interesting one. Kate E. Brown has been my primary interlocutor throughout. Her work on mourning has deeply influenced my understanding of loss. At any number of places, this book channels her thinking.

Conversations with numerous other colleagues at Boulder and beyond have helped me to refine ideas and develop new insights. I thank Emily Bartels, Anna Brickhouse, Scarlet Bowen, Jonathan Burton, Arnab Chakladar, Joanna Cheetham, Barbara Fuchs, Patrick Greaney, Jeremy Green, Donna Goldstein, Jonathan Gil Harris, Rose Hentzell, Jill Heydt-Stevenson, Bruce Holsinger, Jean Howard, Zachary Lesser, Nina Levine, Raphael Lyne, Subha Mukherji, Jeffrey Robinson, Barbara Seebek, Scott Shershow, Charlotte Sussman, Henry Turner, Dan Vitkus, William West, Mike Witmore, Christopher Worley, Sue Zemka, and Michael Zimmerman. All of the above read or heard sections of the book when it was in process; their responses have led me to a better understanding of my own project. My students at Boulder, especially members of my graduate seminar "Genre, History, and the Early Modern Theater," will see that many of our discussions have been incorporated into these pages.

Fleet of foot and strong of mind and back, my two research assistants—Pete Remien and Kat Rutkowski—provided much needed help in gathering and organizing materials with gracious efficiency. Without them I would have gotten much less sleep. Jerry Singerman, editor at the University of Pennsylvania Press, will forever have my gratitude for taking a potentially stressful process and transforming it into a pleasure.

Though I began writing this book after my student days were over, I owe a great intellectual debt to my generous teachers. Harry Berger has influenced how I think and read in ways I am only beginning to understand. In a serendipitous full circle, he was teaching at Boulder when I finished the manuscript, and I treasured the renewal of our intellectual and comradely bonds. With her dedication to intellectual pursuits, Carla Freccero remains my model of what it means to be a scholar. From her, I also learned the importance of social history for literary studies. Wendy Brown introduced me to the political theory that provides the foundation for so much of my thinking and continues to inspire me. I remain grateful to Janet Adelman for introducing me to Renaissance studies and for the generosity with which she recognized and supported my potential.

A number of people have helped me to make Colorado home. Anna Brickhouse, Jane Garrity, Bruce Holsinger, and Karen Jacobs are like a second family. Tony Robinson introduced me to the activist community in Denver. The salsa communities of Boulder and Denver have kept my spirits high and my body in motion. I can't imagine having written this book without the love and support of friends and family: Daniel Brown, Joe Cahn, Edmund Campos, Jeffrey DeShell, June Forman, Leila Gomez, Bonnie Greenwald, Dennis Greenwald, Jessica Guaranda, Kerri Honaker, Dennis Jaramillo, Valerie Kaussen, Jenny Knight, Laura Michaelis, Mark Porter, James Reed, Jodi Reed, Lindsey Sage Reed, Marc Schachter, Jeff Schweinfest, Elisabeth Sheffield, and Rebecca Stern. I cherish their many and varied gifts. Finally, I want to thank my parents, Sidney Forman and Laurie Porter, for, among other things, making sure that I could dance without having to sell my books.

Sections of chapters appeared first in a different form in "Transformations of Value and the Production of 'Investment' in the Early History of the English East India Company," *Journal of Medieval and Early Modern Studies* 34 (2004). I am grateful to Duke University Press for permission to reprint that material here. A section of Chapter 1 appeared in "Material Dispossessions and Counterfeit Investments: The Economies of *Twelfth Night*" in *Money and the Age of Shakespeare: Essays in New Economic Criticism,* ed. Linda Woodbridge (New York: Palgrave Macmillan, 2003). It is here reproduced with permission of Palgrave Macmillan.